PENGUIN BOOKS

EYEWITNESS TO THE AMERICAN WEST

David Colbert, editor of the highly-acclaimed *Eyewitness to . . .* series, began digging through libraries and pushing great authors upon his friends while at Brown University, and has been doing so ever since, through a stint editing books at a large publishing house and now as an author and editor. The first volume in the series, *Eyewitness to America,* was a main selection of the Book-of-the-Month Club and the History Book Club.

EYEWITNESS TO THE AMERICAN WEST

500 Years of Firsthand History

EDITED BY

DAVID COLBERT

PENGUIN BOOKS

PENGUIN BOOKS
Published by the Penguin Group
Penguin Putnam Inc., 375 Hudson Street,
New York, New York 10014, U.S.A.
Penguin Books Ltd, 27 Wrights Lane, London W8 5TZ, England
Penguin Books Australia Ltd, Ringwood, Victoria, Australia
Penguin Books Canada Ltd, 10 Alcorn Avenue,
Toronto, Ontario, Canada M4V 3B2
Penguin Books (N.Z.) Ltd, 182–190 Wairau Road,
Auckland 10, New Zealand

Penguin Books Ltd, Registered Offices:
Harmondsworth, Middlesex, England

First published in the United States of America by Viking Penguin,
a member of Penguin Putnam Inc. 1998
Published in Penguin Books 1999

1   3   5   7   9   10   8   6   4   2

Copyright © David Colbert, 1998
All rights reserved

Acknowledgments for permission to reprint copyrighted texts appear on pages 473–81.

Care has been taken to trace the ownership of the selections included in this work and to make full acknowledgment for their use. If errors or omissions have occurred, they will be corrected in subsequent editions, provided written notification is sent to the publisher.

THE LIBRARY OF CONGRESS HAS CATALOGED THE HARDCOVER EDITION AS FOLLOWS:
Eyewitness to the American West: from the first frontier to the New Age seekers
in the words of those who saw it happen / edited by David Colbert.
p.   cm.
Included bibliographical references and index.
ISBN 0-670-88103-1 (hc)
ISBN 0 14 02.8054 5 (pbk.)
I. West (U.S.)—History—Sources.   I. Colbert, David.
F591.E94   1998
978—dc21   98–18724

Printed in the United States of America
Set in Perpetua

in memory of Alan D. Williams

CONTENTS

INTRODUCTION

All the eyewitnesses assembled here have one thing in common: they were at the right place at the right time, with their eyes wide open and a gift for telling about what they saw. Beyond that, they differ widely. Some are famous, some are anonymous. Some were caught in the rush of events, others kept their distance. Their accounts are gathered from a variety of sources: memoirs, diaries, letters, oral history interviews, transcripts of trials and congressional debates, and reportage. Some knew they were writing for the public record. Others recorded thoughts they never expected to share.

Their stories describe more than cowboys and Indians. Although I was born there, to me the West is more than Big Sky country and Pacific sunsets. Culture, not geography, set the editorial boundaries for this book. A strict historian might say I am more interested in the frontier than the West. That would be accurate. My idea of the prototypical Western state is just a half hour's drive from Boston. When preacher Roger Williams stormed out of Massachusetts in 1636 in a huff about religious freedom and settled in the wild frontier forty miles west of Boston, founding Rhode Island as a haven for dissenters, he played out a drama that has been repeated by religious and political and social dissenters ever since: Americans get angry and then head west to live as they please.

Historian Frederick Jackson Turner wrote, "What the Mediterranean Sea was to the Greeks, breaking the bonds of custom, offering new experiences, calling out new institutions and activities, that, and more, the ever retreating frontier has been to the United States." American life was shaped, he said, "at the meeting point between savagery and civilization."

Just as the book covers unusual territory for a "Western" anthology, it covers an unusual stretch of time. It begins long before the mythic Old

West of gunfights and saloons, and extends to the present day. More than half the book is devoted to events of the twentieth century.

For all the astonishing events that have occurred in the five centuries of history covered here, much has remained the same. For instance, the impulse to move west has followed consistent patterns:

—*Americans head west to escape their past.* Thomas Morton, the hedonist nemesis of the Puritan colony, left behind a lawsuit and bad debts when he sailed from England in the 1620s. Many of the gangsters who built Las Vegas went there, as crime writer Nicholas Pileggi wrote, because "Las Vegas was a city with no memory. It was the place you went for a second chance. . . ."

—*One type of escapism stands out: Americans head west after they go bust.* Two hundred years ago Benjamin Rush, one of the signers of the Declaration of Independence, observed, "The first settler in the woods is generally a man who has outlived his credit or fortune in the cultivated parts of the state." When pioneer Moses Austin went broke in Missouri he got permission from the Mexican government to establish the first American settlement in Texas. When vacuum tube inventor Lee De Forest went bust in 1912, and needed to get away from creditors in New York City, he went to Palo Alto, taking a salaried job at Stanford University, which led to the birth of Silicon Valley.

—*Americans head west for sanctuary.* The Mormons did this several times, starting in New York State and finally settling in Utah and the Pacific coast. Abolitionist John Brown's master plan was to create a republic in the West populated by freed slaves—and the thousands who settled in the loosely governed Oklahoma Territory after the Civil War showed he was on to something. The gay men who moved to San Francisco after World War II created enclaves free from the stigma and violence they had experienced elsewhere.

—*Americans head west for the quick buck.* This was true before and after the Gold Rush or the oil drilling boom. Daniel Boone's famous autobiography, written to promote land sales in Kentucky, was published three years before the U.S. Constitution was written.

—*Americans head west to be the boss.* The unclaimed or undefended land of the West has cried out a siren song to would-be empire builders since the Spanish conquistadors. Aaron Burr tried to create a new republic in the Southwest because he had failed to win the presidency from Thomas Jefferson. William Walker, the "Gray-Eyed Man of Destiny," first tried to conquer Mexico and then took over Nicaragua, which was a gateway to the West. *Los Angeles Times* publisher Harrison Gray Otis ambitiously exploited his paper to promote the city and the San Fernando Valley, much of which he owned.

Despite the changing cast of characters, from conquistadors and missionaries to venture capitalists and new age therapists, it seems there is little new under the setting sun. These are some of the patterns of Western culture that endure:

—*The West has predicted many of the nation's social crises and the social shifts that followed.* The creation of each new state opened the question of new rules. The slavery conflict first led to open skirmishes in Kansas, when that new state tried to decide the matter by popular vote. Women's suffrage was first enacted in the West, long before it became a national law. Social Security had precursors in California's EPIC and Townsend plans. And of course the youth movement and the environmental movement of the modern era both got their start in the West. "The West," wrote novelist and essayist Wallace Stegner, "has had a way of warping well-carpentered habits, and raising the grain on exposed dreams."

—*The story of the American West can be told as the story of religious movements.* Roger Williams sought sanctuary in the wilderness just as all the Puritans had, and the Quakers and Mormons would after him. And the West spawned its own brand of religion. The Great Revival began in Tennessee in 1800. Evangelists Aimee Semple McPherson and Bob Shuler had huge congregations in Los Angeles in the 1930s. Aldous Huxley was searching for enlightenment when, inspired by the Indians of the Southwest, he began experimenting with mescaline and LSD in Los Angeles in the 1950s. Even the mass therapy movements that have sprung up to briefly take the place of religion for some people, like Werner Erhard's est in the 1970s, began in the West.

—Even when it was a few dozen miles from the east coast, the western frontier has fought political battles for independence from the East. The conspiracy theorists living in isolated western camps today are simply extreme examples of a type that has always existed in areas distant from their government. (Witness the colonists on the Atlantic coast in 1776.) And though the phenomenon isn't uniquely American, it has been a characteristic of the West from the time of Cortés, who fought against a Spanish army that had been sent to remove him from his post in Mexico. Shortly before the Revolutionary War, the "Regulators" of the western Carolinas rebelled against the colonial government on the coast. Soon after arriving in Utah in the 1850s, the Mormons fought against federal troops. In 1979, state politicians in Nevada attempted the "Sagebrush Revolt," a legal maneuver to reclaim the federal land that consitutes most of their state.

Although these patterns and others appear throughout the book, the accounts are arranged as the adventures unfolded, with no thematic chapters or sections. I've followed author Daniel Boorstin's observation, "The historian's neat categories parse experience in ways never found among living people." Jumping from era to era and being surprised by what one finds is part of the fun, and this book is meant to entertain. Or to use the westernism: don't fence me in. This isn't a book about objective theories, and couldn't be. Often it's the subjectivity of the eyewitness that makes an account so compelling.

Here is frontier trader Alexander Henry, who escaped death three times while witnessing the first day of Pontiac's Rebellion in 1763: *"The door was unlocked, and opening, and the Indians ascending the stairs, before I had completely crept into a small opening, which presented itself at one end of the heap. An instant after four Indians entered the room, all armed with tomahawks, and all besmeared with blood upon every part of their bodies."*

Utah native Terry Tempest Williams, thinking about why so many women in her family suddenly developed cancer after the nearby atomic bomb tests of the 1950s: *"When the Atomic Energy Commission described the country north of the Nevada Test Site as 'virtually uninhabited desert terrain,' my family were some of the 'virtual uninhabitants.' "*

John Gregory Dunne's sarcastic commentary on the superficial view of Los Angeles held by New Yorkers: *"A year ago a reporter from Time telephoned my wife and said that the magazine was preparing a new cover story on California; he wondered if she had noticed any significant changes in the state since Time's last California cover."*

These are people with a passion for what they've seen and experienced, and a desire to express it. In the early 1970s, reporter Charles Kuralt visited Independence Rock in Wyoming, which got its name because emigrants crossing the country were told to reach it by July 4th if they hoped to cross the Sierra Nevada before winter. "This rock," he said, "was an invitation no passerby could resist. . . . It begs to be written upon. And so they wrote upon it, and some of them did such a careful job with hammer and chisel that their names are still plainly visible. . . . It was graffiti when it was written. But it is history now, very personal and affecting history. . . . It was a way of saying, 'You see, I have made it this far. . . . Think of that!' "

Nearly every eyewitness in this book—including Kuralt, whose full account of Independence Rock appears on page 386—was participating in a great adventure, whether it be political or commercial or spiritual or personal. Their stories form a portrait of one of the most vital, enterprising aspects of the American story: The need to head into the new territory of the West, to shape it and be shaped by it.

"When Moctezuma was told all this, he was terror-struck."

THE RETURN OF QUETZALCOATL

April 1519
Mexico

AZTEC EYEWITNESSES

During the sixteenth century, the Aztec empire extended as far south as present-day Guatemala. When Spanish conquistador Hernando Cortés arrived, the empire was ruled by Moctezuma II. Thanks to another Spaniard who had made a brief landing a year earlier, Cortés knew the Aztecs believed a god named Quetzalcoatl would one day return from the east. He claimed to be that god.

The Aztecs were a literate culture; their version of the Spanish arrival and conquest was recorded soon after the events. About 1555, the various stories were rendered into Spanish by Bernadino de Sahagún, a Franciscan missionary, as part of his General History of the Things of New Spain.

The Mexicans climbed up [the ship], carrying the godly array as a gift of greeting. Each one went through the motions of kissing the earth before Cortes. . . .

Then they dressed Cortes in the array of Quetzalcoatl: in the turquoise mosaic snake mask with the head fan of quetzal feathers and with the jadeite snake-head earplugs suspended from it; the sleeveless jerkin; the plaited jadeite neckband with the golden disc resting in its midst. On the small of his back they put the mirror; over his shoulders they bound the cape; about the calf of his leg they arranged the jadeite band with the golden shells. And on his arm they laid the shield with bands of gold and shells crisscrossed and with outspread quetzal feathers on the lower rim and a quetzal feather flag. In front of him they laid the black "obsidian" sandals.

27

"Are these all your gifts of greeting, all your gifts for coming before one?" asked Cortes through interpreters, after all this had been done.

"These are all the things we have brought," they answered.

Then Cortes ordered them to be bound. The Spaniards put irons about their necks; they fettered them. Then they shot off the great lombard gun. At this, Moctezuma's emissaries fainted dead away—fell—knew no more, until the Spaniards sat each one up, revived them with a drink of wine, and made them eat some food.

. . . Cortes and the Spaniards then let them climb down to their boats. They paddled off furiously, each one as hard as he could. Some paddled with their hands, so as to flee as fast as they could. They said to one another, "Warriors! All your strength, now! Row hard, lest something evil befall us! . . . We must warn Moctezuma; we must report what we saw. . . ."

So they hastened on, reaching Mexico deep in the night.

Meanwhile Moctezuma had been unable to rest, to sleep, to eat. He would speak to no one. He seemed to be in great torment. He sighed. He felt weak. He could enjoy nothing.

"What will happen now?" he kept asking. "Who will be lord as I have been until now? My heart is burning as if dipped in chili sauce. Where can we go, O lord?"

Then the five emissaries arrived. "Even if he is asleep," they told the guards, "wake him. Tell him that those he sent to the sea have returned."

But Moctezuma said, "I shall not hear them in this place. Have them go to the Coacalli building." Further he commanded, "Have two captives covered with chalk."

So the messengers went to the Coacalli, the house of snakes.

Moctezuma came later. In front of the messengers, the captives were killed—their hearts torn out, their blood sprinkled over the messengers; for they had gone into great danger; they had looked into the very faces of the gods; they had even spoken to them.

After this they reported to Moctezuma all the wonders they had seen, and they showed him samples of the food the Spaniards ate.

Moctezuma was shocked, terrified by what he heard. He was much puzzled by their food, but what made him almost faint away was the telling of how the great lombard gun, at the Spaniards' command, expelled the shot which thundered as it went off. The noise weakened one, dizzied one. Something like a stone came out of it in a shower of fire and sparks. The smoke was foul; it had a sickening, fetid smell. And the shot, which struck a mountain, knocked it to bits—dissolved it. It reduced a tree to sawdust—the tree disappeared as if they had blown it away.

And as to their war gear, it was all iron. They were iron. Their head pieces were of iron. Their swords, their crossbows, their shields, their lances were of iron.

The animals they rode—they looked like deer—were as high as roof tops. [Horses were unknown in America before the Spanish arrived.]

They covered their bodies completely, all except their faces.

They were very white. Their eyes were like chalk. Their hair—on some it was yellow, on some it was black.

They wore long beards; they were yellow, too. And there were some black-skinned ones with kinky hair.

What they ate was like what Aztecs ate during periods of fasting: it was large, it was white, it was lighter than tortillas; it was spongy like the inside of corn stalks; it tasted as if it had been made of a flour of corn stalks; it was sweetish.

Their dogs were huge. Their ears were folded over; their jowls dragged; their eyes blazed yellow, fiery yellow. They were thin—their ribs showed. They were big. They were restless, moving about panting, tongues hanging. They were spotted or varicolored like jaguars.

When Moctezuma was told all this, he was terror-struck.

Although Moctezuma is now a symbol of resistance to colonial aggression, many of his subjects were not happy with his rule. Many Aztecs believed Moctezuma had usurped the throne, and become a despot. As well, the empire was feared by non-Aztec natives in the region, who were made to pay tributes and were often captured to be offered as live sacrifices to the Aztec gods.

Cortés was savvy in making alliances with the non-Aztecs. With their help he advanced toward the Aztec capital of Tenochtitlan—now Mexico City.

"The city is as large as Seville or Cordova. . . ."

THE AZTEC METROPOLIS

1520
Tenochtitlan

HERNANDO CORTÉS

Because of his Quetzalcoatl ruse, Cortés and his men were allowed to enter Tenochtitlan without a fight. The city was already a thousand years old when he saw it, and had a population of more than 150,000, comparable to the larger cities of Europe. His men likened it to Venice, remarking on the canals and causeways

*that linked the city's center island to the mainland, and on the ten-mile-long
system of dikes that controlled the surrounding lake and flood plain.*

Cortés wrote this description to Emperor Charles V.

There are four avenues or entrances to the city, all of which are
formed by artificial causeways, two spears' length in width.

The city is as large as Seville or Cordova; its streets, I speak of the
principal ones, are very wide and straight; some of these, and all the
inferior ones, are half land and half water, and are navigated by canoes.

All the streets at intervals have openings, through which the water
flows, crossing from one street to another; and at these openings, some
of which are very wide, there are also very wide bridges, composed of
large pieces of timber, of great strength and well put together; on many
of these bridges ten horses can go abreast.

This city has many public squares, in which are situated the markets
and other places for buying and selling. There is one square twice as
large as that of the city of Salamanca, surrounded by porticoes, where
are daily assembled more than sixty thousand souls, engaged in buying
and selling; and where are found all kinds of merchandise that the world
affords, embracing the necessaries of life, as for instance articles of food,
as well as jewels of gold and silver, lead, brass, copper, tin, precious
stones, bones, shells, snails, and feathers. . . .

There are apothecary shops, where prepared medicines, liquids,
ointments, and plasters are sold; barber shops, where they wash and
shave the head; and restaurants, that furnish food and drink at a certain
price. . . .

Every kind of merchandise is sold in a particular street or quarter
assigned to it exclusively, and thus the best order is preserved.

A building in the great square is used as an audience house, where
ten or twelve magistrates sit and decide all controversies that arise in the
market, and order delinquents to be punished.

Other persons go constantly about among the people observing
what is sold, and the measures used in selling; and they have been seen
to break measures that were not true.

. . . This great city contains a large number of temples, or houses
for their idols. . . . Among these temples there is one which far sur-
passes all the rest. . . . There are full forty towers, which are lofty and
well built, the largest of which has fifty steps leading to its main body,
and is higher than the tower of the principal church at Seville. The stone
and wood of which they are constructed are so well wrought in every
part, that nothing could be better done. . . .

I precipitated [the Aztec idols] from their pedestals, and cast them down the steps of the temple, purifying the chapels in which they had stood, as they were all polluted with human blood, shed in the sacrifices.

In the place of these I put images of Our Lady and the Saints, which excited not a little feeling in Moctezuma and the inhabitants, who at first remonstrated, declaring that if my proceedings were known throughout the country, the people would rise against me.

They believed that their idols bestowed on them all temporal good, and if they permitted them to be ill-treated, they would be angry and withhold their gifts, and by this means the people would be deprived of the fruits of the earth and perish with famine.

I answered, through the interpreters, that they were deceived in expecting any favors from idols, the work of their own hands, formed of unclean things, and that they must learn there was but one God.

Moctezuma replied, the others assenting to what he said, "That they had already informed me they were not the aborigines of the country, but that their ancestors had emigrated to it many years ago; and they fully believed that after so long an absence from their native land, they might have fallen into some errors; that I having more recently arrived must know better than themselves what they ought to believe and that if I would instruct them in these matters, and make them understand the true faith, they would follow my directions, as being for the best."

. . . In regard to the domestic appointments of Moctezuma, and the wonderful grandeur and state that he maintains, there is so much to be told. . . . As nearly as I have been able to learn, his territories are equal in extent to Spain itself. He is also dressed every day in four different suits, entirely new, which he never wears a second time. Whenever Moctezuma appeared in public, which was seldom the case, all those who accompanied him, or whom he accidentally met in the streets, turned away without looking towards him, and others prostrated themselves until he had passed.

Within a week Cortés was holding Moctezuma prisoner, and governing through him. Moctezuma was killed about a year later during an unsuccessful uprising.

In the century that followed, Spanish explorers trekked throughout the West. Most of them were in search of gold. Others built Catholic missions and converted tens of thousands of Native Americans.

In 1540, Francisco Vásquez de Coronado, governor of a Mexican province, led a large expedition in search of the Seven Cities of Cibola, rumored to be made of gold and jewels. They found only the less-than-glittering Zuñi pueblos of pre-

sent-day New Mexico, and the simple village of Quivara near what is now Wichita, Kansas. But the two-year quest was the first organized European journey into what is now Texas, Oklahoma, Kansas, and Nebraska.

Along the way, they had a few surprises. They were shocked to discover a strange animal, the buffalo: "There was not one of the horses that did not take flight when he [first] saw [a buffalo], for they have a narrow, short face, the brow two palms across from eye to eye, the eyes sticking out at the side, so that, when they are running, they can see who is following them. They have very long beards, like goats, and . . . a great hump, larger than a camel's." And Coronado's men were the first Europeans to see the Grand Canyon: "[We] came to the banks of the [Colorado] river, which seemed to be more than three or four leagues across to the other bank of the stream which flowed between them. . . . We spent three days on this bank looking for a passage down to the river, which looked from above as if the water was six feet across, although the Indians said it was half a league wide. It was impossible to descend."

While Coronado was exploring on land, a naval expedition, led by Portuguese sailor Juan Rodriguez Cabrillo, sailed along the Pacific coast as far as the present-day Oregon border. Cabrillo noted San Diego Bay—the probable site of his landing there is a national monument—and a bit farther up the coast encountered "a large bay which [we] called Bay of Los Fumos, (Bay of the Smokes), because of the many smokes on it." That's probably the first eyewitness account of Los Angeles smog, a combination of smoke and fog trapped by the surrounding mountains. It plagued the area long before today's industrial-grade smog from factories and car exhaust.

At the end of the century, the Spanish began to settle north of the Rio Grande. In a ceremony near what is now El Paso, Texas, Don Juan de Oñate, a descendant of both Cortés and Moctezuma II, claimed a territory encompassing what is now several southwestern states. He was a cruel governor—in a notable battle, he destroyed the Acoma pueblo, considered the oldest city in the United States—but he left an important legacy: The wild horses and cattle herds of the West are thought to have descended from his livestock.

All these endeavors occurred before the founding of the first permanent British settlements on the Atlantic coast. With its head start on the other Europeans powers, Spain dominated the West politically for the next three hundred years, until Mexican independence in 1821. Almost another two centuries later, it remains one of the West's strongest cultural influences.

"A great number of weak and distressed souls . . . are flying hither from Old and New England."

THE WILD WEST OF THE EAST

1636
Rhode Island

ROGER WILLIAMS

About a hundred years after the Spanish began exploring from the south, the British began to settle along the Atlantic coast. It wasn't long before factions began to develop among the British colonists, leading some to move inland to the wilderness.

In New England, the most notable rebel faction was led by a minister named Roger Williams. He was either a madman or a visionary, depending on whether you agreed with him or not. He believed no one could mediate between an individual and God, which set him against the leaders of Massachusetts, who enjoyed both civil and church authority. They quickly decided that Williams wasn't a visionary, and banished him.

As both madmen and dreamers have done in the centuries since, Williams headed west to start fresh. Of course, in 1636 the Far West was about forty miles outside of Boston. Williams founded a new colony there, now the state of Rhode Island, in many ways the prototypical "Western" state.

When I was unkindly and unchristianly, as I believe, driven from my house and land and wife and children (in the midst of New England winter, now about 35 years past) at Salem, that ever-honored Governor Mr. Winthrop privately wrote to me to steer my course to Nahigonset-Bay [Narragansett Bay] and Indians for many high and heavenly and public ends, encouraging me [because of] the freeness of the place from any English claims or patents. I took his prudent motion as a hint and voice from God and waving all other thoughts and motions, I steered my course from Salem (though in winter snow which I feel yet) unto these parts, wherein I may say I have seen the face of God.

I first pitched, and begun to build and plant at Sekonk, now Rehoboth, but I received a letter from my ancient friend Mr. Winslow, then Governour of Plymouth, professing his own and others love and respect to me, yet lovingly advising me, since I was fallen into the edge of their bounds and they were loath to displease the Bay, to remove but to the other side of the water and then he said I had the country free before me and might be as free as themselves and we should be loving neighbors together. These were the joint understandings of these two eminently wise and Christian Governors and others, in their day, together with their council and advice as to the freedom and vacancy of this place, which in this respect and many other Providences of the most holy and only wise, I called *Providence*.

Sometime after Plymouth, great Sachim Ousamaquin [Wampanoag chief Massasoit], upon occasion affirming that Providence was his land and therefore Plymouth's land and some resenting it, the then prudent and godly Governor Mr. Bradford and others of his godly council, answered that if after due examination it should be found true what the barbarian said, yet having, to my loss of a harvest that year, been now (though by their gentle advice) as good as banished from Plymouth as from the Massachusetts; and I had quietly and patiently departed from them, at their motion, to the place where now I was, I should not be molested and tossed up and down again while they had breath in their bodies; and surely between those my friends of the Bay and Plymouth, I was sorely tossed for fourteen weeks, in a bitter winter season, not knowing what bread or bed did mean; beside the yearly loss of no small matter in my trading with English and natives, being debarred from Boston, the chief mart and port of New England. . . .

Upon frequent exceptions against Providence men that we had no authority for civil government, I went purposely to England and upon my report and petition, the Parliament granted us a charter of government for these parts, so judged vacant on all hands.

Here all over this colony, a great number of weak and distressed souls, scattered are flying hither from Old and New England, the Most High and only wise hath in his infinite wisdom provided this country and this corner as a shelter for the poor and persecuted, according to their several persuasions. . . .

We must part with lands and lives before we part with such a jewel.

The 1663 Rhode Island charter states: ". . . noe person within the said colonye, at any tyme hereafter shall be any wise molested, punished, disquieted or called in question for any differences in opinion in matters of religion [that] doe not actually disturb the civil peace. . . ."

Along with the Baptist followers of Williams, the first colony dedicated to religious freedom and to the separation of church and state became a sanctuary for Jews and Quakers who had been persecuted by the Puritans. Providence, the capital, is the site of the first Baptist church in America, and Newport is the home of the first American synagogue.

". . . A monument of revenging Justice."

KING PHILIP'S WAR: THE DEATH OF PHILIP

August 12, 1676
Mt. Hope, Rhode Island

INCREASE MATHER

In 1621, the Wampanoag Indians and the Pilgrims celebrated their friendship with the first Thanksgiving ceremony. In 1675–6, they fought one of the bloodiest wars in American history.

As the European settlements expanded westward from the Massachusetts coast, the Indians found that the colonists considered them trespassers. When the tension turned to war, there were about ten thousand Indians in the region, and about fifty thousand colonists.

Several Indian tribes allied to fight the colonists. The conflict was named "King Philip's War" because "Philip" was the English name of Metacomet, the Wampanoag chief. He was the son of chief Massasoit, who had welcomed the first arrivals from the Mayflower.

This account of Philip's death, by clergyman and Harvard College fellow Increase Mather, reveals the blood lust of the war.

This is the memorable day wherein Philip, the perfidious and bloody author of the war and woeful miseries that have thence ensued, was taken and slain. And God brought it to pass, chiefly by Indians themselves.

One of Philip's men (being disgusted at him, for killing an Indian who had propounded an expedient for peace with the English) ran away from him, and coming to Rhode-Island, informed that Philip was now returned again to Mount-Hope [now Bristol], and undertook to bring them to the Swamp where he hid himself. Divine Providence so disposed, as that Captain Church of Plymouth was then in Rhode-Island, in order to recruit his soldiers, who had been wearied with a tedious march that week. But immediately upon this intelligence, he set forth again, with a small company of English and Indians.

It seemeth that night Philip (like the man in the host of Midian) dreamed that he was fallen into the hands of the English, and just as he was saying to those that were with him, that they must fly for their lives that day, lest the Indian that was gone from him should discover where he was our soldiers came upon him and surrounded the swamp (where he with forty-seven of his men absconded). Thereupon he betook himself to flight; but as he was coming out of the swamp, an Englishman and an Indian endeavored to fire at him, the Englishman missed his aim, but the Indian shot him through the heart, so as that he fell down dead.

. . . And in that very place where he first contrived and began his mischief, was he taken and destroyed, and there was he (like as Agag was hewed in pieces before the Lord) cut into four quarters, and is now hanged up as a monument of revenging Justice, his head being cut off and carried away to Plymouth, his hands were brought to Boston.

So let all thine enemies perish, O Lord!

The war devastated both the colonists and the Indians. Among the colonists, one of every sixteen adult men was killed. The Indians fared worse, and after the war many were sold into slavery in the Caribbean. Some of the dozen European settlements destroyed in the war were not fully resettled for twenty years. Westward expansion was halted for twenty more.

"The rebels were numerous and we were very few . . ."

THE PUEBLO UPRISING

June 13–14, 1680
Santa Fe, New Mexico

ANTONIO DE OTERMIN AND PEDRO NARANJO

In 1680, a medicine man named Popé led a Pueblo uprising against Spanish Jesuits in New Mexico. The Jesuits, who had converted more than 100,000 Indians and built chapels in more than 100 villages, had not been gentle conquerors. Their brutality appalled even their Franciscan colleagues.

Eyewitness Pedro Naranjo, of the San Felipe Pueblo, was taken prisoner and interrogated by the Spanish, who recorded his testimony. Eyewitness Antonio de Otermin was governor of New Mexico.

NARANJO

Under oath Pedro Naranjo declared that . . . in an estufa [sacred meeting place] of the pueblo of Los Taos there appeared to the said Popé three figures of Indians who never came out of the estufa. They gave the said Popé to understand that they were going underground to the lake of Copala. He saw these figures emit fire from all the extremities of their bodies . . . and these three beings spoke to the said Popé. . . . They told him to make a cord of maguey fiber and tie some knots in it which would signify the number of days that they must wait for the rebellion. He said that the cord was passed through all the pueblos of the kingdom so that those which agreed to it [the rebellion] might untie one knot in sign of obedience. . . . As a sign of agreement and notice of having concurred in the treason and perfidy they were to send up smoke signals to that effect in each one of the pueblos singly. The said cord was taken from pueblo to pueblo by the swiftest youths under the penalty of death if they revealed the secret.

DE OTERMIN

About nine o'clock in the morning, there came in sight of us . . . all the Indians of the Tanos and Pecos nations and the Querez of San Marcos, armed and giving war-whoops. As I learned that one of the Indians who was leading them was from the villa and had gone to join them shortly before, I sent some soldiers to summon him and tell him on my behalf that he could come to see me in entire safety, so that I might ascertain from him the purpose for which they were coming.

Upon receiving this message he came to where I was, and, since he was known, as I say, I asked him how it was that he had gone crazy too— being an Indian who spoke our language, was so intelligent, and had lived all his life in the villa among the Spaniards, where I had placed such confidence in him—and was now coming as a leader of the rebels.

He replied to me that they had elected him as their captain, and that they were carrying two banners, one white and the other red, and that the white one signified peace and the red one war. Thus we should choose the white if we agreed to leave the country, and if we chose the red, we must perish, because the rebels were numerous and we were very few. . . .

I spoke to him very persuasively, to the effect that he and the rest of his followers were Catholic Christians, [asking] how they expected to live without the religious [leaders]. . . . I told him (having given him all the preceding admonitions as a Christian and a Catholic) to return to his people and say to them that unless they immediately desisted from sacking the houses and dispersed, I would send to drive them away from there. Whereupon he went back, and his people received him with peals of bells and trumpets, giving loud shouts in sign of war.

On the next day, Friday, the nations of the Taos, Pecuries, Hemes, and Querez having assembled during the past night, when dawn came more than 2,500 Indians fell upon us in the villa. . . .

. . . Two days before the time set for its execution, because his lordship had learned of it and had imprisoned two Indian accomplices from the pueblo of Tesuque, it was carried out prematurely that night, because it seemed to them that they were now discovered; and they killed religious, Spaniards, women, and children. . . .

. . . An order came from the said Indian, Popé, in which he commanded all the Indians to break the lands and enlarge their cultivated fields, saying that now they were as they had been in ancient times, free from the labor they had performed for the religious and the Spaniards, who could not now be alive. . . .

. . . Popé . . . ordered in all the pueblos through which he passed that they instantly break up and burn the images of the holy Christ, the Virgin Mary and the other saints, the crosses, and everything pertaining to Christianity, and that they burn the temples, break up the bells, and separate from the wives whom God had given them in marriage and take those whom they desired.

In order to take away their baptismal names, the water, and the holy oils, they were to plunge into the rivers and wash themselves with amole, which is a root native to the country, washing even their clothing, with the understanding that there would thus be taken from them the character of the holy sacraments. . . . He saw to it that they at once erected and rebuilt their houses of idolatry which they call estufas, and made very ugly masks in imitation of the devil in order to dance the dance of the cacina [kachina]; and he said likewise that the devil had given them to understand that living thus in accordance with the law of their ancestors, they would harvest a great deal of maize, many beans, a great abundance of cotton, calabashes, and very large watermelons and cantaloupes; and that they could erect their houses and enjoy abundant health and leisure.

This incident began the most successful revolt in the long history of clashes between Native Americans and Europeans. The Indians forced a Spanish retreat from Santa Fe, the provincial capital, to El Paso, and held off the Spanish for twelve years. The Spanish eventually reclaimed their territories and brought the New Mexico Pueblos back into the fold, but some Indians, such as the Hopi, remained free of Spanish government.

"The whole assembly responded with
shouts of **Vive le Roi . . ."**

LA SALLE CLAIMS LOUISIANA

April 9, 1682
near the Gulf of Mexico

JACQUES DE LA METAIRIE

While the Spanish were colonizing the desert Southwest, and the British were set-
tling along the Atlantic coast, the French entered via the St. Lawrence River,
north of New England. Eventually they would establish claims throughout the
Great Lakes region, building outposts and forging alliances with Indian tribes
such as the Miami and Illinois.

Among the intrepid Frenchmen was Robert Cavelier, Sieur de la Salle, who
voyaged down the Mississippi, grandly claiming the river and all of its surround-
ing lands on behalf of King Louis of France. His now-forgotten name for the
Mississippi, the "River Colbert," was a gracious attempt to honor Louis's powerful
finance minister and advisor, Jean-Baptiste Colbert.

Jacques de la Metairie was the expedition's notary.

We continued our voyage till the 6th, when we discovered three
channels by which the River Colbert discharges itself into the sea. On
the 8th, we reascended the river, a little above its confluence with the
sea, to find a dry place, beyond the reach of inundations. Here we prepared a column and a cross, and to the said column were affixed the
arms of France, with this inscription:

LOUIS LE GRAND, ROI DE FRANCE ET DE NAVARRE, REGNE
LE NEUVIEME, AVRIL, 1682

The whole party, under arms, chanted the *Te Deum,* the *Exaudiat,* the
Domine salvum fac Regem; and then, after a salute of firearms and cries of
Vive le Roi, the column was erected by M. de la Salle, who, standing near
it, said, with a loud voice, in French: "In the name of the most high,
mighty, invincible, and victorious Prince, Louis the Great, by the Grace
of God, King of France and of Navarre, Fourteenth of that name, this
ninth day of April, one thousand six hundred and eighty-two, I do now
take, in the name of his Majesty, possession of this country of Louisiana,
the seas, harbours, ports, bays, adjacent straits; and all the nations, people, provinces, cities, towns, villages, mines, minerals, fisheries,

streams, and rivers, comprised in the extent of the said Louisiana, from the mouth of the great river St. Louis on the eastern side, otherwise called Ohio, Alighin [Allegheny], Chikachas [Chickasaws], and this with the consent of the Chaouanons [Shawnee], Chikachas, and other people dwelling therein, with whom we have made alliance; as also along the River Colbert, or Mississippi, from its source . . . as far as its mouth at the sea, or Gulf of Mexico, upon the assurance which we have received from all these [Indian] nations, that we are the first Europeans who have descended or ascended the said River Colbert. . . .

To which the whole assembly responded with shouts of *Vive le Roi,* and with salutes of firearms. Moreover, the Sieur de la Salle caused to be buried at the foot of the tree, to which the cross was attached, a leaden plate, on one side of which were engraved the arms of France.

Actually, Hernando de Soto had explored the Mississippi on behalf of Spain in 1542. But the French built outposts in the region, giving them control of the all-important fur trade and leading to French settlement.

"The Governor persuaded them to continue on . . ."

THE KNIGHTS OF THE GOLDEN HORSESHOE

September 5–7, 1716
Virginia Colony

JOHN FONTAINE

The English colonists did not leave western exploration to the Spanish and French. Virginia's lieutenant governor Alexander Spotswood led a party of gentleman explorers over the Blue Ridge Mountains into the Shenandoah Valley, the Far West to the colonists. When they returned he gave each of them a golden horseshoe and dubbed them knights of that order, to "encourage gentlemen to venture backwards and make new settlements."

"Sir" John Fontaine lived in Virginia from 1715 to 1719.

5th.—A fair day. At nine we were mounted; we were obliged to have axe-men to clear the way in some places. We followed the windings of James River, observing that it came from the very top of the mountains. . . . In some places it was very steep, in others, it was so that we could ride up. About one of the clock we got to the top of the mountain; . . . and we came to the very head spring of James River, where it runs no bigger than a man's arm, from under a large stone. We drank King George's health, and all the Royal Family's, at the very top of the Appalachian mountains. About a musket-shot from the spring there is another, which rises and runs down on the other side; it goes westward, and we thought we could go down that way, but we met with such prodigious precipices, that we were obliged to return to the top again. We found some trees which had been formerly marked, I suppose, by the Northern Indians, and following these trees, we found a good, safe descent. Several of the company were for returning; but the Governor persuaded them to continue on. About five, we were down on the other side, and continued our way for about seven miles further, until we came to a large river, by the side of which we encamped. . . .

6th.——We crossed the river, which we called Euphrates. It is very deep; the main course of the water is north; it is fourscore yards wide in the narrowest part. We drank some healths on the other side, and returned; after which I went a swimming in it. . . . the Governor buried a bottle with a paper inclosed, on which he writ that he took possession of this place in the name and for King George the First of England. We had a good dinner, and after it we got the men together, and loaded all their arms, and we drank the King's health in champagne, and fired a volley—the Princess's health in Burgundy, and fired a volley, and all the rest of the Royal Family in claret, and a volley. We drank the Governor's health and fired another volley. We had several sorts of liquors, viz., Virginia red wine and white wine, Irish usquebaugh, brandy, shrub, two sorts of rum, champagne, canary, cherry, punch, water, cider, &c. . . .

7th.——At seven in the morning we mounted our horses, and parted with the rangers, who were to go farther on, and we returned homewards.

Spotswood's efforts sparked the settlement of the southern Piedmont. He is remembered in the name of Spotsylvania County, formerly part of his estate.

*"I may conclude the inhabitants of this American coast
are of the same origin as the Kamchadals. . . ."*

BERING REACHES ALASKA

July 15, 1741

GEORG STELLER

*Along with the Spanish, British, and French, a fourth European power made a
significant effort to settle the West. Russia established a foothold in a territory
that included Alaska, the Aleutian Islands, and some of what is now British
Columbia.*

*Russian America, as the territory became known, grew out of the voyages of
Vitus Bering in the seas northeast of Siberia. Bering discovered the strait that now
bears his name in 1730, exciting the interest of his patron, Tsar Peter I, for an
expedition to explore America. Ten years were devoted to planning before two ships
finally left Kamchatka in 1741.*

Georg Steller, a German who had studied botany and medicine, was the voyage's naturalist.

We saw land as early as July 15 . . . the mountains, observed extending inland, were so lofty that we could see them quite plainly at sea
at a distance of sixteen Dutch miles. I cannot recall having seen higher
mountains anywhere in Siberia and Kamchatka. The coast was everywhere much indented and therefore provided with numerous bays and
inlets close to the mainland.

. . . It can easily be imagined how happy every one was when land
was finally sighted; nobody failed to congratulate the Captain Commander, whom the glory for the discovery mostly concerned. He, however, received it all not only very indifferently and without particular
pleasure, but in the presence of all he even shrugged his shoulders while
looking at the land. . . . The good Captain Commander was much superior to his officers in looking into the future, and in the cabin he
expressed himself to me and Mr. Plenisner as follows: "We think now we
have accomplished everything, and many go about greatly inflated, but
they do not consider where we have reached land, how far we are from
home, and what may yet happen, who knows but that perhaps trade
winds may arise, which may prevent us from returning? We do not
know this country; nor are we provided with supplies for a wintering."

. . . On Monday the 20th we came to anchor among numerous
islands. . . . I struck out in the direction of the mainland in the hopes of

finding human beings and habitations. I had not gone more than a verst [about two-thirds of a mile] along the beach before I ran across signs of people and their doings.

Under a tree I found an old piece of a log hollowed out in the shape of a trough, in which, a couple of hours before, the savages, for lack of pots and vessels, had cooked their meat by means of red-hot stones, just as the Kamchadals did formerly. . . . There were also strewn about the remains of yukola, or pieces of dried fish, which, as in Kamchatka, has to serve the purpose of bread at all meals. There were also great numbers of very large scallops over eight inches across, also blue mussels similar to those found in Kamchatka and, no doubt, eaten raw as the custom is there. In various shells, as on dishes, I found sweet grass completely prepared in Kamchadal fashion, on which water seemed to have been poured in order to extract the sweetness. I discovered further, not far from the fireplace, beside the tree, on which there still were the live coals, a wooden apparatus for making fire, of the same nature as those used in Kamchatka. . . .

From all this I think I may conclude that the inhabitants of this American coast are of the same origin as the Kamchadals, with whom they agree completely in such peculiar customs and utensils, particularly the preparation of the sweet grass, which have not been communicated even to the Siberian natives nearest to Kamchatka, for instance the Tunguses and Koryaks.

But if this is so, then it may also be conjectured that America extends farther westward and, opposite Kamchatka, is much nearer in the north, since in view of such a great distance as we traveled of at least 500 miles, it is not credible that the Kamchadals would have been able to get there in their miserable craft. . . .

These, then, are all our achievements and observations, and these not even from the mainland, on which none of us set foot, but only from an island which seemed to be three miles long and a half mile wide and the nearest to the mainland (which here forms a large bay studded with many islands) and separated from it by a channel less than half a mile wide. The only reason why we did not attempt to land on the mainland is a sluggish obstinacy and a dull fear. . . . The time here spent in investigation bears an arithmetical ratio to the time used in fitting out: ten years the preparations for this great undertaking lasted, and ten hours were devoted to the work itself. Of the mainland we have a sketch on paper; of the country itself an imperfect idea, based upon what could be discovered on the island and upon conjectures.

. . . The animals occurring there and supplying the natives with their meat for food and with their skins for clothing are, so far as I had opportunity to observe, hair seals, large and small sharks, whales, and plenty of sea otters. . . . Of birds I saw only two familiar species, the raven and the magpie; however, of strange and unknown ones I noted more than ten different kinds, all of which were easily distinguished from the European and Siberian [species] by their very particularly bright coloring. Good luck, thanks to my huntsman, placed in my hands a single specimen, of which I remember to have seen a likeness painted in lively colors and described in the newest account of the birds and plants of the Carolinas published in French and English, the name of the author of which, however, does not occur to me now. This bird proved to me that we were really in America.

The bird Steller saw was a blue jay. (He recognized it from The Natural History of Carolina, Florida, and the Bahama Islands, *by Mark Catesby.) Steller's other insightful hypotheses were also confirmed. And his descriptions of four unknown animals—the fur seal, the sea otter, the sea lion, and the sea cow—sparked the Russian fur trade in Alaska.*

On the way back to Russia after just a brief exploration, Bering's ship was wrecked on the shore of an Alaskan island, where Bering died of scurvy. The following summer the surviving crew built a boat out of the wreckage and returned to Russia.

Although the fur trade flourished, Russia was unable to establish large settlements throughout the territory. America bought it in 1867. The deal, negotiated by Secretary of State William Henry Seward, was known as "Seward's Folly," because the price of $7,200,000 was widely considered to be outrageously high. Eventually the public realized it was dirt cheap.

"The chief officers retired to hold a council of war. . . ."

WASHINGTON PARLEYS WITH THE FRENCH

November 25–December 4, 1753
Fort Le Boeuf, in the Ohio Valley

GEORGE WASHINGTON

As European settlement continued, the rival claims and ambitions of Spain, England, and France encroached on one another, unrestrained by the vague boundaries of western territories.

Although historian Samuel Eliot Morison said the early 1700s was a period of "cold war maneuvering for the west," tempers often flared red hot. The French massacred the English at Fort Schenectady in 1690, the English took Louisbourg in 1745, and so on. Back-and-forth skirmishes went on for decades. In the late 1740s, when several Virginia land companies were formed to settle the Ohio Valley, the French resisted the incursion. They sent a flotilla to secure claims along the Ohio River, and built a chain of forts in the region. A French royal document of the time says, "It is of the greatest importance to arrest the progress of the pretensions and expeditions of the English in that quarter. Should they succeed there, they would cut off communication between the two colonies of Canada and Louisiana, and would be in a position to trouble them, and to ruin both one and the other. . . ."

Enter George Washington. Just twenty-two, he was chosen by Virginia governor Robert Dinwiddie to protest the French actions. This diplomatic assignment was a prelude to the French and Indian War of 1755–63, the conflict that gave Washington the experience and reputation that led to his command of the colonial army twenty years later.

NOVEMBER 25

I inquired [of some Indians] into the situation of the French on the Mississippi—their number, and what forts they had built. They informed me that there were four small forts between New Orleans and the Black Islands garrisoned with about thirty or forty men, and a few small pieces in each.

DECEMBER 4

We found the French colors hoisted at a house from which they had driven Mr. John Frazier, an English subject. I immediately repaired to it to know where the commander resided. There were three officers, one of whom, Captain Joncaire, informed me that he had the command of the Ohio, but that there was a general officer at the near fort, where he advised me to apply for an answer. He invited us to sup with them, and treated us with the greatest complaisance.

The wine, as they dosed themselves pretty plentifully with it, soon banished the restraint which at first appeared in their conversation, and gave a license to their tongues to reveal their sentiments more freely.

They told me that it was their absolute design to take possession of the Ohio, and, by G——, they would do it. For that, although they were sensible the English could raise two men for their one, yet they knew [the British] motions were too slow to prevent any undertaking of theirs. They pretend to have an undoubted right to the river from a discovery made by one La Salle sixty years ago, and the rise of this expedition is to prevent our settling on the river or waters of it, as they had heard of some families moving out in order thereto.

DECEMBER 12TH

[At the fort,] I prepared early to wait upon the commander, and was received and conducted to him by the second in command. I acquainted him with my business, and offered my commission and letter.

DECEMBER 13

The chief officers retired to hold a council of war, which gave me an opportunity of taking the dimensions of the fort and making what observations I could.

I could get no certain account of the number of men here, but, according to the best judgment I could form, there are an hundred exclusive of officers, of which there are many. I also gave orders to the people who were with me to take an exact account of the canoes which were hauled up to convey their forces down in the spring. This they did, and told fifty of birchbark and one hundred and seventy of pine, besides many others which were blocked out in readiness to make.

DECEMBER 14

As I found many plots to retard the Indians' business and prevent their returning with me, I endeavored all that lay in my power to frustrate their schemes and hurry them on. . . . I was inquiring of the commander by what authority he had made prisoners of several of our English subjects. He told me that the country belonged to them; that no Englishman had a right to trade upon those waters and that he had orders to make every person prisoner who attempted it on the Ohio, or the waters of it.

DECEMBER 16

The French were not slack in their inventions to keep the Indians this day also. . . . But I urged and insisted with the Half-King [an Indian ally of the American colonists] so closely upon his word that he refrained and set off with us as he had engaged.

Our horses were now so weak and feeble and the baggage so heavy, that . . . myself and others . . . gave up our horses to assist with the baggage. I put myself in an Indian walking dress, and continued with them three days till I found there was no probability of their getting home in any reasonable time. . . . As I was uneasy to get back to make report of my proceedings to his Honor the Governor, I determined to journey the nearest way through the woods on foot. Accordingly I left Mr. Vanbraam in charge of our baggage, with money and directions, . . . took my necessary papers, pulled off my clothes, and tied myself up in a matchcoat. Then with gun in hand and pack at my back, in which were my papers and provisions, I set out. . . .

". . . The commandant only smiled at my suspicions."

PONTIAC'S REBELLION BEGINS

June 2, 1763
Fort Michilimackinac

ALEXANDER HENRY

On paper, England's 1759 defeat of French forces on the Plains of Abraham at Quebec City secured success in the French and Indian War. The British colonists appeared to have gained control of Canada, the Great Lakes region, and the Mississippi Valley from the rival French forces. But the war was only half won. The Indians wouldn't play along.

Led by the charismatic Ottawa chief Pontiac, a confederacy of tribes waged war with the British colonists for eighteen months. The rebellion included a daring simultaneous attack on several British forts along a thousand-mile stretch of western wilderness. Within a month, Pontiac held nine of the eleven British forts in the West.

Pontiac's Rebellion was not a gentleman's war. The Indians mutilated their prisoners. The British used germ warfare. "Could it not be contrived," Sir Jeffery Amherst, commander of the British army, asked one of his field officers, "to send the Small Pox among those disaffected tribes of Indians? We must on this occasion use every stratagem in our power to reduce them."

Fort Michilimackinac, the site of this account, was located in what is now northern Michigan, at the meeting point of Lake Michigan and Lake Huron. It was essential to the fur trade, which was itself essential to the economy of North America.

Eyewitness Alexander Henry was a trader from New Jersey.

The morning was sultry. A Chipewa came to tell me that his nation was going to play at baggatiway with the Sacs or Saakies, another Indian nation, for a high wager. He invited me to witness the sport, adding that the commandant was to be there, and would bet on the side of the Chipewa. In consequence of this information I went to the commandant and expostulated with him a little, representing that the Indians might possibly have some sinister end in view; but the commandant only smiled at my suspicions.

I did not go myself to see the match which was now to be played without the fort, because there being a canoe prepared to depart on the following day for Montreal I employed myself in writing letters to my friends; and even when a fellow trader, Mr. Tracy, happened to call upon me, saying that another canoe had just arrived from Detroit, and proposing that I should go with him to the beach to inquire the news, it so happened that I still remained to finish my letters, promising to follow Mr. Tracy in the course of a few minutes. Mr. Tracy had not gone more than twenty paces from my door when I heard an Indian war cry and a noise of general confusion.

Going instantly to my window I saw a crowd of Indians within the fort furiously cutting down and scalping every Englishman they found. In particular I witnessed the fate of Lieutenant Jemette.

I had in the room in which I was a fowling piece, loaded with swanshot. This I immediately seized and held it for a few minutes, waiting to hear the drum beat to arms. In this dreadful interval I saw several of my countrymen fall, and more than one struggling between the knees of an Indian, who, holding him in this manner, scalped him while yet living.

At length, disappointed in the hope of seeing resistance made to the enemy, and sensible, of course, that no effort of my own unassisted arm could avail against four hundred Indians, I thought only of seeking shelter. Amid the slaughter which was raging I observed many of the Canadian inhabitants of the fort calmly looking on, neither opposing the Indians, nor suffering injury; and from this circumstance I conceived a hope of finding security in their houses.

Between the yard door of my own house and that of M. Langlade, my next neighbor, there was only a low fence, over which I easily climbed. At my entrance I found the whole family at the windows, gazing at the scene of blood before them. I addressed myself immediately to M. Langlade, begging that he would put me into some place of safety until the heat of the affair should be over; an act of charity by which he might perhaps preserve me from the general massacre; but while I uttered my petition M. Langlade, who had looked for a moment at me, turned again to the window, shrugging his shoulders and intimating that he could do nothing for me:—*"Que voudriez-vous que j'en ferais?"* [What would you like me to do?]

This was a moment for despair; but the next a Pani woman, a slave of M. Langlade's, beckoned me to follow her. She brought me to a door which she opened, desiring me to enter, and telling me that it led to the garret, where I must go and conceal myself. I joyfully obeyed her directions; and she, having followed me up to the garret door, locked it after me and with great presence of mind took away the key.

This shelter obtained, if shelter I could hope to find it, I was naturally anxious to know what might still be passing without. Through an aperture which afforded me a view of the area of the fort I beheld, in shapes the foulest and most terrible, the ferocious triumphs of barbarian conquerors. The dead were scalped and mangled; the dying were writhing and shrieking under the unsatiated knife and tomahawk; and from the bodies of some, ripped open, their butchers were drinking the blood, scooped up in the hollow of joined hands and quaffed amid shouts of rage and victory. I was shaken not only with horror, but with fear. The sufferings which I witnessed I seemed on the point of experiencing. No long time elapsed before every one being destroyed who could be found, there was a general cry of "All is finished!" At the same instant I heard some of the Indians enter the house in which I was.

The garret was separated from the room below only by a layer of single boards, at once the flooring of the one and the ceiling of the other. I could therefore hear everything that passed; and the Indians no sooner came in than they inquired whether or not any Englishman were in the house. M. Langlade replied that he could not say—he did not know of any—answers in which he did not exceed the truth, for the Pani woman had not only hidden me by stealth, but kept my secret and her own. M. Langlade was therefore, as I presume, as far from a wish to destroy me as he was careless about saving me, when he added to these answers that they might examine for themselves, and would soon be satisfied as to the object of their question. Saying this, he brought them to the garret door.

The state of my mind will be imagined. Arrived at the door some delay was occasioned by the absence of the key and a few moments were thus allowed me in which to look around for a hiding place. In one corner of the garret was a heap of those vessels of birch bark used in maple sugar making. . . .

The door was unlocked, and opening, and the Indians ascending the stairs, before I had completely crept into a small opening, which presented itself at one end of the heap. An instant after four Indians entered the room, all armed with tomahawks, and all besmeared with blood upon every part of their bodies.

The die appeared to be cast. I could scarcely breathe; but I thought that the throbbing of my heart occasioned a noise loud enough to betray me. The Indians walked in every direction about the garret, and one of them approached me so closely that at a particular moment, had he put forth his hand, he must have touched me. Still I remained undiscovered, a circumstance to which the dark color of my clothes and the want of light in a room which had no window, and in the corner in which I was, must have contributed.

In a word, after taking several turns in the room, during which they told M. Langlade how many they had killed and how many scalps they had taken, they returned down stairs, and I with sensations not to be expressed, heard the door, which was the barrier between me and my fate, locked for the second time.

There was a feather bed on the floor, and on this, exhausted as I was by the agitation of my mind, I threw myself down and fell asleep. In this state I remained till the dusk of the evening, when I was awakened by a second opening of the door. The person that now entered was M. Langlade's wife, who was much surprised at finding me, but advised me not to be uneasy, observing that the Indians had killed most of the English, but that she hoped I might myself escape. A shower of rain having begun to fall, she had come to stop a hole in the roof. On her going away, I begged her to send me a little water to drink, which she did.

As night was now advancing I continued to lie on the bed, ruminating on my condition, but unable to discover a resource from which I could hope for life. A flight to Detroit had no probable chance of success. The distance from Michilimackinac was four hundred miles; I was without provisions; and the whole length of the road lay through Indian countries, countries of an enemy in arms, where the first man whom I should meet would kill me. To stay where I was threatened nearly the same issue. As before, fatigue of mind, and not tranquillity, suspended my cares and procured me further sleep. . . .

The respite which sleep afforded me during the night was put an end to by the return of morning. I was again on the rack of apprehension. At sunrise I heard the family stirring, and presently after, Indian voices informing M. Langlade they had not found my hapless self among the dead, and that they supposed me to be somewhere concealed.

M. Langlade appeared from what followed to be by this time acquainted with the place of my retreat, of which no doubt he had been informed by his wife. The poor woman, as soon as the Indians mentioned me, declared to her husband in the French tongue that he should no longer keep me in his house, but deliver me up to my pursuers, giving as a reason for this measure that should the Indians discover his instrumentality in my concealment, they might revenge it on her children, and that it was better that I should die than they.

M. Langlade resisted at first this sentence of his wife's; but soon suffered her to prevail, informing the Indians that he had been told I was in his house, that I had come there without his knowledge, and that he would put me into their hands. This was no sooner expressed than he began to ascend the stairs, the Indians following upon his heels.

I now resigned myself to the fate with which I was menaced; and regarding every attempt at concealment as vain, I arose from the bed and presented myself full in view to the Indians who were entering the room. They were all in a state of intoxication, and entirely naked, except about the middle. One of them, named Wenniway, whom I had previously known, and who was upward of six feet in height, had his entire face and body covered with charcoal and grease, only that a white spot of two inches in diameter encircled either eye. This man, walking up to me, seized me with one hand by the collar of the coat, while in the other he held a large carving knife, as if to plunge it into my breast; his eyes, meanwhile, were fixed steadfastly on mine. At length, after some seconds of the most anxious suspense, he dropped his arm, saying, "I won't kill you!" To this he added that he had been frequently engaged in wars against the English, and had brought away many scalps; that on a certain occasion he had lost a brother whose name was Musinigon, and that I should be called after him.

A reprieve upon any terms placed me among the living, and gave me back the sustaining voice of hope. . . .

Thus far secure I reascended my garret stairs in order to place myself the furthest possible out of the reach of insult from drunken Indians; but I had not remained there more than an hour, when I was called to the room below in which was an Indian who said that I must go with him out of the fort. . . . This man, as well as Wenniway himself, I had seen before. In the preceding year I had allowed him to take goods on credit, for which he was still in my debt; and some short time previous to the surprise of the fort he had said upon my upbraiding him with want of honesty that he would pay me before long. This speech now came fresh into my memory and led me to suspect that the fellow had formed a design against my life. . . .

I was now told to proceed; and my driver followed me close until I had passed the gate of the fort, when I turned toward the spot where I knew the Indians to be encamped. This, however, did not suit the purpose of my enemy, who seized me by the arm and drew me violently in the opposite direction to the distance of fifty yards above the fort. Here, finding that I was approaching the bushes and sand hills, I determined to proceed no farther, but told the Indian that I believed he meant to murder me, and that if so he might as well strike where I was as at any greater distance.

He replied with coolness that my suspicions were just, and that he meant to pay me in this manner for my goods. At the same time he produced a knife and held me in a position to receive the intended blow. Both this and that which followed were necessarily the affair of a moment. By some effort, too sudden and too little dependent on thought to be explained or remembered, I was enabled to arrest his arm and give him a sudden push by which I turned him from me and released myself from his grasp.

This was no sooner done than I ran toward the fort with all the swiftness in my power, the Indian following me, and I expecting every moment to feel his knife. I succeeded in my flight; and on entering the fort I saw Wenniway standing in the midst of the area, and to him I hastened for protection.

Wenniway desired the Indian to desist; but the latter pursued me round him, making several strokes at me with his knife, and foaming at the mouth with rage at the repeated failure of his purpose.

At length Wenniway drew near to M. Langlade's house; and, the door being open, I ran into it. The Indian followed me; but on my entering the house he voluntarily abandoned the pursuit.

The rebellion ended with a peace treaty signed in 1766. Pontiac himself was assassinated a few years after he surrendered.

Eyewitness Alexander Henry stayed at Fort Michilimackinac another year. The site of the fort is now Mackinaw City, Michigan.

"I was happy in the midst of dangers . . ."

THE DISCOVERY OF PARADISE

May 1769–March 1771
Kentucky

DANIEL BOONE

Daniel Boone, while serving under George Washington during the French and Indian War, was captivated by stories he heard from a fellow soldier about the western wilderness. After Pontiac's Rebellion was quashed in 1766 (see page 47), he began exploring Kentucky.

Boone's memoir, from which this account comes, was ghostwritten by John Filson, a land speculator who wanted to attract people to Kentucky. First published as part of a promotional booklet in 1784, it became an American origin myth three years before the Constitution was written.

It was on the first of May in the year 1769, that I resigned my domestic happiness for a time, and left my family and peaceable habitation on the Yadkin river, in North Carolina, to wander through the wilderness of America, in quest of the country of Kentucky, in company with John Finley, John Stewart, Joseph Holden, James Monay, and William Cool.

We proceeded successfully; and after a long and fatiguing journey, through a mountainous wilderness, in a westward direction, on the seventh day of June following we found ourselves on Red river, where John Finley had formerly been trading with the Indians, and, from the top of an eminence, saw with pleasure the beautiful level of Kentucky.

We found everywhere abundance of wild beasts of all sorts, through this vast forest. The buffalo were more frequent than I have seen cattle in the settlements, browsing on the leaves of the cane, or cropping the herbage on those extensive plains, fearless, because ignorant, of the violence of man. Sometimes we saw hundreds in a drove, and the numbers about the salt springs were amazing. In this forest, the habitation of beasts of every kind natural to America, we practiced hunting with great success, until the 22d day of December following.

This day John Stewart and I had a pleasing ramble, but fortune changed the scene in the close of it. We had passed through a great forest, on which stood myriads of trees, some gay with blossoms, others rich with fruits. Nature was here a series of wonders, and a fund of delight. We were diverted with innumerable animals presenting themselves perpetually to our view.

In the decline of the day, near Kentucky river, as we ascended the brow of a small hill, a number of Indians rushed out of a thick cane-brake upon us, and made us prisoners. The time of our sorrow was now arrived, and the scene fully opened. The Indians plundered us of what we had, and kept us in confinement 7 days, treating us with common savage usage. During this time we discovered no uneasiness or desire to escape, which made them less suspicious of us; but in the dead of the night, as we lay in a thick cane-brake by a large fire, when sleep had locked up their senses, my situation not disposing me for rest, I touched my companion, and gently awoke him. We improved this favourable opportunity, and departed, leaving them to take their rest, and speedily directed our course towards our old camp, but found it plundered, and the company dispersed and gone home.

About this time, my brother, Squire Boon, with another adventurer, who came to explore the country shortly after us, was wandering through the forest, determined to find me if possible, and accidentally found our camp. So much does friendship triumph over misfortune, that sorrows and sufferings vanish at the meeting not only of real friends, but of the most distant acquaintances.

Soon after this, my companion in captivity, John Stewart, was killed by the savages, and the man that came with my brother returned home by himself. We were then in a dangerous, helpless situation, exposed daily to perils and death, amongst savages and wild beasts, not a white man in the country but ourselves.

Thus situated, many hundred miles from our families, in the howl-ing wilderness, I believe few would have equally enjoyed the happiness we experienced. I often observed to my brother, You see now how little nature requires to be satisfied. Felicity, the companion of content, is rather found in our own breasts than in the enjoyment of external things: and I firmly believe it requires but a little philosophy to make a man happy in whatsoever state he is. This consists in a full resignation to the will of providence; and a resigned soul finds pleasure in a path strewed with briars and thorns. . . .

One day I undertook a tour through the country, and the diversity and beauties of nature I met with in this charming season, expelled every gloomy and vexatious thought. Just at the close of day the gentle gales retired, and left the place to the disposal of a profound calm. Not a breeze shook the most tremulous leaf. I had gained the summit of a commanding ridge, and, looking round with astonishing delight, beheld the ample plains, the beauteous tracts below. On the other hand, I sur-veyed the famous river Ohio, that rolled in silent dignity, marking the western boundary of Kentucky with inconceivable grandeur.

At a vast distance I beheld the mountains lift their venerable brows, and penetrate the clouds. All things were still. I kindled a fire near a fountain of sweet water, and feasted on the loin of a buck, which a few hours before I had killed. The sullen shades of night soon overspread the whole hemisphere, and the earth seemed to gasp after the hovering moisture. My roving excursion this day had fatigued my body, and diverted my imagination. I laid me down to sleep, and I awoke not until the sun had chased away the night.

. . . Thus I was surrounded with plenty in the midst of want. I was happy in the midst of dangers and inconveniences. In such a diversity it was impossible I should be disposed to melancholy. No populous city, with all the varieties of commerce and stately structures, could afford so much pleasure to my mind, as the beauties of nature I found here.

. . . Soon after, I returned home to my family, with a determination to bring them as soon as possible to live in Kentucky, which I esteemed a second paradise, at the risk of my life and fortune.

In 1775, working for Richard Henderson's Transylvania Company, Boone began to blaze a trail to Kentucky through the Cumberland Gap, a natural passage through the Cumberland Mountains that had been created by an ancient stream. His Wilderness Road, which followed Indian trails, gave settlers their first route from the east to Kentucky and Ohio. In 1795 the road opened to wagon traffic. Millions of settlers would follow it in the next century.

The Wilderness Road is now part of U.S. Route 25.

"Is it admissible to think that it has been filled up, or destroyed . . . ?"

THE SACRED EXPEDITION FACES DISASTER

December 4–5, 1769
Alta California

MIGUEL COSTANSO

While the French and English were skirmishing in the interior of the continent, the Spanish were strengthening their hold on the west coast. In 1769, worried about incursions from the north by Russia, the Spanish sent a land and sea expedition into Alta ("Upper") California to establish missions and settlements.

The first mission was established at San Diego. Part of the expeditionary force, led by Mexican governor Gaspar de Portolá, then continued north in search of Monterey Bay, which had been explored and mapped more than 150 years earlier. But Monterey had mysteriously disappeared.

Eyewitness Costanso was the navigator and cosmographer for the march.

Our commander, somewhat confused by these reports [from scouts who had failed to see Monterey], determined to call a meeting of his officers to consider what action was most suitable in the present exigency. He drew attention to the scarcity of provisions that confronted us; to the large number of sick we had among us (there were seventeen men half-crippled and unfit for work); to the seasons already far advanced; and to the great suffering of the men who remained well, on account of the unlimited work required in looking after the horses, and watching them at night, in guarding the camp, and in the continual excursions for exploration and reconnaissance. The meeting was held after we had heard the mass of the Holy Ghost, and all the officers voted unanimously that the journey be continued . . . and, if God willed that in the search for Monterey we should all perish, we would have performed our duty towards God and man, laboring together until death for the success of the undertaking upon which we had been sent.

. . . We did not know what to think of the situation. A port so famous as that of Monterey, so celebrated, and so talked of in its time, by energetic, skillful, and intelligent men, expert sailors who came expressly to reconnoiter these coasts by order of the monarch who at that time governed the Spains—is it possible to say that it has not been found after the most careful and earnest efforts, carried out at the cost of much toil and fatigue? Or, is it admissible to think that it has been filled up, or destroyed in the course of time?

The explorers were not hopelessly lost. They had simply passed Monterey Bay without recognizing it, continuing north as far as San Francisco. They found it on their return trip. (The Monterey settlement became the capital of Upper California and remained so until five years after U.S. statehood, when it was replaced by Sacramento.)

Thanks in part to extraordinary efforts by Father Junipero Serra, the religious leader of the Sacred Expedition, twenty-one Franciscan missions were founded. The mission system lasted sixty-five years, by which time it had led to the baptism of nearly 90,000 Indians and the Catholic marriages of 24,000. The first Americans in California thought little of the missions, which appeared to be managed in the imperious style of a southern plantation. Later California boosters romanticized them: Popular plays mythologized the mission era; the energetic Charles F. Lummis, an author, magazine editor, and founder of the Landmarks

Club, promoted a revival of mission architecture. For better and for worse, the effect of the missions on the culture of the region persists today.

El Camino Réal ("the Royal Road"), the trail linking the missions, stretched from San Diego to Sonoma. It established the route of present-day Highway 101.

"They also charged the Court with injustice . . ."

RIOT OF THE NORTH CAROLINA REGULATORS

1770
Hillsborough, North Carolina

JUDGE RICHARD HENDERSON

Historian Carl Van Doren once noted that victory in the French and Indian War strengthened the self-confidence of the colonists, leading to the independent spirit that resulted in the Revolution. This was especially true in the western territories. Having fought for the freedom to live in the West, the frontiersmen would now demand a voice in government.

In the western Carolinas, the more radical frontiersmen formed gangs called Regulators, similar to the vigilante groups of the Far West during the 1849 Gold Rush (see page 132). Although they lived far from the rule of law that prevailed closer to the coast, the Regulators wanted to ensure honest government and safety from outlaws. In South Carolina, they even established their own courts.

This riot in North Carolina was sparked by the failure of the court to punish Edmund Fanning, a hated official.

On Monday last being the second day of Hillsborough Superior Court, early in the morning the Town was filled with a great number of these people shouting, hallooing & making a considerable tumult in the streets. At about 11 o'clock the Court was opened, and immediately the House filled as close as one man could stand by another, some with clubs others with whips and switches, few or none without some weapon. When the House had become so crowded that no more could well get in, one of them (whose name I think is called Fields) came forward and told me he had something to say before I proceeded to business. . . . Upon my informing Fields that he might speak on he proceeded to let me know that he spoke for the whole body of the people called Regulators. That they understood that I would not try their causes, and their determination was to have them tried, for they had come down to see justice done and justice they would have, and if I would proceed to try those causes it might prevent much mischief. They also charged the Court with injustice at the preceding term and objected to the jurors appointed by the Inferior Court and said they would have them altered and others appointed in their room, with many other things too tedious to mention here. Thus I found myself under a necessity of attempting to soften and turn away the fury of this mad people, in the best manner in my power, and as much as could well be, pacify their rage and at the same time preserve the little remaining dignity of the Court. The consequence of which was that after spending upwards of half an hour in this disagreeable situation the mob cried out "Retire, retire, and let the Court go on." Upon which most of the Regulators went out and seemed to be in consultation in a party by themselves.

The little hopes of peace derived from this piece of behaviour were very transient, for in a few minutes Mr. Williams an Attorney of that Court was coming in and had advanced near the door when they fell on him in a most furious manner with clubs and sticks of enormous size and it was with great difficulty he saved his life by taking shelter in a neighbouring Store House. Mr. Fanning was next the object of their fury, him they seized and took with a degree of violence not to be described from off the bench where he had retired for protection and assistance and with hideous shouts of barbarian cruelty dragged him by the heels out of doors, while others engaged in dealing out blows with such violence that I made no doubt his life would instantly become a sacrifice to their rage and madness. However Mr. Fanning by a manly exertion miraculously broke free and fortunately jumped into a door that saved him from immediate dissolution. During the uproar several of them told me with oaths of great bitterness that my turn should be next.

I took advantage of this proposal and made no scruple at promising what was not in my intention to perform for the Terms they would admit me to hold Court on were that no Lawyer, the King's Attorney excepted, should be admitted into Court, and that they would stay and see justice impartially done.

. . . In about four or five hours their rage seemed to subside a little and they permitted me to adjourn Court and conducted me with great parade to my lodgings. Colonel Fanning whom they had made a prisoner of was in the evening permitted to return to his own house on his word of honour to surrender himself next day. At about ten o'clock that evening, I took an opportunity of making my escape by a back way, and left poor Col. Fanning and the little Borough in a wretched situation.

The number of Insurgents that appeared when the riot first began was, I think, about one hundred and fifty, though they constantly increased for two days and kept a number with fire arms at about a mile distance from town ready to fall on whenever they were called for.

This riot was not the end of the violence. In 1771, the North Carolina militia fought the Regulators at Alamance Creek, capturing and executing seven rebel leaders. Some of the remaining Regulators packed up and moved farther west to Tennessee, where they formed the Watauga Association, an independent local government.

Eyewitness Richard Henderson, an associate justice of the province of North Carolina at the time of this riot, was one of the most influential pioneers of his era. In 1775 he employed his neighbor, Daniel Boone, to blaze a trail through the Cumberland Gap (see page 53). He later helped colonize Tennessee, and established the settlement that became Nashville. Cities in Kentucky, North Carolina, and Tennessee bear his name.

". . . The water, instead of getting shallower,
became continually deeper."

THE REVOLUTIONARY WAR:
THE CONQUEST OF THE OLD NORTHWEST

February 5–24, 1779
Vincennes, Illinois Territory

COLONEL GEORGE ROGERS CLARK

In the West, the Revolutionary War was a struggle for strategic outposts and forts such as Detroit, Vincennes, and Kaskaskia, all within what is now called the "Old Northwest"—the region that includes present-day Ohio, Indiana, Illinois, Michigan, Wisconsin, and part of Minnesota.

The hero of the war's western front was George Rogers Clark, older brother of William Clark of the Lewis and Clark expedition. In May 1778 he set out with a force of fewer than 200 men and captured a string of British forts: Kaskaskia, Cahokia, and Vincennes were his within two months. But as he advanced, British troops from Fort Detroit reclaimed Vincennes, so Clark returned in the middle of winter, crossing through 180 miles of deadly conditions to surprise the British and retake his prize.

Everything being ready, on the 5th of February after receiving a lecture and absolution from a priest, we crossed the Kaskaskia River with one hundred and seventy men and at a distance of about three miles encamped until February 8. The weather was wet and a part of the country was covered with several inches of water. Progress under these conditions was difficult and fatiguing, although, fortunately, it was not very cold considering the time of year. My object now was to keep the men in good spirits. I permitted them to shoot game on all occasions and to feast on it like Indians at a war dance, each company taking turns in inviting the other to its feast. A feast was held every night, the company that was to give it being always supplied with horses for laying in a sufficient store of meat in the course of the day. I myself and my principal officers conducted ourselves like woodsmen, shouting and running through the mud and water the same as the men themselves.

Thus, insensible of their hardships and without complaining, our men were conducted through difficulties far surpassing anything we had ever experienced before. . . .

Shortly after sunrise [on the 23rd] I addressed the men. What I said to them I do not now remember, but it may be easily imagined by anyone who can understand my affection for them at that time. I concluded by informing them that by surmounting the plain, now in full view, and reaching the woods opposite, they would put an end to their suffering and in a few hours would have sight of their long-wished-for goal.

Without waiting for any reply, I stepped into the water, and a hurrah was raised. We commonly marched through the water in single file as it was much easier to advance in this way. When about a third of the men had entered, I halted them, and further to prove the men and because I had some suspicion of three or four of them, I called to Major Bowman to fall into the rear with twenty-five men and to put to death any of the men who refused to march, saying that we wished to have no such person among us. The whole force raised a cry of approbation, and on we went.

This was the most trying difficulty of all we had experienced. I had fifteen or twenty of the strongest men follow after me, and, judging from my own sensations what must be those of the men, on reaching the middle of the plain where the water was about knee-deep I realized that I was failing. There being no trees or bushes here for the men to support themselves by, I did not doubt but that many of the weaker ones would be drowned. I therefore ordered the canoes to make the land, discharge their loads, and then ply backward and forward with all possible diligence, picking up the men.

To encourage the party I sent some of the strongest men ahead with orders to pass the word back when they reached a certain distance that the water was getting shallower and on approaching the woods to cry out "Land." This stratagem produced the desired effect. Encouraged by it, the men exerted themselves to the limit of their ability, the weaker holding on to the stronger ones and frequently one man being upheld by two. This was a great advantage to the weak, but the water, instead of getting shallower, became continually deeper.

On reaching the woods, where they expected land, the water was up to my shoulders. All the weak and short men clung to the trees and floated on logs until they were taken off by the canoes. The strong and tall men got ashore and started fires. Many would reach the bank and fall with their bodies half in the water, not being able to support themselves outside it. The only way to restore the men was for two strong ones to take a weak one by the arms and exercise him and by this means they soon recovered.

We were now in the situation I had been laboring to attain. The idea of being taken prisoner was foreign to almost all of our men. In the event of capture they looked forward to being tortured by the savages. Our fate was now to be determined, probably within the next few hours, and we knew that nothing but the boldest conduct would insure success. I knew that some of the inhabitants wished us well, while many more were lukewarm to the interest of the British and Americans alike. I also learned that the grand chief, the son of Tobacco, had within a few days openly declared, in council with the British, that he was a brother and friend of the Big Knives [the Americans]. These circumstances were in our favor. . . .

Shortly before sunset we advanced, displaying ourselves in full view of the crowds in the town. We were plunging headlong either to certain destruction or to success.

I ordered Lieutenant Bailey with fourteen men to advance and open fire on the fort while the main body moved in a different direction and took possession of the strongest part of the town. The firing now commenced against the fort, but since drunken Indians often saluted it after nightfall, the garrison did not suppose it to be from an enemy until one of the men, lighting his match, was shot down through a porthole. The drums now sounded and the conflict was fairly joined on both sides.

The garrison was now completely surrounded, and the firing continued without intermission (except for about fifteen minutes shortly before dawn) until nine o'clock the following morning. Our entire force, with the exception of fifty men kept as a reserve in case of some emergency, participated in the attack, being joined by a few young men.

Since we could not afford to lose any of our men, great pains were taken to keep them sufficiently sheltered and to maintain a hot fire against the fort in order to intimidate the enemy as well as to destroy them. The embrasures for their cannon were frequently closed, for our riflemen, finding the true direction, would pour in such volleys when they were open that the artillerymen could not stand to the guns. Seven or eight of them were shot down in a short time.

Our men frequently taunted the enemy in order to provoke them into opening the portholes and firing the cannon so that they might have the pleasure of cutting them down with their rifles. Fifty rifles would be leveled the instant the port flew open, and had the garrison stood to their artillery, most of them, I believe, would have been destroyed during the night, as the greater part of our men, lying within thirty yards of the walls and behind some houses, were as well sheltered as those within the fort and were much more expert in this mode of fighting.

The enemy fired at the flash of our guns, but our men would change their position the moment they had fired. On the instant of the least appearance at one of their loopholes a dozen guns would be fired at it. At times an irregular fire as hot as could be maintained was poured in from different directions for several minutes. This would be continually succeeded by a scattering fire at the portholes, and a great uproar and laughter would be raised by the reserve parties in different parts of the town to give the impression that they had only fired on the fort for a few minutes for amusement, while those who were keeping up a continuous fire were being regularly relieved.

The firing immediately recommenced with redoubled vigor on both sides, and I do not believe that more noise could possibly have been made by an equal number of men. Their shouting could not be heard amid the discharge of the muskets, and a continual line of fire around the garrison was maintained until shortly before daylight.

The attack continued until nine o'clock on the morning of the 24th.

Toward evening a flag of truce appeared.

Clark's life took some hard turns after the war. Like many officers of the time, he had used his own savings to pay the expenses of his command. When the land grant he was due for his services failed to materialize, he was left with large debts. Perhaps because of circumstance, or from an allegiance to the Old Northwest rather than the new federal government, Clark eventually became a soldier of fortune, taking part in French and Spanish schemes to settle the West.

"This is, in a sense, the birthday of this Western World."

NEW SETTLEMENTS ON THE OHIO

May–July 1788
Marietta, Ohio

JOHN MAY

The settlement of the Ohio Valley was the first great land grab in the new nation. The region was well known as a valuable piece of real estate, but decades passed between the first British entrepreneurial schemes and the first significant settlements, because the French and the Indians weren't welcoming. Some wealthy colonists also resisted settling the region. Their concerns were voiced by John Dunmore, colonial governor of Virginia, who said "the people of property" were "justly apprehensive . . . of an infinite number of the lower class of inhabitants, who, the desire of novelty alone will induce to change their situation."

Dunmore was right; but victories in the French and Indian War, Pontiac's Rebellion, and the Revolution eliminated the obstacles for the entrepreneurs.

Eyewitness John May moved to Ohio from Boston with the first party of settlers, Revolutionary War veterans from New England.

May 12th, Monday. I am still in quarters opposite Pittsburg, living as cheaply as if I was at Muskingum. Am waiting for the boat to carry us all down. Yesterday two boats for Kentucky hauled in at our landing having on board twenty-nine whites, twenty-four negroes, nine dogs, twenty-three horses, cows, hogs, etc., besides provision and furniture. Several have passed to-day equally large.

Wednesday, 21st. At 2 o'clock our boat—oh, be joyful!—hove in sight, coming around the point, and, in half an hour, was made fast at Pittsburg. She is forty-two feet long and twelve feet wide, with cover. She will carry a burden of forty-five tons, and draws only two and one-half feet water. . . .

Saturday, 24th. At 12 ½ o'clock we cast off our fasts, and committed ourselves to the current of the Ohio. The scene was beautiful. Without wind or waves, we, insensibly almost, make more than five miles an hour. . . .

Monday, 26th. Thus we moved on, constantly espying new wonders and beauties, till 3 o'clock, when we arrived safely on the banks of the delightful Muskingum.

Tuesday, 27th. Slept on board last night, and rose early this morning. Have spent the day in reconnoitering the spot where the city is to be laid out, and find it to answer the best descriptions I have ever heard of it. The situation delightfully agreeable, and well calculated for an elegant city. As to our surveying, buildings, etc., they are in a very backward way. Little appears to be done, and a great deal of time and money misspent.

Wednesday, 28th. The directors and agents present agreed to lease the ministerial lot to different persons, in lots of ten acres each, for a term not less than one hundred years, at the option of the lessee—to be without rent the first ten years, and then a fixed rent the remainder of the time. This was done to accommodate a number of proprietors present, whose eight-acre lots were drawn at a distance. Went this afternoon to survey the ten-acre lots, and drew them in the evening.

Thursday, 29th. This day the axe is laid to the root of the trees. In order to do this my people were armed with the suitable tool, and went forth to smite the ancient tenants of the woods. Venison plenty at one copper per pound. I was engaged in the afternoon with the surveyors. Find the soil very good, but was tormented beyond measure by myriads of gnats. They not only bit surprisingly, but get down one's throat.

This evening, arrived two long boats from the Rapids, with officers and soldiers, the number about one hundred. On their passage up the river they were fired upon by a strong party of Indians, headed by a white man. They returned the fire, and had two men killed. They were obliged to drop down the river a piece, and come by the place in the night. There are various reports about the hostilities of the savages, but nothing to be depended on. The Indians are frequently in here, and seem to be on friendly terms. I have shaken hands with many of them. My people employed in clearing land. I have been, this afternoon, sowing garden-seeds.

Sunday, 15th. A number of poor devils—five in all—took their departure homeward this morning. They came from home moneyless and brainless, and have returned as they came.

Tuesday, 17th. This evening Judge Parsons' and General Varnum's commissions were read; also, regulations for the government of the people. In fact, by-laws were much wanted. Officers were named to command the militia; guards to be mounted every evening; all males more than fifteen years old to appear under arms every Sunday.

Friday, [July] 4th. All labor comes to a pause to-day in memory of the Declaration of Independence. Our long bowery is built on the east bank of the Muskingum; a table laid sixty feet long, in plain sight of the garrison, one-quarter of a mile distant. At 1 o'clock General Harmer and his lady, Mrs. McCurders, and all the officers not on duty came over, and several other gentlemen. An excellent oration was delivered by

Judge Varnum, and the cannon fired a salute of fourteen guns.

Wednesday, 9th. This is, in a sense, the birthday of this Western World. Governor St. Clair arrived at the garrison. His landing was announced by the discharge of fourteen cannon; and all rejoiced at his coming. . . .

As an aside, it is worth noting that one of the largest landholders in the region was George Washington. His family had been among the founders of the Ohio company, and he had received more land as payment for his services during the French and Indian War. He spent much time and energy on the settlement of the Ohio.

". . . Our rout laid through a beatifull high leavel and fertile prarie. . . ."

LEWIS AND CLARK'S JOURNEY

May 20, 1804
St. Charles, Missouri;
near Fort Mandan;
Lemhi Pass, at the Montana-Idaho border;
and Fort Clatsop, near the Pacific coast

MERIWETHER LEWIS, WILLIAM CLARK, AND SACAGAWEA

Instructions for Lewis and Clark's expedition came from Jefferson himself: Explore the vast Louisiana Territory and follow the Columbia River to the Pacific Ocean.

Almost as interesting as what the men saw on their journey was the story of the men themselves. Meriwether Lewis had been President Thomas Jefferson's secretary. Though he was in charge as far as officials in Washington were concerned, he shared the command equally with William Clark, younger brother of Revolutionary War hero George Rogers Clark. Because he could not convince officials to grant Clark a military rank equal to his own, he coined the unofficial term "Corps of Discovery," and gave Clark and himself the equal titles of "Captain." This gracious and democratic leadership continued throughout the journey, despite many crises.

For much of the journey they were guided by Sacagawea, a Shoshone who had been kidnapped as a child by the Mandans of the upper Missouri River Valley, where Lewis and Clark met her when wintering near what is now Bismarck, North

Dakota. With a newborn son, she guided Lewis and Clark into Shoshone territory by August of 1805, and continued with them to the Oregon coast. She and her family remained in North Dakota when the expedition passed through on its return trip.

Many different versions of the Lewis and Clark journals exist, because several editors have tried to smooth the rough edges. These accounts come from the edition prepared by Reuben Thwaites, which maintains the personal idiosyncrasies of grammar and spelling.

Sacagawea's account comes from a book billed as "her own story" as related by a Canadian trapper and by the daughter of one of the Mandan chiefs.

The men had left St. Louis on the 13th, along with some well-wishers, stopping first at St. Charles before heading into the wild.

ST. CHARLES, MISSOURI
MAY 20, 1804
LEWIS

The morning was fair, and the weather pleasant; at 10 OCk. A M. agreably to an appointment of the proceeding day, I was joined by Capt Stoddard, Lieuts. Milford & Worrell together with Messrs. A. Chouteau, C. Gratiot, and many other rispecrable inhabitants of St. Louis, who had engaged to accompany me to the Vilage of St. Charles; accordingly at 12 OCk., after bidding an affectionate adieu to my Hostis, that excellent woman the spouse of Mr. Peter Chouteau, and some of my fair friends of St. Louis, we set forward to that vilage in order to join my friend companion and fellow labourer Capt. William Clark, who had previously arrived at that place with the party destined for the discovery of the interior of the continent of North America the first 5 miles of our rout laid through a beatifull high leavel and fertile prarie which incircles the town of St. Louis from N. W. to S. E. the lands through which we then passed are somewhat broken less fertile the plains and woodlands are here indiscriminately interspersed untill you arrive within three miles of the vilage when the woodland commences and continues to the Missouri the latter is extreemly fertile. At half after one P. M. our progress was interrupted by the near approach of a violent thunderstorm from the N. W. and concluded to take shelter in a little cabbin hard by untill the rain should be over; accordingly we alighted and remained about an hour and a half and regaled ourselves with a could collation which we had taken the precaution to bring with us from St. Louis.

I did not, of course, attend the great council of our chiefs with the Long Knife chiefs; women were not allowed in it. But my man was there, and when it was over he told me: "The Long Knife chiefs will winter here with us, and when they go on westward they want a guide to show them the way, and some one to take them to the Snakes, in order to purchase horses from them. They will need many horses for riding and for carrying their goods when they arrive at the head of the river and leave their boats."

"They cannot take their boats to the head of the river," I told him. "They will not be able to get them up over the big falls, a long way this side of the mountains."

"Oh, well, wherever they abandon the boats, they must have horses with which to go on. I shall tell them that I will be their guide and interpreter."

"But you do not know the way, you cannot even understand my Snake language!" I told him.

"Fool!" he cried. "You shall show me the way—and I will lead them to your people!"

Can you imagine how my heart beat when he said that? Here, after all the years, was a chance to see my own people again! At the thought of it I was so happy that I cried. And Otter Woman was happy, too. She sprang up and danced around and around, crying, "We are going to the mountains! We are going to the mountains! We shall see our Snake people, our dear relations!"

"Come! Let us go to the Long Knives at once, and tell them that we will guide them, and interpret for them," I said.

"No! We shall let them find out that we are the only ones that can do this for them. Then they will come to us about it, and so we shall get bigger pay than if we ran to them to offer our services," our man answered.

As our man said, so it had to be. Oh, how anxious Otter Woman and I became as the days passed and we had no word from the white men! Our man became anxious, too, and one day went down and visited the white men, where they were building a fort, some distance below the lower Mandan village. They said nothing to him about engaging us at that time. More and more long days passed. We became more and more uneasy, and finally our man took us down to visit the whites and to see their fort. It was not completed, but we were filled with wonder at it, the first white men's building that we had ever seen. It was wonderful how they had put heavy logs one on top of another, up and up to make the walls. As a great rock is in the middle of a river's swift current, so was that fort there in the timbered bottom. Storms could not even shake it. Nor could all the warriors of our three tribes take it by attack, for there were cunningly cut holes in the walls through which the whites could shoot their many guns and kill off the attackers as they came!

The great white chiefs, Long Knife [Lewis] and Red Hair [Clark], greeted us very pleasantly, and made us feel that we were really welcome in their camp. They showed their many strange things, things beautiful and useful, and made us presents of some of them. They had us eat with them, and at that evening meal Otter Woman and I first tasted bread; we thought it the best-flavored food that we had ever eaten.

Just as soon as I looked at those two white chiefs, and put my hand in theirs, my heart went out to them, for I knew that, although very brave, truly fearless of all things, yet were they of gentle heart. I could not keep my eyes off them. I felt that I wanted to work for them; to do all that I could for them. Think how happy I was when, that very evening, it was arranged that we should all come and live with them as soon as their fort was completed, our man to be their Minnetaree interpreter, and hunter at times.

Nothing was then said about our going west with them in the spring, but I felt sure that would be asked of us later.

A few days later the fort was completed, and we moved down with our belongings and were given a room in it. Oh, what a pleasant place that room was, with its fireplace, its windows of oiled skin, and its comfortable couches! The white men visited us in it, and we often visited in their rooms, especially the room of the two chiefs. They were always having visitors from the villages above, and were always getting them to describe what they knew of the country and the people who inhabited it, especially those to the west of us.

Night after night they got me to tell them about my Snake people and their country, and I told them all, even to telling them how my people were persecuted by the Blackfeet, the Minnetarees, the Assiniboines, and how I, myself, had been taken into captivity. I told them, too, that my people starved more than half the time, because, without guns, they were driven from the plains by their powerful enemies every time that they came out after buffalo.

At that Long Knife and Red Hair both told me that one of their objects in coming to the country was to make peace between all the tribes in it, and, anyhow, if they would not agree to that, the traders who would follow the trail that they were to make would furnish my Snake people plenty of guns, and they would then be able to hold their own against all enemies.

LEMHI PASS—THE CONTINENTAL DIVIDE
AUGUST 12, 1805
LEWIS

This morning I sent Drewyer [Drouillard] out as soon as it was light, to try and discover what rout the Indians had taken. he followed the track of the horse we had pursued yesterday to the mountain wher it had ascended, and returned to me in about an hour and a half. I now determined to pursue the base of the mountains which form this cove to the S.W. in the expectation of finding some Indian road which lead over the Mountains

after eating we continued our rout through the low bottom of the main stream along the foot of the mountains on our right the valley for 5 Mls. further in a S.W. direction was from 2 to 3 miles wide the main stream now after discarding two stream[s] on the left in this valley turns abruptly to the West through a narrow bottom betwe[e]n the mountains. the road was still plain, I therefore did not dispair of shortly finding a passage over the mountains and of taisting the waters of the great Columbia this evening.

at the distance of 4 miles further the road took us to the most distant fountain of the waters of the Mighty Missouri in surch of which we have spent so many toilsome days and wristless nights. thus far I had accomplished one of those great objects on which my mind has been unalterably fixed for many years, judge then of the pleasure I felt in all[a]ying my thirst with this pure and ice-cold water which issues from the base of a low mountain or hill of a gentle ascent for ½ a mile. the mountains are high on either hand leave this gap at the head of this rivulet through which the road passes. I here I halted a few minutes and rested myself. two miles below Mc.Neal had exultingly stood with a foot on each side of this little rivulet and thanked his god that he had lived to bestride the mighty & heretofore deemed endless Missouri. after refreshing ourselves we proceeded on to the top of the dividing ridges from which I discovered immence ranges of high mountains still to the West of us with their tops partially covered with snow. I now decended the mountain about ¾ of a mile which I found much steeper than on the opposite side, to a handsome bold runing Creek of cold Clear water. here I first tasted the water of the great Columbia river. [Actually a stream that fed the Lemhi River, which in turn fed the Salmon River, then the Snake River, and finally the Columbia.]

I compleated a map of the Countrey through which we have been passing from the Mississippi at the Mouth of Missouri to this place.

. . . We now discover that we have found the most practicable and navigable passage across the Continent of North America; it is . . . by way of the Missouri to the Falls; thence to Clarks river at the enterance of Travellers rest Creek, from thence up travillers rest Creek to the forks, from whence you prosue a range of mountains which divides the waters of the two forks of this Creek, and which still Continues it's westwardly course on the Mountains which divides the waters of the two forks of the Kooskooske river to their junction; from thence to decend this river to the S. E. branch of the Columbia, thence down that river to the Columbia, and down the Latter to the Pacific Ocian.

During the 8,000-mile journey to the Oregon coast and back, the explorers encountered more than fifty Native American tribes, saw the vast buffalo herds of the West, and even discovered a dinosaur fossil. Although the men had been given up for lost before returning to St. Louis in 1806, only one had died, and that was the result of appendicitis.

Lewis was appointed governor of the Louisiana Territory shortly after his return, but two years later he died mysteriously, perhaps a suicide. Clark was put in charge of the militia and of Indian affairs in the territory, and in 1813 was made governor of the new Missouri Territory. The rest of Sacagawea's life is unclear. She may have died in 1812, but in 1875 a Shoshone woman in Wyoming claimed to be Sacagawea. That woman died in 1884, when Sacagawea would have been almost 100 years old.

*"They met us with open arms,
crowding round to touch and embrace us."*

ZEBULON PIKE IS ROBBED

November 22, 1806
Colorado

ZEBULON PIKE

Pike was a career army officer, sent to explore the Southwest shortly after Lewis and Clark left on their expedition. He is remembered in the name of Pikes Peak, which he "discovered." He didn't name it after himself. In fact, it was called James' Peak for several decades afterwards.

Marched early, and with rather more caution than usual. After having proceeded about five miles on the prairie, and as those in front were descending into the bottom, Baroney cried out, *"Voila un sauvage,"* when we observed a number of Indians running from the woods towards us.

We advanced towards them, and, on turning my head to the left, I observed several running on the hill, as it were to surround us; one of them bearing a stand of colours. This caused a momentary halt, but perceiving those in front reaching out their hands, and without arms, we again advanced.

They met us with open arms, crowding round to touch and embrace us. They appeared so anxious that I dismounted from my horse, and in a moment a fellow had mounted him and driven off. I then observed the Doctor and Baroney in the same predicament. The Indians were embracing the soldiers.

After some time tranquillity was so far restored, they having returned our horses all safe, as to enable us to learn they were a war party from the Grand Pawnees, who had been in search of the Ietans, but, not finding them, were now on their return. An unsuccessful war party on their way home are always ready to embrace an opportunity of gratifying their disappointed vengeance on the first persons they meet.

It was with great difficulty they got them tranquil, and not until there had been a bow or two bent on the occasion. When in some order, we found them to be sixty warriors, half with fire arms, and half with bows, arrows, and lances. Our party was in all sixteen. In a short time they were arranged in a ring, and I took my seat between the two leaders: our colours were placed opposite each other; the utensils for smoking, & c., being prepared on a small seat before us. Thus far all was well.

I then ordered half a carrot of tobacco, one dozen knives, sixty fire steels, and sixty flints to be presented to them. They demanded corn, ammunition, blankets, kettles, &c., all of which they were refused, notwithstanding the pressing instances of my interpreter to accede to some points. The pipes yet lay unmoved, as if they were undetermined whether to treat us as friends or as enemies; but after some time we were presented with a kettle of water, drank, smoked, and ate together.

During this time Dr. Robinson was standing up to observe their actions, in order that, if necessary, we might be ready to commence hostilities as soon as they. The Indians now took their presents and commenced distributing them, but some malcontents threw them away, as if out of contempt. We began to load our horses, when they encircled us and commenced stealing everything they could. Finding it was difficult to preserve my pistols, I mounted my horse, when I found myself frequently surrounded, during which some were endeavouring to steal the pistols.

The doctor was equally engaged in another quarter, and all the soldiers at their several posts, taking things from them.

One having stolen my tomahawk, I informed the chief, but he paid no respect to my remonstrance, except to reply that "they were pitiful." Finding this, we determined to protect ourselves as far as was in our power, and the affair began to wear a serious aspect.

I ordered my men to take their arms, and separate themselves from the savages, at the same time declaring to them I would kill the first man who touched our baggage, on which they commenced filing off immediately. We marched about the same time, and found after they had left us that they had contrived to steal one sword, a tomahawk, a broad axe, five canteens, and sundry other small articles. When I reflected on the subject, I felt sincerely mortified that the smallness of my number obliged me thus to submit to the insults of lawless banditti, it being the first time a savage had ever taken anything from me with the least appearance of force.

When the sponsor of the Pike expedition, territorial governor James Wilkinson, was implicated in a conspiracy led by Aaron Burr to establish a new republic in the area, Pike was suspected of scouting for the conspirators. (For the conspiracy, see the following account.) If his expedition was actually a scouting mission for Burr and Wilkinson, he did not know it. He was eventually cleared of charges.

"... Designs were in agitation in the Western country. ..."

THE AARON BURR CONSPIRACY

January 16, 1807
Washington, D.C.

THOMAS JEFFERSON

*"This was the most formidable secession conspiracy prior to 1860," wrote histori-
an Samuel Eliot Morison, "one which probably would have succeeded had not
[Louisiana Territory governor James] Wilkinson ratted on Burr."*

*At the time, the United States was on the verge of falling apart. Less than
twenty years had passed since the creation of the Constitution, and states were still
jockeying for power with the federal government and among themselves. Thomas
Jefferson was in the White House, which frightened the New England establishment, who saw Jefferson's belief in the rights of the individual as contrary to peace
and order.*

*When Jefferson bought Louisiana, several important New England politicians
(including a former secretary of state) worried about a change in the north-south
balance of states. They advocated the North's seccession from the U.S., and the
creation of a new country, the "Northern Confederacy of New England and New
York."*

*Add to this volatile political mixture an ambitious, ruthless catalyst, Aaron
Burr, who had already double-crossed Jefferson. When they ran together in the
1800 federal election, Burr used a technicality to try to become president rather
than serve as vice-president, bringing the government to a standstill for three
months.*

*Burr then looked westward for the fulfillment of his ambition. But a slippery
co-conspirator, worried he would be caught, leaked the news to Jefferson.*

This account comes from a message Jefferson sent Congress.

To the Senate and House of Representatives of the United States:
I proceed to state . . . information received touching an illegal combination of private individuals against the peace and safety of the Union,
and a military expedition planned by them against the Territories of a
Power in amity with the United States. . . .
. . . Neither safety nor justice will permit the exposing names,
except that of the principal actor, whose guilt is placed beyond question.
Some time in the latter part of September, I received intimations
that designs were in agitation in the Western country, unlawful and
unfriendly to the peace of the Union; and that the prime mover in these

was Aaron Burr, heretofore distinguished by the favor of his country. The ground of these intimations being inconclusive . . . the only measure taken was to urge the informants to use their best endeavors to get further insight into the designs.

It was not until the latter part of October, that the objects of the conspiracy began to be perceived; but still so blended, and involved in mystery, that nothing distinct could be singled out for pursuit. . . .

By this time it was known that many boats were under preparation, stores of provisions collecting, and an unusual number of suspicious characters in motion on the Ohio and its waters. . . .

[We intercepted] a letter . . . partly written in cypher . . . explaining his designs . . . different parts of which only had been revealed to different informants. It appeared that he contemplated two distinct objects, which might be carried on either jointly or separately.

One of these was the severance of the Union of these States by the Alleghany mountains; the other an attack on Mexico.

A third object, the settlement of a pretended purchase of a tract of country on the Washita, was to serve as the pretext for all his preparations, an allurement for such followers as really wished to acquire settlements in that country, and a cover under which to retreat in the event of a final discomfiture of his real design. . . .

This was the state of my information of his proceedings about the last of November, at which time, therefore, it was first possible to take specific measures to meet them.

Orders were despatched to every interesting point on the Ohio and Mississippi, from Pittsburg to New Orleans, for the employment of such force, either of the regulars or of the militia, and of such proceedings also, of the civil authorities, as might enable them to seize on all boats and stores provided for the enterprise, to arrest the persons concerned, and to suppress effectually the further progress of the enterprise. . . .

At the time, Jefferson did not know that the source of his information, Louisiana Territory governor James Wilkinson, had been Burr's ally.

Burr was captured and tried for treason. Wilkinson testified against him, but Burr was acquitted for lack of hard evidence.

"Every one who could, . . . clung for life to the rigging."

A VICIOUS CAPTAIN
LEADS ASTOR'S ADVENTURERS

March 22–25, 1811

at the mouth of the Columbia River, Oregon

ALEXANDER ROSS

The first permanent American settlement on the Pacific coast was established on the orders of fur tycoon John Jacob Astor. His hired team of pioneers set sail from Boston in 1810, headed for the mouth of the Columbia River, where Lewis and Clark had established their winter headquarters five year earlier.

Oregon's vague boundaries, which included what is now the state of Washington and the Canadian province of British Columbia, were the subject of rival claims by the Americans and the British, who controlled Canada at the time. Astor's plan was to compete with Canadian fur companies already in the area.

But, with the adventurers in sight of the coast, it seemed as if the plan would literally be sunk. By then, Captain Jonathan Thorn, in command of the Tonquin, had already proven himself to be a sullen and rigid disciplinarian. Faced with the difficulty of safely sailing the Tonquin to the shore, he proved especially brutal.

Eyewitness Alexander Ross, a Scotsman who had been a farmer in Canada, joined Astor's expedition to make a fortune in the more lucrative fur trade.

On the 22nd of March, we came in sight of land, which, on a nearer approach, proved to be Cape Disappointment, a promontory forming the north side of the Great Oregon or Columbia River. The sight filled every heart with gladness. But the cloudy and stormy state of the weather prevented us seeing clearly the mouth of the river; being then about ten miles from land.

. . . The mouth of Columbia River is remarkable for its sand-bars and high surf at all seasons, but more particularly in the spring and fall. . . . These sand-bars frequently shift, the channel of course shifting along with them, which renders the passage at all times extremely dangerous.

The bar, or rather the chain of sand banks, over which the huge waves and foaming breakers roll so awfully, is a league broad, and extends in a white foaming sheet for many miles, both south and north of the mouth of the river, forming as it were an impracticable barrier to the entrance, and threatening with instant destruction everything that comes near it.

. . . Mr. Fox, the first mate, was ordered to go and examine the channel on the bar. At half-past one o'clock in the afternoon, Mr. Fox left the ship, having with him one sailor, a very old Frenchman, and three Canadian lads, unacquainted with sea service—two of them being carters from La Chine, and the other a Montreal barber.

Mr. Fox objected to such hands; but the captain refused to change them, adding that he had none else to spare. Mr. Fox then represented the impossibility of performing the business in such weather, and on such a rough sea, even with the best seamen, adding, that the waves were too high for any boat to live in.

The captain, turning sharply round, said—"Mr. Fox, if you are afraid of water, you should have remained at Boston."

On this Mr. Fox immediately ordered the boat to be lowered, and the men to embark. If the crew was bad, the boat was still worse—being scarcely seaworthy, and very small. While this was going on, the partners, who were all partial to Mr. Fox, began to sympathize with him, and to intercede with the captain to defer examining the bar till a favourable change took place in the weather. But he was deaf to entreaties, stamped, and swore that a combination was formed to frustrate all his designs. The partners' interference, therefore, only riveted him the more in his determination, and Mr. Fox was peremptorily ordered to proceed.

He, seeing that the captain was immovable, turned to the partners with tears in his eyes and said—"My uncle was drowned here not many years ago, and now I am going to lay my bones with his." He then shook hands with all around him, and bade them adieu. Stepping into the boat—"Farewell, my friends!" said he; "we will perhaps meet again in the next world." And the words were prophetic.

The moment the boat pushed off, all hands crowded in silence to take a last farewell of her. The weather was boisterous, and the sea rough, so that we often lost sight of the boat before she got 100 yards from the ship; nor had she gone that far before she became utterly unmanageable, sometimes broaching broadside to the foaming surges, other times almost whirling round like a top, then tossing on the crest of a huge wave would sink again for a time and disappear altogether.

At last she hoisted the flag; the meaning could not be mistaken; we knew it was a signal of distress. At this instant all the people crowded round the captain, and implored him to try and save the boat; but in an angry tone he ordered about ship, and we saw the ill-fated boat no more.

. . . [Still looking for a safe channel three days later,] captain now called on Mr. Aikens, the third mate, and ordered him to go and sound in a more northerly direction, and if he found 3½ fathoms water to hoist a flag as a signal. At three o'clock in the afternoon, Mr. Aikens, together with the sailmaker, armourer, and two Sandwich Islanders, embarked in the pinnace, and proceeded to the bar.

As soon as the pinnace hoisted the flag agreed upon, the ship weighed anchor and stood in for the channel; at the same time the boat, pulling back from the bar, met the ship about half a mile from the breakers, in eight fathoms, going in with a gentle sea breeze, at the rate of three knots an hour.

As the ship and boat drew near to each other, the latter steered a little aside to be out of the ship's way, then lay upon her oars in smooth water, waiting to be taken on board, while the ship passed on within twenty yards of them in silence; nor did the people in the boat speak a single word.

As soon as the ship had passed, and no motion made to take the boat on board, every one appeared thunderstruck, and Mr. M' Kay was the first that spoke,—"Who," said he, "is going to throw a rope to the boat?"

No one answered; but by this time she had fallen astern, and began to pull after the ship. Every one now called out, "The boat, the boat!" The partners, in astonishment, entreated the captain to take the boat on board, but he coolly replied, "I can give them no assistance."

Mr. Mumford said it would not be the work of a minute "Back a sail, throw a rope overboard," cried the partners, the answer was, "No, I will not endanger the ship." We now felt convinced that the boat and crew were devoted to destruction—no advice was given them, no assistance offered, no reasons assigned for risking so cruel a sacrifice of human life—for the place where the boat met us was entirely free from the influence of the breakers, and a long way from the bar. . . .

During this time the ship was drawing nearer and nearer to the breakers, which called our attention from the boat to look out for our own safety; but she was seen for some time struggling hard to follow the ship as we entered the breakers, the sight of which was appalling. On the ship making the first plunge, every countenance looked dismay; and the sun, at the time just sinking below the horizon, seemed to say, "Prepare for your last." . . . She struck tremendously on the second reef or shoal; and the surges breaking over her stern overwhelmed everything on deck. Every one who could, sprang aloft, and clung for life to the rigging. The waves at times broke ten feet high over her, and at other times she was in danger of foundering: she struck again and again, and, regardless of her helm, was tossed and whirled in every direction, and became completely unmanageable. Night now began to spread an impenetrable gloom over the turbulent deep. . . . At this instant, some one called out, "We are all lost, the ship is among the rocks."

. . . But there is a limit to all things: hour after hour had passed, and terrific was the sight; yet our faithful bark still defied the elements, until the tide . . . brought about our deliverance by carrying the ship along with it into Baker's Bay, snug within the Cape, where we lay in safety.

In the morning of the 26th, Captain Thorn, Mr. M'Kay, myself, and a few men, left the ship, to take a view of the coast from the top of Cape Disappointment, to try if we could learn any tidings of the boats. We had proceeded fifty yards when we saw Steven Weeks, the armourer, standing under the shelter of a rock, shivering and half-dead with cold. . . . He appeared so overpowered with grief and vexation, that we could scarcely get a word from him; in short, he seemed to reproach us bitterly. "You did it purposely," said he, in great agitation, but after some time, and when we had first told him what we had suffered, he seemed to come round, as if his feelings were soothed by the recital of our dangers; and then he related his melancholy tale, in the following words:—

"After the ship passed us we pulled hard to follow her, thinking every moment you would take us on board; but when we saw her enter the breakers we considered ourselves as lost. We tried to pull back again, but in vain; for we were drawn into the breakers in spite of all we could do. We saw the ship make two or three heavy plunges but just at this time we ourselves were struck with the boiling surf, and the ship went reeling in every direction; in an instant a heavy sea swamped her— poor Mr. Aikens and John Coles were never seen after.

"As soon as I got above the surface of the water, I kept tossing about at the mercy of the waves. While in this state I saw the two Sandwich Islanders struggling through the surf to get hold of the boat, and being expert swimmers they succeeded. After long struggles they got her turned upon her keel, bailed out some of the water, and recovered one of the oars.

"I made several attempts to get near them, but the weight of my clothes and the rough sea had almost exhausted me. I could scarcely keep myself above water, and the Owhyhees ['Hawaiis'—the Sandwich Islanders] were so much occupied about the boat, that they seemed to take no notice of anything else. In vain I tried to make signs, and to call out; every effort only sank me more and more.

"The tide had drawn the boat by this time out to sea, and almost free of the breakers, when the two islanders saw me, now supporting myself by a floating oar, and made for me. The poor fellows tried to haul me into the boat, but their strength failed them. At last, taking hold of my clothes in their teeth, they fortunately succeeded.

"We then stood out to sea as night set in, and a darker one I never saw. The Owhyhees, overcome with wet and cold, began to lose hope, and their fortitude forsook them, so that they lay down despairingly in the boat, nor could I arouse them from their drowsy stupor.

"When I saw that I had nothing to expect from them, I set to sculling the boat myself, and yet it was with much ado I could stand on my legs. During the night one of the Indians died in despair, and the other seemed to court death, for he lost all heart, and would not utter a single word.

"When the tide began to flow I was roused by the sense of my danger, for the sound of the breakers grew louder and louder, and I knew if I got entangled in them in my exhausted state all was lost; I, therefore, set to with might and main, as a last effort, to keep the boat out to sea, and at daylight I was within a quarter of a mile of the breakers, and about double that distance short of the Cape.

"I paused for a moment, 'What is to be done?' I said to myself; 'death itself is preferable to this protracted struggle.' So, turning the head of my boat for shore, I determined to reach the land or die in the attempt.

"Providence favoured my resolution, the breakers seemed to aid in hurrying me out of the watery element; and the sun had scarcely risen when the boat was thrown up high and dry on the beach. I had much ado to extricate myself from her, and to drag my benumbed limbs along.

"On seeing myself once more on dry land, I sat down and felt a momentary relief. . . . Seeing the poor islander still alive, but insensible, I hauled him out of the boat. . . ." Such was Weeks's melancholy story: himself and the Indian being the only survivors of the last boat, it follows that eight men in all lost their lives in entering this fatal river.

The men did found a trading post, which they named Fort Astoria. Although the War of 1812 left Oregon in British hands, and Astor was compelled to sell Astoria to his Canadian competitors, mergers and partnerships after the war brought him back into the western fur trade.

Missionaries followed the traders, and, in the early 1840s, thousands of settlers arrived via the Oregon Trail. Another war with Britain seemed possible as the growing number of settlers demanded a border at 54°40′ N., well into what is now British Columbia. (One slogan in the 1844 election was "Fifty-four forty or fight!") But the dispute was settled by diplomats, establishing the present border and leaving the U.S. army free to fight Mexico for control of the Southwest.

Eyewitness Alexander Ross stayed in Oregon more than a decade, then moved back to Canada. Captain Jonathon Thorn was killed shortly after Astoria was founded, when a gunpowder explosion destroyed the Tonquin.

"A thousand tomahawks were brandished in the air."

TECUMSEH

GENERAL SAM DALE

The last great Indian resistance to white settlement of the midwest was led by Tecumseh, a charismatic Shawnee chief. In the style of Pontiac, he forged a coalition of tribes that fought together against the Americans.

His legal basis for the resistance was sound: No one disputes that William Henry Harrison, governor of the Indiana Territory, had secured land grants by means of dubious treaties with tribes that had no real claims. But legal arguments could never have stopped the westward movement.

Tecumseh eventually turned to force. He was supported by the British, who were happy to harass the Americans.

Frontiersman Sam Dale saw Tecumseh in present-day Alabama.

In October, 1811, the annual grand council of the Creek Indians assembled at Took-a-batcha, a very ancient town on the Tallapoosa River. At those annual assemblies the United States Agent for the Creeks always attended, besides many white and half-breed traders, and strangers from other tribes. I accompanied Colonel Hawkins, the United States Agent. A flying rumor had circulated far and near that some of the north-western Indians would be present, and this brought some five thousand people to Took-a-batcha, including many Cherokees and Choctaws.

The day after the council met, Tecumseh, with a suite of twenty-four warriors, marched into the centre of the square, and stood still and erect as so many statues. They were dressed in tanned buckskin hunting shirt and leggings, fitting closely, so as to exhibit their muscular development, and they wore a profusion of silver ornaments; their faces were painted red and black. Each warrior carried a rifle, tomahawk and war-club. They were the most athletic body of men I ever saw. The famous Jim Bluejacket was among them. Tecumseh was about six feet high, well put together, not so stout as some of his followers, but of an austere countenance and imperial mien. He was in the prime of life.

The Shawnees made no salutation, but stood facing the council house, not looking to the right or the left. Throughout the assembly there was a dead silence. At length, the Big Warrior, a noted chief of the Creeks and a man of colossal proportions, slowly approached, and handed his pipe to Tecumseh. It was passed in succession to each of his warriors; and then the Big Warrior—not a word being spoken—pointed to a large cabin, a few hundred yards from the square, which had previously been furnished with skins and provisions. Tecumseh and his band, in single file, marched to it.

. . . Next day, precisely at twelve, Bill (a half-breed) summoned me. I saw the Shawnees issue from their lodge; they were painted black, and entirely naked except the flap about their loins. Every weapon but the war-club—then first introduced among the Creeks—had been laid aside. An angry scowl sat on all their visages: they looked like a procession of devils.

Tecumseh led, the warriors followed, one in the footsteps of the other. The Creeks, in dense masses, stood on each side of the path, but the Shawnees noticed no one; they marched to the pole in the centre of the square, and then turned to the left. At each angle of the square Tecumseh took from his pouch some tobacco and sumach, and dropped it on the ground; his warriors performed the same ceremony. This they repeated three times as they marched around the square. Then they approached the flag-pole in the centre, circled round it three times, and, facing the north, threw tobacco and sumach on a small fire, burning, as usual, near the base of the pole. On this they emptied their pouches. They then marched in the same order to the council, or king's house (as it was termed in ancient times), and drew up before it.

. . . At length Tecumseh spoke, at first slowly and in sonorous tones; but soon he grew impassioned, and the words fell in avalanches from his lips. His eyes burned with supernatural luster, and his whole frame trembled with emotion—his voice resounded over the multitude—now sinking in low and musical whispers, now rising to its highest key, hurling out his words like a succession of thunderbolts.

His countenance varied with his speech: its prevalent expression was a sneer of hatred and defiance; sometimes a murderous smile; for a brief interval a sentiment of profound sorrow pervaded it; and, at the close, a look of concentrated vengeance, such, I suppose, as distinguished the arch-enemy of mankind.

I have heard many great orators, but I never saw one with the vocal powers of Tecumseh, or the same command of the muscles of his face. Had I been deaf, the play of his countenance would have told me what he said. Its effect on that wild, superstitious, untutored, and warlike assemblage may be conceived: not a word was said, but stern warriors, the "stoics of the woods," shook with emotion, and a thousand tomahawks were brandished in the air. Even the Big Warrior, who had been true to the whites, and remained faithful during the war, was, for the moment, visibly affected, and more than once I saw his huge hand clutch, spasmodically, the handle of his knife. All this was the effect of his delivery; for, though the mother of Tecumseh was a Creek, and he was familiar with the language, he spoke in the northern dialect, and it was afterwards interpreted by an Indian linguist to the assembly. His speech has been reported, but no one has done or can do it justice. I think I can repeat the substance of what he said, and, indeed, his very words.

In defiance of the white warriors of Ohio and Kentucky, I have travelled through their settlements, once our favorite hunting grounds.

No war whoop was sounded, but there is blood on our knives. The Palefaces felt the blow, and knew not whence it came.

Accursed be the race that has seized our country, and made women of our warriors! Our fathers, from their tombs, reproach us as slaves and cowards; I hear them now in the wailing winds.

The Muscogee was once a mighty people. The Georgians trembled at your war whoop, and the maidens of my tribe, on the distant lakes, seeing the prowess of your warriors, sighed for their embraces. Now your blood is white; your tomahawks have no edge; your bows and arrows were buried with your fathers. Oh, Muscogees, brush from your eyelids the sleep of slavery; once more strike for vengeance, once more for your country. The spirits of the mighty dead complain. The tears drop from the weeping skies. Let the white race perish.

They seize your land; they corrupt your women; they trample on the ashes of your dead. Back, whence they came, upon a trail of blood, they must be driven. Back! back, ay, into the great water whose accursed waves brought them to our shores! Burn their dwellings! Destroy their stock! Slay their wives and children! The Red Man owns the country. War now! War forever! War upon the living! War upon the dead! Dig their very corpses from the grave. Our country must give no rest to a white man's bones!

This is the will of the Great Spirit, revealed to my brother, his familiar, the Prophet of the Lakes. He sends me to you. All the tribes of the north are dancing the war-dance. Two mighty warriors across the seas will send us arms. Tecumseh will soon return to his country. My prophets shall tarry with you. They will stand between you and the bullets of your enemies. When the white men approach you the yawning earth shall swallow them up.

Soon shall you see my arm of fire stretched athwart the sky. I will stamp my foot at Tippecanoe, and the very earth shall shake.

When he resumed his seat the northern pipe was again passed round in solemn silence. The Shawnees then simultaneously leaped up with one appalling yell, and danced their tribal war-dance, going through the evolutions of battle, the scout, the ambush, the final struggle, brandishing their war-clubs, and screaming in terrific concert an infernal harmony fit only for the regions of the damned.

The resistance ended when Tecumseh's brother-in-law, a mystical visionary known as The Prophet, foolishly attacked Harrison when Tecumseh was away. The battle, at Tippecanoe, was a rout.

Harrison's victory was so important to westward migration that he successfully ran for president in 1840 on its fame, using the slogan "Tippecanoe and Tyler too." (John Tyler was the candidate for vice president.)

But perhaps one of Tecumseh's prophecies did come to pass. Shortly after his threat that, "I will stamp my foot . . . and the very earth shall shake," an earthquake hit the Mississippi Valley—the strongest ever in the United States. Although few people lost their lives because the area was so sparsely populated, the physical devastation was astounding. The upward thrust forced the Mississippi River to flow backward. The ground rose or sank from one to three yards in an area of more than 8,000 square miles. Chimneys fell down in Cincinnati, 350 miles from the epicenter in New Madrid, Missouri. Shock waves could be felt from the Gulf Coast to Canada. Seismologists estimate it would have measured 8.0 on the Richter scale.

In any case, Tecumseh died at the Battle of the Thames in Ontario, during the War of 1812. Holding the rank of brigadier general, he fought with the British. Their earlier support of his cause had aggravated America's anger, and helped prompt the war.

"This is the way I live in the wilderness."

JOHNNY APPLESEED

1826–1840
Ohio

ANONYMOUS, S.C. COFFINBURY,
AND FRANKLIN VANDORN

*Yes, there was a Johnny Appleseed. John Chapman was born in Massachusetts in
1774. Not much is known about his early life except that sometime in his twen-
ties he left Philadelphia for the Ohio Valley, carrying a supply of apple seeds. His
work as a nurseryman was inseparable from his devotion to the teachings of
Emanuel Swedenborg (1688–1772), a scientist who claimed to have received a
personal communication of the true spirit of the Scriptures.*

*The first account is from a letter to a Swedenborg society; the second is a
response to a fictionalized profile in* Harper's *magazine; the last recalls a meeting near the farm of Amos Harding, great-grandfather to President Warren
Harding.*

ANONYMOUS

There is in the western country a very extraordinary missionary of
the New Jerusalem. A man has appeared who seems to be almost independent of corporal wants and sufferings. He goes barefooted, can sleep
anywhere, in house or out of house, and live upon the coarsest and most
scanty fare. He has actually thawed the ice with his bare feet.

He procures what books he can of the New Church; travels into the
remote settlements, and lends them wherever he can find readers, and
sometimes divides a book into two or three parts for more extensive
distribution and usefulness.

This man for years past has been in the employment of bringing into
cultivation, in numberless places in the wilderness, small patches (two
or three acres) of ground, and then sowing apple seeds and rearing nurs-
eries. These become valuable as the settlements approximate, and the
profits of the whole are intended for the purpose of enabling him to
print all the Writings of Emanuel Swedenborg, and distribute them
through the western settlements of the United States.

John Chapman was a small man, wiry and thin in habit. His cheeks were hollow; his face and neck dark and skinny from exposure to the weather. His mouth was small; his nose small and turned up quite so much as apparently to raise his upper lip. His eye was [sic] dark and deeply set in his head, but searching and penetrating. His hair was black and straight which he parted in the middle, and permitted to fall about his neck. His hair, withal, was rather thin, fine and glossy. He never wore a full beard, but shaved all clean except a thin roach at the bottom of his throat. His beard was lightly set, sparse, and very black.

In 1840, when the writer last saw him in Mansfield this was his appearance, and at the time he had changed but little, if any, in his general appearance, since he first remembered seeing him when the writer was a small boy.

The dress of this strange man was unique. The writer here assumes to say that he never wore a coffee sack as a part of his apparel. He may have worn the offcast clothing of others; he probably did so. Although often in rags and tatters, and at best in the most plain and simple wardrobe he was always clean, and in his most desolate rags comfortable, and never repulsive.

He generally, when the weather would permit, wore no clothing on his feet, consequently his feet were dark, hard, and horny. He was frequently seen with shirts, pants, and a kind of a long tailed coat of tow-linen then much worn by the farmers. This coat was a device of his own ingenuity and in itself was a curiosity. It consisted of one width of the coarse fabric, which descended from his neck to his heels. It was without collar. In this robe were cut two arm holes into which were placed two straight sleeves. The mother of the writer made it up for him under his immediate direction and supervision.

VANDORN

I never shall forget how pleased he appeared to be when we came up to him in the wilderness, four miles from a living soul but Indians, among bears, wolves, catamounts, serpents, owls and porcupines, yet apparently contented and happy. Here Johnny had some poles put on crotches, covered with elm bark. Some five or six rods from this were logs cut for a cabin and some clapboards for a roof.

After sitting down and chatting for a while, Johnny poked in the ashes with a stick and dragged out some potatoes, saying, "This is the way I live in the wilderness."

"Well," one of the boys replied, "you appear to be as happy as a king."

"Yes," said Chapman, "I could not enjoy myself better anywhere—I can lay on my back, look up at the stars, and it seems almost as though I can see the angels praising God, for he has made all things for good."

"I shall take with me about 30 young men to commence the settlement...."

MOSES AUSTIN REVEALS HIS PLANS FOR TEXAS

April 8, 1821
St. Louis, Missouri

MOSES AUSTIN

Moses Austin had ventured several businesses, each one a bit farther west, by the time he thought of establishing an American settlement in the Mexican territory of Texas. He had been a dry goods merchant in Philadelphia and Richmond, had owned lead mines in Virginia and Missouri, and had been a banker in St. Louis. Left bankrupt by the financial panic of 1819, his wanderlust stirred again, and he asked the Mexican government for a land grant.

Shortly after conceiving the plan Austin described it in a letter to one of his sons, J. E. B. Austin, revealing the motivation behind his own decision and that of innumerable Americans before and since.

. . . I much wish to see you return to this country before I leave it for the Spanish province of Texas. I have made a visit to St. Antonio and obtained liberty to settle in that country—*as I am, ruined, in this,* I found nothing I could do would bring back my property again and to remain in a Country where I had enjoyed *welth* in a state of *poverty* I could Not submit to I therefore made an *exertion* and obtained what I asked for a right of settlement for myself and family the situation I have marked out is on the *Colorado* about 3 Days sale from New Orleans or rather from the *Belise* a *most* delightful situation. . . . I have asked for leave of settlement for 300 families and 200 Thousand Acres of Land to open a Port *Town* at the *mouth of the River* which has been granted me by the Governor of the Province of Texas and has gone on to the Vice King for his confirmation, I have been offered as many *Names* of respectable families as will make up the Number but until I return I shall not admit any as my wish is to have the lands surveyed before I introduce any families at all. I shall take with me about 30 young men to commence the settlement and return after your mother next year. . . .

Though he died shortly after receiving the grant, another son, Stephen Austin, established the settlement in 1823.

"The line of tents is pitched, and the religious city grows up in a few hours. . . ."

REVIVAL MEETINGS

1828
Mississippi Valley

REVEREND TIMOTHY FLINT

"A Methodist preacher," wrote Peter Cartwright, an energetic minister, "instead of hunting up a college or a Biblical institute, hunted up a hardy pony, or a horse, and some travelling apparatus, and with his library always at hand, namely the Bible . . . went through storms of wind, hail, snow, and rain; climbed hills and mountains, traversed valleys, plunged through swamps, swam swollen streams, lay out at night, wet, weary and hungry. He slept with his saddle blanket for a bed, his saddle or saddle-bags for his pillow, and his old big coat or blanket, if he had any, for covering."

Cartwright's description of what became known as "muscular Christianity" held true for other sects as well. The eyewitness of this account, Reverend Timothy Flint, was a Massachusetts native and Harvard graduate who became a Congregationalist missionary in the West about 1815. This account comes from a memoir of ten years of traveling through the Mississippi Valley.

None but one who has seen can imagine the interest, excited in a district of country, perhaps, fifty miles in extent, by the awaited approach of the time for a camp meeting. The notice has been circulated two or three months. On the appointed day, coaches, chaises, wagons, carts, people on horseback, and multitudes travelling from a distance on foot, wagons with provisions, mattresses, tents, and arrangements for the stay of a week, are seen hurrying from every point towards the central spot.

The line of tents is pitched; and the religious city grows up in a few hours under the trees, beside the stream. Lamps are hung in lines among the branches; and the effect of their glare upon the surrounding forest is, as of magic. Meantime the multitudes, with the highest excitement of social feeling added to the general enthusiasm of expectation, pass from tent to tent, and interchange apostolic greetings and embraces, and talk of the coming solemnities. An old man, in a dress of the quaintest simplicity, ascends a platform, wipes the dust from his spectacles, and in a voice of suppressed emotion, gives out the hymn, of which the whole assembled multitude can recite the words. The hoary orator talks of God, of eternity, a judgment to come, and all that is impressive beyond. He speaks of his "experiences," his toils and travels, his persecutions and welcomes, and how many he has seen in hope, in peace and triumph, gathered to their fathers; and when he speaks of the short space that remains to him, his only regret is, that he can no more proclaim, in the silence of death, the mercies of his crucified Redeemer.

There is no need of the studied trick of oratory, to produce in such a place the deepest movements of the heart.

Whatever be the cause, the effect is certain, that through the state of Tennessee, parts of Mississippi, Missouri, Kentucky, Ohio, Indiana and Illinois, these excitements have produced a palpable change in the habits and manners of the people. The gambling and drinking shops are deserted; and the people, that used to congregate there, now go to the religious meetings.

"The arrival produced a great deal of bustle and excitement."

THE SANTA FE TRAIL

1831
Santa Fe

JOSIAH GREGG

The Santa Fe Trail began as an annual caravan in 1822, after news of Mexico's independence from Spain reached the United States. The Spanish government had prohibited trade with the U.S.; the new Mexican government welcomed it.

The wagons started the 780-mile route in Independence, Missouri, or Council Grove, Kansas, usually reaching their destination in forty to sixty days.

By the time the trail began, Santa Fe, which had been the capital of New

Mexico since 1609, had already been long established as the trading center of the Southwest. Though it had only about 3,000 permanent residents, as many as 40,000 buyers and sellers met there to haggle.

The eyewitness of this account, Josiah Gregg, made many trips. His first, in 1831, was with 100 wagons carrying about $200,000 worth of goods. By the 1850s, several million dollars of goods were transported annually.

Some distance beyond the Colorado a party of about a dozen (which I joined) left the wagons to go ahead to Santa Fe.

A few miles before reaching the city the road emerges into an open plain. Ascending a table-ridge, we spied in an extended valley to the northwest occasional groups of trees skirted with verdant corn and wheat fields, with here and there a square block-like protuberance reared in the midst. A little farther and just ahead of us to the north irregular clusters of the same opened to our view. "Oh, we are approaching the suburbs!" thought I, on perceiving the cornfields and what I supposed to be brick-kilns scattered in every direction.

These and other observations of the same nature becoming audible, a friend at my elbow said, "It is true those are heaps of unburnt bricks, nevertheless they are houses—this is the city of Santa Fe."

Five or six days after our arrival the caravan at last hove in sight, and wagon after wagon was seen pouring down the last declivity at about a mile distance from the city.

To judge from the clamorous rejoicings of the men and the state of agreeable excitement which the muleteers seemed to be laboring under, the spectacle must have been as new to them as it had been to me. It was truly a scene for the artist's pencil to revel in.

Even the animals seemed to participate in the humor of their riders, who grew more and more merry and obstreperous as they descended towards the city. I doubt whether the first sight of the walls of Jerusalem was beheld by the crusaders with much more tumultuous and soul-enrapturing joy.

The arrival produced a great deal of bustle and excitement among the natives. *"Los Americanos!"—"Los cargos!"—"La entrada de caravana!"* were to be heard in every direction; and crowds of women and boys flocked around to see the new-comers; while crowds of *leperos* hung about, as usual, to see what they could pilfer. The wagoners were by no means free from excitement on this occasion. Informed of the ordeal they had to pass, they had spent the previous morning in rubbing up; and now they were prepared, with clean faces, sleek-combed hair, and their choicest Sunday suit to meet the fair eyes of glistening black that were sure to stare at them as they passed. There was yet another preparation to be made in order to show off to advantage. Each wagoner must tie a brand new cracker to the lash of his whip; for on driving through the streets and the *plaza publica* every one strives to outvie his comrades in the dexterity with which he flourishes this favorite badge of authority.

Our wagons were soon discharged in the ware-rooms of the custom house; and a few days' leisure being now at our disposal, we had time to take that recreation which a fatiguing journey of ten weeks had rendered so necessary. The wagoners and many of the traders, particularly the novices, flocked to the numerous fandangoes which are regularly kept up after the arrival of a caravan. But the merchants generally were anxiously and actively engaged in their affairs—striving who should first get his goods out of the custom house and obtain a chance at the hard chink of the numerous country dealers, who annually resort to the capital on these occasions.

The wagon trail was made obsolete by the Santa Fe railroad, completed in 1880, which followed much of the old route.

"I can't contrive where the devil
all these well-dressed people have come from!"

A BALL IN CHICAGO

1834

CHARLES FENNO HOFFMAN

"Chicago," wrote a British traveler in 1833, "consists of 150 wooden houses, placed irregularly on both sides of the river. . . . There is already a place of considerable trade, supplying salt, tea, coffee, sugar, and clothing to a large tract of the country to the south and west; and when connected with the navigable point of the river Illinois, by canal or railway, cannot fail of rising to importance."
Eyewitness Charles Hoffman visited at about the same time.

We had not been here an hour before an invitation to a public ball was courteously sent to us by the managers; and though my soiled and travel-worn riding dress was not exactly the thing to present one's self in before ladies of an evening, yet, in my earnestness to see life on the frontier, I easily allowed all objections to be overruled by my companions, and we accordingly drove to the house in which the ball was given.

It was a frame building, one of the few as yet to be found in Chicago; which, although one of the most ancient French trading-posts on the Lakes, can only date its growth as a village since the Indian war, eighteen months since.

When I add that the population has quintupled last summer, and that but few mechanics have come in with the prodigious increase of residents, you can readily imagine that the influx of strangers far exceeds the means of accommodation; while scarcely a house in the place, however comfortable looking outside, contains more than two or three finished rooms. In the present instance, we were ushered into a tolerably sized dancing-room, occupying the second story of the house, and having its unfinished walls so ingeniously covered with pine-branches and flags borrowed from the garrison, that, with the white-washed ceiling above, it presented a very complete and quite pretty appearance. It was not so warm, however, that the fires of cheerful hickory, which roared at either end, could have been readily dispensed with.

. . . As for the company, it was such a complete medley of all ranks, ages, professions, trades, and occupations, brought together from all parts of the world, and now for the first time brought together, that it was amazing to witness the decorum with which they commingled on this festive occasion. The managers (among whom were some officers of the garrison) must certainly be *au fait* at dressing a lobster and mixing regent's punch, in order to have produced a harmonious compound from such a collection of contrarieties. The gayest figure that was ever called by quadrille playing Benoit never afforded me half the amusement that did these Chicago cotillions.

Here you might see a veteran officer in full uniform balancing to a tradesman's daughter still in her short frock and trousers, while there the golden aiguillette of a handsome surgeon flapped in unison with the glass beads upon a scrawny neck of fifty. In one quarter, the high-placed buttons of a linsey-woolsey coat would be dos a dos to the elegantly turned shoulders of a delicate-looking Southern girl; and in another, a pair of Cinderella-like slippers would chassez cross with a brace of thick-soled broghans, in making which, one of the lost feet of the Colossus of Rhodes may have served for a last.

Those raven locks, dressed a la Madonne, over eyes of jet, and touching a cheek where blood of a deeper hue, mingling with the less glowing current from European veins, tell of a lineage drawn from the original owners of the soil; while these golden tresses, floating away from eyes of heaven's own colour over a neck of alabaster, recall the Gothic ancestry of some of "England's born." How piquantly do these trim and beaded leggins peep from under that simple dress of black, as its tall, nut-brown wearer moves, as if unconsciously, through the graceful mazes of the dance. How divertingly do those inflated gigots, rising like windsails from the little Dutch-built hull, jar against those tall plumes which impend over them like a commodore's pennant on the same vessel.

But what boots all these incongruities, when the spirit of festive good humor animates every one present. "It takes all kinds of people to make a world" (as I hear it judiciously observed this side of the mountains), and why should not all these kinds of people be represented as well in a ball-room as in a legislature?

At all events, if I wished to give an intelligent foreigner a favourable opinion of the manners and deportment of my countrymen in the aggregate, I should not wish a better opportunity, after explaining to him the materials of which it was composed, and the mode in which they were brought together from every section of the Union, than was afforded by this very ball. "This is a scene of enchantment to me, sir," observed an officer to me, recently exchanged to this post, and formerly stationed here. "There were but a few traders around the fort when I last visited Chicago, and now I can't contrive where the devil all these well-dressed people have come from!"

"Such a stupid and greasy-looking set . . ."

RUSSIAN FUR TRADERS ON THE PACIFIC COAST

1834
San Francisco, Alta California

RICHARD HENRY DANA

Dana, scion of a prominent Boston family, left Harvard because of illness and signed aboard a trading ship to restore his health. He saw the Pacific coast while it was still primarily Spanish, with just a few American and Russian traders.

Here, at anchor, and the only vessel, was a brig under Russian colors, from Sitka, in Russian America, which had come down to winter, and to take in a supply of tallow and grain, great quantities of which latter article are raised in the Missions at the head of the bay. The second day after our arrival we went on board the brig, it being Sunday, as a matter of curiosity; and there was enough there to gratify it. Though no larger than the *Pilgrim*, she had five or six officers, and a crew of between twenty and thirty; and such a stupid and greasy-looking set, I never saw before. Although it was quite comfortable weather and we had nothing on but straw hats, shirts, and duck trousers, and were barefooted, they had, every man of them, double-soled boots, coming up to the knees, and well greased; thick woollen trousers, frocks, waistcoats, pea-jackets, woollen caps, and everything in true *Nova Zembla* rig; and in the warmest days they made no change. The clothing of one of these men would weigh nearly as much as that of half our crew. They had brutish faces, looked like the antipodes of sailors, and apparently dealt in nothing but grease. They lived upon grease; ate it, drank it, slept in the midst of it, and their clothes were covered with it. To a Russian, grease is the greatest luxury. They looked with greedy eyes upon the tallow-bags as they were taken into the vessel, and, no doubt, would have eaten one up whole, had not the officer kept watch over it. The grease appeared to fill their pores, and to come out in their hair and on their faces. It seems as if it were this saturation which makes them stand cold and rain so well. If they were to go into a warm climate, they would melt and die of the scurvy.

His report of his adventures, Two Years Before the Mast, *has never been out of print since publication in 1840. It is credited with influencing President James Polk's decision to wage war with Mexico to gain California.*

"*. . . Both almost at the same instant fired.*"

KIT CARSON FIGHTS AT A RENDEZVOUS

August 12–15, 1835
near the Green River, Colorado

SAMUEL PARKER

A paid notice in the Missouri Intelligencer *of October 6, 1826, read as follows: "Christopher Carson, a boy about sixteen years old, small of his age, but thickset, light hair, ran away from the subscriber, living in Franklin, Howard County, Mo., to whom he had been bound to learn the saddler's trade, on or about the first day of September last. He is supposed to have made his way toward the upper part of the state. All persons are notified not to harbor, support, or subsist said boy under penalty of the law. One cent reward will be given to any person who will bring back the said boy."*

Christopher "Kit" Carson was never returned to his master. He became a trapper, settling near Taos, New Mexico, and working as far as away as California and Montana.

Eyewitness Samuel Parker saw him at a "rendezvous"—a meeting place for trappers and buyers from the fur companies. Parker, a Presbyterian preacher, was crossing the country to found a missionary settlement in Oregon.

The American Fur Company have between two and three hundred men constantly in and about these mountains, engaged in trading, hunting and trapping. These all assemble at rendezvous upon the arrival of the caravan, bring in their furs, and take new supplies for the coming year, of clothing, ammunition, and goods for trade with the Indians. But few of these men ever return to their country and friends. Most of them are constantly in debt to the company, and are unwilling to return without a fortune; and year after year passes away, while they are hoping in vain for better success. . . .

A few days after our arrival at the place of rendezvous, and when all the mountain men had assembled, another day of indulgence was granted to them, in which all restraint was laid aside. These days are the climax of the hunter's happiness. I will relate an occurrence which took place near evening, as a specimen of mountain life. A hunter, who goes technically by the name of the great bully of the mountains, mounted his horse with a loaded rifle, and challenged any Frenchman, American, Spaniard, or Dutchman, to fight him in single combat. Kit Carson, an American, told him if he wished to die, he would accept the challenge. Shunar defied him. C. mounted his horse, and with a loaded pistol, rushed into close contact, and both almost at the same instant fired. C's ball entered S's hand, came out at the wrist, and passed through the arm above the elbow. Shunar's ball passed over the head of Carson; and while he went for another pistol, Shunar begged that his life might be spared. Such scenes, sometimes from passion, and sometimes for amusement, make the pastime of their wild and wandering life. They appear to have sought for a place where, as they would say, human nature is not oppressed by the tyranny of religion, and pleasure is not awed by the frown of virtue. . . . Their toils and privations are so great, that they more readily compensate themselves by plunging into such excesses, as in their mistaken judgment of things, seem most adapted to give them pleasure.

A few years after the rendezvous described in this account, Carson met John

Frémont and agreed to become a guide for Frémont's western expeditions. On a later trip back east he learned to his surprise that accounts of his exploits had made him a national hero. Eventually the mythmakers took over completely, even publishing a fictionalized "autobiography."

"We have given over all hopes of receiving assistance. . . ."

DAVY CROCKETT DEFENDS THE ALAMO

February 19–March 5, 1836
San Antonio, Texas

DAVY CROCKETT

Davy Crockett parlayed his frontier reputation into a seat in the Tennessee State House and then three terms in the U.S. Congress. When he lost the next election he said of his detractors, "They can go to hell. I'm going to Texas."

Unfortunately, he was soon besieged at the Alamo with 186 other doomed men. This last testament has been both quoted and disputed by historians since it first appeared, but it is considered faithful to the facts and is irresistibly colorful.

FEBRUARY 19

We are all in high spirits, though we are rather short of provisions, for men who have appetites that could digest anything but oppression; but no matter, we have a prospect of soon getting our bellies full of fighting, and that is victuals and drink to a true patriot any day.

FEBRUARY 22

The Mexicans, about sixteen hundred strong with their President Santa Anna at their head, aided by Generals Almonte, Cos, Sesma, and Castrillon, are within two leagues of Bexar. . . .

FEBRUARY 23

Early this morning the enemy came in sight, marching in regular order, and displaying their strength to the greatest advantage, in order to strike us with terror. But that was no go; they'll find that they have to do with men who will never lay down their arms as long as they can stand on their legs. We held a short council of war, and, finding that we should be completely surrounded, and overwhelmed by numbers, if we remained in the town, we concluded to withdraw to the fortress of Alamo, and defend it to the last extremity. We accordingly filed off, in good order, having some days before placed all the surplus provisions, arms, and ammunition in the fortress. We have had a large national flag made; it is composed of thirteen stripes, red and white, alternately, on a blue ground with a large white star, of five points, in the center, and between the points the letters texas. As soon as all our little band, about one hundred and fifty in number, had entered and secured the fortress in the best possible manner, we set about raising our flag on the battlements.

FEBRUARY 24

Very early this morning the enemy commenced a new battery on the banks of the river, about three hundred and fifty yards from the fort, and by afternoon they amused themselves by firing at us from that quarter.

MARCH 3

We have given over all hopes of receiving assistance from Goliad or Refugio. Colonel Travis harangued the garrison, and concluded by exhorting them, in case the enemy should carry the fort, to fight to the last gasp, and render their victory even more serious to them than to us. This was followed by three cheers.

MARCH 4

Shells have been falling into the fort like hail during the day, but without effect. About dusk, in the evening, we observed a man running toward the fort, pursued by about half a dozen of the Mexican cavalry. The bee-hunter immediately knew him to be the old pirate who had gone to Goliad, and, calling to the two hunters, he sallied out of the fort to the relief of the old man, who was hard pressed. I followed close after.

Before we reached the spot the Mexicans were close on the heel of the old man, who stopped suddenly, turned short upon his pursuers, discharged his rifle, and one of the enemy fell from his horse.

The chase was renewed, but finding that he would be overtaken and cut to pieces, he now turned again, and, to the amazement of the enemy became the assailant in his turn.

He clubbed his gun, and dashed among them like a wounded tiger, and they fled like sparrows. By this time we reached the spot, and, in the ardor of the moment, followed some distance before we saw that our retreat to the fort was cut off by another detachment of cavalry.

Nothing was to be done but to fight our way through. We were all of the same mind. "Go ahead!" cried I, and they shouted, "Go ahead, Colonel!"

We dashed among them, and a bloody conflict ensued. They were about twenty in all, and they stood their ground. After the fight had continued about five minutes, a detachment issued from the fort to our relief, and the Mexicans scampered off, leaving eight of their comrades dead upon the field.

But we did not escape unscathed, for both the pirate and the bee-hunter were mortally wounded, and I received a saber cut across the forehead.

The old man died, without speaking, as soon as we entered the fort. We bore my young friend to his bed, dressed his wounds, and I watched beside him. He lay, without complaint or manifesting pain, until about midnight, when he spoke, and I asked him if he wanted anything. "Nothing," he replied, but drew a sigh that seemed to rend his heart, as he added, "Poor Kate of Nacogdoches!"

His eyes were filled with tears, as he continued: "Her words were prophetic, Colonel"; and then he sang in a low voice that resembled the sweet notes of his own devoted Kate,

> But toom cam' the saddle, all bluidy to see,
> And hame cam' the steed, but hame never cam' he.

He spoke no more, and a few minutes after, died. Poor Kate, who will tell this to thee?

MARCH 5

Pop, pop, pop! Bom, bom, bom! throughout the day. No time for memorandums now. Go ahead! Liberty and independence forever! (Here ends Colonel Crockett's manuscript.)

———————————

"Our line advanced without a halt. . . ."

"REMEMBER THE ALAMO!"

April 21, 1836
the San Jacinto River, Texas

SAM HOUSTON

While the Alamo was under siege, the declaration of Texan independence was made at Washington-on-the-Bravos. Less than two months later, Sam Houston, previously a congressman and governor of Tennessee, led the Texan forces into this decisive battle at the San Jacinto riverbank near present-day Houston. The defeat of the Mexicans, commanded by President Antonio Lopez de Santa Anna, made Texas truly independent.

This account is from a report Sam Houston sent to David G. Burnet, who had been selected provisional president of Texas when independence was declared.

The enemy withdrew to a position on the bank of the San Jacinto, about three-quarters of a mile from our encampment, and commenced fortification. . . . About nine o'clock on the morning of the 21st the enemy were reinforced by five hundred choice troops, under the command of General Cos, increasing their effective force to upwards of fifteen hundred men, while our aggregate force for the field numbered seven hundred and eighty-three.

At half past three o'clock in the evening I ordered the officers of the Texan army to parade their respective commands, having in the meantime ordered the bridge on the only road communicating with the Brazos, distant eight miles from our encampment, to be destroyed, thus cutting off all possibility of escape. Our troops paraded with alacrity and spirit, and were anxious for the contest. Their conscious disparity in numbers seemed only to increase their enthusiasm and confidence, and heightened their anxiety for the conflict.

Our situation afforded me an opportunity of making the arrangements preparatory to the attack without exposing our designs to the enemy. Our cavalry was first dispatched to the front of the enemy's left, for the purpose of attracting their notice, while an extensive island of timber afforded us an opportunity of concentrating our forces and deploying from that point, agreeably to the previous design of the troops.

Every evolution was performed with alacrity, the whole advancing rapidly in line, through an open prairie, without any protection whatever for our men. The artillery advanced and took station within two hundred yards of the enemy's breastwork, and commenced an effective fire with grape and canister.

Colonel Sherman, with his regiment, having commenced the action upon our left wing, the whole line, at the centre and on the right, advancing in double-quick time, raising the war-cry, "Remember the Alamo!" received the enemy's fire, and advanced within point-blank shot, before a piece was discharged from our lines.

Our line advanced without a halt, until they were in possession of the woodland and the enemy's breastwork—the right wing of Burleson's and the left wing of Millard's taking possession of the breastwork, our artillery having gallantly charged up within seventy yards of the enemy's cannon, when it was taken by our troops.

The conflict lasted about eighteen minutes from the time of close action until we were in possession of the enemy's encampment, taking one piece of cannon (loaded), four stands of colors, all their camp equipage, stores and baggage. Our cavalry had charged and routed that of the enemy upon the right, and given pursuit to the fugitives, which did not cease until they arrived at the bridge which I have mentioned before, Captain Karnes, always among the foremost in danger, commanding the pursuers.

The conflict in the breastwork lasted but a few moments; many of the troops encountered hand to hand, and, not having the advantage of bayonets on our side, our riflemen used their pieces as war-clubs, breaking many of them off at the breech. The rout commenced at half-past four, and the pursuit by the main army continued until twilight. . . . Every officer and man proved himself worthy of the cause in which he battled. . . .

There were about 50,000 Americans in Texas at the time of its independence, most of whom wanted to join the United States immediately. But Texas permitted slavery, so antislavery forces blocked its admission. Almost ten years of politicking passed before Texas became the twenty-eighth state in 1845, just as the Mexican War approached.

Shortly after the battle he describes here, eyewitness Sam Houston became Texas's first elected president. After statehood he was its governor and then a senator.

JOHN DEERE'S PLOW

1837
Grand Detour, Illinois

JOHN DEERE

*The thick black soil that made midwest farms so fertile also drove farmers crazy.
It stuck to everything. When plowing, they had to stop every few yards and use
wooden paddles to scrape the soil off the plow.*

*Blacksmith John Deere was making some repairs at a local sawmill when he
saw an old steel sawblade and got an idea. The blade had become polished with
use. Maybe its surface would move smoothly through the soil.*

*Deere told the story of the invention to a friend, Frank Kern, who recounted
it many years later in this version.*

I cut the teeth off with a hand chisel with the help of a striker and
sledge, then laid them on the fire of the forge and heated what little I
could at a time and shaped them as best I could with the hand hammer.
After making the upright standard out of bar iron, I was ready for the
wood parts. I went out to the timber, dug up a sapling and made the
crooks of the roots for handles, shaped the beam out of a stick of timber
with an ax and drawing-knife, and finally succeeded in constructing a
very rough plow. I set it on a box by the side of the shop-door. A few days
after, a farmer from across the river drove up. Seeing the plow, he asked:

"Who made that plow?"

"I did, such as it is, wood work and all."

"Hell," said the farmer, "that looks as though it would work. Let me
take it home and try it, and if it works all right, I will keep it and pay you
for it. If not I will return it."

"Take it" said I, "and give it a thorough trial."

About two weeks later, the farmer drove up to the shop, without the
plow, and paid for it, and said: "Now get a move on you, and make me
two more plows just like the other one."

*By 1847, Deere's factory was turning out a thousand plows a year; a decade
later, ten thousand. Today the John Deere Company is one of the world's largest
farm machinery makers.*

"They threaten Death and Distruction . . .
saying that I was the cause of the small pox."

A SMALLPOX EPIDEMIC

July 14–September 22, 1837
Fort Clark, Dakota Territory

FRANCIS AUGUSTE CHARDON

According to some estimates, smallpox killed more than fifty times the number of Indians killed in battles with European settlers, starting soon after the first Europeans arrived. Several tribes were essentially wiped out by the disease.

Obviously a virus knows no politics, and the disease was as hated by the Europeans as by the Indians. But each epidemic sparked fear, and a human enemy was usually blamed. Because some Europeans used the disease as a weapon, offering infected gifts to Indians in an early form of chemical warfare, the blame was sometimes deserved.

Fort Clark was about fifty miles north of Bismarck, North Dakota. Chardon, a native of Philadelphia, headed the trading firm there.

JULY 14

A young Mandan died to day of the Small Pox—several others has caught it—the Indians all being out Makeing dried Meat has saved several of them.

JULY 26

The Rees [Arickarees] and Mandans all arrived to day well loaded with Meat. The 4 Bears [a Mandan chief] has caught the small pox, and got crazy and has disappeared from camp—he arrived here in the afternoon. . . .

JULY 28

Rain in the morning—This day was very Near being my last—a young Mandan came to the Fort with his gun cocked, and secreted under his robe, with the intention of Killing me. After hunting me in 3 or 4 of the houses he at last found me. The door being shut, he waited some time for me to come out. Just as I was in the act of going out, Mitchel caught him, and gave him in the hands of two Indians who conducted him to the Village. Had not Mitchel perceived him the instant he did, I would not be at the trouble of Makeing this statement—I am upon my guard.

The Rees are outrageous against the Mandans. They say that the first Mandan that kills a white, they will exterminate the whole race. I have got 100 Guns ready and 1,000 lb Powder, ready to hand out to them when the fun commences.

The Mandans & Rees gave us two splendid dances. They say dance, on account of their Not haveing a long time to live, as they expect to all die of the small pox—and as long as they are alive, they will take it out in dancing.

JULY 30

Another report from the Gros Ventres to day say that they are arrived at their Village, and that 10 or 15 of them have died, two big fish among them. They threaten Death and Distruction to us all at this place, saying that I was the cause of the small pox Makeing its appearance in this country. One of our best friends of the Village (The Four Bears) died to day, regretted by all who Knew him.

JULY 31

Mandans are getting worse, Nothing will do them except revenge. Three of the war party that left here on the 26th of last Month arrived to day, with each of them one horse that they stole from the Yanctons on White river.

Speech of the 4 Bears a Mandan Warrior to the Arricarees and Mandans, 30th July 1837—

> My Friends one and all, Listen to what I have to say. Ever since I can remember, I have loved the Whites. I have lived With them ever since I was a Boy, and to the best of my Knowledge I have never Wronged a White Man; on the Contrary, I have always protected them from the insults of Others, Which they cannot deny.
>
> The 4 Bears never saw a White Man hungry, but what he gave him to eat, Drink, and a buffaloe skin to sleep on, in time of Need. I was always ready to die for them, which they cannot deny. I have done every thing that a red Skin could do for them, and how have they repaid it!
>
> What ingratitude! I have Never Called a White Man a Dog, but to day I do Pronounce them to be a set of Black harted

Dogs. They have deceivd me, them that I always considered as Brothers has turned out to be My Worst Enemies.

I have been in Many Battles, and often Wounded, but the Wounds of My enemies I exhalt in. But to day I am Wounded, and by Whom, by those same White Dogs that I have always Considered and treated as Brothers. I do not fear Death, my friends. You know it. But to die with my face rotten, that even the Wolves will shrink with horror at seeing Me, and say to themselves, that is the 4 Bears the Friend of the Whites—

Listen well what I have to say, as it will be the last time you will hear Me. Think of your Wives, Children, Brothers, Sisters, Friends, and in fact all that you hold dear, are all Dead, or Dying, with their faces all rotten, caused by those dogs the whites. Think of all that, My friends, and rise all together and Not leave one of them alive.

The 4 Bears will act his Part.

AUGUST 12

Cool and pleasant weather. One of my best friends of the Little Village died to day. . . .

AUGUST 15

The War Party of Rees and Mandans that left here the 26th of June, all came back to day, haveing Killed seven Sioux, men, women and children. It appears that the small pox has broke out amongst the Sioux, as some of the Party, on their way back, was taken sick at Grand River, haveing caught the disease from those that they butchered.

AUGUST 17

The Rees started out after buffaloe, the Indians dying off every day. Where the disease will stop, I know not. We are badly situated, as we are threatened to be Murdered by the Indians every instant; however we are all determined, and prepared for the worst.

A Young Ree for several days has been lurking around the Fort, watching a good opportunity to Kill me, but not finding a good chance, this Morning he came, full intent to sit himself down in front of the Fort gate, and waited a few Minutes for me to go out.

In the Mean time one of my Men a Dutchman, John Cliver— stepped out and sat himself down a long side of the Indian. After setting a few Minutes, he got up to come in the Fort. He only Made five paces, when the Indian shot him in the back bone and Killed him instantaneously. He made off immediately. We pursued after him shooting at him, but without effect. He got as far as the little river, where one of his Brothers is entered. On arriving there he made a stop, and hollowed to us that that was the place he wanted to die.

Garreau approached in 15 paces of him and shot. The contents knocked him over. He then rushed on him with his large Knife and ripped his body open. They were both [Cliver and the Indian] entered at 2 P.M. I hoisted the Black flag.

. . . The Mother of the fellow we Killed came to the Fort crying, saying that she wanted to die also, and wished for us to Kill her.

Garreau stepped up, and with his tommahawk would of Made short work of the Old Woman, but was prevented.

AUGUST 29

An Indian Vaccinated his child by cutting two small pieces of flesh out of his arms, and two on the belly—and then takeing a Scab from one that was getting well of the disease, and rubbing it on the wounded part. Three days after, it took effect, and the child is perfectly well.

AUGUST 31

A young Mandan that died 4 days ago, his wife haveing the disease also, killed her two children, one a fine Boy of eight years, and the other six. To complete the affair she hung herself.

The Number of Deaths up to the Present is very near five hundred—the Mandans are all cut off, except 23 young and Old Men.

SEPTEMBER 1

This Morning two dead bodies, wrapped in a White skin, and laid on a raft passed by the Fort, on their way to the regions below. May success attend them.

SEPTEMBER 4

A young Mandan that was given over for dead, and abandoned by his Father, and left alone in the bushes to die, came to life again, and is now doing well. He is hunting his Father, with the intent to Kill him, for leaveing him alone.

I was visited by a young fellow from the Little Village. He assures me that there is but 14 of them liveing, the Number of deaths Cannot be less than 800.

SEPTEMBER 21

The Mandans fearing their Allies, the Rees, should unite with the Sioux, have all fled to the opposite side of the river. What their intention is, I Know not, but the few that are left (41) are Miserable, surrounded on all sides.

SEPTEMBER 22

My youngest son died to day.

---

*". . . Aged females, apparently nearly ready to drop
into the grave, were traveling with heavy burdens. . . ."*

THE TRAIL OF TEARS

December 1838
Kentucky

ANONYMOUS

In 1824 about 77,000 Indians were living east of the Mississippi River, according to estimates given to the secretary of war. By 1840, almost all the tribes had been "removed," pushed westward to make room for new settlers.

"Have we done any wrong?" asked John Ross, a Cherokee. "We are not charged with any. We have a country which others covet. This is the only event we have ever yet been charged with."

In the series of forced marches that have become known as the Trail of Tears, 14,000 Cherokees were driven out of Georgia and Tennessee into Oklahoma.

[We saw a] detachment of the poor Cherokee Indians . . . about eleven hundred Indians—sixty waggons—six hundred horses, and perhaps forty pairs of oxen. We found them in the forest camped for the night by the road side under a severe fall of rain accompanied by heavy wind.

With their canvas for a shield from the inclemency of the weather, and the cold wet ground for a resting place, after the fatigue of the day, they spent the night. Many of the aged Indians were suffering extremely from the fatigue of the journey, and the ill health consequent upon it. . . . Several were then quite ill, and an aged man we were informed was then in the last struggles of death.

We met several detachments in the southern part of Kentucky on the 4th, 5th, and 6th of December. The last detachment which we passed on the 7th embraced rising two thousand Indians with horses and mules in proportion. The forward part of the train we found just pitching their tents for the night, and notwithstanding some thirty or forty waggons were already stationed, we found the road literally filled with the procession for about three miles in length. The sick and feeble were carried in waggons—about as comfortable for traveling as a New England ox cart with a covering over it—a great many ride on horseback and multitudes go on foot—even aged females, apparently nearly ready to drop into the grave, were traveling with heavy burdens attached to the back—on the sometimes frozen ground, and sometimes muddy streets, with no covering for the feet except what nature had given them.

We learned from the inhabitants on the road where the Indians passed, that they buried fourteen or fifteen at every stopping place, and they make a journey of ten miles per day only on an average.

About 4,000 Indians died along the way. Perhaps 1,000 escaped.

"No men on earth . . . could withstand a shock from a hundred others with such arms in their hands!"

COLT'S REVOLVER

October 22, 1840
New York City

J. D. WILLIAMSON AND JAMES McINTOSH

"Treat them well," an early ad for Colt revolvers gushed, "and they will treat your enemies badly. They are always worth what they cost—in the Far West much more, almost a legal tender! If you buy a Colt's Rifle or Pistol, you feel certain you have one true friend, with six hearts in his body, who can always be relied on."

Samuel Colt thought up the revolver when he was just a teenager. He later whittled a model and built a working version, receiving French, English and U.S. patents.

Although the U.S. Army decided not to buy the gun after testing it in 1837, some soldiers used it in that year's Seminole War in Florida. Word of mouth helped Colt sell it to individuals, but he struggled to keep his business alive.

A few years later he convinced the military to test it again. The eyewitness report here comes from J. D. Williamson and James McIntosh, navy commanders.

In obedience to your order of the 22d instant, we have the honor to report, that, after witnessing the very interesting trial of Colt's carbines and pistols, with the common ship muskets and pistols now in use, on that day, we feel no hesitation in recommending them for use on board all ships in the United States navy.

The expense of adopting Colt's patent arms, and laying aside those now in use, we think, should be no consideration with a Government wishing to place their army and navy in a superior condition to those of other nations.

Eight of Colt's carbines were fired by eight of Colt's men, or mechanics, as rapidly as they could load and fire, for ten minutes. In that time, 371 balls were thrown, and two seconds more must have added another round of 48 balls, as the eight men had nearly reloaded their cylinders. Had extra cylinders been employed, in preference to reloading, it is probable double the number of balls would have been thrown, or discharged, as they can be replaced in about half the time of reloading a cylinder.

No accident occurred, and no failure in the discharge of the carbines. . . .

Eight marines, with their muskets, were selected from the marine guard of the Fulton, and desired to load and fire in the same manner for ten minutes: the number of balls discharged was 147. The muskets, after a few fires, snapped and blowed frequently and one of them went off accidentally in the act of loading, burning the hand of the marine using it.

The accuracy was very much in favor of the carbine; although officers of the army, who were present, declared they had never witnessed better firing with muskets by soldiers of any description. The penetration was probably a shade less; but no practical man will doubt the efficiency of the carbines, in that respect, for all useful purposes.

The pistols were then tested, and we feel that a comparison between them cannot be instituted. Colt's pistols went off regularly, and the accuracy was astonishing; striking frequently at mark less than a dollar, and scares a ball passing outside a circle of ten inches.

The common ship pistols were tried, and went very wide of the mark the balls never striking within the circle, and seldom hitting the board, of four feet long and eighteen inches wide. It was with difficulty the officers using the ship's pistols could get them off, in consequence of their being so very hard on the trigger. . . . And the reaction was great, as almost to cripple those who used them.

Some of the cylinders of the carbines and pistols were immersed for two hours in a tub of water, and, although the caps were rather large for the nipples, nearly half of them went off.

We cannot conclude this report without recording a remark made on the ground by a gallant and experienced officer of the army, who witnessed the commencement of the firing of the eight carbines: "There are no men on earth," he observed, "who could withstand a shock from a hundred others with such arms in their hands!" and we believe it would be next to impossible to board a ship where Colt's arms were used by the marines and small-arms men.

The report's recommendation was not followed. Colt endured a bankruptcy while waiting for the gun to catch on, but success arrived in 1847 with the start of the Mexican War, when the army placed an order for a thousand pistols.

**"The kindness and hospitality
of the native Californians have not been overstated."**

HOSPITALITY IN SPANISH CALIFORNIA

1841

JOHN BIDWELL

In 1841, eyewitness John Bidwell led the first wagon train along the famous Oregon Trail from Independence, Missouri, to California. He had lost his land in Missouri to a claim jumper, and wanted to start fresh in California, which had been described to him as "perennial spring and boundless fertility."

He organized an expedition with 500 other prospective emigrants; but by the departure day, every one of them had dropped out. After some scrambling he found six willing adventurers, and on the trail sixty more joined. "Our ignorance of the route was complete," Bidwell later said. "We knew that California lay west, and that was the extent of our knowledge." The harsh trip took twenty-four weeks. The emigrants had to eat their mules to survive.

The kindness and hospitality of the native Californians have not been overstated. Up to the time the Mexican regime ceased in California they had a custom of never charging for anything; that is to say, for entertainment—food, use of horses, etc. You were supposed, even if invited to visit a friend, to bring your blankets with you, and one would be very thoughtless if he traveled and did not take a knife with him to cut his meat. When you had eaten, the invariable custom was to rise, deliver to the woman or hostess the plate on which you had eaten the meat and beans—for that was about all they had—and say, *"Muchas gracias Senora,"* ("Many thanks, madame"); and the hostess as invariably replied, *"Buen Provecho,"* ("May it do you much good"). The Missions in California invariably had gardens with grapes, olives, figs, pomegranates, pears, and apples, but the ranches scarcely ever had any fruit. When you wanted a horse to ride, you would take it to the next ranch—it might be twenty, thirty, or fifty miles—and turn it out there, and sometime or other in reclaiming his stock the owner would get it back. In this way you might travel from one end of California to the other.

Bidwell lived in Sacramento, found gold in the Feather River, and ran California's largest ranch. After U.S. statehood he represented California in Congress.

". . .They were to be decimated, and each tenth man shot."

A DEADLY LOTTERY

1843
Salado, Mexico

THOMAS JEFFERSON GREEN

Mexico never gave the young Republic of Texas a rest. Mexican president Santa Anna had told one American diplomat that he "would war for ever for the reconquest of Texas, and that if he died in his senses his last words should be an exhortation to his countrymen never to abandon the effort to reconquer the country." Mexico invaded in 1842, capturing San Antonio. Fighting continued until the middle of 1843.

Eyewitness Thomas Jefferson Green, a leader of the Texan volunteers, was ignoring orders when he attacked the Mexican town of Mier, where he and his

*troops were defeated and taken prisoner. On the order of Santa Anna, 193
Texans were marched to Salado and made to pay an enormous price.*

Soon after they arrived, our men received the melancholy intelligence that they were to be decimated, and each tenth man shot.

It was now too late to resist this horrible order. Our men were closely ironed [chained] and drawn up in front of all their guards, who were in readiness to fire. Could they have known it previously they would have again charged their guards, and made them pay dearly for the last breach of faith. It was now too late! A manly gloom and a proud defiance filled all faces. They had but one resort, and that was to invoke their country's vengeance upon their murderers, consign their souls to God, and die like men.

The decimator, Colonel Domingo Huerta, had arrived at Salado ahead of our men. The "Redcap" company were to be the executioners; those men whose lives had been so humanely spared by our men at this place on the 11th of February.

The decimation took place by the drawing of black and white beans from a small earthen mug. The white ones signified life and the black death. One hundred and fifty-nine white beans were placed in the bottom of the mug with seventeen black ones upon the top of them. The beans were not stirred, and had so slight a shake that it was perfectly clear that they had not been mixed together. Such was [the Mexicans'] anxiety to execute Captain Cameron, and perhaps the balance of the officers, that first Cameron, and afterward the other officers, were made to draw a bean each from the mug in this condition.

Cameron said, with his usual coolness: "Well, boys, we have to draw; let's be at it." He then thrust his hand into the mug and drew out a white bean. Next came Colonel Wilson, then Captain Ryan, and then Judge Gibson, all of whom drew white beans. Next came Captain Eastland, who drew the first black one, and then the balance of the men. The knocking off the irons from the unfortunates alone told who they were.

They all drew their beans with that manly dignity and firmness which showed them superior to their condition. None showed change of countenance; and as the black beans failed to depress so did the white beans fail to elate. Some of lighter temper jested over the tragedy. One would say: "Boys, this beats raffling all to pieces"; another would say: "This is the tallest gambling scrape I ever was in."

Major Cocke, when he first drew the fatal bean, held it up before his forefinger and thumb, and with a smile of contempt said: "Boys, I told you so; I never failed in my life to draw a prize."

Soon after, the fated men were placed in a separate courtyard, where about dark they were executed. Several of our men were permitted to visit the unfortunates to receive their dying requests.

Just previous to the firing they were bound together with cords, and their eyes being bandaged they were set upon a log near the wall with their backs to the executioners. They all begged the officer to shoot them in front and at a short distance. This he refused; and, to make his cruelty as refined as possible, he fired at several paces.

During the martyrdom of these patriots the main body of our men were separated from them by a stone wall some fifteen feet high. The next morning, as they marched on the road to Mexico, they passed the bodies of their dead comrades, whose bones now lie upon the plains of Salado, a perishing remembrance of exalted patriotism.

The survivors were released by the Mexicans about a year later.

"I walked through the solitary streets...."

THE MORMON GHOST TOWN

October 1846
Nauvoo, Illinois

THOMAS L. KANE

The Mormon town of Nauvoo, with 15,000 citizens, was once the largest and wealthiest in the state of Illinois. Resentment of the sect, and fear of its power, grew with the success of the town. By the time Mormon founder Joseph Smith grandiosely declared his candidacy for president of the United States, anti-Mormon violence had became common. Smith was killed by a mob in 1844.

His successor, Brigham Young, decided to lead his followers across the plains to escape further persecution. The effort to found the state of Deseret, now Utah, was extraordinary: The last of the Mormons to start the trek had no animals to pull their wagons, so they dragged handcarts across the country.

Eyewitness Kane, though never a member of the church, was fascinated by the Mormons, and became an important middleman between them and the U.S. government.

I was descending the last hillside upon my journey, when a land-scape . . . broke upon my view. Half encircled by a bend of the river, a beautiful city lay glittering in the fresh morning sun; its bright new dwellings, set in cool green gardens, ranging up around a stately dome-shaped hill, which was crowned by a noble marble edifice, whose high tapering spire was radiant with white and gold.

The city appeared to cover several miles; and beyond it, in the background, there rolled off a fair country, checquered by the careful lines of fruitful husbandry. The unmistakable marks of industry, enterprise and educated wealth, everywhere, made the scene one of singular and most striking beauty.

It was a natural impulse to visit this inviting region. I procured a skiff, and rowing across the river, landed at the chief wharf of the city. No one met me there. I looked, and saw no one. I could hear no one move; though the quiet everywhere was such that I heard the flies buzz, and the water ripples break against the shallow of the beach.

I walked through the solitary streets. The town lay as in a dream, under some deadening spell of loneliness, from which I almost feared to wake it. For plainly it had not slept long. There was no grass growing up in the paved ways. Rains had not entirely washed away the prints of dusty footsteps.

Yet I went about unchecked. I went into empty workshops, rope walks and smithies. The spinner's wheel was idle; the carpenter had gone from his work-bench and shavings, his unfinished sash and casing. Fresh bark was in the tanner's vat, and the fresh-chopped lightwood stood piled against the baker's oven.

The blacksmith's shop was cold; but his coal heap and ladling pool and crooked water horn were all there, as if he had just gone off for a holiday. No work people anywhere looked to know my errand.

If I went into the gardens, clinking the wicket-latch loudly after me, to pull the marygolds, heart's-ease and lady-slippers, and draw a drink with the water sodden well-bucket and its noisy chain; or, knocking off with my stick the tall heavy-headed dahlias and sunflowers, hunted over the beds for cucumbers and love-apples, no one called out to me from any opened window, or dog sprang forward to bark an alarm.

I could have supposed the people hidden in the houses, but the doors were unfastened; and when at last I timidly entered them, I found dead ashes white upon the hearths, and had to tread a tiptoe, as if walking down the aisle of a country church, to avoid rousing irreverent echoes from the naked floors.

Honoring Kane's work to secure government protection for the exodus, Council Bluffs, Iowa, an important Mormon settlement, was once named Kanesville.

> *"The necessary mutilation of the bodies*
> *of those who had been my friends...."*

LAST OF THE DONNER PARTY

February 1847
near Truckee Lake, California

LEWIS KESEBERG

The Donner Party, almost ninety emigrants from several families, headed west from Springfield, Illinois, in the summer of 1846. The inexperience of its leaders and some petty arguments delayed its attempt to cross the Sierra Nevada range until late October, when deep snows had already fallen on the mountains. The emigrants had to stop at Truckee Lake.

Some of them made a courageous descent to California in December, and sent back help. An interim relief party came with some food, but not everyone could follow it back.

By the time rescuers could make a second trip to Truckee, some of those left behind had resorted to the cannibalism that made their ordeal notorious.

A heavy storm came on in a few days after the last relief party left. Mrs. George Donner had remained with her sick husband in their camp, six or seven miles away. Mrs. Murphy lived about a week after we were left alone. When my provisions gave out, I remained four days before I could taste human flesh. There was no other resort—it was that or death. My wife and child had gone on with the first relief party. I knew not whether they were living or dead. They were penniless and friendless in a strange land. For their sakes I must live, if not for my own. Mrs. Murphy was too weak to revive.

The flesh of starved beings contains little nutriment. It is like feeding straw to horses. I can not describe the unutterable repugnance with which I tasted the first mouthful of flesh. There is an instinct in our nature that revolts at the thought of touching, much less eating, a corpse. It makes my blood curdle to think of it!

It has been told that I boasted of my shame—said that I enjoyed this horrid food, and that I remarked that human flesh was more palatable than California beef. This is a falsehood. It is a horrible, revolting falsehood. This food was never otherwise than loathsome, insipid, and disgusting. For nearly two months I was alone in that dismal cabin. No one knows what occurred but myself—no living being ever before was told of the occurrences. Life was a burden. The horrors of one day succeeded those of the preceding.

Five of my companions had died in my cabin, and their stark and ghastly bodies lay there day and night, seemingly gazing at me with their glazed and staring eyes. I was too weak to move them had I tried. The relief parties had not removed them. These parties had been too hurried, too horror-stricken at the sight, too fearful lest an hour's delay might cause them to share the same fate. I endured a thousand deaths. To have one's suffering prolonged inch by inch, to be deserted, forsaken, hopeless; to see that loathsome food ever before my eyes, was almost too much for human endurance.

I am conversant with four different languages. I speak and write them with equal fluency; yet in all four I do not find words enough to express the horror I experienced during those two months, or what I still feel when memory reverts to the scene. Suicide would have been a relief, a happiness, a godsend! Many a time I had the muzzle of my pistol in my mouth and my finger on the trigger, but the faces of my helpless, dependent wife and child would rise up before me, and my hand would fall powerless. I was not the cause of my misfortunes, and God Almighty had provided only this one horrible way for me to subsist.

But to go into details—to relate the minutiae—is too agonizing! I can not do it! Imagination can supply these. The necessary mutilation of the bodies of those who had been my friends, rendered the ghastliness of my situation more frightful. . . .

At midnight, one cold, bitter night, Mrs. George Donner came to my door. It was about two weeks after Reed had gone, and my loneliness was beginning to be unendurable. I was most happy to hear the sound of a human voice. . . . She was going, alone, across the mountains. She was going to start without food or guide. She kept saying, "My children! I must see my children!" She feared she would not survive, and told me she had some money in her tent. It was too heavy for her to carry. She said, "Mr. Keseberg, I confide this to your care." She made me promise sacredly that I would get the money and take it to her children in case she perished and I survived. She declared she would start over the mountains in the morning. She said, "I am bound to go to my children." She seemed very cold, and her clothes were like ice. I think she had got in the creek in coming. She said she was very hungry, but refused the only food I could offer. She had never eaten the loathsome flesh.

She finally lay down, and I spread a feather-bed and some blankets over her. In the morning she was dead. I think the hunger, the mental suffering, and the icy chill of the preceding night, caused her death.

I have often been accused of taking her life. Before my God, I swear this is untrue! Do you think a man would be such a miscreant, such a damnable fiend, such a caricature on humanity, as to kill this lone woman? There were plenty of corpses lying around. He would only add one more corpse to the many!

Some time after Mrs. Donner's death, I thought I had gained sufficient strength to redeem the pledge I had made her before her death. I started to go to the camps at Alder Creek to get the money. . . . I searched carefully among the bales and bundles of goods, and found five hundred and thirty-one dollars. Part of this sum was silver, part gold. The silver I buried at the foot of a pine tree, a little way from the camp. One of the lower branches of another tree reached down close to the ground, and appeared to point to the spot. I put the gold in my pocket, and started to return to my cabin. I had spent one night at the Donner tents.

On my return I became lost. . . . Some time after dark I reached my own cabin. My clothes were wet by getting in the creek, and the night was so cold that my garments were frozen into sheets of ice. I was so weary, and chilled, and numbed, that I did not build up a fire, or attempt to get anything to eat, but rolled myself up in the bedclothes and tried to get warm. Nearly all night I lay there shivering with cold; and when I finally slept, I slept very soundly. I did not wake up until quite late the next morning. To my utter astonishment my camp was in the most inexplicable confusion. My trunks were broken open, and their contents were scattered everywhere. Everything about the cabin was torn up and thrown about the floor. My wife's jewelry, my cloak, my pistol and ammunition were missing. I supposed Indians had robbed my camp during my absence. Suddenly I was startled by the sound of human voices. I hurried up to the surface of the snow, and saw white men coming toward the cabin.

I was overwhelmed with joy and gratitude at the prospect of my deliverance. I had suffered so much, and for so long a time, that I could scarcely believe my senses. Imagine my astonishment upon their arrival to be greeted, not with a "good morning" or a kind word, but with the gruff, insolent demand, "Where is Donner's money?"

I told them they ought to give me something to eat, and that I would talk with them afterwards, but no, they insisted that I should tell them about Donner's money. I asked them who they were, and where they came from, but they replied by threatening to kill me if I did not give up the money. They threatened to hang or shoot me, and at last I told them I had promised Mrs. Donner that I would carry her money to her children, and I proposed to do so, unless shown some authority by which they had a better claim. This so exasperated them, that they acted as though they were going to kill me.

I offered to let them bind me as a prisoner, and take me before the alcalde at Sutter's Fort, and I promised that I would then tell all I knew about the money. They would listen to nothing, however, and finally I told them where they would find the silver buried, and gave them the gold. After I had done this, they showed me a document from Alcalde Sinclair, by which they were to receive a certain proportion of all moneys and property which they rescued.

These men treated me with the greatest unkindness. Mr. Tucker was the only one who took my part or befriended me. When they started over the mountains, each man carried two bales of goods. They had silks, calicoes, and delaines from the Donners, and other articles of great value. Each man would carry one bundle a little way, lay it down, and come back and get the other bundle. In this way they passed over the snow three times. I could not keep up with them because I was so weak, but managed to come up to their camp every night.

One day I was dragging myself slowly along behind the party, when I came to a place which had evidently been used as a camping-ground by some of the previous parties. Feeling very tired, I thought it would be a good place to make some coffee. Kindling a fire, I filled my coffee-pot with fresh snow and sat waiting for it to melt and get hot. Happening to cast my eyes carelessly around, I discovered a little piece of calico protruding from the snow. Half thoughtlessly, half out of idle curiosity, I caught hold of the cloth, and finding it did not come readily, I gave it a strong pull. I had in my hands the body of my dead child Ada! She had been buried in the snow, which, melting down, had disclosed a portion of her clothing. I thought I should go frantic! It was the first intimation I had of her death, and it came with such a shock!

About half the party finally reached California. Despite his energetic explanations, Eyewitness Lewis Keseberg never escaped the infamy of his cannibalism, in part because of the suspicion that he had murdered Mrs. George Donner.

"The Mexican can say, 'There I bled for liberty!' . . ."

AGAINST WAR WITH MEXICO

February 11, 1847
Washington, D.C.

SENATOR THOMAS CORWIN

The Mexican War (1846–1848) was a simple battle for real estate, not a grand conflict about ideas or liberty. The Americans had annexed Texas, and now wanted to buy California and New Mexico. The Mexicans wanted Texas back, and weren't in the mood to sell anything else. Senator Corwin, a Whig from Ohio, made this speech in opposition to an appropriation bill for the war effort.

Mr. President: . . . You have overrun half of Mexico—you have exasperated and irritated her people—you claim indemnity for all expenses incurred in doing this mischief, and boldly ask her to give up New Mexico and California; and, as a bribe to her patriotism, seizing on her property, you offer three millions to pay the soldiers she has called out to repel your invasion, on condition that she will give up to you at least one-third of her whole territory. . . .

But, sir, let us see what, as the chairman of the Committee on Foreign Relations explains it, we are to get by the combined processes of conquest and treaty.

What is the territory, Mr. President, which you propose to wrest from Mexico? It is consecrated to the heart of the Mexican by many a well-fought battle with his old Castilian master. His Bunker Hills, and Saratogas, and Yorktowns, are there! The Mexican can say, "There I bled for liberty! and shall I surrender that consecrated home of my affections to the Anglo-Saxon invaders? What do they want with it? They have Texas already. They have possessed themselves of the territory between the Nueces and the Rio Grande. What else do they want? To what shall I point my children as memorials of that independence which I bequeath to them when those battle-fields shall have passed from my possession?"

Sir, had one come and demanded Bunker Hill of the people of Massachusetts, had England's Lion ever showed himself there, is there a man over thirteen and under ninety who would not have been ready to meet him? Is there a river on this continent that would not have run red with blood?

The Senator from Michigan says he must have this [land]. Why, my worthy Christian brother, on what principle of justice? "I want room!"

The Senator from Michigan says we will be two hundred millions in a few years, and we want room. . . .

Why, says the chairman of this Committee on Foreign Relations, it is the most reasonable thing in the world! We ought to have the Bay of San Francisco. Why? Because it is the best harbor on the Pacific! It has been my fortune, Mr. President, to have practised a good deal in criminal courts in the course of my life, but I never yet heard a thief, arraigned for stealing a horse, plead that it was the best horse that he could find in the country!

. . . Let [the Americans who want western lands] go and seek their happiness in whatever country or clime it pleases them. All I ask of them is, not to require this Government to protect them with that banner consecrated to war waged for principles—eternal, enduring truth.

The principles for which Corwin argued meant little to the proponents of "manifest destiny," the idea that Americans were somehow endowed by God with the purpose of expanding across the continent.

But there were also arguments on the other side. Five years before the war, the U.S. minister to Mexico made this note: "Whenever the [Americans] in California make the movement of separation [from Mexico], it must succeed. The department of Sonora, not half the distance from Mexico, has been in a state of revolt for four years, and the government has been unable to suppress it. . . . A leading member of the Mexican cabinet once said to me that he believed that the tendency of things was towards the annexation of Texas to the United States, and that he greatly preferred that result either to the separate independence of Texas or any connection or dependence of Texas upon England; that if Texas was an independent power, other departments of Mexico would unite with it either voluntarily or by conquest, and if there was any connection between Texas and England, that English manufactures and merchandise would be smuggled into Mexico through Texas to the utter ruin of the Mexican manufactures and revenue."

A bit more than a decade after the war, Corwin, then a Republican, was named by President Lincoln to be the U.S. minister to Mexico.

THE MEXICAN WAR:
AT THE HALLS OF MONTEZUMA

September 11–12, 1847
Mexico City

SECOND LIEUTENANT ULYSSES S. GRANT

Chapultepec ("Hill of the Grasshopper") rises 200 feet on the western edge of Mexico City. Its strategic importance was noticed hundreds of years ago. The Aztecs first fortified it even before they began their rule of Mexico in 1325. A castle was built there a few hundred years later, and the Mexican National Military Academy took it over a few years before the Mexican War.

The advancing Americans, led by General Winfield Scott, had to pass Chapultepec to reach Mexico City. Five thousand Mexican troops stood ready at Chapultepec to stop them.

During the night of the 11th batteries were established which could play upon the fortifications of Chapultepec. The bombardment commenced early on the morning of the 12th, but there was no further engagement during this day than that of the artillery. General Scott assigned the capture of Chapultepec to General Pillow, but did not leave the details to his judgment. Two assaulting columns, two hundred and fifty men each, composed of volunteers for the occasion, were formed. They were commanded by Captains McKinzie and Casey respectively. The assault was successful, but bloody. . . .

Worth's command gradually advanced to the front. . . . Later in the day in reconnoitering I found a church off to the south of the road, which looked to me as if the belfry would command the ground back of the garita San Cosme. I got an officer of the voltigeurs, with a mountain howitzer and men to work it, to go with me. The road being in possession of the enemy, we had to take the field to the south to reach the church. This took us over several ditches breast deep in water and grown up with water plants. These ditches, however, were not over eight or ten feet in width. The howitzer was taken to pieces and carried by the men to its destination. When I knocked for admission a priest came to the door, who, while extremely polite, declined to admit us. With the little Spanish then at my command, I explained to him that he might save property by opening the door, and he certainly would save himself from becoming a prisoner, for a time at least; and besides, I intended to go in whether he consented or not. He began to see his duty in the same light that I did, and opened the door, though he did not look as if it gave him special pleasure to do so. The gun was carried to the belfry and put together. We were not more than two or three hundred yards from San Cosme. The shots from our little gun dropped in upon the enemy and created great confusion. Why they did not send out a small party and capture us, I do not know. We had no infantry or other defences besides our one gun.

The effect of this gun upon the troops about the gate of the city was so marked that General Worth saw it from his position. He was so pleased that he sent a staff officer, Lieutenant Pemberton . . . to bring me to him. He expressed his gratification at the services the howitzer in the church steeple was doing, saying that every shot was effective, and ordered a captain of voltigeurs to report to me with another howitzer to be placed along with the one already rendering so much service. I could not tell the General that there was not room enough in the steeple for another gun, because he probably would have looked upon such a statement as a contradiction from a second lieutenant. I took the captain with me, but did not use his gun.

After two days of hard fighting, the Americans took Chapultepec, then discovered that Mexico City itself had few defenses. The quick thinking of Ulysses Grant captured the attention of several superior officers, including Robert E. Lee, and earned him a promotion to captain.

The capture of Mexico City essentially ended the war. Despite pressure from his Cabinet to advance and conquer all of Mexico, President James Polk decided the political risks weren't worth the possible gain. The United States paid Mexico $15 million for the 525,000 square miles that now include Arizona, California, western Colorado, Nevada, New Mexico, Texas, and Utah.

The addition of the new land and citizens altered the balance of power between free and slave states, and contributed to the tensions that led to the Civil War. A period of political extremism also followed in Mexico, which endured a civil war in 1857.

_____

"After we was alone in a private Room
he showed me the first Specimens of Gold. . . ."

GOLD!

January 28–May 19, 1848
Coloma, California

JOHN AUGUSTUS SUTTER

America's timing couldn't have been better. As soon as it captured California, the dreams of fortune hunters dating back to Columbus came true there.

Eyewitness John Sutter was already one of California's wealthiest men when workers building a sawmill on his Sacramento Valley estate found a lump of gold. The crew chief, John Marshall, hurried to tell him the news that would change the West overnight.

JANUARY 28TH

Marshall arrived in the evening, it was raining very heavy, but he told me he came on important business. After we was alone in a private Room he showed me the first Specimens of Gold, that is he was not certain if it was Gold or not, but he thought it might be; immediately I made the proof and found that it was Gold. I told him even that most of all is 23 Carat Gold; he wished that I should come up with him immediately, but I told him that I have to give first my orders to the people in all my factories and shops.

FEBRUARY 1ST

Left for the Sawmill attended by a Baquero (Olimpio). I examined myself everything and picked up a few Specimens of Gold myself in the tail race of the Sawmill; this Gold and others which Marshall and some of the other laborers gave to me (it was found while in my employ and Wages) I told them that I would a Ring got made of it so soon as a Goldsmith would be here. I had a talk with my employed people all at the Sawmill. I told them that as they do know now that this Metal is Gold, I wished that they would do me the great favor and keep it secret only 6 weeks, because my large Flour Mill at Brighton would have been in Operation in such a time, which undertaking would have been a fortune to me, and unfortunately the people would not keep it secret, and so I lost on this Mill at the lowest calculation about $25,000.

The first party of Mormons, employed by me left for washing and digging Gold and very soon all followed and left me only the sick and the lame behind. And at this time I could say that every body left me from the Clerk to the Cook. What for great Damages I had to suffer in my tannery which was just doing a profitable and extensive business, and the Vatts was left filled and a quantity of half finished leather was spoiled, likewise a large quantity of raw hides collected by the farmers and of my own killing. The same thing was in every branch of business which I carried on at the time. I began to harvest my wheat, while others was digging and washing Gold, but even the Indians could not be keeped longer at Work. They was impatient to run to the mines, and other Indians had informed them of the Gold and its Value; and so I had to leave more than ⅔ my harvest in the fields.

MARCH 21ST

Threatened by a band of Robbers, from the Red Woods at San Francisquito near Santa Clara.

APRIL 2ND

Mr. Humphrey a regular Miner arrived, and left for Coloma with Wimmer & Marshall. Entered with them in Mining, furnished Indians, teams and provisions to this Company, and as I was loosing instead making something, I left this Company as a Partner. Some of the neighbors, while the Mormons left, became likewise the Gold fever and went to the Mountains prospecting and soon afterwards moved up to digg and wash Gold, and some of them with great success.

APRIL 16TH

Mr. Gray (from Virginia) who purchased Silver Mines in the San Jose Valley for a Compy and was interested himself. At the fort he learned the news of the Gold discovery. I presented him some Speciments of Gold. He left for the States across the Mountains. Some families are moving in the Mountains to camp and settle there.

APRIL 18TH

More curious people arrived, bound for the Mountains. I left for

Coloma, in Company with Major P. B. Reading and Mr. Kembel (Editor of the *Alta California*) we were absent 4 Days. We was prospecting and found Silver and iron ore in abundance.

APRIL 28TH

A great many people more went up to the Mountains. This day the Saw mill was in Operation and the first Lumber has been sawed in the whole upper Country.

MAY 1ST

Saml Brannan was building a store at Natoma, Mormon Islands, and have done a very large and heavy business.

MAY 15TH

Paid off all the Mormons which has been employed by me, in building these Mills and other Mechanical trades, all of them made their pile, and some of them became rich & wealthy, but all of them was bound to the great Salt Lake, and spent there their fortunes to the honor and Glory of the Lord!

MAY 19TH

The great Rush from San Francisco arrived at the fort, all my friends and acquaintances filled up the houses and the whole fort, I had only a little Indian boy, to make them roasted Ripps etc. as my Cooks left me like every body else. The Merchants, Doctors, Lawyers, Sea Captains, Merchants etc. all came up and did not know what to do, all was in a Confusion, all left their wives and families in San Francisco, and those which had none locked their Doors, abandoned their houses, offered them for sale cheap, a few hundred Dollars House & Lot (Lots which are worth now $100,000 and more), some of these men were just like greazy. Some of the Merchants has been the most prudentest of the Wholes visited the Mines and returned immediately and began to do a very profitable business, and soon Vessels came from every where with all Kind of Merchandise, the whole old trash which was laying for Years unsold, on the Coasts of South & Central America, Mexico, Sandwich Islands etc. All found a good Market here.

By 1849, the whole nation was in on the Gold Rush. Immigration to

California had totaled less than 1,000 in 1848; but the next year an estimated 90,000 arrived. San Francisco had about 2,000 residents in 1848; two years later it had 25,000.

Few miners struck it rich. The real fortunes were made by the merchants who outfitted the miners, not the miners themselves. Some of them, like Mark Hopkins, Collis Huntington, Leland Stanford, Charles Crocker, Sam Brannan, and Levi Strauss, built fortunes and institutions that last to this day.

The unluckiest person in the Gold Rush may have been John Sutter. His estate was overrun, his livestock was eaten by the miners, and he could not find ranch workers willing to stay away from the mines. He went from being extraordinarily wealthy to flat broke.

"Soon we came upon a scene of wreck that surpassed anything preceding it."

WAGON TRAIN

1849
The Humbolt Sink, Nevada

SARAH ROYCE

Sarah Bayliss Royce and her husband joined the Gold Rush, crossing the country with their two-year-old daughter. It was slow going, because the Royces would not travel on the Sabbath, so to shorten the journey they risked a route through the Nevada desert. Traveling by night to avoid the heat, they missed an important turnoff to pastures where they could prepare their cattle and themselves for the crossing. When day broke they were in the desert, with signs everywhere of other travelers who had made the same mistake and perished.

Royce's now-famous account of the crossing, A Frontier Lady, *was written in the 1880s as a family record for her son Josiah, a renowned philospher at the University of California at Berkeley and then Harvard. It was published about fifty years later.*

By a strong effort of will, backed by the soothing influence of prayer, I fell asleep, but only for a few minutes. I was roused by the stopping of the wagon, and then my husband's voice said, "So you've given out, have you, Tom?" and at the same moment I knew by the rattling chains and yokes that some of the cattle were being loosed from the team. I was out of the wagon in a minute. One of the oxen was prostrate on the ground, and his companion, from whose neck the yoke was just being removed, looked very likely soon to follow him. It had been the weak couple all along. Now we had but two yoke. How soon would they, one by one, follow?

Nothing could induce me to get into the wagon again. I said I would walk by the team, and for awhile I did; but by and by I found myself yards ahead. An inward power urged me forward; and the poor cattle were so slow, it seemed every minute as if they were going to stop. When I got so far off as to miss the sound of footsteps and wheels, I would pause, startled, wait and listen, dreading lest they had stopped, then as they came near, I would again walk beside them awhile, watching, through the darkness, the dim outlines of their heads and horns to see if they drooped lower. But soon I found myself again forward and alone.

. . . From near midnight, on through the small hours, it appeared necessary to stop more frequently, for both man and beast were sadly weary, and craved frequent nourishment. Soon after midnight we finished the last bit of meat we had; but there was still enough of the biscuit, rice and dried fruit to give us two or three more little baits.

The waning moon now gave us a little melancholy light, showing still the bodies of dead cattle, and the forms of forsaken wagons as our grim way-marks. In one or two instances they had been left in the very middle of the road; and we had to turn out into the untracked sand to pass them.

Soon we came upon a scene of wreck that surpassed anything preceding it. As we neared it, we wondered at the size of the wagons, which, in the dim light, looked tall as houses, against the sky. Coming to them, we found three or four of them to be of the make that the early Mississippi Valley emigrants used to call "Prairie Schooners": having deep beds, with projecting backs and high tops.

One of them was especially immense, and, useless as we felt it to be to spend time in examining these warning relics of those who had gone before us, curiosity led us to lift the front curtain which hung down, and by the light of our candle which we had again lit, look in. There from the strong, high bows, hung several sides of well cured bacon, much better in quality than that we had finished, at our last resting place. So we had but a short interval in which to say we were destitute of meat, for, though, warned by all we saw not to add a useless pound to our load, we thought it wise to take a little to eke out our scanty supply of food. And, as to the young men, who had so rarely, since they joined us, had a bit of meat they could call their own, they were very glad to bear the burden of a few pounds of bacon slung over their shoulders.

After this little episode, the only cheering incident for many hours, we turned to look at what lay round these monster wagons. It would be impossible to describe the motley collection of things of various sorts, strewed all about. The greater part of the materials, however, were pasteboard boxes, some complete, but most of them broken, and pieces of wrapping paper still creased, partially in the form of packages. But the most prominent objects were two or three, perhaps more, very beautifully finished trunks of various sizes, some of them standing open, their pretty trays lying on the ground, and all rifled of their contents; save that occasionally a few pamphlets, or, here and there, a book remained in the corners.

We concluded that this must have been a company of merchants hauling a load of goods to California, that some of their animals had given out, and, fearing the rest would they had packed such things as they could, and had fled for their lives toward the river.

There was only one thing, (besides the few pounds of bacon) that, in all these varied heaps of things, many of which, in civilized scenes, would have been valuable, I thought worth picking up. That was a little book, bound in cloth and illustrated with a number of small engravings. Its title was "Little Ella." I thought it would please Mary, so I put it in my pocket. It was an easily carried souvenir of the desert; and more than one pair of young eyes learned to read its pages in after years.

"I kept my eye on the movements of the agents. . . ."

THE PANAMA LOTTERY

May 1849
Panama, Central America

R. R. TAYLOR

Many forty-niners decided to sail to California rather than cross the country by wagon or stagecoach. But, too impatient for the long trip around South America, they first sailed to the Atlantic coast of Central America, then crossed overland to the Pacific, and finally caught a board heading north. Competition for a berth was fierce.

My Dear Wife:
Today has been the most exciting day I think I ever spent. I have had

more pending upon a *game of chance* them I ever had before, or probably ever shall again. To explain. When I last wrote you I had almost concluded to leave here in the "Wilhelmine." But I felt I could not afford the time to go in a sailing craft. I felt the necessity of getting into some situation where I could be earning something for you, & if I did not go in a steamer it would very likely be three months before I got to California. Finally therefore, I positively refused to go in any other way until I was certain no passage could be got in the steamers. . . .

From the moment of the arrival of the "Panama" I kept my eye on the movements of the agents, in order that no tickets should be sold without my knowledge. I made it a rule to be about the office of the company at least every two hours in the day, & nothing escaped my attention.

At last it was given out yesterday afternoon just before the closing of the office that the tickets remaining would be disposed of to-day. At daylight I was "on hand," confident of being able to get near enough to the front of the crowd to get a ticket.

But a new notice came out. Persons wishing tickets were to register their names & then they were to draw lots for the 50 tickets to be disposed of. Fifty pieces of paper were to be numbered & put into a hat, & as there were over a hundred applications there were of course to be as many blanks as there was a surplus of names. . . .

The stake you will see was a great one;—if I drew a blank, I must take a sailing vessel & run my risk of getting to California, "sometime" in a crowded hold, with the worst fare possible, or remain 3 or 4 weeks longer in this miserable place, for the Oregon & perhaps after all not get a passage in her—if I won I should probably get to California in 3 weeks.

The drawing was to take place at one o'clock & the intermediate time was an exciting period for me. A great crowd was collected to witness the drawing & a good deal of trouble was experienced in correcting the list & making sure that none were there who already had tickets, or who were known to be speculators etc.

Lt. [Edward E.] Beale, whose name you will see in the papers often, presided at the hat, & when my name was called & he put in his hand, I believe my heart fairly stood still. He drew a ticket & the way I jumped about and shook hands with friends & acquaintances who crowded around with their congratulations was "a caution." Had he drawn a blank, I am afraid I should have sunk under it—my spirits & my courage which I have managed thus far to preserve good, would have deserted me under so great a disappointment.

Eyewitness R. R. Taylor's ship reached San Francisco on June 4. By December, just under 700 ships had brought about 40,000 forty-niners to San Francisco. Many of those ships were abandoned and left to rot by their crews, who went off to the diggings.

"There are many ways of evading the law."

AT THE GOLD MINES

1851
Feather River Canyon, California

LOUISE A. CLAPPE

Louise Clappe was "Dame Shirley" to the readers of her "Shirley Letters" in the Pioneer *magazine. She had come west from New England with her doctor husband in 1851.*

First, let me explain to you the "claiming" system. As there are no State laws upon the subject, each mining community is permitted to make its own. Here, they have decided that no man may "claim" an area of more than forty feet square. This he "stakes off" and puts a notice upon it, to the effect that he "holds" it for mining purposes. If he does not choose to "work it" immediately, he is obliged to renew the notice every ten days; for without this precaution, any other person has a right to "jump it," that is, to take it from him.

There are many ways of evading the above law. For instance, an individual can "hold" as many "claims" as he pleases, if he keeps a man at work in each, for this workman represents the original owner. I am told, however, that the laborer, himself, can "jump" the "claim" of the very man who employs him, if he pleases so to do. This is seldom, if ever, done; the person who is willing to be hired, generally prefers to receive the six dollars *per diem,* of which he is *sure* in any case, to running the risk of a "claim" not proving valuable. But there are many ways of really outwitting this [claiming] rule, which give rise to innumerable arbitrations, and nearly every Sunday, there is a "miners' meeting" connected with this subject.

Having got our gold mines discovered and "claimed," I will try to give you a faint idea of how they "work" them. Here, in the mountains, the labor of excavation is extremely difficult, on account of the immense rocks which form a large portion of the soil.

Of course, no man can "work out" a "claim" alone. For that reason, and also for the same that makes partnerships desirable, they congregate in companies of four or six, generally designating themselves by the place from whence the majority of the members have emigrated; for example, the "Illinois," "Bunker Hill," "Bay State," etc., companies.

In many places the surface-soil, or in mining phrase, the "top dirt," "pays" when worked in a "Long Tom." This machine, (I have never been able to discover the derivation of its name,) is a trough, generally about twenty feet in length, and eight inches in depth, formed of wood, with the exception of six feet at one end, called the "riddle," which is made of sheet-iron perforated with holes about the size of a large marble. Underneath this cullender-like portion of the "long-tom," is placed another trough, about ten feet long, the sides six inches perhaps in height, which divided through the middle by a slender slat, is called the "riffle-box."

It takes several persons to manage, properly, a "long-tom." Three or four men station themselves with spades, at the head of the machine, while at the foot of it, stands an individual armed "wid de shovel and de hoe." The spadesmen throw in large quantities of the precious dirt, which is washed down to the "riddle" by a stream of water leading into the "long-tom" through wooden gutters or "sluices." When the soil reaches the "riddle," it is kept constantly in motion by the man with the hoe.

Of course, by this means, all the dirt and gold escapes through the perforations into the "riffle-box" below, one compartment of which is placed just beyond the "riddle." Most of the dirt washes over the sides of the "riffle-box," but the gold being so astonishingly heavy remains safely at the bottom of it. When the machine gets too full of stones to be worked easily, the man whose business it is to attend to them throws them out with his shovel, looking carefully among them as he does so for any pieces of gold, which may have been too large to pass through the holes of the "riddle." I am sorry to say that he generally loses his labor. At night they "pan out" the gold, which has been collected in the "riffle-box" during the day.

Many of the miners decline washing the "top dirt" at all, but try to reach as quickly as possible the "bed-rock," where are found the richest deposits of gold. The river is supposed to have formerly flowed over this "bed-rock," in the "crevices" of which, it left, as it passed away, the largest portions of the so eagerly sought for ore. . . .

---

*". . . The old chief made a sudden spring to the right
and attempted to escape . . ."*

AMERICAN NAMES

LAFAYETTE HOUGHTON BUNNELL

*Bunnell, a doctor and gold miner, was a member of the Mariposa Battalion,
formed to capture the Yosemite and Chowchilla Indians who had been skirmishing with miners. He was competent in several Indian languages.*

We suddenly came in full view of the valley. . . . The immensity of
the rock I had seen in my vision on the Old Bear Valley trail was here
presented to my astonished gaze. The mystery of that glimpse was here
disclosed and my awe was increased by this nearer view of that stupendous cliff, now known as El Capitan. None but those who have visited
this wonderful valley can even imagine the feelings with which I looked
upon the view that was there presented. The grandeur of the scene was
but softened by the haze that hung over the valley—light as gossamer—
and by the clouds which partially dimmed the higher cliffs and mountains. An exalted sensation seemed to fill my whole being and I found my
eyes in tears with emotion.

. . . In the morning our Indian guide brought word from Tenieya
that the old chief refused to consider any plan which would involve leaving the valley, and our scouts were sent out with instructions to bring
him in, alive if possible. Knowing where Tenieya had talked with the
messenger, scouting parties started out and cutting off his retreat on all
sides, brought him in, unharmed.

The first sight which greeted him as he entered the camp was the
dead body of his favorite son, shot while attempting to escape. At the
sight he halted without visible emotion, except a slight quivering of the
lips. As he raised his head, his feelings were exhibited in the glaring
expression of deadly hatred with which he gazed at Capt. Boling and cast
his eyes over the camp as though in search of his other sons.

Boling expressed his regret and had the circumstances explained to
him, but not a word did Tenieya utter. Passively he accompanied us to
our camp on the south side of the valley. The boy's body was left where
he had fallen, and permission was given for the Indians to take it away
for burial. The following night, unobserved by us, the body disappeared.

For days Tenieya rebuffed all attempts to talk to him. Finding that nothing could be accomplished through the old chief, the captain gave orders to recommence our search for his people. Scouts were sent out who explored all the ravines of the valley but without finding any trace of the Yosemites, so Capt. Boling sent back for a pack train with supplies and we started over the high Sierras, Tenieya firmly tied with a rope whose other end I held.

Over trails, seemingly impossible for a man to follow, from which some of our party turned back, we climbed out of the valley to the north. Savage had despatched a new Indian guide to us, Cowchitty, a traditional enemy of the Yosemites; and partly by following his counsel and partly by doing the opposite of what Tenieya wished at critical moments, we at length wound around a mountain spur and saw opposite a dim circle of blue smoke. Old Tenieya was standing in front of me, but he exhibited no interest in the discovery.

Resting in fancied security, upon the border of a most beautiful little lake, to which I later gave the name of Tenieya, the village was seemingly not more than half a mile away. As the captain was studying the location and planning how to capture the village, our scouts were discovered in full chase of an Indian picket who was running toward the village as though his life depended upon his efforts.

In the excitement of the moment Capt. Boling ordered us to double quick and charge, thinking that the huts were not more than half a mile away. Such a mistake could originate only in the transparent air of the mountains. The village was fully two miles or more away; we did, however, double quick, and I kept a gait that soon carried Tenieya and myself ahead of our scattered column.

Finding the rope with which I held Tenieya an encumbrance in our rapid march, I wound it around his shoulder and kept him in front of me. While passing a steep slope of overlapping granite rock, the old chief made a sudden spring to the right and attempted to escape down the ragged precipice. His age was against him for I caught him just as he was about to let himself drop from the projecting ledge to the ground below; angered at the trick of the old fellow in attempting to relieve himself of my custody, I resumed our advance at a gait that hurried the old sachem forward less carefully than comported with his years and dignity.

The Yosemites discovered our approach too late for either concerted resistance or successful escape, for Lieutenant Crawford at the head of a portion of the command, dashed at once into the center of the encampment and the terror-stricken Indians threw up their bare hands in token of submission and piteously cried out "Peace! Peace!" No show of resistance was offered us, neither did any escape.

Finding themselves completely surprised, notwithstanding their extreme vigilance, and comparing the well-kept appearance of their old chief with their own worn out dilapidated condition, the Indians expressed a willingness to live in the future at peace with the Americans. All hopes of avoiding a treaty or of preventing their transfer to the reservation appeared to be at once abandoned. "Where can we now go that the Americans will not follow us?" asked the young chief in charge of that particular band. "Where can we make our homes that you will not find us?"

Before dawn, unable to sleep because of the penetrating cold, Boling aroused the camp and began preparations to start for the valley. . . . As we climbed the mountains I looked back on the lovely little lake from which we were leading the last remnant of the once dreaded Yosemites to a territory from which it was designed they should never return as a people.

I waited for Tenieya to come up and told him that we had given his name to the lake and the river. At first he seemed unable to comprehend our purpose, repeating: "It already has a name." Upon telling him that we had named it Tenieya because it was upon the shores of the lake that we had found his people, who would never return to it to live, his countenance fell, and he at once left us and rejoined his own family circle. His expression as he left us indicated that he thought the naming of the lake no equivalent for the loss of the territory.

"Protecting ourselves from . . . this hoard of ruffians . . ."

THE COMMITTEE OF VIGILANCE

June 1851
San Francisco

JAMES NEALL, JR., WILLIAM T. COLEMAN, AND GARRETT W. RYCKMAN

It was impossible to maintain a police force in San Francisco, because everyone wanted to find a fortune at the mines. With thousands of new arrivals each week, few of whom had social ties, lawlessness became inevitable. To keep the peace, 103 of the most respectable businessmen in town became vigilantes.

Eyewitness James Neall, a lumber merchant, helped conceive the committee.

William Coleman, a merchant, was a leader of both the original committee and later vigilante efforts. Garrett Ryckman was a landlord.

Samuel Brannan, whom Neal mentions, was San Francisco's leading citizen. A printer, merchant, and landlord, he was the man who first brought the news to San Francisco of the gold strike at Sutter's Mill—after stocking up on mining supplies to sell to prospectors.

FROM THE CALIFORNIA *COURIER*, JUNE 10, 1851

It is clear to every man that San Francisco is partially in the hands of criminals, and that crime has reached a crisis where the fate of life and property are in imminent jeopardy. There is no alternative now left us but to lay aside business and direct our whole energies as a people to seek out the abodes of these villains and execute summary vengeance upon them. . . . No man, since we became a city, has been hung in San Francisco. Some fifty murders have been committed, but no murderer has suffered death for his crimes. . . . We are in the midst of a revolution, and we should meet the emergencies of our condition with firm hearts and well-braced nerves. We have no time to talk about the defects of the laws—of the dangers which beset us; but we must act, and act at once—act as men do in revolutionary times.

NEALL

On Sunday [June 8] . . . George [Oakes] . . . in conversation with me, upon the perilous condition of society at that time, said we ought to take some steps to see if we could not change these things, and suggested that we should go up and have a talk with Sam Brannan, and we went up to Brannan's office. . . . We there found Mr. Brannan and his clerk, and sat down and talked the matter [over]. . . . We . . . concluded that something must be done, and it was suggested that each one of us should give Mr. Brannan's clerk, Mr. Wardwell, the names of such men as we could mention, whom we knew to be reliable, to invite them to meet us at 12 o'clock noon the next day, at the California Engine House . . . to devise some means of protecting ourselves from the depredations of this hoard of ruffians, who seemed to have possession of the city. There was no such thing as doing anything with them before the courts; that had been tried in vain. Notices were sent out to parties to the effect that they were nominated, each as chairman of a committee for his neighborhood, to invite their fellow citizens, good reliable men, to meet . . . as above indicated. . . .

I was early at the building, and found a number of gentlemen there, probably thirty or forty already. An organization was formed, and the objects of the meeting stated, with a brief discussion. Articles had been already prepared for the mode of organization, and some thirty or forty names were enrolled, and it was styled the Committee of Vigilance of San Francisco, the avowed objects of the Committee being to vigilantly watch and pursue the outlaws and criminals who were infesting the city and bring them to justice, through the regularly constituted courts, if that could be, through more summary and direct process, if must be. Each member pledged his word of honor, his life and fortune if need be, for the protection of his fellow members, for the protection of life and property of the citizens and of the community, and for purging the city of the bad characters who were making themselves odious in it. After arranging for a concert of action, watchwords, and a signal to be used to call the members to the rendezvous . . . and detailing officers for immediate duty, enrolling a number of members, all among the most respectable, substantial and well-known citizens of the place, and the disposition of some needed business,—the Committee adjourned for the evening. . . .

RYCKMAN

When any men were arrested and turned over to the Committee, they were tried by the Executive and such trials were as honest and impartial as ever a man had, and no man was convicted without an abundance of testimony, such as would convict any human being in any court of justice; only we could not allow any alibis to come in to screen these fellows. After the trial and conviction of the prisoner, the case was referred to the General Committee for its action, and the testimony was sent to them. They invariably confirmed the decisions of the Executive Committee, and it was impossible for them to do otherwise, in the face of such proofs as were offered.

The Committee was composed mostly of our best men; the salt of San Francisco joined us. Everything was organized in a proper and unmistakable shape, so that every man had his duty to perform, and he had to report daily to the Committee, and if anything had transpired it was properly noted. Every man had his place, and there was a place for every man; there were no drones there. . . .

In about a hundred days, the committee hanged four men, whipped one, ordered twenty-eight to be deported, gave fifteen to the police for legal trials, and, surprisingly, let forty-one go free. Order was restored, for a while. More vigilante groups arose from time to time in San Francisco and other towns.

"We then hauled down the Mexican flag. . . ."

THE GRAY-EYED MAN OF DESTINY

1853
La Paz, Baja California

WILLIAM WALKER

In late 1853, the leader of a band of American adventurers sent a surprising letter to a newspaper in San Francisco. It announced the conquest of Baja ("Lower") California, the Mexican peninsula south of Tijuana.

Headquarters Republic Lower California
November 7th, 1853.

On the morning of the 15th of October we sailed with the First Independent Battalion for Lower California. The command consisted of forty-five men. Our voyage was a prosperous one to Cape St. Lucas, where we landed on the 28th of October. Here we gained some little information of importance, and proceeded on our journey to La Paz. On the 3d day of November our vessel cast anchor opposite the town. A party were ordered by Col. Walker to land, take possession of the town, and secure the person of the Governor—Lieut. Gilman commanding the party. In less than thirty minutes the town was taken and the Governor secured. We then hauled down the Mexican flag in front of the Governor's house, proclaimed the Independence of Lower California, and our flag floated triumphantly where but a few minutes previous that of Mexico waved in supposed security. Our men, provisions and munitions of war were now landed, the town fortified, and Col. Walker entered upon his duties as President of the Republic of Lower California, issuing such decrees as were most congenial to the citizens, as well as to the comfort and security of his command.

Here we remained until Sunday, the 6th, when the President determined to remove the seat of Government to St. Lucas. In accordance with this determination we re-embarked, taking with us Ex-Governor Espanosa and the public documents. Shortly after our embarkation a vessel came into port, having on board Col. Robollero, who was sent by the Government of Mexico to supersede Ex-Governor Espanosa. A small detachment was dispatched to bring Col. Robollero on board our vessel. This order was promptly executed. About an hour after this occurrence, a party was sent on shore to procure wood, and while in the act of returning to their boats they were fired upon by a large party. Thus commenced the first action.

The party consisted of but six men, who retired to the vessel under a heavy fire of musketry without losing a man. In the meantime a fire was opened upon the town with our ordnance, which was kept up until Col. Walker landed with thirty men, when the fighting became general. From the time of landing until the close of the action (a signal defeat of the enemy), was about one hour and a half. The enemy's loss was six or seven killed and several wounded. Our men did not receive so much as a wound, except from cacti, while pursuing the enemy through the chapparal, in the rear of the town.

Thus ended the battle of La Paz, crowning our efforts with victory, releasing Lower California from the tyrannous yoke of declining Mexico, and establishing a new Republic.

The commercial resources—the mineral and agricultural wealth of the Republic of Lower California, destines her to compare favorably with her sister Republic.

Our men are all in fine health and spirits, and are as noble and determined a body of men as ever were collected together.

. . . Our Government has been formed upon a firm and sure basis.

Wm. Walker, Col.,
President of Lower California.

Who was this grandiose schemer? Trained as a doctor and a lawyer, William Walker had briefly worked as a journalist in San Francisco before founding his new "republic." Because he had earlier used his dramatic gray eyes to practice mesmerism and faith healing, newspapers dubbed him "The Gray-Eyed Man of Destiny." Although he might be considered an oddity today, he was once a hero to many in the South, who hoped he would establish a slaveholding state on the west coast, providing the key to a southern route for the all-important transcontinental railroad.

His first empire disappeared within months, because a U.S. blockade led to a lack of supplies. He was tried by the U.S. for violating neutrality laws, but was acquitted.

He next set out to conquer Nicaragua, an important shortcut between the Atlantic and the Pacific in the decades before the Panama Canal was built. He won control of the country, but soon isolated himself by making alliances with proslavery forces in the U.S. and passing laws to reestablish the slave trade.

His rule ended when he took over a private railroad that crossed Nicaragua. The owner, tycoon Cornelius Vanderbilt, sent a private army to kill Walker. Walker had to surrender to the U.S. Navy to escape death.

While attempting to return to Nicaragua in 1860 he was captured in Honduras, where the government executed him.

**"On the day previous to the election . . .
armed men . . . came into town."**

"BLEEDING KANSAS"

March 29–30, 1855
Lawrence, Kansas

ERASTUS D. LADD

Westward expansion was tightly bound to the slavery question. Would new territories permit slavery or prohibit it? The South chafed under the restrictions of the Missouri Compromise (1820), which set a boundary for slavery. The balance of power among the northern and southern states was at risk each time a new settler arrived in the West.

In 1854, Kansas became the war front in the abolition battle. Congress waffled while free-state and proslavery factions skirmished. Eventually a compromise in Congress created the Kansas Territory (which included the present-day state and most of what is now Colorado), and the Nebraska Territory (present-day Nebraska and pieces of what are now North and South Dakota, Wyoming, and Colorado). It also threw the slavery decision back to each territory's citizens.

Nebraska, it was accurately assumed, would choose slavery. But in Kansas the direction was not as clear. It had a chance of becoming the first state north of the Missouri Compromise's boundary to allow slavery.

Abolition societies rushed to finance the settlement of emigrants who would vote "free-soil," and their side seemed to hold a majority as the election approached. But the situation changed suddenly as thousands of angry Missourians who wanted Kansas to become a slave state crossed the border.

Eyewitness Erastus Ladd, who saw the mayhem of that election, was a Free State candidate who later became a notable public official.

On the day previous to the election a number of teams and wagons loaded with armed men, and men on horseback, came into town. They were strangers here; they came in from the south and south-west, and were preceded by two or three men, one of whom was called Colonel

Samuel Young, of Missouri, who appeared to be the chief in command. They were armed; I saw private arms, and I saw rifles and other arms of that kind, double-barrelled shotguns, revolvers, and knives. The strangers continued to come in during the evening, and next morning there had been a very large addition made to their number.

I went to the place of voting in the morning, and was there at the opening of the polls, and remained all day, except time for dinner. A very large company came from the camp in the ravine to the place of voting and surrounded it.

There was some difficulty in the organization of the board, and delay in commencing the voting. Mr. Abbott, one of the judges, resigned. A vote was offered, which I saw, and a question of the legality of the vote was raised and was discussed some time.

During the discussion Colonel Young said he would settle the matter. He crowded up to the front, the place being thronged with people. The other vote was then withdrawn and he offered his vote.

The question was raised as to the legality of his vote. He said he was ready to swear that he was a resident of the Territory. His oath was received. He then mounted the window-sill and proclaimed to the crowd around that the matter was all settled and they could vote. I cannot repeat his exact words, but that was the sentiment; and they proceeded to vote.

At noon I went to their camp, and passed along the ravine from one extremity to the other, and counted the number of wagons and conveyances of different kinds then on the ground and in sight. They had then commenced leaving. I counted very near one hundred conveyances, such as wagons and carriages.

There were, besides, a large number of saddle horses. I estimate that there were then on the ground about seven hundred of the party; in the estimate I do not include those who had left for home.

I heard a conversation a short distance from where I stood, and approached pretty nearly. I stepped up on a small rise of ground and saw quite a violent contest going on, of which Mr. Stearns of this place was the object. It was a contest of words and threats but not of blows or force; while it was going on, I heard some one cry out "There is the Lawrence bully."

A rush was immediately made in another direction, towards Mr. Bond of this town, and a cry was raised to shoot him. He ran for the bank of the river, and the crowd followed him. During the running I think one or two shots were fired.

When he got to the bank of the river, he sprang off out of sight. They rushed to the bank, and guns were pointed at him while below. But the cry was raised to let him go, and he was permitted to go on without being fired at.

Another circumstance occurred in the latter part of the day. Mr. Willis, who was then a resident of this town, was on the ground, and a cry was raised that he was one of the men concerned in abducting a black woman about which there had been some difficulty in the town a short time previous.

Several men raised the cry to hang him. Some were on horseback, and some were on foot. Movements were made towards him by strangers armed with rifles and smaller arms. The cry was repeated by a large number of persons to "hang him," "get a rope" etc. At the suggestion of some friends he left. . . .

The result of the election was a mess. The legislature voted for slavery, but the abolitionists set up a second state government and appealed to Washington for recognition. More elections were held with equally chaotic results, and the conflict turned deadly. Guerrilla skirmishes were fought back and forth for a few years, and about 200 people were killed.

Kansas became a state in 1861, without slavery. In the Civil War, it fought with the Union.

"Denver . . . can boast of no antiquity beyond September or October last."

DENVER AND AURARIA

June 1859

HORACE GREELEY

Greeley, founder and editor of the New York Tribune, *was the country's most influential journalist. When John Soule, editor of the* Terre Haute Express, *wrote "Go west, young man, go west, and grow up with the land," Greeley reprinted the editorial in the* Tribune *and the phrase earned a permanent place in American legend. (Greeley credited Soule, but the remark is attributed to Greeley anyway.)*

Greeley himself took Soule's advice, at least for a tour across the country as a reporter.

The rival cities of Denver and Auraria front on each other from either bank of Cherry Creek, just before it is lost in the South Platte. The Platte has its sources in and around the South Park of the Rocky Mountains, a hundred miles southwest of this point; but Cherry Creek is headed off from them by that river, and, winding its northward course of forty or fifty miles over the plains, with its sources barely touching the Mountains, is a capricious stream, running quite smartly when we came here, but whose broad and thirsty sands have since drank it all up at this point, leaving the log foot-bridges which connect the two large cities as useless as an ice-house in November. . . .

Of these rival cities, Auraria is by far the more venerable—some of its structures being, I think, fully a year old, if not more. Denver, on the other hand, can boast of no antiquity beyond September or October last.

In the architecture of the two cities there is, notwithstanding, a striking similarity. . . . There is a new hotel nearly finished in Auraria, which has a second story (but no first story) floor; beside this, mine eyes have never yet been blessed with the sight of any floor whatever in either Denver or Auraria. The last time I slept or ate with a floor under me (our wagon-box and mother earth excepted) was at Junction City, nearly four weeks ago.

The "Denver House," which is the Astor House of the gold region, has walls of logs, a floor of earth, with windows and roof of rather flimsy cotton-sheeting; while every guest is allowed as good a bed as his blankets will make.

The charges are no higher than at the Astor and other first-class hotels, except for liquor—twenty-five cents a drink for dubious whisky, colored and nicknamed to suit the taste of customers—being the regular rate throughout this region.

Still, a few days of such luxury surfeited me, mainly because the main or drinking-room was also occupied by several blacklegs as a gambling-hall, and their incessant clamor of "Who'll go me twenty? The ace of hearts is the winning card. Whoever turns the ace of hearts wins the twenty dollars," etc. etc., persisted in at all hours up to midnight, became at length a nuisance, from which I craved deliverance at any price.

Then the visitors of that drinking and gambling-room had a careless way, when drunk, of firing revolvers, sometimes at each other, at other times quite miscellaneously, which struck me as inconvenient for a quiet guest with only a leg and a half, hence in poor condition for dodging bullets. So I left.

"How do you live in Denver?" I inquired of a New York friend some weeks domiciled here, in whose company I visited the mines. "O, I've jumped a cabin," was his cool, matter-of-course reply. As jumping a cabin was rather beyond my experience, I inquired further, and learned that, finding an uninhabited cabin that suited him, he had quietly entered and spread his blankets, eating at home or abroad as opportunity might suggest.

I found, on further inquiry, that at least one-third of the habitations in Denver and Auraria were desolate when we came here (they have been gradually filling up since), some of the owners having gone into the mountains, digging or prospecting, and taken their limited supply of household goods along with them.

On every side, I note signs of progress—improvement—manifest destiny:—there was a man about the city yesterday with lettuce to sell—and I am credibly assured that there will be green peas next month—actually peas! . . . But I must turn my back on this promise of luxuries, and take the road to Laramie to-day.

---

*"San Francisco is in instant communication
with New York. . . ."*

DEATH OF THE PONY EXPRESS

August 16, 1861
San Francisco

ANONYMOUS *ALTA CALIFORNIAN* REPORTER
AND *SAN FRANCISCO HERALD* ADVERTISEMENT

The Pony Express carried the mail 2,000 miles from St. Joseph, Missouri, to Sacramento, California, in about two weeks, using stage riders who traveled ten to fifteen miles at a time.

Despite its enduring image, it lasted just a year and never turned a profit. One day after the transcontinental telegraph's final cable was connected, these notices appeared.

FROM THE *ALTA CALIFORNIAN*

The overland telegraph is completed. San Francisco is in instant communication with New York and the other great cities of the Atlantic seaboard. It is a great change for us. A few years ago we received intelligence from the other side only semi-monthly by steamer, and generally from 25 to 30 days old, at that. Then followed the semi-weekly mail, by the overland route, which brought us news twice a week, on the average 18 or 20 days old. And last came the Pony, sweeping across the Continent by the Central route, in everlasting gallop, with dates varying from 14 to 4 days after its departure. . . .

FROM THE *SAN FRANCISCO HERALD*

NOTICE

By Orders from the East Coast the

PONY EXPRESS

WILL BE DISCONTINUED

The Last Pony Coming This Way Left
Atchison, Kansas,
Yesterday

WELLS, FARGO & CO., Agents.

"Captain Stokes had a spy in the camp. . . ."

THE CIVIL WAR IN THE WEST: THE ST. LOUIS ARSENAL

April 24, 1861

ANONYMOUS *CHICAGO TRIBUNE* REPORTER

"The war in the Trans-Mississippi West has been unjustly neglected by historians," remarked historian Henry Steele Commager in 1955. *"The outcome of the war was decided, to be sure, in the East—at Gettysburg and Vicksburg, at Chattanooga and Atlanta and the Wilderness—yet the fighting in the West profoundly influenced the course of these Eastern campaigns, and some of these campaigns, in turn, were directed to the severance of the Confederacy along the Mississippi River."*

Missouri was the crucial state. "Had that state gone with the Confederacy,"
Commager wrote, "the consequences would have been grave and might have been
decisive. It outflanked Illinois and the Northwest; controlled the Mississippi; con-
ditioned the fighting in Kentucky and Tennessee."

All evidence suggested Missouri would side with the Confederacy. It was a
slave state, and most of its citizens supported slavery. The governor, Claiborne
Jackson, wanted to secede.

Within two weeks of the fall of Fort Sumter on April 13, Confederate sup-
porters, including Governor Jackson, planned to raid the federal arsenal at St.
Louis, which held tens of thousands of arms. A plan to move the arms from
Missouri to Illinois was rushed into action by Governor Richard Yates of Illinois
and General Nathaniel Lyon.

Captain James H. Stokes, of Chicago, late of the regular army, volunteered to undertake the perilous mission, and Governor Yates placed
in his hands the requisition of the Secretary of War for 10,000 muskets.
Captain Stokes went to St. Louis, and made his way as rapidly as possible to the arsenal. He found it surrounded by an immense mob, and the
postern gates all closed. His utmost efforts to penetrate the crowd were
for a long time unavailing. The requisition was shown. Captain Lyon
doubted the possibility of executing it. He said the arsenal was surrounded by a thousand spies, and every movement was watched and
reported to the headquarters of the Secessionists, who could throw an
overpowering force upon them at any moment. Captain Stokes represented that every hour's delay was rendering the capture of the arsenal
more certain, and the arms must be moved to Illinois now or never.
Major Callender agreed with him, and told him to take them at his own
time and in his own way. This was Wednesday night, 24th April (1861).

Captain Stokes had a spy in the camp, whom he met at intervals in a
certain place in the city. On Thursday, he received information that Gov.
Jackson had ordered two thousand armed men from Jefferson City,
whose movements could only contemplate a seizure of the arsenal, by
occupying the heights around it, and planting batteries thereon. The job
would have been an easy one. They had already planted one battery on
the St. Louis levee, and another at Powder Point, a short distance below
the arsenal. Capt. Stokes immediately telegraphed to Alton to have the
steamer *City of Alton* drop down to the arsenal landing about midnight.
He then returned to the arsenal, and commenced moving the boxes of
guns, weighing some three hundred pounds each, down to the lower
floor.

About 700 men were employed in the work. He then took 500
Kentucky flint-lock muskets, which had been sent there to be altered,

and sent them to be placed on a steamer as a blind to cover his real movements. The Secessionists nabbed them at once, and raised a perfect Bedlam over the capture. A large portion of the outside crowd left the arsenal when this movement was executed; and Capt. Lyon took the remainder, who were lying around as spies, and locked them up in the guard-house. About 11 o'clock the steamer *City of Alton* came alongside, planks were shoved out from the windows to the main deck, and the boxes slid down. When the 10,000 were safely on board, Capt. Stokes went to Capt. Lyon and Major Callender, and urged them, by the most pressing appeals, to let him empty the arsenal. They told him to go ahead and take whatever he wanted. Accordingly, he took 10,000 more muskets, 500 new rifle carbines, 500 revolvers, 110,000 musket cartridges, to say nothing of the cannon and a large quantity of miscellaneous accoutrements, leaving only 7,000 muskets in the arsenal to arm the St. Louis volunteers.

When the whole were on board, about 2 o'clock on Friday morning the order was given by the captain of the steamer to cast off. Judge of the consternation of all hands when it was found that she would not move. The arms had been piled in great quantities around the engines to protect them against the battery on the levee, and the great weight had fastened the bows of the boat firmly on a rock, which was tearing a hole through the bottom at every turn of the wheels. A man of less nerve than Capt. Stokes would have gone crazy on the spot. He called the arsenal men on board, and commenced moving the boxes to the stern.

Fortunately, when about two hundred boxes had been shifted, the boat fell away from the shore, and floated in deep water. "Which way?" said Captain Mitchell, of the steamer. "Straight to Alton, in the regular channel," replied Captain Stokes. "What if we are attacked?" said Captain Mitchell. "Then we will fight," said Captain Stokes. "What if we are overpowered?" said Captain Mitchell. "Run her to the deepest part of the river, and sink her," replied Captain Stokes. "I'll do it," was the heroic answer of Capt. Mitchell; and away they went past the secession battery, past the entire St. Louis levee, and on to Alton, in the regular channel, where they arrived at five o'clock in the morning.

When the boat touched the landing, Capt. Stokes, fearing pursuit by some two or three of the Secession military companies by which the city of St. Louis is disgraced, ran to the market-house and rang the fire-bell, The citizens came flocking pell-mell to the river, in all sorts of habiliments. Capt. Stokes informed them of the situation of things, and pointed out the freight cars. Instantly, men, women, and children boarded the steamer, seized the freight, and clambered up the levees to the cars. Rich and poor tugged together with might and main for two hours, when the cargo was all deposited in the cars, and the train moved off, amid their enthusiastic cheers, for Springfield.

Although Claiborne Jackson tried to lead a shadow government in the state, Missouri stayed in the Union. About 110,000 of its citizens fought for the Union; about 30,000 for the Confederacy.

General Lyon went on to perform other crucial tasks, such as seizing the camp where Jackson was quartering Missouri's state militia. He died in battle later in 1861.

One might say that Governor Yates of Illinois won the war. After Washington ignored a store clerk's request for an army posting, Yates granted the man a commission in the Illinois state militia. That man was Ulysses S. Grant.

". . . He leveled his pistol at me and said,
'Are you union or secesh?' "

THE CIVIL WAR IN THE WEST: QUANTRILL'S RAIDERS RIDE INTO LAWRENCE

August 21, 1861
Lawrence, Kansas

GURDON GROVENOR

William C. Quantrill has been described as a Jekyll and Hyde character. Although occasionally a schoolteacher, by the time the Civil War began he had already been charged with horse stealing, theft, and murder. In one telling incident, he posed as an abolitionist to infiltrate a cabal plotting to help some slaves escape; then he sold the information to the slaves' owner, who had three of the abolitionists shot.

He formed a band of guerrillas at the outbreak of the war. Together they fought for the Confederacy and for themselves, robbing mail coaches and murdering Union sympathizers in Kansas and Missouri. The U.S. government put a price on his head in 1862; that same year the Confederates commissioned him a captain and made his guerrilla band an official unit.

His most infamous act was the raid described here, when he and 450 men rode into Lawrence, Kansas.

It was a clear, warm, still morning, in the midst of one of the hot, dry, dusty spells of weather common in Kansas in the month of August.

The guerrillas reached Lawrence just before sunrise after an all night's ride from the border of Missouri. Myself and family were yet in bed and asleep. They passed directly by our house, and we were awakened by their yelling and shouting.

I thought at first that the noise came from a company of colored recruits who were camped just west of our house; thought that they had got to quarrelling among themselves. I got up and went to the window to see what was the matter, and as I drew aside the curtain the sight that met my eyes was one of terror—one that I never shall forget. The bush-whackers were just passing by my house. There were 350 of them, all mounted and heavily armed; they were grim and dirty from their night's ride over the dusty roads and were a reckless and bloodthirsty set of men. It was a sight we had somewhat anticipated, felt that it might come, and one that we had dreaded ever since the commencement of the war. I turned to my wife and said: "The bushwhackers are here."

They first made for the main street, passing up as far as the Eldridge House to see if they were going to meet with any opposition, and when they found none they scattered out all over town, killing, stealing and burning. We hastily dressed ourselves and closed up the house tightly as possible and began to talk over what was best to do. My first thought was to get away to some hiding place, but on looking out there seemed no possibility of that as the enemy were everywhere, and I had a feeling that I ought not to leave my family, a young wife and two children, one a babe of three months old, and so we sat down and awaited developments. We saw men shot down and fires shooting up in all directions.

Just on the north of our house, a half a block away and in full view was a camp of recruits twenty-two in all, not yet mustered into service and unarmed. They were awakened by the noise, got up and started to run but were all shot down but five. I saw this wholesale shooting from my window, and it was a sight to strike terror to a stouter heart than mine. But we had not long to wait before our time came. Three of the guerrillas came to the house, stepped up on the front porch, and with the butt of a musket smashed in one of the front windows; my wife opened the door and let them in. They ransacked the house, talked and swore and threatened a good deal, but offered no violence. They set the house on fire above and below, took such things as they fancied, and left. After they had gone I put the fire out below, but above it had got too strong a hold, and I could not put it out.

Not long after a single man rode up to the front gate; he was a vil-lainous looking fellow, and was doubly villainous from too much whiskey. He saw me standing back in the hall of the house, and with a terrible oath he ordered me to come out. I stepped out on the piazza, and he leveled his pistol at me and said; "Are you union or secesh?"

It was my time of trial; my wife with her little one in her arms, and our little boy clinging to her side, was standing just a little ways from me. My life seemingly hung on my answer, my position may be imagined but it cannot be described. The thought ran through me like an electric shock, that I could not say that I was a secessionist, and deny my loyalty to my country; that I would rather die than to live and face that disgrace; and so I answered that I was a union man. He snapped his pistol but it failed to fire. I stepped back into the house and he rode around to the north door and met me there, and snapped his pistol at me again, and this time it failed. Was there a providence in this?

Just then a party of a half dozen of the raiders came riding towards the house from the north, and seeing my enemy, hallooed to him "Don't shoot that man." They rode up to the gate and told me to come there; I did so and my would be murderer came up to me and placed the muzzle of his revolver in my ear. It was not a pleasant place to be in, but the leader of the new crowd told him not to shoot, but to let me alone until he could inquire about me, so he asked me if I had ever been down in Missouri stealing niggers or horses; I told him "No that I never had been in Missouri, except to cross the state going and coming from the east." This seemed to be satisfactory so he told my old enemy to let me alone and not to kill me. This seemed to make him very angry, and he cursed me terribly, but I ventured to put my hand up and push away his revolver. The leader of the party then told me if I did not expect to get killed, I must get out of sight, that they were all getting drunk, and would kill everybody they saw; I told him that that was what I had wanted to do all the morning, but I could not; "Well," he says, "you must hide or get killed." And they all rode away.

After they had gone I told my wife that I would go into the cellar, and stay until the fire reached me, and if any more of the raiders inquired for me to tell them that I had been taken a prisoner and carried off. Some years ago I read an article in the Sunday School Times, saying that a lie under any circumstances was a sin. I thought then that I should like to see that writer try my experiences at the time of the raid and see what he would think then; I did not feel my lie a sin then and never have since.

The cellar of my house was under the [building's wing] and the fire was in the front and in the upper story. There was an outside bulk-head door, where I knew I could get out after the fire had reached the floor above me. I had not been in the cellar long before my wife came and said they had just killed my neighbor across the street.

Soon after the notorious Bill Anderson, passing by the house, saw my wife standing in the yard, stopped and commenced talking with her; told her how many men he had killed that morning, and inquiring where her husband was; she told him that he had been taken prisoner and carried away—was it my wife's duty to tell him the truth, tell him where I was and let him come and shoot me as he would a dog, which he would have done? Awhile after my wife came and said she thought the raiders had all gone, and so I came out of my prison just as the fire was eating through the floor over my head, thankful that I had passed through that dreadful ordeal and was safe.

Such was my experience during those four or five terrible hours. Our home and its contents was in ashes, but so thankful were we that my life was spared that we thought but little of our pecuniary loss. After the raiders had left and the people could get out on the street, a most desolate and sickening sight met their view. The whole business part of the town, except two stores, was in ashes. The bodies of dead men, some of them partly burned away, were laying in all directions. A large number of dwellings were burned to the ground, and the moaning of the grief stricken people was heard from all sides. Gen. Lane, who was in the city at the time, told me that he had been over the battleground of Gettysburg a few days before, but the sight was not so sickening as the one which the burned and sacked city of Lawrence presented. The exact number killed was never known, but it was about 150, many of them of the best citizens.

Some estimates of the dead approached 180, including women and children. The author of this account was one of the few men to escape.

Quantrill was severely wounded in the spring of 1865, and died in a federal prison. But he left behind an outlaw legacy that outgrew even his own fame. A certain teenager in his gang continued to create all sorts of trouble for the authorities for years after the war: Jesse James.

———————————————

> *"...We descended into Gold Hill with drums beating and colors flying, enveloped in imposing clouds of dust...."*

THE CIVIL WAR IN THE WEST:
THE $150,000 SACK OF FLOUR

1862
Nevada

MARK TWAIN

This odd event was sparked by the mania of the Comstock Lode, a huge silver deposit discovered in 1859. Boomtowns sprang up immediately. Eventually the output from the mines was so great—$36 million a year at the peak—that the federal government built a mint at Carson City.

Mark Twain was still Samuel Clemens when the Comstock Lode lured him to Nevada in 1861. He soon realized he was a failure as a miner, and took a job at a newspaper, where he assumed his now famous pseudonym and gathered the stories that became the book from which this account comes, Roughing It.

Money was wonderfully plenty. The trouble was not how to get it but how to spend it, how to lavish it, get rid of it, squander it. And so it was a happy thing that just at this juncture the news came over the wires that a great United States Sanitary Commission had been formed and money was wanted for the relief of the wounded sailors and soldiers of the Union languishing in the Eastern hospitals. Right on the heels of it came word that San Francisco had responded superbly before the telegram was half a day old. Virginia [City] rose as one man!

A sanitary committee was hurriedly organized, and its chairman mounted a vacant cart in C Street and tried to make the clamorous multitude understand that the rest of the committee were flying hither and thither and working with all their might and main, and that if the town would only wait an hour, an office would be ready, books opened, and the commission prepared to receive contributions. His voice was drowned and his information lost in a ceaseless roar of cheers and demands that the money be received now—they swore they would not wait. The chairman pleaded and argued, but, deaf to all entreaty, men plowed their way through the throng and rained checks of gold coin into the cart and scurried away for more.

Hands clutching money were thrust aloft out of the jam by men who hoped this eloquent appeal would cleave a road their strugglings could not open. The very Chinamen and Indians caught the excitement and dashed their half dollars into the cart without knowing or caring what it was all about. Women plunged into the crowd, trimly attired, fought their way to the cart with their coin, and emerged again, by and by, with their apparel in a state of hopeless dilapidation. It was the wildest mob Virginia had ever seen and the most determined and ungovernable, and when at last it abated its fury and dispersed, it had not a penny in its pocket. To use its own phraseology, it came there flush and went away busted.

After that the commission got itself into systematic working order, and for weeks the contributions flowed into its treasury in a generous stream. Individuals and all sorts of organizations levied upon themselves a regular weekly tax for the sanitary fund, graduated according to their means, and there was not another grand universal outburst till the famous "Sanitary Flour Sack" came our way.

Its history is peculiar and interesting. A former schoolmate of mine, by the name of Reuel Gridley, was living at the little city of Austin in the Reese River country at this time and was the Democratic candidate for mayor. He and the Republican candidate made an agreement that the defeated man should be publicly presented with a fifty-pound sack of flour by the successful one and should carry it home on his shoulder. Gridley was defeated. The new mayor gave him the sack of flour, and he shouldered it and carried it a mile or two from lower Austin to his home in upper Austin, attended by a band of music and the whole population. Arrived there, he said he did not need the flour and asked what the people thought he had better do with it. A voice said:

"Sell it to the highest bidder for the benefit of the sanitary fund."

The suggestion was greeted with a round of applause, and Gridley mounted a dry goods box and assumed the role of auctioneer. The bids went higher and higher as the sympathies of the pioneers awoke and expanded, till at last the sack was knocked down to a millman at two hundred and fifty dollars and his check taken. He was asked where he would have the flour delivered, and he said:

"Nowhere—sell it again."

Now the cheers went up royally, and the multitude were fairly in the spirit of the thing. So Gridley stood there and shouted and perspired till the sun went down, and when the crowd dispersed he had sold the sack to three hundred different people and had taken in eight thousand dollars in gold. And still the flour sack was in his possession.

The news came to Virginia and a telegram went back:

"Fetch along your flour sack!"

. . . Telegrams had [also] gone ahead to Gold Hill, Silver City, and Dayton, and those communities were at fever heat and ripe for the conflict. It was a very hot day and wonderfully dusty. At the end of a short half hour we descended into Gold Hill with drums beating and colors flying, and enveloped in imposing clouds of dust. The whole population—men, women, and children, Chinamen and Indians—were massed in the main street, all the flags in town were at the masthead, and the blare of the bands was drowned in cheers. Gridley stood up and asked who would make the first bid for the National Sanitary Flour Sack. General W. said:

"The Yellow Jacket silver mining company offers a thousand dollars, coin!"

A tempest of applause followed. A telegram carried the news to Virginia, and fifteen minutes afterward that city's population was massed in the streets devouring the tidings—for it was part of the program that the bulletin boards should do a good work that day. Every few minutes a new dispatch was bulletined from Gold Hill, and still the excitement grew. Telegrams began to return to us from Virginia beseeching Gridley to bring back the flour sack, but such was not the plan of the campaign. At the end of an hour Gold Hill's small population had paid a figure for the flour sack that awoke all the enthusiasm of Virginia when the grand total was displayed upon the bulletin boards.

Then the Gridley cavalcade moved on, a giant refreshed with new lager beer and plenty of it—for the people brought it to the carriages without waiting to measure it—and within three hours more the expedition had carried Silver City and Dayton by storm and was on its way back covered with glory. Every move had been telegraphed and bulletined, and as the procession entered Virginia and filed down C Street at half past eight in the evening the town was abroad in the thoroughfares, torches were glaring, flags flying, bands playing, cheer on cheer cleaving the air, and the city ready to surrender at discretion.

The auction began; every bid was greeted with bursts of applause, and at the end of two hours and a half a population of fifteen thousand souls had paid in coin for a fifty-pound sack of flour a sum equal to forty thousand dollars in greenbacks! It was at a rate in the neighborhood of three dollars for each man, woman, and child of the population. The grand total would have been twice as large, but the streets were very narrow, and hundreds who wanted to bid could not get within a block of the stand and could not make themselves heard. These grew tired of waiting, and many of them went home long before the auction was over. This was the greatest day Virginia ever saw, perhaps.

Gridley sold the sack in Carson City and several California towns; also in San Francisco. Then he took it east and sold it in one or two Atlantic cities, I think. I am not sure of that, but I know that he finally carried it to St. Louis, where a monster sanitary fair was being held, and after selling it there for a large sum and helping on the enthusiasm by displaying the portly silver bricks which Nevada's donation had produced, he had the flour baked up into small cakes and retailed them at high prices.

It was estimated that when the flour sack's mission was ended it had been sold for a grand total of a hundred and fifty thousand dollars in greenbacks! This is probably the only instance on record where common family flour brought three thousand dollars a pound in the public market.

As early as 1864, President Lincoln was exploiting the growth of Nevada to push through statehood, so the pro-Union Nevadans would vote their support for his reelection and for the Constitutional amendment to end slavery.

But by 1898, the mines were abandoned, in part because the federal government stopped using silver to back currency.

"The inhabitants all made preparations to live under the ground during the siege...."

THE CIVIL WAR IN THE WEST: THE SIEGE OF VICKSBURG

May–July 1863

ANONYMOUS VICKSBURG RESIDENT AND ANONYMOUS *CLEVELAND HERALD* REPORTER

In the West the chief goal of the Union was control of the Mississippi River, to cut the Confederate supply lines from Texas and Mexico. General Ulysses S. Grant achieved that goal with a forty-seven-day siege of Vicksburg, Mississippi. Along with the Battle of Gettysburg, Vicksburg finished the Confederacy.

WITHIN VICKSBURG

So constantly dropped the shells around the city, that the inhabitants all made preparations to live under the ground during the siege. M. sent over and had a cave made in a hill near by. We seized the opportunity one evening, when the gunners were probably at their supper, for we had a few moments of quiet, to go over and take possession. We were under the care of a friend of M., who was paymaster on the staff of the same General with whom M. was Adjutant. We had neighbors on both sides of us; and it would have been an amusing sight to a spectator to witness the domestic scenes presented without by the number of servants preparing the meals under the high bank containing the caves.

Our new habitation was an excavation made in the earth, and branching six feet from the entrance, forming a cave in the shape of a T. In one of the wings my bed fitted; the other I used as a kind of a dressing room; in this the earth had been cut down a foot or two below the floor of the main cave; I could stand erect here; and when tired of sitting in other portions of my residence, I bowed myself into it, and stood impassively resting at full height—one of the variations in the still shell-expectant life. M.'s servant cooked for us under protection of the hill. Our quarters were close, indeed; yet I was more comfortable than I expected I could have been made under the earth in that fashion.

We were safe at least from fragments of shell—and they were flying in all directions; though no one seemed to think our cave any protection, should a mortar shell happen to fall directly on top of the ground above us.

Still, we had nothing to complain of in comparison with the soldiers: many of them were sick and wounded in a hospital in the most exposed parts of the city, with shells falling and exploding all around them.

OUTSIDE VICKSBURG

Let us climb the parapet and see the siege by moonlight. In front of us, beyond the enemy's works, but hidden from us, lies the city of Vicksburg. Look carefully, and you can distinguish the spires of the courthouse and two or three churches. The rebels had a signal station on the former when we came, but our shells made it too warm for them, and they withdrew. The mortars are playing tonight, and they are well worth seeing. We watch a moment, and in the direction of Young's Point, beyond the city, suddenly up shoots a flash of light, and in a moment the ponderous shell, with its fuse glowing and sparkling, rises slowly from behind the bluffs; up, up, it goes, as though mounting to the zenith, over it comes towards us, down through its flight trajectory into the city, and explodes with a shock that jars the ground for miles. There are women and tender children where those shells fall, but war is war.

Sherman's eight-inch monsters are grumbling far away on the right. Nearer, McPherson's, too, are playing—we can even see the cannoneers beside them at each flash. Ours will open at midnight; then there will be music to your heart's content. Meanwhile, let us go to the front.

A hundred yards to the right of where we now are we enter a deep trench. Following this, as it winds down around the hill, we reach the opening of a cave or mine. The air within is damp and close, like that of a vault. Candles are burning dimly at intervals, and we hear a hum of voices far within and out of sight. We proceed, and presently meet two men carrying a barrow of earth, for our boys are at work night and day. Finally, we reach the moonlight again, and emerge into a wide, deep trench, cut across the line of the covered way. This is open, and filled with troops, who protect the working party. A heavy parapet of cotton bales and earth is built on the side towards the enemy, and we must mount them to look over.

We are now within sociable distance of the chivalry. Those men lying on the ground, ten to thirty yards from us, are our boys, our advance pickets; but that grey fellow, with the bright musket, which glistens so, a few steps beyond, is a "reb," long-haired and hot-blooded, one of Wall's famous Texas legion—a bulldog to fight, you may be sure.

Now jump down and enter the mouth of the other mine, which leads toward the salient of the enemy's work. Stumbling along, we reach the end where the men are digging. The candle burns very dimly—the air is almost stifling. Never mind, let us watch them. See that slender, bright-looking fellow swinging that pick. Great beaded drops of perspiration trickle down his face; there is not a dry thread in his coarse, grey shirt; but no matter, the pick swings, and each stroke slices down six inches of the tough subsoil of Mississippi. That fellow was "Jim," once a tender-handed, smooth-faced, nice young man, whose livery-stable, billiard and cigar bills were a sore trial to his worthy governor. Jim says that he used to wear gloves and "store-clothes," and that girls called him good-looking, but that's played out now; he is going for Uncle Sam.

But we return to the fresh air. Look over the parapet again towards the turret, where we saw the rebel picket. Do you see the little grey mounds which cover the hillside so thickly?—ten, twenty, thirty, you can count on a few square rods. Ah, my friend, this is sacred ground you are looking upon. There our boys charged; there they were slain in heaps; but they pressed on, and leaped into the ditch. They climbed the parapet, and rolled back into eternity. Others followed them; their flag was planted, and they sprang over, to meet their certain death. An hour passed, and one returned; the rest were dead.

"Come to the big house, quick."

THE CIVIL WAR IN THE WEST: EMANCIPATION ARRIVES

September 1865
Texas

ANONYMOUS

Many slave owners had sent slaves to Texas to avoid liberation by the advancing Union army. The date of this account, months after the South ceded defeat, reveals that slave owners were slow to catch on to the idea of defeat.

I heard about freedom in September and they were picking cotton and a white man rode up to master's house on a big, white horse and the houseboy told master a man wanted to see him and he hollered, "Light, stranger." It was a government man and he had the big book and a bunch of papers and said why hadn't master turned the n——s loose. Master said he was trying to get the crop out and he told master to have the slaves in. Uncle Steven blew the cow horn that they used to call to eat and all the n——s came running, because that horn meant, "Come to the big house, quick." The man read the paper telling us we were free, but master made us work several months after that. He said we would get 20 acres of land and a mule but we didn't get it.

Lots of n——s were killed after freedom, because the slaves in Harrison County were turned loose right at freedom and those in Rusk County weren't. But they heard about it and ran away to freedom in Harrison County and their owners had them bushwhacked, then shot down. You could see lots of n——s hanging from trees in Sabine bottom right after freedom, because they caught them swimming across Sabine River and shot them. There sure are going to be lots of souls crying against them in judgment!

The arrival of the army in Texas in mid-June to enforce emancipation is now marked by "Juneteenth" celebrations in many parts of the country.

"... It is a matter of great economy to put some of these colored regiments into the field in the Indian country...."

BUFFALO SOLDIERS

1866
Washington, D.C.

SENATE RECORDS

The Ninth and Tenth Cavalry units, known as the "Buffalo Soldiers," were like the Tuskegee Airmen of World War II: Black soldiers accepted only reluctantly, and then distinguished far beyond expectations. But as this debate reveals, only the unique demands of the western wilderness were sufficient to sway the politicians, despite the fine performance of black troops during the Civil War.

MR. [JAMES] MCDOUGALL [DEMOCRAT-UNIONIST OF CALIFORNIA]: I wish to express my thought that the people of my country are able to maintain themselves, and do not need to be maintained by an inferior race. . . . Soldiers are men of arms, as are their officers and commanders. They must belong to ruling forces, and not to the inferior forces. These are simple men that all men who have read history should have learned, and where it has not been learned there is ignorance.

I do not care to say all I think, for it would be thought by some unkind, and I do not care to be unkind; I would rather be generous; but this undertaking to place a lower, inferior, different race upon a level with the white man's race, in arms, is against the laws that lie at the foundation of true republicanism.

MR. [IRA] HARRIS [REPUBLICAN OF NEW YORK]: I am not in favor of compelling an officer to make the election either to resign or serve in a colored regiment. . . . I have no objection that any officer should serve in a colored regiment if he pleases to do so, but many feel disinclined to do that, and I do not feel disposed to drive them to the alternative of either doing that or leaving the Army.

MR. [JAMES] GRIMES [REPUBLICAN OF IOWA]: The Senator and I are diametrically opposed to each other on that subject. I want to compel that officer, if he is receiving and has been receiving a salary from the government of the United States during a series of years, and is entitled to promotion in the regular order of promotion, and is not willing to be transferred from the command of a white regiment to the command of a colored regiment, to leave the service. He has no business in the service. He is not a man to whom I would intrust the honor of the flag or the defense of the country. It is not for him to determine whether he shall command a black or a white regiment or whether there shall be a colored regiment in the Army or not. That is a question for us to determine; and when he says he will not take command of a colored regiment, if we put him in charge of it, he is not longer fit to be an officer of the Army of the United States, and ought to be turned out. . . .

MR. [BENJAMIN FRANKLIN] WADE [WHIG-REPUBLICAN OF OHIO]: I am informed that while we lose greatly by desertion all the time from the white regiments on the frontier, there is scarcely anything of the kind among colored troops. When you get our regiments off among the gold regions or on the frontier, there is a great waste of white troops by desertion; but experience has shown us that there is scarcely anything of the kind among the colored troops. For this reason, and also because experience has shown that they are just as good troops as the whites, and because we want to make no distinction between the one and the other, I think there should be in each arm of the service a certain portion of colored troops. . . .

MR. [HENRY] WILSON [REPUBLICAN OF MASSACHUSETTS]: I certainly do not think there is any objection. . . . Our cavalry regiments will be mostly our frontier regiments; and while we have desertions, and have had lately since the war has been over, to the extent of thirty or forty per cent, from our white regiments that go on the frontiers, there are no desertions from the colored regiments stationed in Arkansas and on the frontiers, and they are the best riders in America connected with our Army. . . . I think it is a matter of great economy to put some of these colored regiments into the field in the Indian country, in the mountains, and in sections of the country where white men desert largely and go to the mines where the temptation is very great.

MR. [WILLARD] SAULSBURY [DEMOCRAT OF DELAWARE]: . . . I hope that the amendment will not be adopted. . . . What would be the effect if you were to send negro regiments into the community in which I live to brandish their swords and exhibit their pistols and their guns? Their very presence would be a stench in the nostrils of the people from whom I come. A negro soldier riding up and down the streets and through your country, dressed in a little brief authority, to insult white men! . . . You must expect collisions. . . .

The Buffalo Soldiers eventually accounted for 20 percent of the troops in the West. Historian William Leckie wrote, "Their stations were among the most lonely and isolated to be found anywhere in the country and mere service at such posts would seem to have called for honorable mention. Discipline was severe, food usually poor, recreation difficult, and violent death always near at hand. Prejudice robbed them of recognition and often of simple justice." Historian William Loren Katz notes that they were often outfitted with cast-off equipment and horses. Nonetheless, eleven of them earned the Medal of Honor.

About thirty years after the debate recounted here the Buffalo Soldiers charged to the top of Cuba's San Juan Hill to end the Spanish-American War and help Teddy Roosevelt win the presidency.

"He who can draw and fire first is the best. . . ."

WILD BILL HICKOK AND CALAMITY JANE

1866–1876
Wyoming and South Dakota

GEORGE ARMSTRONG CUSTER
AND MARTHA JANE CANARY

Trail driver James Butler "Wild Bill" Hickok became a legendary scout during and after the Civil War. He played along with the pulp novelists who exaggerated his reputation, briefly joining Buffalo Bill Cody's Wild West Show. But soon he was back to his true love, gambling. As for his gunfighting, his friend Cody said, "Well, [Wild] Bill was a pretty good shot, but he could not shoot as quick as half a dozen men we all knew in those days. Nor as straight, either. But Bill was cool, and the men he went up against were rattled, I guess. Bill beat them to it. He made up his mind to kill the other man before the other man had finished thinking, and so Bill would just quietly pull his gun and give it to him."

Martha Jane Canary, having lost both her parents by the time she was about fifteen years old, embarked on a life of adventure that was unconventional even in the freewheeling West. She also became a scout, earning her nickname when she saved the life of her post commander, who had been wounded in a skirmish with some Indians. "I saw the Captain reeling in his saddle as though about to fall. I turned my horse and galloped back with all haste to his side and got there in time to catch him as he was falling. I lifted him onto my horse in front of me and succeeded in getting him safely to the Fort. . . . On recovering, [he] laughingly said, 'I name you Calamity Jane, the heroine of the plains.'"

Wild Bill and Calamity Jane met and became companions in Deadwood, South Dakota, after the 1876 gold strike in the Black Hills.

Eyewitness George Armstrong Custer was one of the army officers for whom Wild Bill scouted (see page 184). Calamity Jane's account comes from a pamphlet billed as her memoir.

"Wild Bill" was a strange character, just the one which a novelist might gloat over. He was a Plainsman in every sense of the word, yet unlike any other of his class. In person he was about six feet one in height, straight as the straightest of the warriors whose implacable foe he was; broad shoulders, well-formed chest and limbs, and a face strikingly handsome; sharp, clear, blue eyes, which stared you straight in the face when in conversation; a finely-shaped nose, inclined to be aquiline; a well-turned mouth, with lips only partially concealed by a handsome moustache. His hair and complexion were those of the perfect blond. The former was worn in uncut ringlets falling carelessly over his powerfully formed shoulders. Add to this figure a costume blending the immaculate neatness of the dandy with the extravagant taste and style of the frontiersman, and you have Wild Bill, then as now the most famous scout on the Plains. Whether on foot or on horseback, he was one of the most perfect types of physical manhood I ever saw.

Of his courage there could be no question; it had been brought to the test on too many occasions to admit of a doubt. His skill in the use of the rifle and pistol was unerring; while his deportment was exactly the opposite of what might be expected from a man of his surroundings. It was entirely free from all bluster or bravado. He seldom spoke of himself unless requested to do so. His conversation, strange to say, never bordered either on the vulgar or blasphemous. His influence among the frontiersmen was unbounded, his word was law; and many are the personal quarrels and disturbances which he has checked among his comrades by his simple announcement that "this has gone far enough" if need be followed by the ominous warning that when persisted in or renewed the quarreler "must settle it with me." Wild Bill is anything but a quarrelsome man; yet no one but himself can enumerate the many conflicts in which he has been engaged, and which have almost invariably resulted in the death of his adversary. I have a personal knowledge of at least half a dozen men whom he has at various times killed, one of these being at the time a member of my command. Others have been severely wounded, yet he always escapes unhurt.

On the Plains every man openly carries his belt with its invariable appendages, knife and revolver, often two of the latter. Wild Bill always carried two handsome ivory-handled revolvers of the large size; he was never seen without them. Where this is the common custom, brawls or personal difficulties are seldom if ever settled by blows. The quarrel is not from a word to a blow, but from a word to the revolver, and he who can draw and fire first is the best man. No civil law reaches him; none is applied for. In fact there is no law recognized beyond the frontier but that of "might makes right." Should death result from the quarrel, as it usually does, no coroner's jury is impaneled to learn the cause of death, and the survivor is not arrested. But instead of these old-fashioned proceedings, a meeting of citizens takes place, the survivor is requested to be present when the circumstances of the homicide are inquired into, and the unfailing verdict of "justifiable," "self-defense," etc., is pronounced, and the law stands vindicated.

That justice is often deprived to a victim there is not a doubt. Yet in all of the many affairs of this kind in which "Wild Bill" has performed a part, and which have come to my knowledge, there is not a single instance in which the verdict of twelve fair-minded men would not be pronounced in his favor. That the even tenor of his way continues to be disturbed by little events of this description may be inferred from an item which has been floating lately through the columns of the press, and which states that "the funeral of 'Jim Bludso,' who was killed the other day by 'Wild Bill,' took place to-day." It then adds: "The funeral expenses were borne by 'Wild Bill.'" What could be more thoughtful than this? Not only to send a fellow mortal out of the world, but to pay the expenses of the transit.

CALAMITY JANE

. . . In spring of 1876 . . . [at] Fort Laramie . . . I met Wm. Hickock, better known as Wild Bill, and we started for Deadwood, where we arrived about June.

During the month of June I acted as a pony express rider carrying the U.S. mail between Deadwood and Custer, a distance of fifty miles, over one of the roughest trails in the Black Hills country. As many of the riders before me had been held up and robbed of their packages, mail and money that they carried, for that was the only means of getting mail and money between these points. It was considered the most dangerous route in the Hills, but as my reputation as a rider and quick shot was well known, I was molested very little, for the toll gatherers looked on me as being a good fellow, and they knew that I never missed my mark. I made the round trip every two days which was considered pretty good riding in that country. Remained around Deadwood all that summer visiting all the camps within an area of one hundred miles. My friend, Wild Bill, remained in Deadwood during the summer with the exception of occasional visits to the camps. On the 2nd of August, while setting at a gambling table in the Bell Union saloon, in Deadwood, he was shot in the back of the head by the notorious Jack McCall, a desperado. I was in

Deadwood at the time and on hearing of the killing made my way at once to the scene of the shooting and found that my friend had been killed by McCall. I at once started to look for the assassin and found him at Shurdy's butcher shop and grabbed a meat cleaver and made him throw up his hands; through the excitement on hearing of Bill's death, having left my weapons on the post of my bed. He was then taken to a log cabin and locked up, well secured as every one thought, but he got away and was afterwards caught at Fagan's ranch on Horse Creek, on the old Cheyenne road and was then taken to Yankton, Dak., where he was tried, sentenced and hung. . . .

The cards Wild Bill was holding when he was shot—two pairs, aces and eights—are still called a "Dead Man's Hand." Calamity Jane died in 1903, and was buried beside him.

"Goods . . . have all disappeared. . . ."

INDIAN AGENTS

1866
Dakota Territory

STRUCK BY THE REE

General William T. Sherman defined an Indian reservation as "a parcel of land set aside for Indians, surrounded by thieves." In theory, the government was supposed to provide the Indians with the means to live on the reservations, because traditonal ways of life couldn't be supported on them. In reality, the Indian agents who managed the reservations schemed to profit from their posts. They often sold supplies to nearby white settlers and pocketed the cash, made deals to sell natural resources from the reservation lands, and received kickbacks from cattle ranchers who delivered substandard beef.

Struck By The Ree was a Yankton Sioux.

The first agent was Redfield; and when he came there he borrowed blankets from me to sleep upon, and agreed to return them, but never did, though I asked for them. Goods have been stored up stairs in the warehouse, and have all disappeared; perhaps the rats eat them; I don't know what became of them. If they bring any goods for the Indians to eat and put them in the warehouse, the agents live out of them, and the mess house where travellers stop has been supplied from the Indians' goods, and pay has been taken by the agents, and they have put the money in their pockets and taken it away with them. I have seen them take the goods from the storehouse of the Indians and take them to the mess-house, and I have had to pay for a meal for myself at the mess-house, and so have others of our Indians had to pay for meals at the mess-house, prepared from their own goods. . . .

When Redfield left the agency, a steamboat came in the night and took away fifteen boxes of goods, so that the Indians would not know it; but the Indians were too sharp for him. . . . Mr. Redfield said to me, "when I am gone you will meet with a great many agents; but you will never meet one like me." I think I never want to see one like him. . . .

The agents weren't the only crooked ones. Many of them had to bribe high-ranking officials to get the posts. By the time of the Civil War, the federal Bureau of Indian Affairs had become so corrupt that Congress created a commission to investigate the problems. President Lincoln said, "If we get through this war and I live, this Indian system shall be reformed."

The system was improved a bit by President Grant in the 1870s. He circum-vented the political patronage of the Indian agencies by giving oversight power to several religious groups and appointing a Board of Indian Commissioners made up of prominent civilians.

"Lava . . . was boiling and surging furiously. . . ."

NATURE SUBLIME AND NATURE RIDICULOUS: A VOLCANO AND AN EARTHQUAKE

December 1866 and October 1868
Hawaii and San Francisco

MARK TWAIN

This San Francisco temblor was of course not as awesome as the great quake of 1906. Twain wasn't the only writer to treat it with some humor.

Twain, as noted earlier, had gone west to become a miner, but soon realized he was more fit for writing (see page 149).

We bought horses and bent our way over the summer-clad mountain terraces, toward the great volcano of Kilauea. . . . I have seen Vesuvius since, but it was a mere toy, a child's volcano, a soup kettle, compared to this. . . . Here was a vast, perpendicular, walled cellar, nine hundred feet deep in some places, thirteen hundred in others, level-floored, and ten miles in circumference! Here was a yawning pit upon whose floor the armies of Russia could camp, with room to spare.

Perched upon the edge of the crater, at the opposite end from where we stood, was a small lookout house—say three miles away. It assisted us, by comparison, to comprehend and appreciate the great depth of the basin—it looked like a tiny martin-box clinging at the eaves of a cathedral. After some little time spent in resting and looking and ciphering, we hurried on to the hotel.

By the path it is half a mile from the Volcano House to the lookout house. After a hearty supper we waited until it was thoroughly dark and then started to the crater.

. . . Arrived at the little thatched lookout house, we rested our elbows on the railing in front and looked abroad over the wide crater and down over the sheer precipice at the seething fires beneath us.

. . . The greater part of the vast floor of the desert under us was as black as ink, and apparently smooth and level; but over a mile square of it was ringed and streaked and striped with a thousand branching streams of liquid and gorgeously brilliant fire! It looked like a colossal railroad map of the State of Massachusetts done in chain lightning on a midnight sky. Imagine it—imagine a coal-black sky shivered into a tangled network of angry fire!

Here and there were gleaming holes a hundred feet in diameter, broken in the dark crust, and in them the melted lava—the color of a dazzling white just tinged with yellow—was boiling and surging furiously; and from these holes branched numberless bright torrents in many directions, like the spoke of a wheel, and kept a tolerably straight course for a while and then swept round in huge rainbow curves, or made a long succession of sharp worm-fence angles, which looked precisely like the fiercest jagged lightning. These streams met other streams, and they mingled with and crossed and recrossed each other in every conceivable direction, like skate tracks on a popular skating ground. Sometimes streams twenty or thirty feet wide flowed from the holes to some distance without dividing—and through the opera glasses we could see that they ran down small, steep hills, and were genuine cataracts of fire, white at their source, but soon cooling and turning to the richest red, grained with alternate lines of black and gold.

Every now and then masses of the dark crust broke away and floated slowly down these streams like rafts down a river. Occasionally, the molten lava flowing under the superincumbent crust broke through— split a dazzling streak, from five hundred to a thousand feet long, like a sudden flash of lightning, and then acre after acre of the cold lava parted into fragments, turned up edgewise like cakes of ice when a great river breaks up, plunged downward and were swallowed in the crimson cauldron. Then the wide expanse of the "thaw" maintained a ruddy glow for a while, but shortly cooled and became black and level again.

SAN FRANCISCO

I was coming down Third Street. The only objects in motion anywhere in sight in that thickly built and populous quarter, were a man in a buggy behind me, and a street car wending slowly up the cross street. Otherwise, all was solitude and a Sabbath stillness. As I turned the corner, around a frame house, there was a great rattle and jar, and it occurred to me that here was an item!—no doubt a fight in that house.

Before I could turn and seek the door, there came a really terrific shock; the ground seemed to roll under me in waves, interrupted by violent jogglings up and down, and there was a heavy grinding noise as of brick houses rubbing together. I fell against the frame house and hurt my elbow.

I knew what it was now, and from mere reportorial instinct, nothing else, took out my watch and noted the time of day; at that moment a third and still severer shock came, and as I reeled about on the pavement trying to keep my footing I saw a sight! The entire front of a tall four-story brick building in Third street sprung outward like a door and fell sprawling across the street, raising a dust like a great volume of smoke! And here came the buggy—overboard went the man, and in less time than I can tell it the vehicle was distributed in small fragments along three hundred yards of street. One could have fancied that somebody had fired a charge of chair-rounds and rags down the thoroughfare.

The street car had stopped, the horses were rearing and plunging, the passengers were pouring out at both ends, and one fat man had crashed half way through a glass window on one side of the car, got wedged fast and was squirming and screaming like an impaled madman.

Every door of each house, as far as the eye could reach, was vomiting a stream of human beings; and almost before one could execute a wink and begin another, there was a massed multitude of people stretching in endless procession down every street my position commanded. Never was solemn solitude turned into teeming life quicker.

. . . The "curiosities" of the quake were simply endless. I could regale you for weeks, but will limit myself a bit. Gentlemen and ladies who were sick, or were taking a siesta, or had dissipated till a late hour and were making up lost sleep, thronged into the public streets in all sorts of queer apparel, and some without any at all. One woman who had been washing a naked child, ran down the street holding it by the ankles as if it were a dressed turkey. Prominent citizens who were supposed to keep the Sabbath very strictly, rushed out of saloons in their shirt-sleeves, with billiard cues in their hands. Dozens of men with necks swathed in napkins, rushed from barber-shops, lathered to the eyes or with one cheek clean shaved and the other still bearing a hairy stubble. Horses broke from stables, and a frightened dog rushed up a short attic ladder and out on to a roof, and when his scare was over had not the nerve to go down again the same way he had gone up. A prominent editor flew down stairs, in the principal hotel, with nothing on but one brief undergarment—met a chambermaid, and exclaimed: "Oh, what shall I do! Where shall I go?"

She responded with naive serenity: "If you have no choice, you might try a clothing-store!"

Such another destruction of mantel ornaments and toilet bottles as the earthquake created, San Francisco never saw before. There was hardly a girl or a matron in the city but suffered losses of this kind. Suspended pictures were thrown down, but oftener still, by a curious freak of the earthquake's humor, they were whirled completely around with their faces to the wall!

". . . Work on as though Heaven were before you and Hell behind you."

RACE TO THE LAST SPIKE

January 1868–January 1869
Sacramento

COLLIS P. HUNTINGTON

Rival businessmen lobbied for more than a decade to win government approval for a transcontinental railroad before construction finally began.

In Congress, debate over the route reflected the schism between the southern and northern states. When the South seceded, the question was settled: The 1862 Pacific Railway Act established the route through the northern states.

The Act also decided the builders. The Union Pacific company would build west from Omaha, Nebraska; the Central Pacific would build east from Sacramento, California.

Then in 1866, Congress granted permission for the Central Pacific to build beyond the California-Nevada border, and the race to the last spike began. Toward the end both companies graded paths along the route, side by side, each hoping to lay down rails first. The stakes were high because the railroads were given fees and land grants for each mile of track they laid.

This account of the race to the last spike comes from letters written by the Central Pacific's Collis P. Huntington to his partners, Charles Crocker, E. P. Crocker, Mark Hopkins, and Leland Stanford. All of them were already established business leaders in California.

TO CHARLES CROCKER, JANUARY 26, 1868

I consider it of the most vital importance that we build to the Wasatch Mountains for many reasons which I have given before. I would build the road in the cheapest possible manner then go back and improve it at once, because the Union Pacific have built the cheapest kind of road.

TO CHARLES CROCKER, APRIL 15, 1868

Keep right on laying rails just as though you did not care a d— for the snow, but were bound to get to Weber Canyon before the Union Company, and if you do that I will forever pray that you will have your reward.

TO MARK HOPKINS, JUNE 10, 1868

I telegraphed you yesterday not to take possession of the line more than 300 miles in advance, as they no doubt have possession, and therefore I thought we had better take high ground and confine ourselves to the law.

TO LELAND STANFORD, JUNE 15, 1868

It is all important we build to Weber Canyon, we all understand that, but I have been sorely troubled about iron. It sometimes seems as though the fates were against us from the mills that have burned and broke, hands striking, etc. But all great enterprises of this kind must have their mishaps. I only hope the Union may have as many as we do.

TO CHARLES CROCKER, JULY 1, 1868

There has left this port in all up to this time, 60,146 tons of rails. I shall continue to ship on fast ships until I have on the way 90,000 to 100,000 tons. I think all the iron that we lay on the Central Pacific (except for repairs) will be laid between this and the first of next February. So work on as though Heaven were before you and Hell behind you.

TO MARK HOPKINS, JULY 6, 1868

I think all these roads being built under the Railroad Act of 1862 will have a terrible overhauling. I hope they will show as clean hands as we can, but I doubt it.

TO E. B. CROCKER, JULY 9, 1868

The Union Company are in a quarrel again, but I think nothing will delay them pushing their track forward. It is a pity other railroad companies do not take high ground as we do.

TO LELAND STANFORD, JULY 17, 1868

Hurry up with all possible speed to reach within 300 miles of Echo Canyon, as it is all important that we make that point.

TO CHARLES CROCKER, OCTOBER 22, 1868

I have got the new line to Echo Summit approved [by the secretary of the interior]. You must lay the track to the tunnel. By God, Charley, you must work as man never worked before. Our salvation is you.

The Central Pacific pushed far past its original boundary, and the race ended with the driving of the last spike at Promontory Point, Utah, on May 10, 1869.

The companies had been granted more than 30 million acres of land. (Eventually they would receive more than 150 million acres—almost the area of Texas. To this day the corporations that descended from the railroad companies are some of the largest private landowners in the West.)

The "quarrels" and "clean hands" to which Huntington refers foreshadow one of the great scandals in American history, the Crédit Mobilier scandal. Crédit Mobilier of America was a phony construction company established by the men who ran the Union Pacific. Its purpose was to overbill the Union Pacific, thus skimming money from the government-financed railroad company into their own private company. Because of this scam the Union Pacific was essentially broke when the last spike in the transcontinental railroad was driven in 1869. Meanwhile, its owners had made millions.

Some congressmen were cut in on the deal by a colleague who was also a Union Pacific shareholder. As he wrote to an associate, he had placed Crédit Mobilier stock "where it will do the most good for us," going on to include a list of congressmen who had been given shares.

A few years later, when he and his associate had a falling out, the letter made its way to the New York Sun newspaper, which broke the story. The investigation implicated many politicians, including Vice President Schuyler Colfax. But in the end only two congressmen were censured, and no one was prosecuted. One congressman tainted by the scandal, James Garfield of Ohio, was elected president a few years later.

Although Huntington and his partners ran a similar scheme in the course of building the Central Pacific, the Union Pacific suffered worse. It eventually went into receivership.

"The members looked at each other in astonishment. . . ."

THE FIRST WOMAN'S SUFFRAGE VICTORY

December 10, 1869
Cheyenne, Wyoming

JOHN WESLEY HOYT

Woman's suffrage became law in the West long before the nation as a whole accepted it. In part this was due to cold sociological facts: The new territories required new constitutions and laws anyway; the rough life for everyone in the West broke down many eastern mannerisms that had separated the sexes; and a smaller population meant fewer minds had to change. But those facts were just context.

When the new territory of Wyoming, with about 9,000 citizens, gave women the right to vote, to own property separate from a husband's, to sit on juries, and to hold public office, a handful of colorful personalities, who were not above sharp dealing, were due the credit. And perhaps the law would not have passed if the politicians behind it had been more reputable. Some people thought the law was a publicity stunt to attract women to the territory, which had just one for every *six men. The* Cheyenne Leader *called it "a shrewd advertising dodge" and "a cunning device." But it stuck.*

Eyewitness John Wesley Hoyt became the territory's governor and later the first president of the University of Wyoming. He describes the backroom deals made by William Bright, president of the state's Council and House of Representatives. Bright, the author of the suffrage bill, was an unlikely politician. "I have never been to school a day in my life," he once said, "and where I learned to read and write I do not know." A friend once said, "His character was not above reproach, but he had an excellent, well-informed wife, and he was a kind, indulgent husband. In fact, he venerated his wife [Betty], and submitted to her judgment and influence more willingly than one could have supposed; and she was in favor of woman suffrage."

"Betty," [Bright said,] "it's a shame that I should be a member of the legislature and make laws for such a woman as you. You are a great deal better than I am; you know a great deal more, and you would make a better member of the Assembly than I, and you know it. I have been thinking about it and have made up my mind that I will go to work and do everything in my power to give you the ballot. Then you may work out the rest in your own way."

So he went over and talked with other members of the legislature. They smiled. But he got one of the lawyers to help him draw up a short bill, which he introduced.

It was considered and discussed. People smiled generally. There was not much expectation that anything of that sort would be done; but this was a shrewd fellow, who managed the party card in such a way as to get, as he believed, enough votes to carry the measure. . . .

He said to the Democrats: "We have a Republican governor and a Democratic Assembly. Now, then, if we can carry this bill through the Assembly and the governor vetoes it, we shall have made a point, you know; we shall have shown our liberality and lost nothing. But keep still; don't say anything about it." They promised.

He then went to the Republicans and told them that the Democrats were going to support his measure, and that if *they* did not want to lose capital they had better vote for it too. He [said he] didn't think there would be enough of them to carry it, but the vote would be on record and thus defeat the game of the other party. And they likewise agreed to vote for it.

So when the bill came to a vote it went right through. The members looked at each other in astonishment, for they hadn't intended to do it, *quite.* Then they laughed and said it was a good joke, but they had "got the governor in a fix."

So the bill went, in the course of time, to John A. Campbell, who was then governor—the first governor of the territory of Wyoming—and he promptly signed it!

His heart was right. He saw that it was long-deferred justice, and so signed it as gladly as Abraham Lincoln wrote *his* name to the Proclamation of Emancipation of the slaves. Of course the women were astounded! If a whole troop of angels had come down with flaming swords for their vindication, they would not have been much more astonished than they were when that bill became a law and the women of Wyoming were thus clothed with the habiliments of citizenship.

In 1890, when Wyoming became a state, it was the first state with women's voting rights. The Nineteenth Amendment to the Constitution, guaranteeing woman's suffrage nationwide, was not passed until 1920.

"Chinatown, wholly surrounded, was in a state of siege...."

LYNCHING THE CHINESE

October 28, 1871
Los Angeles, California

P. S. DORNEY

Chinese laborers who built the transcontinental railroad were not welcome in western cities after the railroad was finished. Their willingness to work for low wages angered many Caucasians. Their neighborhoods, almost exlusively male because of alien exclusion laws, turned into rough ghettoes.

This incident began with a battle between rival Chinese gangs. After two days of open warfare in Chinatown, the Los Angeles police moved in. The gang fight stopped temporarily only because the gangs joined forces to repel the police. When the police made a second attempt to control the quarter, they were joined by a few civilians, one of whom, Bob Thompson, was mortally wounded. He was pulled into a drugstore away from the fighting, where a Caucasian mob gathered.

Eyewitness P. S. Dorney was a journalist.

About 8 o'clock the death of Thompson was announced. The announcement was received in sullen silence; but in a moment the crowd melted away, and Main Street was deserted. In another moment, armed men were seen hastening, singly and in clusters, from every street and avenue, all heading toward Chinatown. The whole city seemed moved by one grim and tacit purpose—men streamed down from the hills and swarmed from the suburbs, while "Sonora" poured forth a horde of swarthy avengers. Businessmen closed their shops and joined the gathering clans, and in less than fifteen minutes after the announcement of "Bob" Thompson's death, the cracking of rifles, the roar of shotguns, and the rattle of small arms proclaimed the investment of Chinatown.

About 9 o'clock the first Chinese was captured. He was armed with a hatchet and was taken while attempting to break through the cordon of whites that surrounded the Chinese quarter. A dozen hands clutched him, and a hundred throats hoarsely shouted: "A rope! To the hill! To the hill!"

A man, then and now of standing and influence, dashed into a neighboring store and presently emerged, shaking aloft the first rope—a smooth, kinky, brand-new coil.

As the maddened men surged up the hill (Temple Street), the little ill-favored prisoner, borne bodily along, was stabbed in the back and side and was dead as a doorstep before General Baldwin's corral was reached, to the gate-beam of which the dead man was hanged. While the rope was being fastened to the neck of the corpse, two burly human beasts held it erect, while an Irish shoemaker known as "Crazy Johnson" stood guard, revolver in hand. (Johnson is now a prominent leader of the San Bernardino Holiness Band.)

By this time, Chinatown, wholly surrounded, was in a state of siege. Mounted men came galloping from the country—the vaquero was in his glory, and the cry was *"Carajo la Chino!"* ["Damned Chinese!"]. . . .

After the assault became general, the Chinese never returned shot or blow; but securely barricading every avenue of approach, each like a badger retired to his den and in sullen silence awaited his fate. But few attempted to escape, and all who made the attempt fell riddled with bullets. Not far from eleven o'clock the Main Street side of Chinatown fell into the hands of the besiegers, and, led by Jesus Martinez, the assailants scaled the low adobe walls and mounted to the asphaltum roof. This achievement was hailed with deafening cheers by the crowd below.

The condition of the Chinese had now become wretched indeed. The "Quarters," it will be remembered, were an old Spanish hacienda one story high, with an open courtyard in the center. Martinez and his companions, armed with axes as well as firearms, cut holes in the asphaltum roof, through which the cowering creatures below were shot in their hiding places or hunted from room to room out into the open courtyard, where death from the bullets of those on the roof was certain. Within or without, death was inevitable. The alternative was terrible. As each separate wretch, goaded from his covert, sought in his despair the open space, a volley from the roof brought him down; a chorus of yells telegraphed that fact to the surrounding mob, and the yells were answered by hoarse roars of savage satisfaction.

A simultaneous rush from Los Angeles Street forced the doors upon that side, and the work of real diabolism began. Men were dragged forth, many of them mortally wounded, and hurled headlong from a raised sidewalk to the ground. To the neck of some of the most helpless the mob fastened ropes and, with a whoop and a hurrah, rushed down Los Angeles Street to the hanging place, dragging some writhing wretch prone upon the ground. More doomed and bleeding miserables were jerked along by as many eager hands as could lay hold of clothing and queue, cuffed and cursed in the meantime by the infuriated multitude. A boy was thus led to the place of slaughter. The little fellow was not above twelve years of age. He had been a month in the country and knew not a word of English. He seemed paralyzed by fear—his eyes were fixed and staring, and his face blue-blanched and idiotic. He was hanged.

Nothing improved after this riot. In 1879, a new California constitution outlawed employment of Chinese workers. In 1882, pressure from California led the U.S. to pass the Chinese Exclusion Act, restricting immigration from China. It was not repealed until 1943.

To make up for the loss of cheap Chinese labor, Japanese immigration was encouraged instead. But the Japanese Americans eventually faced the same problems. By 1900, immigration limits were established. In 1924, Japanese immigration was halted.

Other restrictions were also aimed at Asians. Immigrants already in the U.S. were prevented from becoming citizens until the 1950s. Laws making it difficult for Asians to own or lease land also stayed on the books until the 1950s.

"'But where do you want to go?' asked the man. . . .
'To any place that is wild,' I said."

THE WONDERS OF YOSEMITE

1871
Yosemite Valley, California

JOHN MUIR

Appropriately, more features of California's geography have been named for John Muir than anyone else. These include the John Muir Trail in the High Sierra, Muir Gorge in Yosemite, Muir Pass in Kings Canyon Park, and Muir Grove in Sequoia National Park.

Muir's adventures began when he dropped out of the University of Wisconsin to experience the natural world he had been studying in botany and geology classes. He wouldn't have received a degree anyway—he had refused to follow the school's curriculum.

These descriptions come from one of his books, The Mountains of California.

Arriving by the Panama steamer, I stopped one day in San Francisco and then inquired for the nearest way out of town. "But where do you want to go?" asked the man to whom I had applied for this important information. "To any place that is wild," I said. This reply startled him. He seemed to fear I might be crazy and therefore the sooner I was out of town the better, so he directed me to the Oakland ferry.

So on the first of April, 1868, I set out afoot for Yosemite. It was the bloom-time of the year over the lowlands and coast ranges; the landscapes of the Santa Clara Valley were fairly drenched with sunshine, all the air was quivering with the songs of the meadow-larks, and the hills were so covered with flowers that they seemed to be painted. Slow indeed was my progress through these glorious gardens, the first of the California flora I had seen. Cattle and cultivation were making few scars as yet, and I wandered enchanted in long wavering curves, knowing by my pocket map that Yosemite Valley lay to the east and that I should surely find it.

Looking eastward from the summit of the Pacheco Pass one shining morning, a landscape was displayed that after all my wanderings still appears as the most beautiful I have ever beheld. At my feet lay the Great Central Valley of California, level and flowery, like a lake of pure sunshine, forty or fifty miles wide, five hundred miles long, one rich furred garden of yellow Compositæ. And from the eastern boundary of this vast golden flower-bed rose the mighty Sierra, miles in height, and so gloriously colored and so radiant, it seemed not clothed with light, but wholly composed of it, like the wall of some celestial city.

Along the top and extending a good way down, was a rich pearl-gray belt of snow; below it a belt of blue and dark purple, marking the extension of the forests; and stretching along the base of the range a broad belt of rose-purple; all these colors, from the blue sky to the yellow valley smoothly blending as they do in a rainbow, making a wall of light ineffably fine.

Then it seemed to me that the Sierra should be called, not the Nevada or Snowy Range, but the Range of Light. And after ten years of wandering and wondering in the heart of it, rejoicing in its glorious floods of light, the white beams of the morning streaming through the passes, the noonday radiance on the crystal rocks, the flush of the alpenglow, and the irised spray of countless waterfalls, it still seems above all others the Range of Light.

In general views no mark of man is visible upon it, nor anything to suggest the wonderful depth and grandeur of its sculpture. . . . Nevertheless the whole range five hundred miles long is furrowed with cañons 2,000 to 5,000 feet deep, in which once flowed majestic glaciers, and in which now flow and sing the bright rejoicing rivers. . . .

The most famous and accessible of these cañon valleys, and also the one that presents their most striking and sublime features on the grandest scale, is the Yosemite, situated in the basin of the Merced River at an elevation of 4,000 feet above the level of the sea. It is about seven miles long, half a mile to a mile wide, and nearly a mile deep in the solid granite flank of the range. The walls are made up of rocks, mountains in size, partly separated from each other by side cañons, and they are so sheer in front, and so compactly and harmoniously arranged on a level floor, that the Valley, comprehensively seen, looks like an immense hall or temple lighted from above.

But no temple made with hands can compare with Yosemite. Every rock in its walls seems to glow with life. Some lean back in majestic repose; others, absolutely sheer or nearly so for thousands of feet, advance beyond their companions in thoughtful attitudes, giving welcome to storms and calms alike, seemingly aware, yet heedless, of everything going on about them. Awful in stern, immovable majesty, how softly these rocks are adorned, and how fine and reassuring the company they keep: their feet among beautiful groves and meadows, their brows in the sky, a thousand flowers leaning confidingly against their feet, bathed in floods of water, floods of light, while the snow and waterfalls, the winds and avalanches and clouds shine and sing and wreathe about them as the years go by, and myriads of small winged creatures—birds, bees, butterflies—give glad animation and help to make all the air into music.

Down through the middle of the Valley flows the crystal Merced, River of Mercy, peacefully quiet, reflecting lilies and trees and the onlooking rocks; things frail and fleeting and types of endurance meeting here and blending in countless forms, as if into this one mountain mansion Nature had gathered her choicest treasures, to draw her lovers into close and confiding communion with her.

Though Muir lived in and traveled through the wilderness for most of his life, he was more than a frontiersman. In 1892 he organized the Sierra Club, and his lobbying efforts helped secure Yosemite's protection as the first national park.

"These looks like a trifle hardley worth speakeing off...."

LEVI'S

July 2, 1872
San Francisco

JACOB W. DAVIS

Jacob W. Davis, a tailor in Reno, Nevada, invented a new kind of trousers by using rivets to secure the pockets and seams. But he couldn't patent the idea, because his wife said he had already spent too much money on his previous inventions, a steam-powered canal boat and a steam-powered ore crusher. Davis decided to seek help from his denim supplier, San Francisco's Levi Strauss & Co. At that time Strauss & Co. was a store rather than a manufacturer, a four-story emporium with traveling salesmen that reached miners at the diggings.

Davis may have been literate in his native Yiddish, but this letter was drafted by Reno's pharmacist.

I also send you by Express 2 ps. Overall as you will see one Blue and one made of the 10 oz Duck which I have bought in greate many Peces of you, and have made it up in to Pents, such as the sample.

The secratt of them Pents is the Rivits that I put in those Pockets and I found the demand so large that I cannot make them up fast enough. I charge for the Duck $3.00 and the Blue $2.50 a pear. My nabors are getting yealouse of these success and unless I secure it by Patent Papers it will soon become a general thing. Everybody will make them up and thare will be no money in it.

Therefore Gentleman, I wish to make you a Proposition that you should take out the Latters Patent in my name as I am the inventor of it, the expense of it will be about $68, all complit and for these $68 will give you half the right to sell all such clothing Revited according to the Patent, for all the Pacific States and Teroterious, the balince of the United States and half of the Pacific Coast I resarve for myself. The investment for you is but a trifle compaired with the improvement in all Coarse Clothing. I use it in all Blankit Clothing such as Coats, Vests and Pents, and you will find it a very salable article at a much advenst rate. . . .

These looks like a trifle hardley worth speakeing off but nevertheless I knew you can make a very large amount of money on it. If you make up Pents the way I do you can sell Duck Pents such as the Sample at $30. per doz. and they will readly retail for $3. a pair.

Strauss decided he would take a chance and started manufacturing rather than just retailing. He must have been convinced by the prices Davis claimed to receive for his new pants, which were about three times the going rate for a regular pair. Davis moved his family to San Francisco to manage production.

In the company's first century, more than 100 million pairs of Levi's pants were sold. The Battery Street offices to which Davis sent the letter is near the site of today's Levi's Plaza, headquarters of one of the most famous brand names in American culture.

"*. . . I could not remember a single word.*"

BUFFALO BILL TAKES THE STAGE

1872
Chicago

WILLIAM F. CODY

William F. "Buffalo Bill" Cody had been an Indian scout, trapper, miner, and Pony Express rider before receiving his nickname, which he was given when hunting buffalo to feed the men building the Kansas Pacific railroad. When his fame grew, his friend Ned Buntline, an adventurer and bestselling author, convinced him to take the stage. Buntline had already made Cody the hero of dime novels, so he knew Cody's marquee value.

Cody went to Chicago with J. B. "Texas Jack" Omohundro—also the hero of dime novels—and Buntline rented a theater for a play, not yet written, which would open just a few days later, before his friends could change their minds.

"Now, come with me boys," said Buntline; and away we went to the hotel. Buntline immediately obtained a supply of pens, ink and paper, and then engaged all the hotel clerks as penmen. In less than an hour after he had rented the theater, he was dashing off page after page of his proposed drama—the work being done in his room at the hotel. He then set his clerks at copying for him, and at the end of four hours, he jumped up from the table, and enthusiastically shouted:

"Hurrah for *The Scouts of the Plains!* That's the name of the play. The work is done. Hurrah!"

The parts were then all copied off separately by the clerks, and handing us our respective portions Buntline said:

"Now, boys, go to work, and do your level best to have this dead-letter perfect for the rehearsal, which takes place to-morrow morning at ten o'clock, prompt. I want to show [theater owner] Nixon that we'll be ready on time."

I looked at my part and then at Jack; and Jack looked at his part and then at me. Then we looked at each other, and then at Buntline. We did not know what to make of the man.

"How long will it take you to commit your part to memory, Bill?" asked Jack.

"About six months, as near as I can calculate. How long will it take you?" answered I.

"It will take me about that length of time to learn the first line," said Jack.

Nevertheless we went to our room and commenced studying. I thought it was the hardest work I had ever done.

"This is dry business," finally remarked Jack.

"That's just what it is," I answered. "Jerk the bell, Jack." The bell-boy soon appeared. We ordered refreshments. . . .

When Monday night came we didn't know much more about it than when we began.

The clock struck seven, and then we put on our buckskin suits, which were the costumes we were to appear in. The theater was being rapidly filled, and it was evident that we were going to make our debut before a packed house. As the minutes passed by, Jack and I became more and more nervous. We occasionally looked through the holes in the curtain, and saw that the people were continuing to crowd into the theatre; our nervousness increased to an uncomfortable degree.

When at length the curtain arose, our courage had returned, so that we thought we could face the immense crowd; yet when the time came for us to go on, we were rather slow in making our appearance. As we stepped forth we were received with a storm of applause, which we acknowledged with a bow.

Buntline, who was taking the part of "Cale Durg," appeared, and gave me the "cue" to speak "my little piece," but for the life of me I could not remember a single word.

Buntline saw I was "stuck," and a happy thought occurred to him. He said—as if it were in the play:

"Where have you been, Bill? What has kept you so long?"

Just then my eye happened to fall on Mr. Milligan [a Chicago businessman recently returned from hunting with Bill out west], who was surrounded by his friends, the newspaper reporters, and several military officers, all of whom had heard of his hunt and "Indian fight"—he being a very popular man and widely known in Chicago. So I said:

"I have been out on a hunt with Milligan."

This proved to be a big hit. The audience cheered and applauded; which gave me greater confidence in my ability to get through the performance all right. Buntline, who is a very versatile man, saw that it would be a good plan to follow this up, and he said:

"Well, Bill, tell us all about the hunt."

I thereupon proceeded to relate in detail the particulars of the affair. I succeeded in making it rather funny, and I was frequently interrupted by rounds of applause. Whenever I began to "weaken," Buntline would give me a fresh start, by asking some question. In this way I took up fifteen minutes, without once speaking a word of my part; nor did I speak a word of it during the whole evening. . . . The next morning there appeared in the Chicago papers some very funny criticisms on our first performance. The papers gave us a better send-off than I expected, for they did not criticise us as actors. The *Chicago Times* said that if Buntline had actually spent four hours in writing that play, it was difficult for any one to see what he had been doing all the time.

Despite the opening-night jitters, the play was a hit in Chicago, St. Louis, and New York, starting Cody on his second career as a showman. About a decade later he created Buffalo Bill's Wild West Show, which toured America and Europe for many years.

"The swimmers pose themselves on the highest edge...."

"SURF-BATHING"

1873
Hilo Beach, Hawaii

ISABELLA BIRD

Ignoring convention, Isabella Bird, the first woman member of the Royal Geographic Society, explored remote parts of Hawaii without an escort.

This account comes from Bird's book, Six Months Among the Palm Groves, Reefs, and Volcanoes of the Sandwich Islands. *("The Sandwich Islands" was the name used by Captain James Cook when he encountered Hawaii in 1778.)*

Let us stand on the Hilo beach, and witness an exhibition of the national sport of surf-bathing, a most exciting pastime, and needing, in a heavy sea, immense nerve and skill. The surf-board is a plank shaped like a coffin-lid, from six to nine feet in length. Legions of forms, moulded with the lithe and sinuous beauty of classic bronzes, are seen sporting in the waves like born denizens of the foam. A party of forty or fifty, with their surf-sliding boards, come out from the dusky throng, and, with much laughing chatter, prepare for the fascinating game of riding astride the breakers.

Wading out from rocks on which the sea is breaking, the islanders push their boards before them, and swim out to the first line of breakers. Suddenly they dive down out of sight, and nothing more is seen of them till their black heads bob up from the smooth seas like corks, half a mile from shore. Now the fun commences.

Watching for a very high roller, they leap on from behind, lying face downward on their surf-boards. As the wave speeds on, and its bottom touches ground, the top curls into a gigantic comber. The swimmers pose themselves on the highest edge by dexterous movement of hand and foot, keeping themselves at the top of the curl, and always seeming to slide down the foaming hillock. So they come on majestically just ahead of the breaker, borne shoreward by its mighty impulse at the rate of forty miles an hour, yet seeming to have a volition of their own, for the more daring riders kneel and even stand on their surf-boards, waving their arms and uttering exultant cries. Always on the verge of engulfment by the fierce breaker, whose white crest rises above them, just as one expects to see them dashed to pieces on the rocks, they quietly disappear, and emerge again out at sea, ready for another perilous race on their foaming coursers. The great art is in mounting the breaker at just the right time, and to keep exactly on its curl. The leading athletes are always vociferously cheered by the spectators, and the presence of the elite rarely fails to stimulate the swimmers to their utmost exertions. Even the maidens and old men often join in this national amusement. Such is Hawaiian life at Hilo.

Hawaii was still independent when Bird visited, although its constitutional monarchy was heavily under the influence of American missionaries. When the monarchy was overthrown at the end of the nineteenth century, the U.S. annexed Hawaii.

"The night before the hunt, my father instructed me. . . ."

A FIRST BUFFALO HUNT

about 1875
Nebraska

LUTHER STANDING BEAR

Author Luther Standing Bear, an Oglala Sioux, wrote several books that combined history and ethnography with personal memoir. This account comes from My People, The Sioux.

A scout had been sent out, and one morning, very early, he reported that there were some buffalo near. Everybody, including myself, began to get ready. While one of my stepmothers was helping me, she said, "Son, when you kill a buffalo, save me the kidney and the skin." I didn't know whether she was trying to poke fun at me or to give me encouragement. But it made me feel proud to have her talk like that to me.

But my father always talked to me as if I were a man. Of course I now felt that I was big enough to do a man's work. The night before the hunt, my father instructed me as follows:

"My son, the land on which these buffalo have been found is reported not to be rough, and you will not have to chase the buffalo into dangerous places, as the land is very level. Whatever you do, watch the buffalo closely. If the one you are after is running straight ahead and not turning, then you can get in very close, and you will stand a good chance to shoot it in the heart. But if you observe the buffalo to be looking at you from the corner of its eye, then look out! They are very quick and powerful. They can get their horns under your horse and toss him high in the air, and you might get killed.

"If you hit in the right spot, you may kill the buffalo with only one arrow, but if not, you will have to use more. If your pony is not fast enough to catch up with the buffalo, the best thing you can do is to shoot an arrow right behind the small ribs. Perhaps it will reach the heart. If the buffalo runs down a hill or into a bank, then you have another chance. Shoot at the joint of the hips, then your buffalo will sit down and you can take your time to kill it.

"Keep your eyes open! In the beginning there will be lots of dust, but after you pass through that, it will be clear, and you will be able to see where you are going."

This was the first time I was to go on a hunt after such large animals. I had killed several small animals, but a buffalo is far from being a small creature, and you can imagine that I was greatly excited.

Early the next morning every one was ready for the start. I carried my bow in my hand, as there was not room for it in my quiver where I kept my arrows. I rode a little black mare, a very fine runner that could cover the ground like a deer. Two men on beautiful horses rode in front of us. This was for the purpose of keeping order in the party. There was no chance of one man getting ahead of the others and scaring the game. We all had to keep together and stay behind these men.

They rode to the top of a hill where they could get a good look at the herd and figure if there was any better place from which to approach it. We always got as close to the buffalo as possible, because it makes the meat tough to run an animal any farther than necessary.

After looking at the herd from various positions, they chose what was considered the most advantageous spot. Here they cautioned the hunters to change to their running-horses and be all ready. I did not have to make any change, as the little black mare was all the animal I had. I saw some of the men tying their two braids of hair back, and others, who wore shirts, began rolling up their sleeves. They wanted their arrows free once they began shooting. They fixed their quivers on the side instead of carrying them on the back. Nobody wore any feathers or carried any spears or lances.

The extra horses were hobbled and left in the charge of an old man. When the two riders gave the command, everybody started right up. Of course I was right at the front with them. I wanted to do something brave. I depended a great deal on my pony, as I knew she was surefooted and could run as I wanted her to.

At the top of the hill, all the hunters turned their horses loose, and the animals started in running like the wind! I whipped up my little black mare and nearly got ahead of the others. Soon I was mixed up in the dust and could see nothing ahead of me. All I could hear was the roar and rattle of the hoofs of the buffalo as they thundered along. My pony shied this way and that, and I had to hold on for dear life.

For a time I did not even try to pull an arrow from my quiver, as I had all I could do to take care of myself. I knew if my pony went down and one of those big animals stepped on me, it would be my last day on earth. I then realized how helpless I was there in all that dust and confusion, with those ponderous buffalo all around me. The sound of their hoofs was frightening. My pony ran like the wind, while I just clung to her mane; but presently we came out of the dust.

Then I observed what my father had told me previously. I was quite a bit ahead of the buffalo now, and when they caught sight of me, they started running in two different directions. When I looked at those big animals and thought of trying to kill one of them, I realized how small I was. I was really afraid of them. Then I thought about what my stepmother had said to me about bringing her a kidney and a skin, and the feeling that I was a man, after all, came back to me; so I turned my pony toward the bunch which was running north. There was no dust now, and I knew where I was going.

I was all alone and I was determined to chase them, whether I killed one or not. By this time I could hear shots fired by some of the hunters who carried guns, and I knew they were killing some. So I rode on after this small bunch, and when I dashed behind them, I pulled out one of my arrows and shot into the middle of them. I did not even know where my arrow went, and was just thinking of quitting when I observed a young heifer running slower than the others.

This encouraged me, so I whipped up my pony again and took after her. As I came in close, she stopped and turned. Then she started running in another direction, but I saw she was losing fast. She was not as big as the others, so I was not afraid. I made up my mind I was going to kill that buffalo if it took all the arrows in my quiver.

I rode right up alongside the buffalo, just as my father had instructed me. Drawing an arrow from my quiver, and holding to my pony with all the strength of my legs, I fitted the arrow and let drive with all my strength. I had expected to kill the buffalo right quick, but the arrow went into the neck—and I thought I had taken such good aim! But the buffalo only shook her head and kept on running. I again caught up with her, and let another arrow loose, which struck near the heart. Although it was not fired with sufficient strength to kill at once, I saw that she was fast weakening and running much slower. Then I pulled my third arrow and fired again. This went into the heart. I began to think that buffalo had all the nine lives of a cat, and was going to prove about as hard as a cat to kill, when I saw blood running from her nose. Then I knew she would have to drop pretty soon. I shot my fourth arrow into her, and she staggered and dropped over on her side, and was soon dead. So I had killed my first buffalo.

When I examined the fallen animal and noted that I had shot five arrows into her, I felt that this was too many arrows for just one buffalo. Then I recalled that my father had once killed two buffalo with only a single arrow. He knew he had hit the first one in the right spot, as the arrow penetrated very deeply and he simply rode up alongside, drew the arrow through, pulled it out again and used it to kill the second one.

As I stood there thinking of this, it made me feel ashamed of my marksmanship. I began to think of pulling all the arrows out but one. In fact, I had started to do this, when a remark that my father had once made to me came into my head. It was, "Son, always remember that a man who tells lies is never liked by anybody." So, instead of trying to cheat, I told the truth; and it made me feel happier.

I took all the arrows out and started in to skin the buffalo. I was doing splendidly until I tried to turn the animal over. Then I discovered that it was too heavy a task for me. As I had but one side skinned I began to think of removing the kidney and cutting out a nice piece of meat for my stepmother. Just then I heard someone call me. I got on my pony and rode to the top of the hill. There I saw my father, who had been looking for me. He called to me, but I just rode back to my buffalo. He knew something had happened, so came over, and then I pointed to the dead buffalo, lying there half-skinned.

He was so pleased that I had tried to do my best. Then I told him about the number of arrows I had had to use, and where each one had struck. I even told him how I had shot my first arrow into the whole bunch, not knowing where it had landed. He laughed, but he was proud of me. I guess it was because I had told the truth, and not tried to cheat or lie, even though I was just a youngster.

Then Father started in on my buffalo. He soon had it all skinned and butchered. He said he had been all ready to go home when he discovered I was missing. He had thought I was with my grandfather, while Grandfather thought I was with him. All that time I was having a hard job all by myself. When we reached home it made me very proud to be able to give my stepmother the skin and kidney. And she was pleased that I had done so well.

My father called the old man of the camp, who always acted as herald, to announce that "Ota Kte" ["Plenty Kill," the boyhood name of Chief Standing Bear] had shot his first buffalo, and that "Standing Bear," his father, was giving away a horse.

". . . I showed my mother my first scalp. . . ."

CUSTER'S LAST STAND

June 25–26, 1876
Little Bighorn, Dakota Territory

BLACK ELK

In 1875, when gold was discovered in the Black Hills, prospectors rushed in. The U.S. government had agreed to reserve the area, a holy land of the Cheyenne and Sioux, but even the army could not stop the flood of prospectors. The Sioux decided to fight, and the army was now opposing them. Sentiment against the Indians ran high in the centennial year, as national pride inflated the rhetoric of manifest destiny; many politicians called for the annihilation of the Indians, and in the Black Hills the army was given permission to kill any found outside the reservation.

The most famous enemy of the Indians, thanks in part to his hunger for publicity, was George Armstrong Custer, lieutenant colonel of the Seventh Cavalry. Papers in the east ran innumerable stories about his colorful campaigns. One tabloid even paid him under the table for exclusive stories.

In June 1876, Custer's Seventh and other troops under the command of General Alfred Terry encountered the largest gathering of Indians ever seen: 10,000 to 15,000 Cheyenne and Sioux, from several different tribes, filled an area that stretched for three miles along the Little Bighorn River. Custer foolishly attacked before the rest of Terry's command was in position, leading fewer than seven hundred men against the Indians.

Eyewitness Black Elk was a Sioux holy man. In 1930 he recounted the scene to anthropologist John Neihardt in the memoir Black Elk Speaks.

My father woke me at daybreak and told me to go with him to take our horses out to graze, and when we were out there he said: "We must have a long rope on one of them, so that it will be easy to catch; then we can get the others. If anything happens, you must bring the horses back as fast as you can, and keep your eyes on the camp." Several of us boys watched our horses together until the sun was straight above and it was getting very hot. Then we thought we would go swimming, and my cousin said he would stay with our horses till we got back. When I was greasing my self, I did not feel well; I felt queer. It seemed that something terrible was going to happen. But I went with the boys anyway. Many people were in the water now and many of the women were out west of the village digging turnips. We had been in the water quite a while when my cousin came down there with the horses to give them a drink, for it was very hot now.

Just then we heard the crier shouting in the Hunkpapa camp, which was not very far from us "The chargers are coming! They are charging! The chargers are coming!" Then the crier of the Ogalalas shouted the same words; and we could hear the cry going from camp to camp northward clear to the Santees and Yanktonais.

Everybody was running now to catch the horses. We were lucky to have ours right there just at that time. My older brother had a sorrel, and he rode away fast toward the Hunkpapas. I had a buckskin. My father came running and said: "Your brother has gone to the Hunkpapas without his gun. Catch him and give it to him. Then come right back to me." He had my six-shooter too—the one my aunt gave me.

I took the guns, jumped on my pony and caught my brother. I could see a big dust rising just beyond the Hunkpapa camp and all the Hunkpapas were running around and yelling, and many were running wet from the river.

Then out of the dust came the soldiers on their big horses. They looked big and strong and tall and they were all shooting. My brother took his gun and yelled for me to go back. There was brushy timber just on the other side of the Hunkpapas, and some warriors were gathering there. He made for that place, and I followed him. By now women and children were running in a crowd downstream. I looked back and saw them all running and scattering up a hillside down yonder.

When we got into the timber, a good many Hunkpapas were there already and the soldiers were shooting above us so that leaves were falling from the trees where the bullets struck. By now I could not see what was happening in the village below. It was all dust and cries and thunder; for the women and children were running there, and the warriors were coming on their ponies.

Among us there in the brush and out in the Hunkpapa camp a cry went up: "Take courage! Don't be a woman! The helpless are out of breath!" I think this was when Gall stopped the Hunkpapas, who had been running away, and turned them back.

I stayed there in the woods a little while and thought of my vision. It made me feel stronger, and it seemed that my people were all thunder-beings and that the soldiers would be rubbed out.

Then another great cry went up out in the dust:

"Crazy Horse is coming! Crazy Horse is coming!" Off toward the west and north they were yelling "Hoka hey!" like a big wind roaring, and making the tremolo; and you could hear eagle bone whistles screaming.

The valley went darker with dust and smoke, and there were only shadows and a big noise of many cries and hoofs and guns. On the left of where I was I could hear the shod hoofs of the soldiers' horses going back into the brush and there was shooting everywhere. Then the hoofs came out of the brush, and I came out and was in among men and horses weaving in and out and going upstream, and everybody was yelling, "Hurry! Hurry!" The soldiers were running upstream and we were all mixed there in the twilight and the great noise. I did not see much; but once I saw a Lakota charge at a soldier who stayed behind and fought and was a very brave man. The Lakota took the soldier's horse by the bridle, but the soldier killed him with a six-shooter. I was small and could not crowd in to where the soldiers were, so I did not kill anybody. There were so many ahead of me, and it was all dark and mixed up.

Soon the soldiers were all crowded into the river, and many Lakotas too; and I was in the water awhile. Men and horses were all mixed up and fighting in the water, and it was like hail falling in the river. Then we were out of the river, and people were stripping dead soldiers and putting the clothes on themselves. There was a soldier on the ground and he was still kicking. A Lakota rode up and said to me: "Boy, get off and scalp him." I got off and started to do it. He had short hair and my knife was not very sharp. He ground his teeth. Then I shot him in the forehead and got his scalp.

Many of our warriors were following the soldiers up a hill on the other side of the river. Everybody else was turning back down stream, and on a hill away down yonder above the Santee camp there was a big dust, and our warriors whirling around in and out of it just like swallows, and many guns were going off.

I thought I would show my mother my scalp, so I rode over toward the hill where there was a crowd of women and children. On the way down there I saw a very pretty young woman among a band of warriors about to go up to the battle on the hill, and she was singing like this:

"Brothers, now your friends have come! Be brave! Be brave! Would you see me taken captive?"

When I rode through the Ogalala camp I saw Rattling Hawk sitting up in his tepee with a gun in his hands, and he was all alone there singing a song of regret that went like this:

"Brothers, what are you doing that I can not do?"

When I got to the women on the hill they were all singing and making the tremolo to cheer the men fighting across the river in the dust on the hill. My mother gave a big tremolo just for me when she saw my first scalp.

I stayed there awhile with my mother and watched the big dust whirling on the hill across the river, and horses were coming out of it with empty saddles.

Historians still debate why Custer attacked. He had been removed from his post a few years earlier, when he testified to Congress about corruption in the army, and may have been eager to prove himself with an act of courage. Or he may have been, as some historians have suggested, a publicity seeker who lacked military skill and simply bungled. Either way, 200 men including Custer were slaughtered.

"The line of railway stretched from horizon to horizon...."

NEBRASKA

1879

ROBERT LOUIS STEVENSON

British novelist Stevenson traveled across America to see his American fiancée, Fanny Osbourne, who lived in California. He wrote about the experience in Across the Plains.

It had thundered on the Friday night, but the sun rose on Saturday without a cloud. We were at sea—there is no other adequate expression—on the plains of Nebraska.

I made my observatory on the top of a fruit-waggon, and sat by the hour upon that perch to spy about me, and to spy in vain for something new. It was a world almost without a feature; an empty sky, an empty earth; front and back, the line of railway stretched from horizon to horizon, like a cue across a billiard-board; on either hand, the green plain ran till it touched the skirts of heaven.

Along the track innumerable wild sunflowers, no bigger than a crown-piece, bloomed in a continuous flower-bed; grazing beasts were seen upon the prairie at all degrees of distance and diminution; and, now and again we might perceive a few dots beside the railroad which grew more and more distinct as we drew nearer till they turned into wooden cabins, and then dwindled and dwindled in our wake until they melted into their surroundings, and we were once more alone upon the billiard-board.

The train toiled over this infinity like a snail; and being the one thing moving, it was wonderful what huge proportions it began to assume in our regard. It seemed miles in length, and either end of it within but a step of the horizon. Even my own body or my own head seemed a great thing in that emptiness. I note the feeling the more readily as it is the contrary of what I have read of in the experience of others. Day and night, above the roar of the train, our ears were kept busy with the incessant chirp of grasshoppers—a noise like the winding up of countless clocks and watches, which began after a while to seem proper to that land.

To one hurrying through by steam there was a certain exhilaration in this spacious vacancy, this greatness of the air, this discovery of the whole arch of heaven, this straight, unbroken, prison-line of the horizon. Yet one could not but reflect upon the weariness of those who passed by there in old days, at the foot's pace of oxen, painfully urging their teams, and with no landmark but that unattainable evening sun for which they steered, and which daily fled them by an equal stride. They had nothing, it would seem, to overtake; nothing by which to reckon their advance; no sight for repose or for encouragement; but stage after stage, only the dead green waste under foot, and the mocking, fugitive horizon.

But the eye, as I have been told, found differences even here; and at the worst the emigrant came, by perseverance, to the end of his toil. It is the settlers, after all, at whom we have a right to marvel. Our consciousness, by which we live, is itself but the creature of variety. Upon what food does it subsist in such a land? What livelihood can repay a human creature for a life spent in this huge sameness? He is cut off from books, from news, from company, from all that can relieve existence but the prosecution of his affairs. A sky full of stars is the most varied spectacle that he can hope. He may walk five miles and see nothing; ten, and it is as though he had not moved; twenty, and still he is in the midst of the same great level, and has approached no nearer to the one object within view, the flat horizon which keeps pace with his advance.

We are full at home of the question of agreeable wall-papers, and wise people are of opinion that the temper may be quieted by sedative surroundings. But what is to be said of the Nebraskan settler? His is a wall-paper with a vengeance—one quarter of the universe laid bare in all its gauntness. His eye must embrace at every glance the whole seeming concave of the visible world; it quails before so vast an outlook, it is tortured by distance; yet there is no rest or shelter, till the man runs into his cabin, and can repose his sight upon things near at hand.

"He came directly towards me. . . ."

PAT GARRETT HUNTS BILLY THE KID

July 15, 1881
Fort Sumner, New Mexico Territory

PAT GARRETT

According to legend, William Bonney, aka "Billy the Kid," killed his first victim when he was twelve years old. He was certainly living a life of crime by then. He was still a teenager when he enjoyed the mayhem of the 1878 Lincoln County War, a glorified gang rumble among cattlemen. After the war, he continued to rustle cattle. Caught in 1880 by Sheriff Pat Garrett, Billy was convicted of murdering a lawman and sentenced to hang. He then made a daring escape, killing two guards, and the hunt was on again.

During the weeks following The Kid's escape, I was censured by some for my seeming unconcern and inactivity in the matter of his re-arrest. I was egotistical enough to think I knew my own business best, and preferred to accomplish this duty, if possible at all, in my own way. I was constantly, but quietly, at work, seeking sure information and maturing my plans of action. I did not lay about The Kid's old haunts, nor disclose my intentions and operations to any one. I stayed at home, most of the time, and busied myself about the ranch.

If my seeming unconcern deceived the people and gave The Kid confidence in his security, my end was accomplished.

It was my belief that The Kid was still in the country and haunted the vicinity of Fort Sumner; yet there was some doubt mingled with my belief. He was never taken for a fool, but was credited with the possession of extraordinary forethought and cool judgment, for one of his age. It seemed incredible that, in his situation, with the extreme penalty of the law, the reward of detection, and the way of successful flight and safety open to him—with no known tie to bind him to that dangerous locality,—it seemed incredible that he should linger in the Territory. My first task was to solve my doubts.

Early in July I received a reply from a letter I had written to Mr. Brazil. I was at Lincoln when this letter came to me. Mr. Brazil was dodging and hiding from The Kid. He feared his vengeance on account of the part which he, Brazil, had taken in his capture. There were many others who "trembled in their boots" at the knowledge of his escape; but most of them talked him out of his resentment, or conciliated him in some manner.

Brazil's letter gave me no positive information. He said he had not seen The Kid since his escape, but, from many indications, believed he was still in the country. He offered me any assistance in his power to recapture him. I again wrote to Brazil, requesting him to meet me at the mouth of Tayban Arroyo, an hour after dark, on the night of the 13th day of July.

[With two deputies, I] went to Roswell, and started up the Rio Pecos from there on the night of July 10th. We rode mostly in the night, followed no roads, but taking unfrequented routes, and arrived at the mouth of Tayban Arroyo, five miles south of Fort Sumner, one hour after dark, on the night of the 13th. Brazil was not there. We waited nearly two hours, but he did not come. We rode off a mile or two, staked our horses and slept until daylight. Early in the morning we rode up into the hills and prospected awhile with our field-glasses.

I then concluded to go and have a talk with Peter Maxwell, Esq., in whom I felt sure I could rely. We had ridden to within a short distance of Maxwell's grounds, when we found a man in camp, and stopped. To Poe's surprise, he recognized in the camper an old friend and former partner, in Texas, named Jacobs. We unsaddled here, got some coffee, and, on foot, entered an orchard which runs from this point down to a row of old buildings, some of them occupied by Mexicans, not more than sixty yards from Maxwell's house.

We approached these houses cautiously, and when within ear shot, heard the sound of voices conversing in Spanish. We concealed ourselves quickly and listened; but the distance was too great to hear words, or even distinguish voices.

Soon a man arose from the ground, in full view, but too far away to recognize. He wore a broad-brimmed hat, a dark vest and pants, and was in his shirtsleeves. With a few words, which fell like a murmur on our ears, he went to the fence, jumped it, and walked down towards Maxwell's house.

Little as we then suspected it, this man was The Kid. We learned, subsequently, that when he left his companions that night, he went to the house of a Mexican friend, pulled off his hat and boots, threw himself on a bed and commenced reading a newspaper. He soon, however, hailed his friend, who was sleeping in the room, told him to get up and make some coffee, adding:——"Give me a butcher knife and I will go over to Pete's and get some beef; I'm hungry." The Mexican arose, handed him the knife, and The Kid, hatless and in his stocking feet, started to Maxwell, which was but a few steps distant.

When the Kid, by me unrecognized, left the orchard, I motioned to my companions, and we cautiously retreated a short distance, and, to avoid the persons whom we had heard at the houses, took another route, approaching Maxwell's house from the opposite direction.

When we reached the porch in front of the building, I left Poe and McKinney at the end of the porch, about twenty feet from the door of Pete's room, and went in. It was near midnight and Pete was in bed. I walked to the head of the bed and sat down on it, beside him, near the pillow. I asked him as to the whereabouts of The Kid.

He said that The Kid had certainly been about, but he did not know whether he had left or not. At that moment a man sprang quickly into the door, looking back, and called twice in Spanish, "Who comes there?" No one replied and he came on in. He was bareheaded. From his step I could perceive he was either barefooted or in his stocking-feet, and held a revolver in his right hand and a butcher knife in his left.

He came directly towards me. Before he reached the bed, I whispered: "Who is it, Pete?" but received no reply for a moment. The intruder came close to me, leaned both hands on the bed, his right hand almost touching my knee, and asked, in a low tone:——"Who are they Pete?"—at the same instant Maxwell whispered to me. "That's him!"

Simultaneously The Kid . . . raised quickly his pistol, a self-cocker, within a foot of my breast. Retreating rapidly across the room he cried: "*Quien es? Quien es?*" (Who's that? Who's that?) All this occurred in a moment.

Quickly as possible I drew my revolver and fired, threw my body aside and fired again. The second shot was useless; The Kid fell dead. He never spoke. A struggle or two, a little strangling sound as he gasped for breath, and The Kid was with his many victims.

Bonney, just shy of his twenty-second birthday when Garrett caught him for the second and last time, had murdered a man for every year of his life.

". . . They would be sure to shoot me. . . ."

LEADVILLE

OSCAR WILDE

The mining town of Leadville, in central Colorado, once had the second-largest population in the state. It rode the boom-and-bust rollercoaster three times, starting with the discovery of gold in the area in 1860. Within two years the gold was mined out, and the diggings were abandoned. But in 1877, prospectors discovered lead with a high silver content, and the town grew to a boisterous 40,000 people. It went bust again in 1893, when the U.S. government stopped backing the dollar with silver. But the story wasn't over. More gold was soon discovered.

The Irish writer Oscar Wilde stopped there during a lecture tour.

From Salt Lake City one travels over the great plains of Colorado and up the Rocky Mountains, on the top of which is Leadville, the richest city in the world. It has also got the reputation of being the roughest, and every man carries a revolver. I was told that if I went there they would be sure to shoot me or my traveling manager. I wrote and told them that nothing they could do to my traveling manager would intimidate me.

They were miners—men working in metals—so I lectured to them on the Ethics of Art. I read them passages from the autobiography of Benvenuto Cellini and they seemed much delighted. I was reproved by my hearers for not having brought him with me. I explained that he had been dead for some time, which elicited the inquiry, "Who shot him?"

They afterwards took me to a dancing saloon where I saw the only rational method of art criticism I have ever come across. Over the piano was printed a notice:

PLEASE DO NOT SHOOT THE PIANIST.

HE IS DOING HIS BEST.

The mortality among pianists in that place is marvelous.

Then they asked me to supper, and having accepted, I had to descend a mine in a rickety bucket in which it was impossible to be graceful. Having got into the heart of the mountain, I had supper, the first course being whiskey, the second whiskey and the third whiskey.

I went to the Theatre to lecture and I was informed that just before I went there two men had been seized for committing murder, and in that theatre they had been brought on to the stage at eight o'clock in the evening and then and there tried and executed before a crowded audience. But I found these miners very charming and not at all rough.

Leadville's mines provided the outsized fortune of Margaret Tobin Brown, who had a flamboyant personality to match. She proved as lucky as the town itself when she survived the Titanic *disaster in 1912. "We're unsinkable," she told reporters. The Unsinkable Mrs. Brown became an international celebrity.*

"We want to tell you something about this Hopi land. . . ."

ALLOTMENT

1887
Arizona

HOPI CLAN CHIEFS

The long-running cultural battle between the communal land claims of various Indian tribes and the individual land deeds of the new settlers ended with a plan called "allotment." By an act of Congress, tribal lands were surveyed and parceled to individual Indian families in 160-acre lots.

The politics behind the plan were complicated. Although it meant the end of a traditional Indian lifestyle, some of its strongest supporters were Indian rights advocates, who hoped a land deed would ensure legal protection.

Many clans were divided on the question of accepting it. Some people agreed with U.S. Senator Henry Teller: "The real aim is to get at the Indians' lands and open them up for resettlement." But some believed that the communal title could not be defended anyway, and allotment would prevent a wholesale loss of land.

The General Allotment Act passed easily in 1887. The following petition, signed by 123 Hopi clan chiefs from Arizona, was written in 1894, after the government had surveyed the land in preparation for the final allotment.

To the Washington Chiefs:
During the last two years strangers have looked over our land with spy-glasses and made marks upon it, and we know but little of what it means. As we believe that you have no wish to disturb our Possessions, we want to tell you something about this Hopi land.

None of us wer[e] asked that it should be measured into separate lots, and given to individuals for they would cause confusion.

The family, the dwelling house and the field are inseparable, because the woman is the heart of these, and they rest with her. Among us the family traces its kin from the mother, hence all its possessions are hers. The man builds the house but the woman is the owner, because she repairs and preserves it; the man cultivates the field, but he renders its harvest into the woman's keeping, because upon her it rests to prepare the food, and the surplus of stores for barter depends upon her thrift.

A man plants the fields of his wife, and the fields assigned to the children she bears, and informally he calls them his, although in fact they are not. Even of the field which he inherits from his mother, its harvests he may dispose of at will, but the field itself he may not. He may permit his son to occupy it and gather its produce, but at the father's death the son may not own it, for then it passes to the father's sister's son or nearest mother's kin, and thus our fields and houses always remain with our mother's family.

According to the number of children a woman has, fields for them are assigned to her, from some of the lands of her family group, and her husband takes care of them. Hence our fields are numerous but small, and several belonging to the same family may be close together, or they may be miles apart, because arable localities are not continuous. There are other reasons for the irregularity in size and situation of our family lands, as interrupted sequence of inheritance caused by extinction of families, but chiefly owing to the following condition, and to which we especially invite your attention.

In the Spring and early Summer there usually comes from the Southwest a succession of gales, oftentimes strong enough to blow away the sandy soil from the face of some of our fields, and to expose the underlying clay, which is hard, and sour, and barren; as the sand is the only fertile land, when it moves, the planters must follow it, and other fields must be provided in place of those which have been devastated.

Sometimes generations pass away and these barren spots remain, while in other instances, after a few years, the winds have again restored the desirable sand upon them. In such event its fertility is disclosed by the nature of the grass and shrubs that grow upon it.

If these are promising, a number of us unite to clear off the land and make it again fit for planting, when it may be given back to its former owner, or if a long time has elapsed, to other heirs, or it may be given to some person of the same family group, more in need of a planting place.

These limited changes in land holding are effected by mutual discussion and concession among the elders, and among all the thinking men and women of the family groups interested. In effect, the same system of holding, and the same method of planting, obtain among the Tewa, and all the Hopi villages, and under them we provide ourselves with food in abundance.

The American is our elder brother, and in everything he can teach us, except in the method of growing corn in these waterless sand valleys, and in that we are sure we can teach him.

. . . We most earnestly desire to have one continuous boundary ring enclosing all the Tewa and all the Hopi lands, and that it shall be large enough to afford sustenance for our increasing flocks and herds. If such a scope can be confirmed to us by a paper from your hands, securing us forever against intrusion, all our people will be satisfied.

A land grab was built into the allotment law: Any land remaining after allotment, in some cases more than half the reservation, was auctioned off to white settlers. It often sold at a rigged price.

"Oh! it was then they shrieked. . . ."

THE STOCKYARDS

1889
Chicago

RUDYARD KIPLING

Chicago was the end of the line for as many as 600,000 head of cattle from the prairies. The trail drives, now a staple of Western movies, usually had about 2,500 head of cattle, and ran about 1,500 miles to the stockyards of the midwest, near the intersections of railroads and rivers that allowed the slaughtered cattle and hogs to be sent across the country.

English journalist and novelist Rudyard Kipling visited Chicago as part of a cross-country tour, from west to east, that he undertook for his newspaper in India, the Allahabad Pioneer. When he saw the city, it had already become what Carl Sandburg would dub three decades later: "Hog Butcher for the World, / Tool Maker, Stacker of Wheat, / Player with Railroads and the Nation's Freight Handler; / Stormy, husky, brawling, / City of the Big Shoulders. . . ."

They say every Englishman goes to the Chicago stock-yards. You shall find them about six miles from the city; and once having seen them will never forget the sight.

As far as the eye can reach stretches a township of cattle-pens, cunningly divided into blocks so that the animals of any pen can be speedily driven out close to an inclined timber path which leads to an elevated covered way straddling high above the pens. These viaducts are two-storied. On the upper story tramp the doomed cattle, stolidly for the most part. On the lower, with a scuffling of sharp hoofs and multitudinous yells, run the pigs. The same end is appointed for each.

Thus you will see the gangs of cattle waiting their turn—as they wait sometimes for days; and they need not be distressed by the sight of their fellows running about in the fear of death. All they know is that a man on horseback causes their next-door neighbors to move by means of a whip. Certain bars and fences are [opened], and, behold, that crowd have gone up the mouth of a sloping tunnel and return no more. It is different with the pigs. They shriek back the news of the exodus to their friends, and a hundred pens skirt responsive.

It was to the pigs I first addressed myself. Selecting a viaduct which was full of them, as I could hear though I could not see, I marked a somber building whereto it ran, and went there, not unalarmed by stray cattle who had managed to escape from their proper quarters. A pleasant smell of brine warned me of what was coming.

I entered the factory and found it full of pork in barrels, and on another story more pork unbarreled, and in a huge room, the halves of swine for whose use great lumps of ice were being pitched in at the window. That room was the mortuary chamber where the pigs lie for a little while in state ere they begin their progress through such passages as kings may sometimes travel.

Turning a corner and not noting an overhead arrangement of greased rail, wheel, and pulley, I ran into the arms of four eviscerated carcasses, all pure white and of a human aspect, being pushed by a man clad in vehement red. When I leaped aside, the floor was slippery under me. There was a flavour of farmyard in my nostrils and the shouting of a multitude in my ears. But there was no joy in that shouting. Twelve men stood in two lines—six aside. Between them and overhead ran the railway of death that had nearly shunted me through the window. Each man carried a knife, the sleeves of his shirt were cut off at the elbows, and from bosom to heel he was blood-red. The atmosphere was stifling as a night in the Rains, by reason of the steam and the crowd.

I climbed to the beginning of things and, perched upon a narrow beam, overlooked very nearly all the pigs ever bred in Wisconsin. They had just been shot out of the mouth of the viaduct and huddled together in a large pen. Thence they were flicked persuasively, a few at the time, into a smaller chamber, and there a man fixed tackle on their hinder legs so that they rose in the air suspended from the railway of death. Oh! it was then they shrieked and called on their mothers and made promises of amendment, till the tackle-man punted them in their backs, and they slid head down into a brick-floored passage, very like a big kitchen sink that was blood-red. There awaited them a red man with a knife which he passed jauntily through their throats, and the full-voiced shriek became a sputter, and then a fall as of heavy tropical rain.

The red man who was backed against the passage wall stood clear of the wildly kicking hoofs and passed his hand over his eyes, not from any feeling of compassion, but because the spurted blood was in his eyes and he had barely time to stick the next arrival.

Then that first stuck swine dropped, still kicking, into a great vat of boiling water, and spoke no more words, but wallowed in obedience to some unseen machinery, and presently came forth at the lower end of the vat and was heaved on the blades of a blunt paddle-wheel-thing which said, "Hough! Hough! Hough!" and skelped all the hair off him except what little a couple of men with knives could remove. Then he was again hitched by the heels to that said railway and passed down the line of the twelve men—each with a knife—leaving with each man a certain amount of his individuality which was taken away in a wheelbar-row, and when he reached the last man he was very beautiful to behold, but immensely unstuffed and limp.

Preponderance of individuality was ever a bar to foreign travel. That pig could have been in no case to visit you in India had he not parted with some of his most cherished notions.

The dissecting part impressed me not so much as the slaying. They were so excessively alive, these pigs. And then they were so excessively dead, and the man in the dripping, clammy, hot passage did not seem to care, and ere the blood of such a one had ceased to foam on the floor, such another, and four friends with him, had shrieked and died. But a pig is only the Unclean animal—forbidden by the Prophet. . . .

Women come sometimes to see the slaughter, as they would come to see the slaughter of men. And there entered that vermilion hall a young woman of large mold, with brilliantly scarlet lips, and heavy eye-brows, and dark hair that came in a "widow's peak" on the forehead. She was well and healthy and alive, and she was dressed in flaming red and black, and her feet (know you that the feet of American women are like unto the feet of fairies?) her feet, I say, were cased in red leather shoes. She stood in a patch of sunlight, the red blood under her shoes, the vivid carcasses tacked round her, a bullock bleeding its life away not six feet away from her, and the death factory roaring all round her. She looked curiously, with hard, bold eyes, and was not ashamed.

Kipling visited shortly after Chicago surpassed Philadelphia to become the second-largest city in America, a sign of the westward shift of the nation's population. It held that place for almost a century, succumbing to the continuing westward shift when Los Angeles edged by it in 1984.

"Unlike Rome the city of Guthrie was built in a day."

BOOMERS AND SOONERS: THE GREAT LAND RUSH

April 22, 1889
Guthrie, Oklahoma

WILLIAM W. HOWARD

In 1880, a group of white settlers defied the federal government by establishing homesteads in Oklahoma. They were politely escorted out by the Ninth Cavalry. Over the next few years they returned several times, challenging the government and then being removed.

At the time, Oklahoma was the Indian Territory. It had a diverse indigenous population, as well as Indians who had been forced from eastern territories on the orders of President Andrew Jackson (see page 105). After the Civil War, thousands of freed slaves had also settled there to avoid white rule (see page 208).

But white homesteaders couldn't be kept out forever. The government eventually relented, announcing a date on which the territory would be open for claims. The promise of free land drew 60,000 eager "Boomers" to the border to wait for the pistol shot that would start the rush. Meanwhile, some "Sooners" had already snuck into the territory.

Eyewitness William Howard wrote this account for Harper's Weekly.

Unlike Rome the city of Guthrie was built in a day. To be strictly accurate in the matter, it might be said that it was built in an afternoon. At twelve o'clock on Monday, April 22d, the resident population of Guthrie was nothing; before sundown it was at least ten thousand. In that time streets had been laid out, town lots staked off, and steps taken toward the formation of a municipal government. At twilight the camp-fires of ten thousand people gleamed on the grassy slopes of the

Cimarron Valley, where, the night before, the coyote, the gray wolf, and the deer had roamed undisturbed. Never before in the history of the West has so large a number of people been concentrated in one place in so short a time. To the conservative Eastern man, who is wont to see cities grow by decades, the settlement of Guthrie was magical beyond belief; to the quick-acting resident of the West, it was merely a particularly lively townsite speculation.

The preparations for the settlement of Oklahoma had been complete, even to the slightest detail, for weeks before the opening day. The Santa Fe Railway, which runs through Oklahoma north and south, was prepared to take any number of people from its handsome station at Arkansas City, Kansas, and to deposit them in almost any part of Oklahoma as soon as the law allowed; thousands of covered wagons were gathered in camps on all sides of the new Territory waiting for the embargo to be lifted.

In its picturesque aspects the rush across the border at noon on the opening day must go down in history as one of the most noteworthy events of Western civilization. At the time fixed, thousands of hungry home-seekers, who had gathered from all parts of the country, and particularly from Kansas and Missouri, were arranged in line along the border, ready to lash their horses into furious speed in the race for fertile spots in the beautiful land before them.

As the expectant home-seekers waited with restless patience, the clear, sweet notes of a cavalry bugle rose and hung a moment upon the startled air. It was noon. The last barrier of savagery in the United States was broken down.

Moved by the same impulse, each driver lashed his horses furiously; each rider dug his spurs into his willing steed, and each man on foot caught his breath hard and darted forward.

A cloud of dust rose where the home-seekers had stood in line, and when it had drifted away before the gentle breeze, the horses and wagons and men were tearing across the open country like fiends.

The horsemen had the best of it from the start. It was a fine race for a few minutes, but soon the riders began to spread out like a fan, and by the time they had reached the horizon they were scattered about as far as eye could see. Even the fleetest of the horsemen found upon reaching their chosen localities that men in wagons and men on foot were there before them.

As it was clearly impossible for a man on foot to outrun a horseman, the inference is plain that Oklahoma had been entered hours before the appointed time. Notwithstanding the assertions of the soldiers that every boomer had been driven out of Oklahoma, the fact remains that the woods along the various streams within Oklahoma were literally full of people Sunday night.

Nine-tenths of these people made settlement upon the land illegally. The other tenth would have done so had there been any desirable land left to settle upon. This action on the part of the first claim-holders will cause a great deal of land litigation in the future, as it is not to be expected that the man who ran his horse at its utmost speed for ten miles only to find a settler with an ox team in quiet possession of his chosen farm will tamely submit to this plain infringement of the law.

Some of the men who started from the line on foot were quite as successful in securing desirable claims as many who rode fleet horses. They had the advantage of knowing just where their land was located. One man left the line with the others, carrying on his back a tent, a blanket, some camp dishes, an ax, and provisions for two days. He ran down the railway track for six miles, and reached his claim in just sixty minutes. Upon arriving on his land he fell down under a tree, unable to speak or see. I am glad to be able to say that his claim is one of the best in Oklahoma.

The rush from the line was so impetuous that when the first railway train arrived from the north at twenty-five minutes past twelve o'clock, only a few of the hundreds of boomers were anywhere to be seen.

The journey of this first train was well-nigh as interesting as the rush of the men in wagons. The train left Arkansas City at 8:45 o'clock in the forenoon. It consisted of an empty baggage car, which was set apart for the use of the newspaper correspondents, eight passenger coaches, and the caboose of a freight train. The coaches were so densely packed with men that not another human being could get on board. So uncomfortably crowded were they that some of the younger boomers climbed to the roofs of the cars and clung perilously to the ventilators. An adventurous person secured at great risk a seat on the forward truck of the baggage car.

Hardly had the train slackened its speed when the impatient boomers began to leap from the cars and run up the slope. Men jumped from the roofs of the moving cars at the risk of their lives. Some were so stunned by the fall that they could not get up for some minutes. The coaches were so crowded that many men were compelled to squeeze through the windows in order to get a fair start at the head of the crowd. Almost before the train had come to a standstill the cars were emptied.

In their haste and eagerness, men fell over each other in heaps, others stumbled and fell headlong, while many ran forward so blindly and impetuously that it was not until they had passed the best of the town lots that they came to a realization of their actions.

It is estimated that between six and seven thousand persons reached Guthrie by train from the north the first afternoon, and that fully three thousand came in by wagon from the north and east, and by train from Purcell on the south, thus making a total population for the first day of about ten thousand.

By taking thought in the matter, three-fourths of these people had provided themselves with tents and blankets, so that even on the first night they had ample shelter from the weather. The rest of them slept the first night as best they could, with only the red earth for a pillow and the starry arch of heaven for a blanket.

At dawn of Tuesday the unrefreshed home-seekers and town-site speculators arose, and began anew the location of disputed claims. The tents multiplied like mushrooms in a rain that day, and by night the building of frame houses had been begun in earnest in the new streets. The buildings were by no means elaborate, yet they were as good as the average frontier structure, and they served their purpose, which was all that was required.

On that day the trains going north were filled with returning boomers, disgusted beyond expression with the dismal outlook of the new country. Their places were taken by others who came in to see the fun, and perhaps pick up a bargain in the way of town lots or commercial speculation.

During the first three days food was nearly as hard to get as water. Dusty ham sandwiches sold on the streets as high as twenty-five cents each, while in the restaurants a plate of pork and beans was valued at seventy-five cents. Few men were well enough provided with funds to buy themselves a hearty meal. One disgusted home-seeker estimated that if he ate as much as he was accustomed to eat back in Missouri his board would cost him $7.75 per day. Not being able to spend that amount of money every day, he contented himself with such stray sandwiches as were within his means. In this manner he contrived to subsist until Wednesday afternoon, when he was forced to return to civilization in southern Kansas in order to keep from starving to death.

A year after the Oklahoma land rush, the federal census showed the physical frontier no longer existed. The population stretched from coast to coast.

———————————————

"The dead are to return. . . . The Dakota people
will get back their own way of life. . . ."

THE GHOST DANCE

December 1890
Wounded Knee, South Dakota

ANONYMOUS PINE RIDGE SIOUX

Desperation bred a messianic movement at the end of the nineteenth century, as
many Indian tribes faced extinction from the combined effects of smallpox,
Indian wars, and the cultural upheaval of allotment and the reservation system
(see pages 161 and 193).

A religious revival arose among Plains Indians, combining elements of native
religion with Christianity and promising the return of the land to the Indians. It
was led by Wovoka, a Paiute who was orphaned as a teenager and taken into the
family of a white rancher. In 1889, he had a mystical vision that led him to cre-
ate and preach the hybrid religion. In short, he said the earth and the Indian way
of life was old and worn, but it would be renewed in 1891, when the whites would
leave, the buffalo would return, the earth would be recreated, and generations of
dead Indians would return to life.

He called on Indians to prepare for that day by dancing the Ghost Dance, a
five-day ceremony of dancing that was to be repeated every six weeks. The dancers
were to wear "ghost shirts," long shirts painted with spiritual symbols, that would
protect them from bullets.

Although Wovoka called for the Indians to live peacefully until the judgment
day came, white settlers were alarmed by the growing popularity of the Ghost
Dance, and saw it, without any apparent cause, as the beginning of an Indian
uprising.

This account was given to anthropologist Ella Deloria, who was also a Sioux.

A big new government school had been put up at Pine Ridge, and
we were kept there, boys and girls *together*—an unheard-of thing. We
wore *Wasicu* [white people's] clothes, which neither fitted nor felt right
on us. In fact, we looked terrible in them, but we had to wear them or
be punished.

The rumor got about: "The dead are to return. The buffalo are to
return. The Dakota people will get back their own way of life. The white
people will soon go away, and that will mean happier times for us once
more!"

That part about the dead returning was what appealed to me. To think I should see my dear mother, grandmother, brothers and sisters again! But, boylike, I soon forgot about it, until one night when I was rudely wakened in the dormitory. "Get up, put on your clothes and slip downstairs, we are running away," a boy was hissing into my ear.

Soon fifty of us, little boys about eight to ten, started out across country over hills and valleys, running all night. I know now that we ran almost thirty miles. There on the Porcupine Creek thousands of Dakota people were in camp, all hurrying about very purposefully. In a long sweat lodge with openings at both ends, people were being purified in great companies for the holy dance, men by themselves and women by themselves, of course.

A woman quickly spied us and came weeping toward us. "These also shall take part," she was saying of us. So a man called out, "You runaway boys, come here." They stripped our ugly clothes from us and sent us inside. When we were well purified, they sent us out at the other end and placed sacred shirts on us. They were of white muslin with a crow, a fish, stars, and other symbols painted on. I never learned what they meant. Everyone wore one magpie and one eagle feather in his hair, but in our case there was nothing to tie them to. The school had promptly ruined us by shaving off our long hair till our scalps showed lighter than our faces!

The people, wearing the sacred shirts and feathers, now formed a ring. We were in it. All joined hands. Everyone was respectful and quiet, expecting something wonderful to happen. It was not a glad time, though. All walked cautiously and in awe, feeling their dead were close at hand.

The leaders beat time and sang as the people danced, going round to the left in a sidewise step. They danced without rest, on and on, and they got out of breath but still they kept going as long as possible. Occasionally someone thoroughly exhausted and dizzy fell unconscious into the center and lay there "dead." Quickly those on each side of him closed the gap and went right on. After a while, many lay about in that condition. They were now "dead" and seeing their dear ones. As each one came to, she, or he, slowly sat up and looked about, bewildered, and then began wailing inconsolably.

One of the leaders, a medicine man, asked a young girl, "My kinswoman, why do you weep?" Then she told him tearfully what she had just seen, and he in turn proclaimed it to the people. Then all wailed with her. It was very dismal.

I remember two of the songs:

Mother, hand me my sharp knife, Mother, hand me my

sharp knife, Here come the buffalo returning—Mother, hand me my sharp knife!

Mother, do come back! Mother, do come back! My little brother is crying for you—My father says so!

The visions varied at the start, but they ended the same way, like a chorus describing a great encampment of all the Dakotas who had ever died, where all were related and therefore understood each other, where the buffalo came eagerly to feed them, and there was no sorrow but only joy, where relatives thronged out with happy laughter to greet the newcomer. That was the best of all!

Waking to the drab and wretched present after such a glowing vision, it was little wonder that they wailed as if their poor hearts would break in two with disillusionment. But at least they had seen! The people went on and on and could not stop, day or night, hoping perhaps to get a vision of their own dead, or at least to hear of the visions of others. They preferred that to rest or food or sleep. And so I suppose the authorities did think they were crazy—but they weren't. They were only terribly unhappy.

The Ghost Dance movement lost momentum after the massacre, but the incident is still a rallying point for Indian activists. In 1973, "the Knee" was the site of another long and deadly standoff between Indians and the government (see page 390).

Wovoka lived and preached—though with less certainty—until 1932.

"They had come from that wilderness only after a ten years' hard, vicious fight. . . ."

WAGONS EAST!

1895
Emporia, Kansas

WILLIAM ALLEN WHITE

Severe drought created a crisis in 1894, with the worst harvest in memory for Kansas, Nebraska, Iowa, and other western states. By 1895, the optimism of many western settlers had disappeared.

William Allen White was a Kansas newspaper editor who rose to national influence as "the Sage of Emporia."

There came through Emporia yesterday, two old-fashioned mover wagons headed east. The stock in the caravan would invoice four horses, very poor and very tired, one mule, more disheartened than the horses, and one sad-eyed dog that had probably been compelled to rustle his own precarious living for many a long and weary day. A few farm implements of the simpler sort were loaded in the wagon, but nothing that had wheels was moving except the two wagons. All the rest of the impedimenta had been left upon the battlefield, and these poor stragglers, defeated but not conquered, were fleeing to another field, to try the fight again. These movers were from western Kansas—from one of those counties near the Colorado line which holds a charter from the state to officiate as the very worst, most desolate, Godforsaken, man-deserted spot on the sad old earth. They had come from that wilderness only after a ten years' hard, vicious fight, a fight which had left its scars on their faces, had beaten their bodies, had taken the elasticity from their steps and left them crippled to enter the battle anew. For ten years they had been fighting the elements. They had seen it stop raining for months at a time. They had heard the fury of the winter wind as it came whining across the short burned grass and cut the flesh from their children huddling in the corner. These movers have strained their eyes, watching through the long summer days for the rain that never came. They have seen that big cloud roll up from the southwest about one in the afternoon, hover over the land, and stumble away with a few thumps of thunder as the sun went down. They have tossed through hot nights, wild with worry, and have arisen only to find their worst nightmares grazing in reality on the brown stubble in front of their sun-warped doors. They had such high hopes when they went out there; they are so desolate now. . . . They have come out of the wilderness, back to the land of promise.

Desperate farmers sold horses for 25 cents. Hay sold for $2 a ton. Then the fall of 1895 brought a near-record harvest—but, in a wicked twist of fate, the surplus drove prices down, making conditions worse for the farmers. Before the century's end, some western areas lost half their population.

"The bandits then threatened to blow up the whole car...."

BUTCH CASSIDY AND THE SUNDANCE KID ROB THE UNION PACIFIC

June 2, 1899
Wilcox, Wyoming

ROBERT LAWSON

Outlaw Robert Leroy Parker, aka Butch Cassidy, thought big. According to legend, in 1896 he gathered more than 200 fellow thieves in a remote Wyoming valley, to organize a syndicate of train robbers.

The gang became known as the Wild Bunch. (Sometimes they were also called the "Hole in the Wall" gang, coined from the name of another hideout in north-central Wyoming.) It wasn't a tightly controlled organization. The outlaws tended to work in small teams to rob banks and trains, and to rustle horses and cattle.

In 1899, Butch teamed up with Harry Longbaugh, the Sundance Kid. Perhaps the fastest and best shot of all the outlaws, Longbaugh got his nickname from a town where he served time in prison.

Eyewitness Robert Lawson was a mail clerk on the Union Pacific, a favorite target of Butch and Sundance.

As soon as we came to a standstill, Conductor Storey went forward to see what was the matter and saw several men with guns, one of whom shouted that they were going to blow up the train with dynamite. The conductor understood the situation at once and, before meeting the bandits, turned and started back to warn the second section. The robbers mounted the engine and at the point of their guns forced the engineer and fireman to dismount, after beating the engineer over the head with their guns, claiming that he didn't move fast enough, and marched them back over to our car.

In a few moments we heard voices outside our car calling for Sherman, and looking out saw Engineer Jones and his fireman accompanied by three masked men with guns.

They evidently thought Clerk Sherman was aboard and were calling him to come out with the crew. Burt Bruce, clerk in charge, refused to open the door, and ordered all lights extinguished. There was much loud talk and threats to blow up the car were made, but the doors were kept shut. In about 15 minutes two shots were fired into the car, one of the balls passing through the water tank and on through the stanchions.

Following close upon the shooting came a terrific explosion, and one of the doors was completely wrecked and most of the car windows broken. The bandits then threatened to blow up the whole car if we didn't get out, so Bruce gave the word and we jumped down, and were immediately lined up and searched for weapons. They said it would not do us no good to make trouble, that they didn't want the mail—that they wanted what was in the express car and was going to have it, and that they had powder enough to blow the whole train off the track.

After searching us they started us back and we saw up the track the headlight of the second section. They asked what was on the train, and somebody said there were two cars of soldiers on the train. This scared them and they hastened back to the engine, driving us ahead. They forced us on the engine, and as Dietrick moved too slowly they assisted him with a few kicks. While on the engine, Dietrick, in the act of closing the furnace door, brushed a mask off one of the men, endeavoring to catch a glimpse of his face. The man quickly grasped his mask and threatened to "plug" Dietrick.

They then ran the train ahead across a gully and stopped. There were two extra cars on the train. They were uncoupled. Others of the gang went to the bridge, attempting to destroy it with their giant powder, or dynamite, which they placed on the timbers. After the explosion at the bridge they boarded the engine with the baggage, express, and mail cars, went on for about two miles, leaving the extra cars.

Upon arriving at the stopping place they proceeded to business again and went to the express car and ordered the messenger, E. C. Woodcock, to open. He refused, and the outlaws proceeded to batter down the doors and blew a big hole in the side of the car. The explosion was so terrific that the messenger was stunned and had to be taken from the car. They then proceeded to the other mail car, occupied by Clerks O'Brien and Skidmore and threatened to blow it up, but the boys were advised to come out, which they did.

The robbers then went after the safes in the express car with dynamite and soon succeeded in getting into them, but not before the car was torn to pieces by the force of the charges. They took everything from the safes and what they didn't carry away they destroyed. After finishing their work they started out in a northerly direction on foot.

[They] found behind a snowfence, blankets and quilts, as well as two sacks of giant powder, each about 50 pounds in weight.

The men all wore long masks reaching below their necks and of the three I observed, one looked to be six foot tall, the others being about ordinary sized men. The leader appeared to be about 50 years old and spoke with a squeaky voice, pitched very high.

They appeared not to want to hurt anyone and were quite sociable and asked one of the boys for a chew of tobacco. . . .

The robberies of the Union Pacific infuriated the railroad's owner, Edward H. Harriman, who hired Pinkerton detectives to hunt for Butch and Sundance. The fugitives escaped to New York and then South America. The Pinkertons reported that Butch and Sundance were killed in 1909, but evidence suggests they returned to the U.S. under new identities and lived into the 1930s. (One report has Sundance living until 1957!)

". . . Communities in which no white man was allowed to live. . . ."

GOING TO THE TERRITORY

1905
Boley, Oklahoma

BOOKER T. WASHINGTON

Toward the end of Reconstruction, as southern states were granted local government, freed slaves left in large numbers. Tens of thousands headed into the Indian Territory, now Oklahoma, from which whites had been barred by Congress when the territory was established in 1828. The tribes of the Indian Territory had supported the Confederacy—and even held about 7,500 black slaves—but they were less able to resist Reconstruction than white governments of the south.

By the 1890s, twenty-eight all-black towns existed in Oklahoma, and blacks held important roles in politics, business, and the professions. (This is the origin of the famous spiritual, "Goin' to the Nation, Goin' to the Terr'tor'.") Political leaders tried to have Oklahoma declared an all-black state, a holy land for freed slaves.

Educator Booker T. Washington, an advocate of separatism, was delighted by what he witnessed in there.

Boley, Indian Territory, is the youngest, the most enterprising and in many ways the most interesting of the negro towns in the United States. A rude, bustling, western town, it is a characteristic product of the negro immigration from the South and Middle West into the new lands of what is now the state of Oklahoma.

The large proportions of the northward and westward movement of the negro population recall the Kansas exodus of thirty years ago, when within a few months more than forty thousand helpless and destitute negroes from the country districts of Arkansas and Mississippi poured into eastern Kansas in search of "better homes, larger opportunities, and kindlier treatment."

It is a striking evidence of the progress made in thirty years that the present northward and westward movement of the negro people has brought into these new lands, not a helpless and ignorant horde of black people, but land-seekers and home-builders, men who have come prepared to build up the country. In the thirty years since the Kansas exodus the southern negroes have learned to build schools, to establish banks and conduct newspapers. They have recovered something of the knack for trade that their foreparents in Africa were famous for. They have learned through their churches and their secret orders the art of corporate and united action. This experience has enabled them to set up and maintain in a raw western community, numbering 2,500, an orderly and self-respecting government.

In the fall of 1905 I spent a week in the Territories of Oklahoma and Indian Territory. During the course of my visit I had an opportunity for the first time to see the three races—the negro, the Indian, and the white man—living side by side, each in sufficient numbers to make their influence felt in the communities of which they were a part, and in the Territory as a whole.

. . . One cannot escape the impression, in traveling through Indian Territory, that the Indians, who own practically all the lands, and until recently had the local government largely in their own hands, are to a very large extent regarded by the white settlers, who are rapidly filling up the country, as almost a negligible quantity. To such an extent is this true that the Constitution of Oklahoma, as I understand it, takes no account of the Indians in drawing its distinctions among the races. For the Constitution there exist only the negro and the white man. The reason seems to be that the Indians have either receded—"gone back," as the saying in that region is—on the advance of the white race, or they have intermarried with and become absorbed with it. Indeed, so rapidly has this intermarriage of the two races gone on, and so great has been the demand for Indian wives, that in some of the Nations, I was informed, the price of marriage licenses has gone as high as $1,000.

The negroes, immigrants to Indian Territory, have not, however, "gone back." One sees them everywhere, working side by side with white men. They have their banks, business enterprises, schools, and churches. There are still, I am told, among the "natives" some negroes who cannot speak the English language, and who have been so thoroughly bred in the customs of the Indians that they have remained among the hills with the tribes by whom they were adopted. But, as a rule, the negro natives do not shun the white man and his civilization, but, on the contrary, rather seek it, and enter, with the negro immigrants, into competition with the white man for its benefits.

This fact was illustrated by another familiar local expression. In reply to my inquiries in regard to the little towns through which we passed, I often had occasion to notice the expression, "Yes, so and so? Well, that is a 'white town.' " Or again, "So and so, that's colored."

I learned upon inquiry that there were a considerable number of communities throughout the Territory where an effort had been made to exclude negro settlers. To this the negroes had replied by starting other communities in which no white man was allowed to live. For instance, the thriving little city of Wilitka, I was informed, was a white man's town until it got the oil mills. Then they needed laborers, and brought in the negroes. There are a number of other little communities—Clairview, Wildcat, Grayson, and Taft—which were sometimes referred to as "colored towns," but I learned that in their cases the expression meant merely that these towns had started as negro communities or that there were large numbers of negroes there, and that negro immigrants were wanted. But among these various communities there was one of which I heard more than the others. This was the town of Boley, where, it is said, no white man has ever let the sun go down upon him.

In 1905, when I visited Indian Territory, Boley was little more than a name. It was started in 1903. At the present time it is a thriving town of 2,500 inhabitants, with two banks, two cotton gins, a newspaper, a hotel, and a "college," the Creek-Seminole College and Agricultural Institute.

There is a story told in regard to the way in which the town of Boley was started, which, even if it is not wholly true as to the details, is at least characteristic, and illustrates the temper of the people in that region.

One spring day, four years ago, a number of gentlemen were discussing, at Wilitka, the race question. The point at issue was the capability of the negro for self-government. One of the gentlemen, who happened to be connected with the Fort Smith Railway, maintained that if the negroes were given a fair chance they would prove themselves as capable of self-government as any other people of the same degree of culture and education. He asserted that they had never had a fair chance. The other gentlemen naturally asserted the contrary. The result of the argument was Boley. Just at that time a number of other town sites were being laid out along the railway which connects Guthrie, Oklahoma, with Fort Smith, Arkansas. It was, it is said, to put the capability of the negro for self-government to the test that in August, 1903, seventy-two miles east of Guthrie, the site of the new negro town was established. It was called Boley, after the man who built that section of the railway. A negro town-site agent, T. M. Haynes, who is at present connected with the Farmers' and Merchants' Bank, was made Town-site Agent, and the purpose to establish a town which should be exclusively controlled by negroes was widely advertised all over the Southwest.

. . . Mr. T. R. Ringe, the mayor, . . . was born a slave in Kentucky, and Mr. E. L. Lugrande, one of the principal stockholders in the new bank, came out in the new country, like so many of the white settlers, merely to get land. Mr. Lugrande came from Denton County, Texas, where he had 418 acres of land. He had purchased this land some years ago for four and five dollars the acre. He sold it for fifty dollars an acre, and, coming to Boley, he purchased a tract of land just outside of town and began selling town lots. Now a large part of his acreage is in the center of the town.

. . . A large proportion of the settlers of Boley are farmers from Texas, Arkansas, and Mississippi. But the desire for western lands has drawn into the community not only farmers, but doctors, lawyers, and craftsmen of all kinds. The fame of the town has also brought, no doubt, a certain proportion of the drifting population. But behind all other attractions of the new colony is the belief that here negroes would find greater opportunities and more freedom of action than they have been able to find in the older communities North and South.

Any ideas of a black state disappeared when the U.S. government opened the territory to all settlers in 1889. But many of the black communities continued to thrive, producing distinguished Oklahomans like novelist Ralph Ellison.

"The deal is riveted."

THE L.A. WATER SWINDLE

July 29, 1905
Owens Valley and Los Angeles

ANONYMOUS *LOS ANGELES TIMES* REPORTERS

The population of Los Angeles began to boom in the 1880s, growing from 11,000 to 100,000 by the century's end, and doubling again in just another four years. But growth was limited by the city's poor water supply. The Los Angeles River was little more than a stream, and the region was prone to droughts.

Fred Eaton, a native son who was a longtime city booster and had served a term as mayor, had a grandiose idea for improving the water supply. He believed water from the Owens Valley, more than 200 miles away, could be brought to the city by a system of aqueducts, pumping stations, and reservoirs.

In 1904, he secured the agreement of William Mulholland, director of the city's water works. Although Eaton briefly tried to buy the Owens Valley himself, figuring he would make a fortune by selling the water, a syndicate of prominent L. A. businessmen nixed that plan. He was to buy the land on behalf of the city; meanwhile, the syndicate, which included newspaper owners like Harrison Gray Otis of the Los Angeles Times, would keep the plan secret so prices in the valley wouldn't escalate.

The syndicate also paid off a federal Reclamation Service employee, Joseph Lippincott, who gave Eaton access to key land records. Lippincott also scuttled the federal government's plans to send the Owens Valley water in the other direction, into the Mojave Desert.

On July 29, 1905, just after Eaton bought the last parcel of land, the Los Angeles Times broke the silence. "Titanic Project to Give City a River," the headline announced. The reports described in detail most of the chicanery that led to the deal, and even admitted Lippincott's role.

The cable that has held the San Fernando Valley vassal for ten centuries to the arid demon is about to be severed by the magic scimitar of modern engineering skill. . . . Back to the headwaters of the Los Angeles River will be turned the flow of a thousand mountain streams that ages ago were tributaries of the current that swept past the site of the ancient pueblo of Los Angeles to the ocean. . . . Then will Los Angeles county indeed become the Promised Land. More precious than milk and honey will be the flow of the pure mountain water—aye, more precious than gold and diamonds.

The *Times* announces this morning the most important movement for the development of Los Angeles in all the city's history—the closing of the preliminary negotiations securing 30,000 inches of water, or about ten times our total supply, enough for a city of 2,000,000 people. In brief, the project is to bring this water to Los Angeles from Owens River in Inyo county, a distance of about 240 miles, at a cost of about $23,000,000. Options on the water-bearing lands have been closed by the city's representatives and a series of bond issues will be asked of the voters. This new water supply, immense and unfailing, will make Los Angeles forge ahead by leaps and bounds and remove every specter of drought. . . . She will have assured her future for a century.

. . . Agents representing Los Angeles city have secured options on about forty miles of frontage on the Owens River north of Owens Lake. Fred Eaton, ex-Mayor of Los Angeles, and the superintendent of the Los Angeles water works were in the valley in an automobile the early part of this week. Two days ago they closed the last outstanding options. The price paid for many of the ranches is three or four times what the owners ever expected to sell them for. Everybody in the valley has money, and everyone is happy.

Three months ago Eaton bought the holdings of the Rickey Cattle Company, comprising about 50,000 acres of water-bearing land. It was then thought that Eaton was going into the stock-raising business here, but it has since been learned that he was securing options for Los Angeles city. Eaton has made every option solid and secured all the land the city wanted. The deal is riveted.

. . . Scorched and browned by the almost intolerable desert wind and sun Superintendent Mulholland returned yesterday afternoon from a daring nine days' automobile trip into the heart of the Owens River country, bearing the glad tidings that "The last spike has been driven; the options are all secured; the deal by which Los Angeles city becomes the owner of thirty thousand inches of the purest snow water has been nailed."

In the excited gratification born of a knowledge that the vexed water question has at last been solved, Mulholland laughed like a schoolboy.

"Fred Eaton did it. He has been working on it for thirteen years. He is the greatest natural engineer that the West has ever known. He has made it possible for us to accomplish the greatest scheme of water development ever attempted in this country."

. . . "As I was returning home through Mojave an old railroad man whom I used to know years ago asked me why I was making so many trips up into the Owens Lake country. I said that I had taken a flyer in the stock-raising business.

"He chuckled gleefully as he told me that the week before he had sold his Owens River ranch to Fred Eaton. He called Fred an easy mark. 'I got about three times what it is worth,' he said. 'I never saw a fellow so daffy about stock land. Why, he actually gave me $10 an acre for it.' The railroad man thought he had handed Fred a gold brick.

"All through the valley they regarded Fred as easy money. Most of the ranchers received what they considered fancy prices for their holdings, and, judged by their agricultural prices, the prices were fancy.

"We just got into the valley in time. Engineers in the employ of the Government Reclamation Bureau were there working on the details of a plan for conserving the waters that flow into Owens Lake, and carrying them away for the reclamation of arid land in the Mojave Desert."

The Times noted only briefly that the value of the San Fernando Valley, located between the Owens Valley water and the city, would "double," thanks to irrigation from water flowing to the city. Actually, the prices immediately rose five times.

This was a very nice development for Times owner Harrison Gray Otis. He had bought much of the land there, figuring he would make a fortune when the aqueduct was completed. Because the aqueduct was built with public money, many people felt he had abused his insider's role to profit from a public works project. Of course he did. But it can't be denied that he bet big on the city, and that he was right.

Fred Eaton was bitter to his death at having given up a fortune on behalf of the city while others got rich. Having retained some of his Owens Valley land, he went back to the valley and led its political battles against Los Angeles.

The aqueduct was completed in 1913. When the first water arrived in the city, William Mulholland announced to the crowd gathered around for the ceremony, "There it is, take it!"

*". . . This center of civilization had become
a scene of indescribable desolation. . . ."*

THE 1906 EARTHQUAKE AND FIRE AND THEIR AFTERMATH

April 18–28, 1906
San Francisco

MAJOR-GENERAL ADOLPHUS GREELY AND ANONYMOUS *SAN FRANCISCO CHRONICLE* REPORTER

Fire burned for three days after the great earthquake, burning one-third of San Francisco—28,000 buildings. San Franciscans of the time usually called this incident just "the Great Fire," as if the earthquake, which seismologists say might have hit 7.9 on today's Richter scale, wasn't much.

Eyewitness Adolphus Greely was the local army commander.

GREELY

On April 18 this was a city of 500,000 inhabitants, the commercial emporium of the Pacific coast, a great industrial and manufacturing center, adorned with magnificent buildings, equipped with extensive local transportation, provided with the most modern sanitary appliances, and having an abundant water supply.

On April 21 these triumphs of human effort, this center of civilization, had become a scene of indescribable desolation, more than 200,000 residents having fled from the burnt district alone, leaving several hundred dead under its smoldering ashes.

The entire community of 450,000, deprived of all modern conveniences and necessities, had, in forty-eight hours, not only been relegated to conditions of primitive life, but were also hampered by ruins and debris. Its entire business districts and adjacent territory had been ravaged by fire.

The burnt area covered 3,400 acres, as against 2,100 in [the 1871 great fire] in Chicago and 50 in Boston [in 1872]. Of the 261 miles of electric and cable railways not a mile remained in operation. While probably 1,500 teams were uninjured, yet, as a whole, they had been withdrawn with the refugees to the outlying districts.

Practically all travel had to be on foot, the few automobiles having been impressed by the authorities. The intricate masses of iron, brick, and debris were supplemented in the unburned area by fallen buildings and chimneys, which made all travel circuitous and extremely difficult.

The city telephone system was interrupted; every telegraph office and station had been destroyed. All the banks, deposit vaults, and trust buildings were in ruins. Not a hotel of note or importance was left standing. The great apartment houses had vanished. Of the thousands of wholesale and large retail establishments scarce half a dozen were saved, and these in remote districts. Even buildings spared by the fire were damaged as to chimneys, so that all food of the entire city was cooked over camp fires in the open streets.

Two hundred and twenty-five thousand people were not only homeless, losing all real and personal property, but also were deprived of their means of present sustenance and future livelihood. Food, water, shelter, clothing, medicines, and sewerage were all lacking. Failing even for drinking purposes, water had to be brought long distances. Every large bakery was destroyed or interrupted. While milk and country produce were plentiful in the suburbs, local transportation was entirely interrupted so that even people of great wealth could obtain food only by charity or public relief. In short, all those things which are deemed essential to the support, comfort, and decency of a well-ordered life were destroyed or wanting.

The quarter of a million people driven into the streets by the flames escaped as a rule only with the clothing they wore. Thousands upon thousands had fled to the open country, but tens of thousands upon tens of thousands remained in the parks, generally in stupor or exhaustion after days of terror and struggle. . . .

This report would be incomplete if it did not recognize the sterling qualities of the people of San Francisco. Almost without exception these people suffered financially, varying from small losses to total ruin. It is safe to say that nearly 200,000 persons were brought to a state of complete destitution, beyond the clothing they wore or carried in their arms. The majority of the community was reduced from conditions of comfort to dependence upon public charity, yet in all my experiences I have never seen a woman in tears, nor heard a man whining over his losses. Besides this spirit of cheerful courage, they exhibited qualities of resourcefulness and self-respect which must command the admiration of the world. Within two months the bread line, which at first exceeded 300,000, was reduced to a comparative handful—less than 5 per cent of the original number.

The town is on the level in every sense of the word. No more ghouls are shot because there is nothing to steal. Yet the smashed buildings and desolate streets do not represent the significant leveling. The material loss is overwhelming, but it does not stagger the imagination. A few hundred millions will mend the hurt and there are many people here today who think the shakeup is worth it. The leveling that they are willing to pay for is social. Society is on the ground, face to face, jowl to jowl. Every artificial barrier is swept away. The conventions, the pride, the show and the ease which these people have been erecting for 50 years have been swept away with the same swiftness and finality shown by the flames toward the property.

The loss of life is small; the loss of social position colossal. Now nothing counts but human love. Money has momentarily lost its purchasing power. Servants, luxury, habits, prestige—yes, and enmity, feuds, hatreds, jealousies and contempt have disappeared. Humanity is in the flat and everyone is on the level.

Up and down the streets one can see curbstone fires where the people are cooking their meals in obedience to the municipal order to light no fires in the houses. They bring out big ranges, small kitchen stoves, improvised sheet-iron ovens and the old brick Dutch ovens, from which are turned out some wonderful concoctions. Most of the servants have either run away or been sent away and the people who get their own meals out of doors are among the best in the city. Cooking their dinners in the street may be seen girls who have been educated at Stanford, Berkeley, Vassar and Bryn Mawr. It's a free start, everyone beginning over again, rich and poor alike. . . .

The earthquake and fire claimed 500 lives.

The social leveling described by the Chronicle *only went so far. The fear that followed the economic ruin of so many citizens led to a new round of anti-Asian ordinances. To induce San Francisco mayor James Phelan to ease off the Asian community, President Theodore Roosevelt cut a deal with the Japanese government to limit emigration to the U.S. (Ironically, Phelan's position was considered liberal: He was trying to protect the working classes. He was a dream of a mayor, if you were white. He battled corruption, promoted the creation of parks, and supported the arts. But his populist politics were closely related to his extreme racism. "The Chinese and Japanese are not bona fide citizens," he once said. "They are not the stuff of which American citizens can be made." Californians elected him a senator in 1915.)*

"I don't claim that this man is an angel."

WHO KILLED GOVERNOR STEUNENBERG?

July 24, 1907
Boise, Idaho

CLARENCE DARROW

The labor struggles of the West were not unique, but one union and one organizer stood out: The Industrial Workers of the World, and its leader, "Big Bill" Haywood, were at the center of the West's labor battles from 1905 to the 1920s. Though never large in comparison to other national unions, the IWW was strong among the West's loggers, farmworkers, miners, and dockworkers

The "Wobblies," as they were dubbed, were formed in 1905 by radical labor groups angered by the American Federation of Labor's refusal to unionize unskilled workers. The IWW aggressively pursued its goals of a single working-man's union and the replacement of capitalism with communism. Along with boy-cotts and the occasional act of sabotage, it conducted 150 strikes.

An early decisive moment for the union came in 1907, when Haywood was tried for allegedly ordering the assassination of Frank Steunenberg, the former governor of Idaho, who had been killed by a bomb rigged to his front gate. In a confession that may have been coerced by Pinkerton agents hired to break the IWW, the man who set the bomb said Haywood had paid him to do it.

This account comes from the eleven-hour summation to the jury by Haywood's defense attorney, the famous Clarence Darrow.

Gentlemen of the jury . . . William D. Haywood is charged with murder. He is charged with having killed ex-Governor Steunenberg.

He was not here. He was fifteen hundred or a thousand miles away, and he had not been here for years. There might be some member of this jury who would hesitate to take away the life of a human being upon the rotten testimony that has been given to this jury to convict a fellow-cit-izen. There might be some who still hold in their minds a lurking suspi-cion that this defendant had to do with this horrible murder. You might say, we will compromise; we cannot take his life upon Orchard's word, but we will send him to the penitentiary; we will find him guilty of manslaughter; we will find him guilty of murder in the second degree instead of the first.

Gentlemen, you have the right to do it if you want to. But I want to say to you twelve men that whatever else you are, I trust you are not cowards, and I want to say to you, too, that William Haywood is not a coward. I would not thank this jury if they found this defendant guilty of assault and battery and assessed a five-dollar fine against him. This murder was cold, deliberate, cowardly in the extreme, and if this man, sitting in his office in Denver, fifteen hundred miles away, employed this miserable assassin to come here and do this cowardly work, then, for God's sake, gentlemen, hang him by the neck until dead. Don't compromise in this case, whatever else you do. If he is guilty—if, under your conscience and before your God, you can say that you believe that man's story, and believe it beyond a reasonable doubt, then take him—take him and hang him. He has fought many a fight—many a fight with the persecutors who are hounding him in this court. He has met them in many a battle in the open field, and he is not a coward. If he is to die, he will die as he has lived, with his face to the foe. This man is either innocent or guilty. If he is guilty, I have nothing to say for him.

Gentlemen, I am not going to apologize in any way or seek to belittle the terrible crime that was committed in Canyon County. My associate said that Governor Steunenberg was a great and a good man. I don't know anything about that, whether he was either one, and I don't care. . . . Governor Steunenberg was a man. He had a right to live. Whether he was a great man or a small man, a good man or a bad man, wise or foolish, cuts no figure in this case.

. . . Let us assume that Bill Haywood is a cutthroat. Nobody ever said he was a fool. His worst enemies have not made that claim. Let us assume that he is like all the rest of us—a Dr. Jekyll and Mr. Hyde, and that the Mr. Hyde preponderates over the Dr. Jekyll; that he would be willing to slay and to kill; and let him be a criminal as bad as Harry Orchard pictures him; he is weaving a net to catch every man who is unfriendly to him; he is making bombs for governors and judges and the strong and the powerful who hate him. He is a plain assassin, and the head of a great labor organization. Is he a fool? Do you suppose a man could carry on those deeds and take no measure to protect himself? Do you think he could leave his doors open to every tramp and every criminal that might enter them, and when this criminal should say to him, I sent two men to eternity, and I blew up a mine, that he could turn to the man, without introduction and without acquaintance, and, slapping him on the back, say, "Well done; here is $300 for your work and we will need more of it in the future." Now do you believe it? Does that look reasonable?

Gentlemen, let me say this: If this jury believes that Haywood and Moyer met Harry Orchard in their room, and without any introduction of any sort, they let Harry Orchard tell them of this murder, and that they then turned and gave him $300—if you believe that story, for God's sake take them out and hang them—they deserve to die. They have not got brains enough to lead any labor movement in the world; they are misfits, and I don't see why they have been alive so long.

Gentlemen, it is not men of that character that could build up a great organization like the Western Federation of Miners; it is not men of that mold that could plant hospitals in all your hills and all your mountains; it is not men of that kind that could dispense a million and a half dollars to widows and orphans in ten years. It is not those men that could take the English and the Irish, the Dutch and the Bohemians and the Italians, and mold this incongruous mass into one great and mighty power so as to make the cause of labor one in the land. It takes brains. It takes courage. It takes devotion. It does not take a man such as Orchard describes. It takes goodness, too, and you cannot make me believe [Orchard's characterization] of Bill Haywood, or of Charley Moyer, or of any other labor leader in the United States.

I don't claim that this man is an angel. The Western Federation of Miners could not afford to put an angel at their head. Do you want to hire an angel to fight the Mine Owners' Association and the Pinkerton detectives, and the power of wealth? Oh, no, gentlemen; you better get a first-class fighting man who has physical courage, who has mental courage, who has strong devotion, who loves the poor, who loves the weak, who hates iniquity and hates it more when it is with the powerful and the great; and you cannot win without it, and I believe that down in your hearts there is not one of you would wish him to be an angel. You know an angel would not be fitted for that place, and I make no claim of that; but he is not a demon. If he were a demon or a bad man he would never be working in this cause, for the prizes of the world are some-where else. The man who enters the labor movement, either as an orga-nizer, a member, or a lawyer, and who enters it in the hope of reward, is a foolish man indeed. The rewards are on the other side—unless you look for your reward to your conscience and to your consciousness of a duty well done. I presume that this big, strong man is a man, a man that has strength and has power, and has weakness; a man of love and affec-tion, a man of strong nature, of strong purposes—I don't know about that, and I don't care about it; I don't look for anything else in man; I want the man of courage and brains and devotion and strength.

. . . Gentlemen, it is not for [Haywood] alone that I speak. I speak for the poor, for the weak, for the weary, for that long line of men, who, in darkness and despair, have borne the labors of the human race. The eyes of the world are upon you—upon you twelve men of Idaho tonight. Wherever the English language is spoken or wherever any tongue makes known the thoughts of men in any portion of the civilized world, men are talking, and wondering and dreaming about the verdict of these twelve men that I see before me now. If you kill him your act will be applauded by many. If you should decree Bill Haywood's death, in the railroad offices of our great cities men will applaud your names. If you decree his death, amongst the spiders of Wall Street will go up paeans of praise for these twelve good men and true. In every bank in the world, where men hate Haywood because he fights for the poor and against that accursed system upon which the favored live and grow rich and fat—from all those you will receive blessings and unstinted praise.

But if your verdict should be "Not Guilty" in this case, there are still those who will reverently bow their heads and thank these twelve men for the life and reputation you have saved. Out on our broad prairies where men toil with their hands, out on the wide ocean where men are tossed and buffeted on the waves, through our mills and factories, and down deep under the earth, thousands of men, and of women and children—men who labor, men who suffer, women and children weary with care and toil—these men and these women and these children will kneel tonight and ask their God to guide your hearts—these men and these women and these little children, the poor, the weak, and the suffering of the world, are stretching out their helpless hands to this jury in mute appeal for Bill Haywood's life.

Haywood was acquitted.

The Steunenberg case was only one of several headline grabbers in the Western labor movement. In 1910, unionists dynamited the offices of the antilabor Los Angeles Times, killing twenty people. Two bombers eventually confessed, implicating other union members. A few years later, songwriter and IWW organizer Joe Hill was executed in Utah on dubious charges. Frank Little, another IWW organizer, was murdered in Montana, probably by Pinkerton agents.

The IWW began to wane during World War I. The union opposed the war, declaring it a battle of capitalists against the working class, which enraged government officials. Haywood and other IWW members were convicted of sedition. Haywood was sentenced to twenty years in prison, but in 1921 he jumped bail and fled to Russia, where he died a few years later. The union's strength dissipated quickly.

The mystery of Governor Steunenberg's assassination has never been solved. Journalist J. Anthony Lukas, who researched the evidence exhaustively for his book Big Trouble, *concluded that Haywood was probably guilty.*

*"It might soon be . . . necessary for me
to seek radio employment on the Pacific Coast."*

THE BIRTH OF SILICON VALLEY

1908–1911
New York City and Palo Alto, California

LEE DE FOREST

*The former garage workshop of Hewlett-Packard co-founder Bill Hewlett is often
called "the birthplace of Silicon Valley." Hewlett says the real beginning of the
region's high-tech hegemony was "a supernova" named Lee De Forest.*

*De Forest, the inventor of the vacuum tube, was originally based in New York
City. But his first radio company went bust, leaving investors feeling conned by
the ephemeral new technology. In 1911, he had to get out of town.*

. . . My last trip to New York had convinced me that I could no longer
look forward to redemption of the sad wreck which had been my second
foundation of fortune and lasting success. I accepted the doom and recon-
ciled myself to the fact that I must at once seek employment. For some time
past I had cultivated the friendship of Cyril F. Elwell of Palo Alto, one of the
most brilliant graduates from Stanford University, who two years previously
had brought from Denmark the American patent rights and specifications of
the Poulsen-arc generator and "tikker" receiver. With these as assets, Elwell
had succeeded in organizing the Poulsen Telegraph and Telephone Company.

Operating on a small scale at Palo Alto with the encouragement and
moral backing of some Stanford professors, he had finally succeeded in interesting several San Francisco capitalists. . . . Therefore when I made the suggestion that it might soon be advisable, or necessary, for me to seek radio
employment on the Pacific Coast, the idea immediately appealed to Elwell,
and without difficulty he obtained authorization from Beach Thompson,
president of the Federal Telegraph Company, to offer me employment at a
fairly lucrative salary in the Palo Alto laboratory of the new company. . . .

*De Forest's work laid the foundation for Stanford's later electronics research
(see page 305). Though Silicon Valley may herald something new under the sun,
the initial reason for its location in the West follows a pattern that includes
Balboa, Moses Austin, John Bidwell, and countless other bankrupt entrepreneurs
who wanted a fresh start.*

*"We pay for the whole actor, Mr. Griffith. We want
to see all of him."*

THE FIRST CLOSE-UP
AND OTHER MOVIE INNOVATIONS

1908–1909
West Orange, New Jersey

LILLIAN GISH

*The first movies premiered in 1896. Within ten years it was obvious that the new
medium "had legs," as they say in Hollywood. But it had not yet developed its own
means of storytelling. Its success was based on ten-minute novelty films. One man,
David Llewelyn Wark Griffith, made the movies larger than life.*

*D. W. Griffith was the master of cinematic innovation who established the
grammar of filmmaking: the close-up, fade-in and fade-out, the flashback, and
shots from high and low angles. He was also the first moviemaker to fight for
full-length plots.*

*Along with his storytelling skills, he had a good eye for talent, making him
among the first directors to cast actors such as Mary Pickford, Lionel Barrymore,
Dorothy Gish, and Lillian Gish.*

This account comes from Lillian Gish's memoir, The Movies, Mr. Griffith,
and Me. *The events she described occurred shortly before Griffith relocated to
California.*

The ten-minute *Adventures of Dollie* was released in July 1908.
Perhaps because Griffith was a reluctant director, *Dollie* scarcely devi-
ated from the [usual] pattern. . . . But the film, which had cost $65 to
make and was sold to film exchanges for nearly $100 a print, had a suc-
cess greater than any previous Biograph production. The front office was
elated.

Soon everyone wanted more films by the man responsible for *Dollie*.
On the momentum of his first success, he turned out ten more pictures
in a month. Soon he was either directing or supervising all Biograph
films.

It was soon evident that Biograph's new director did not intend to
blindly follow the established rules of film making. In one of his early
projects, the story's climax depended on a circumstance that could not
be shown by action alone.

"The audience must see that these two thieves are beginning to distrust each other," Griffith said.

"Why not use a balloon?" suggested Billy Bitzer, who was now working closely with Griffith. Thoughts at that time were always shown in double exposure, a "dream balloon" being inserted in a corner of the film.

"It's been done too often," Mr. Griffith said, impatient with what had already become a cliche. "Perhaps there's another way." He turned to a young actor standing nearby and suggested, "Let's see some distrust on your face."

The actor obliged.

"That's good!" Griffith exclaimed. "Everyone will understand it."

Billy Bitzer objected, as he was to do often when Griffith attempted something new: "But he's too far away from the camera. His expression won't show up on the film."

"Let's get closer to him then. Let's move the camera."

"Mr. Griffith, that's impossible! Believe me, you can't move the camera. You'll cut off his feet—and the background will be out of focus."

"Get it, Billy," Griffith ordered.

When it came time to film the scene, Billy shot it first from the normal distance. Then he moved the heavy camera much nearer to the actors. Although the performers' feet weren't visible in the second shot, it would be clear to the audience that the two thieves in the film were near a falling out.

After the rushes were viewed, Griffith was summoned to the front office. Henry Marvin was furious. "We pay for the whole actor, Mr. Griffith. We want to see all of him."

Griffith patiently explained the reason for this shot.

Marvin was not satisfied. He complained, "The background's fuzzy."

Griffith strode toward him. "Look at me Mr. Marvin," he said. "Do you see all of me? No! You see half of me, is that correct? Now, while you are looking at me, the door in back of me is indistinct, isn't it? Good Lord, Mr. Marvin, what I showed on the screen is something you and everyone else sees a thousand times a day—and you don't even know it!"

As he continued to make pictures, Griffith brought the camera closer and closer to the actors until he was taking close-ups of their faces. As a result of the close-up, the style of acting became less exaggerated, for the audience, seeing the actor's face, could read his expression and interpret the action for itself. Griffith also used close shots of objects to contribute to the development of the story.

Mr. Griffith then tried another experiment. He interrupted a scene with a visual comma; that is, he broke the scene into separate shots, showing one actor's face, another's reaction, then perhaps an object, thus giving depth and dimension to the moment. Later he would make sense of the assorted shots in the cutting room, giving them drama and continuity.

In October, after less than four months of picture making, he filmed an adaptation of *Enoch Arden,* renaming it *After Many Years.* The shipwrecked husband, finally rescued, comes home to find that his once-grieving wife has remarried. To show the wife's feelings as she thinks of her first husband, Mr. Griffith ordered the camera to close in on her face. Then, to make certain that the audience understood her thoughts, he switched to a scene of the husband on the desert island. He thus violated continuity of time and space.

Mr. Marvin thought Griffith had gone mad.

"You can't jump around like that," he said angrily. "It doesn't make sense! The audience will never understand it."

"Of course they will!" insisted Griffith. "Wait and see."

As with each Griffith invention, audiences not only understood it; they loved it.

The technique Griffith used in *After Many Years* was not entirely new. Nor was the close-up technically a Griffith discovery. Porter's *Life of an American Fireman* had contained a close shot of a fire alarm. Griffith's genius lay in his understanding of the interrelationships of separate shots, each contributing to clarity and pace, adding substance, mood, and emotion to the bare story outline.

In *Ramona* he further extended the film idiom by introducing the extreme long shot of distant horizons, used for atmosphere and later for panoramic action shots.

"I began to seek after atmosphere and effects and the clues to causes," he said later. "If I have had a measure of success, that effort was largely responsible, for it started me in the right direction."

Griffith also experimented with lighting. He disliked the flat sterile lighting that was then in use. In *Edgar Allan Poe*, *The Politician's Love Story*, *A Drunkard's Reformation,* and *Pippa Passes* he arranged for light to come from odd angles. He shot into the bright sun to obtain the effect of the rising sun; he photographed his cast by firelight. He was particularly captivated by the beauty of a scene when it was backlighted by the sun, which cast long, dramatic shadows in front of the actors. He was eager to capture that radiance on film.

"You can't do it!" Billy Bitzer and Arthur Marvin assured him emphatically. "Shoot into the sun, and the actors' faces will come out black on the screen!"

Bitzer and Marvin were capable cameramen, but their point of view was conventional and circumscribed. D. W. did not believe them. Surreptitiously he tried out his theory. They were right.

But it was not in his nature to write off an idea as a failure. A few weeks later, when he and his company were on location in Fort Lee, New Jersey, several actors joined him for lunch in a nearby restaurant. As they were eating, he suddenly noticed the dazzling effect of the sun as it created a halo over the men across the table from him. Yet their faces remained distinct. Why the clarity? Could the reflection of the white tablecloth cast light on their faces?

Back in the studio he experimented with white reflectors and found the answer. The new style aroused more complaints from the front office. His new technique was bad, he was told, because the actors appeared shadowy. But an influential man suddenly took his part. Jeremiah J. Kennedy, a vice president of the Empire State Trust Company, which had a financial interest in Biograph, voiced his delight with the effects D. W. had achieved. "They look just like engravings, Mr. Griffith," he said. "Keep it up."

Mr. Kennedy was a collector of steel engravings.

For *Pippa Passes* Griffith had a sliding panel built into the wall of the set. Beyond it he mounted a powerful light. As Pippa lay sleeping on camera, the panel was lowered a crack, and the morning light Griffith had so adroitly created touched her face. She opened her eyes. The panel was lowered slowly, completely, until the room was flooded with light. Griffith had re-created the movements of the sun.

He ignored the complaints of Henry Marvin and continued to take plots from the classics. Primitive as they were, his twelve-minute versions of *The Taming of the Shrew* and *Resurrection* brought the film industry critical recognition. He also tackled social problems. Mr. Griffith was deeply sympathetic to the sufferings of the poor, to the injustices inflicted on them, and before he marked his first anniversary as a director he had used social problems as the themes of two fine pictures: *The Song of the Shirt* and *A Corner in Wheat*.

In 1909, almost a year after his first film, he elaborated the technique he had first used in *After Many Years*.

"I found," he said, "that pictures could carry not merely two but even three or four simultaneous threads of action without confusing the spectator."

In *The Lonely Villa,* which he made in the same year, a mother and her two children are trapped in a house by burglars. The heroine manages to telephone her husband. He rushes to the rescue. In a succession of short shots Griffith switches from the mother and her children to the burglars to the husband dashing homeward. As the film nears its climax, each shot becomes shorter. The tempo is thus increased and the suspense heightened. This device, which became known technically as "cross-cutting," became a staple in his directorial repertoire.

In *The Lonedale Operator,* two years later, he refined the devices for building suspense. Blanche Sweet, as the heroine held captive in a railroad station, taps out a telegraph message to her father and the man she loves, both of them railroad men. They rush to her rescue by engine. To increase suspense and to build up to the climax, Mr. Griffith again employed cross-cutting, switching from the girl to her sweetheart. Then he moved in even closer with a series of short, meaningful shots—to the smokestack, the screeching whistle, the turning wheels, the heart of the train that becomes a living creature in this race to save the girl. He thus created emotion out of motion.

Every refinement of technique proved costly, for it added to the length of the movie. Mr. Griffith was soon using every inch of film on a 1,000-foot reel. The front office was aghast. Mr. Marvin screamed that Griffith was ruining Biograph. The company officers hampered and impeded Griffith whenever he attempted something new, which was too often for their comfort. That his devices all proved extraordinarily successful did not change their attitude toward him. True, he made money for them, but they considered him extravagant and fanciful. Why experiment with a good thing when it made profits just as it was?

Their screams grew hysterical when Griffith presented them in 1911 with a movie in two cans—Biograph's first two-reel film. It was [the] remake of the *Enoch Arden* story, and it would barely fill a half-hour on today's television screen. But Biograph released it in two weekly installments. When audiences clamored to see the entire film at one screening, Griffith was vindicated. Again he was in the vanguard, and other companies soon followed his lead.

In his lifetime, Griffith directed almost 500 films. Today he is remembered primarily for one, The Birth of a Nation. *Since its first release in 1915, Griffith has been both celebrated and reviled for that film. It is a masterpiece of technical skill; it is also a throwback to slavery days, racist even by the standards of the era in which it was made.*

". . . They'd shoot a hole through the camera. . . ."

ON THE RUN

ALLAN DWAN

The story of how the movie business ended up in California is a shoot-'em-up. Thomas Edison invented the movie camera in New Jersey, and filmed the first movies there, making the New York City area the world's first movie capital. But Edison wanted to control all aspects of his amazingly successful invention, from shooting the pictures to distributing them. So he organized a group of companies to monopolize the business. That made a criminal of anyone who wanted to use a movie camera without paying a royalty to Edison and his partners.

Allan Dwan, an independent filmmaker, described the battles to film historian Kevin Brownlow, author of The War, the West, and the Wilderness.

The [Motion Picture] Patents Company hired goons for gunmen. If they saw a bunch of people working, and it wasn't one of their companies, they'd shoot a hole through the camera. Without the camera you couldn't work, and cameras were impossible to get. The reason we came to places like California was to get away from these goons. Around Chicago and New York, your life was in your hands if you went out with a camera. You'd find a bullet whizzing by your ear—bang, a hole in your camera. And so we sneaked out to California and hid away in little places. We worked in areas where you could see everything around you, and we stationed sentinels. I got my cowboys, the three Morrison brothers [Pete, Carl, and Chick Morrison, who came from Colorado, were among Hollywood's first and most talented cowboys], together with one or two they hired in the neighborhood, and told them, "If these fellows bother you, pop at them. Hit them in the foot, or something, but don't kill. Just let them know you're there."

So I was more or less protected, until one day this character got off the train at San Juan Capistrano, and wanted to see the boss in charge. "I'm the boss," I said. "What do you want?" He said, "I'd like to have a talk with you." So we walked up the road and he said, "Get out of here and quit making pictures." We walked across a little arroyo, a ditch, and people as usual had tossed some tin cans out there as they went by. He took out his sidearm and took a crack at a tin can down in the gully, and missed it. God took me by the hand and I pulled out my gun and hit the can twice. And the fellow looked at me and put his gun away. He turned away to go back and he ran straight into the Morrison brothers with their Winchesters. They stuck these rifles in his fanny and walked him back to the train. He got on and left and we never saw a goon again. Our reputation was abroad—we had an army. People wouldn't even come to watch us work. They were scared. "Don't go near them—they'll shoot you!"

"You simply cannot sell a Western picture at any price...."

A COWBOY STAR IS BORN

1911
Los Angeles

WILLIAM S. HART

Western movies were popular long before the movie business moved west in the 1910s. Thomas Edison filmed Cripple Creek Ballroom *in 1898, and the classic* The Great Train Robbery *in 1903.*

Most of the early efforts were laughable. They had been made by people who knew little or nothing about the West and the way the West looked. Indians might be dressed in gingham shirts. Cowboys might ride along paved streets in English saddles. The audiences, especially foreign audiences, watched them anyway.

But like all Hollywood trends, Westerns started to wane. Then William S. Hart, an experienced actor who had been born in the East but had lived out West as a young man, decided to give movies a try.

Here Hart recounts how he first decided to make Westerns, and his early days in Hollywood when he met up with an old friend, director Thomas Ince.

While playing in Cleveland, I attended a picture show. I saw a Western picture. It was awful! I talked with the manager of the theater and he told me it was one of the best Westerns he had ever had. None of the impossibilities or libels on the West meant anything to him—it was drawing the crowds. The fact that the sheriff was dressed and characterized as a sort of cross between a Wisconsin wood-chopper and a Gloucester fisherman was unknown to him. I did not seek to enlighten him. I was seeking information. In fact, I was so sure that I had made a big discovery that I was frightened that someone would read my mind and find it out.

Here were reproductions of the Old West being seriously presented to the public—in almost a burlesque manner—and they were successful. It made me tremble to think of it. I was an actor and I knew the West. . . . The opportunity that I had been waiting for years to come was knocking at my door.

Hundreds of ideas seemed to rush in from every direction. They assumed form. It was engendered—the die was cast. Rise or fall, sink or swim, I had to bend every endeavor to get a chance to make Western motion pictures. Usually when I was stirred by ambition I became afraid. But surely this could not be the valor of ignorance. I had been waiting for years for the right thing, and now the right thing had come! I was a part of the West—it was my boyhood home—it was in my blood. I had a thorough training as an actor. I was considered the outstanding portrayer of Western roles everywhere on the American stage.

It was the big opportunity that a most high Power, chance, or fixed law, had schooled me for. It had been many years in coming, but it was here. And I would go through hell on three pints of water before I would acknowledge defeat.

The remainder of the season I visited all picture shows wherever possible. During the summer at Westport and on trips to New York, I did the same. I talked to my actor friends in The Lambs Club who were working everyday playing Western parts in pictures being made over in Jersey. I was secretive. I told them nothing of my great plans. When it came time for "The Trail of the Lonesome Pine" to open again, my reluctance to take an engagement before trying my pet scheme caused me to raise my salary to $175 a week. While waiting for their answer, I met an actor who was going to California to work in Western pictures.

"The Trail of the Lonesome Pine" was going to California. I was frightened! They might refuse to give me the part on account of the raise in salary. I was on the point of writing them that I would go for any salary, when they wrote me O.K.

The finger of Fate was pointing in the right direction. Fortunately, we came West immediately after opening. At San Francisco I learned that all the principal studios were in Los Angeles; that the principal companies making Westerns were the Universal Picture Corporation in Hollywood, and the New York Motion Picture Company working in conjunction with the 101 Ranch [an Oklahoma-based Wild West show].

When we reached Los Angeles, while a friend was registering for me, I went into a telephone booth, called up the New York Motion Picture Company and asked for Joe Miller. A man who said his name was Brooks answered, and said that Mr. Miller was not there, but that he represented him.

I then said, "I am an actor and I want to see about making some Western pictures."

He replied: "Mr. Miller only owns the stock and the cowboy end of the company. If you want to see about acting, call up Thomas H. Ince—he is manager of the picture company."

I did so.

"Hello, Tom."

"Hello, Bill."

The next day Tom called and took me out to see the camp. I was enraptured and told him so. The very primitiveness of the whole life out there, the cowboys and the Indians, staggered me. I loved it.

They had everything to make Western pictures. The West was right there!

I told Tom of my hopes, of my plans. I told him everything.

"Bill," he said, "it's a damn shame, but you're too late! The country has been flooded with Western pictures. They are the cheapest pictures to make and every company out here has made them. You simply cannot sell a Western picture at any price. They are a drug on the market."

And to prove his statement, he showed me all the sets they were photographing on. The scenes were all laid in Ireland.

"But, Tom," I cried, "this means everything on earth to me. It is the one big opportunity of my life. Why all these cowboys? Why all these Indians?"

"Bill," he said, "it's a contract. The owners of this company, have a contract with the 101 Show that has another year to run."

"Fine," I said. "Let me make some Western pictures and use these people."

"Bill," he said, "I know you; I know, if there was any possible chance, that you could put it over, but it just can't be done. I made a picture when I came out here, a Western picture, Custer's Last Fight, and I had all these Indians and cowboys. It was a fine picture, but it didn't sell."

I looked at him, and he answered, "Sure, Bill, I used the story you told me [when they last saw each other]—that is why I'm telling you this—to show you that it won't go."

I didn't have any more to say. We walked all round the camp. When we were leaving, I talked in Sioux to some of the Indians, and Tom was so astonished. He walked back and said to a young Indian: "What did he say?"

The Indian just smiled and would not answer, until I told him in Sioux to do so, and then he replied, truthfully, that I had said that I was going away from here, but that I wanted to stay here.

I was late leaving (they had to hold the curtain at the theater for me), but just as Tom was putting me in his car he said: "Bill, if you want to come out next spring and take a chance, I'll give you seventy-five dollars a week to cover your expenses and direct you in a picture myself."

"Tom," I replied, "I'll be here just as soon as we close. . . ."

We closed at the Grand Opera House in New York. An actor called to see his brother in our company, to say good-bye. He was leaving to take the train for California to work in pictures for the New York Motion Picture Company. He showed us his ticket and sleeper. I said nothing. No one knew I was going. I bought my own ticket and rode in a tourist car.

The quality of Hart's work revived the genre. Hart became one of the first movie stars; to an earlier generation he was as famous as John Wayne. When United Artists was formed by the most powerful stars in the movie business— Mary Pickford, Douglas Fairbanks, Charlie Chaplin, and director D. W. Griffith—Hart was supposed to be the fifth partner. He pulled out at the last minute.

———————————

"I whirled to escape, pointed my skees down the slope, and went. . . ."

RACING AN AVALANCHE

1912
San Juan Mountains, Colorado

ENOS A. MILLS

The first American ski club was formed in 1872, and the National Ski Association was formed in 1904, but by 1920 there were only about 4,000 skiers in the whole country. Now there are perhaps 5 million.

As a general rule, it's stupid to race an avalanche. They reach speeds of 200 miles per hour and kill several people a year. Mills, a popular nature writer, was lucky.

I had gone into the San Juan Mountains during the first week in March to learn something of the laws which govern snow slides, to get a fuller idea of their power and destructiveness, and also with the hope of seeing them in wild, magnificent action.

Everywhere, except on wind-swept points, the winter's snows lay deep. Conditions for slide movement were so favorable it seemed probable that, during the next few days at least, one would "run" or chute down every gulch that led from the summit. I climbed on skees well to the top of the range. By waiting on spurs and ridges I saw several thrilling exhibitions.

. . . Broken clouds and a glowing eastern sky claimed all attention until it was light enough to get off the promontory.

Planning to go down the west side, I crossed the table-like top, found, after many trials, a break in the enormous snow-cornice, and started down the steep slope. It was a dangerous descent, for the rock was steep and smooth as a wall, and was overladen with snow which might slip at any moment.

I descended slowly and with great caution, so as not to start the snow, as well as to guard against slipping and losing control of myself. It was like descending a mile of steep, snow-covered barn roof,—nothing to lay hold of and omnipresent opportunity for slipping. I went sideways, with my long skees, which I had now regained, at right angles to the slope; slowly, a few inches at a time, I eased myself down, planting one free skee firmly before I moved the other.

At last I reached a point where the wall was sufficiently tilted to be called a slope, though it was still too steep for safe coasting. The clouds lifted and were floating away, while the sun made the mountains of snow still whiter. I paused to look back and up, to where the wall ended in the blue sky, and could not understand how I had come safely down, even with the long tacks I had made, which showed clearly up to the snow-corniced, mist-shrouded crags at the summit. I had come down the side of a precipitous amphitheatre which rose a thousand feet or more above me. A short distance down the mountain, the slopes of this amphitheatre concentrated in a narrow gulch that extended two miles or more. Altogether it was like being in an enormous frying-pan laying face up. I was in the pan just above the place where the gulch handle joined.

It was a bad place to get out of, and thousands of tons of snow clinging to the steeps and sagging from corniced crests ready to slip, plunge down, and sweep the very spot on which I stood, showed most impressively that it was a perilous place to be in.

As I stood gazing upward and wondering how the snow ever could have held while I came down over it, there suddenly appeared on the upper steeps an upburst as from an explosion. Along several hundred feet of cornice, sprays and clouds of snow dashed and filled the air. An upward breeze curled and swept the top of this cloud over the crest in an inverted cascade.

All this showed for a few seconds until the snowy spray began to separate and vanish in the air. The snow-cloud settled downward and began to roll forward. Then monsters of massed snow appeared beneath the front of the cloud and plunged down the slopes. Wildly, grandly they dragged the entire snow-cloud in their wake. At the same instant the remainder of the snow-cornice was suddenly enveloped in another explosive snow-cloud effect.

A general slide had started. I whirled to escape, pointed my skees down the slope,—and went. In less than half a minute a tremendous snow avalanche, one hundred or perhaps two hundred feet deep and five or six hundred feet long, thundered over the spot where I had stood.

There was no chance to dodge, no time to climb out of the way. The only hope of escape lay in outrunning the magnificent monster. It came crashing and thundering after me as swift as a gale and more all-sweeping and destructive than an earthquake tidal wave.

I made a desperate start. Friction almost ceases to be a factor with skees on a snowy steep, and in less than a hundred yards I was going like the wind. For the first quarter of a mile, to the upper end of the gulch, was smooth coasting, and down this I shot, with the avalanche, comet-tailed with snow-dust, in close pursuit. A race for life was on.

The gulch down which I must go began with a rocky gorge and continued downward, an enormous U-shaped depression between high mountain-ridges. Here and there it expanded and then contracted, and it was broken with granite crags and ribs. It was piled and bristled with ten thousand fire-killed trees. To coast through all these snow-clad obstructions at breakneck speed would be taking the maximum number of life-and-death chances in the minimum amount of time. The worst of it all was that I had never been through the place. And bad enough, too, was the fact that a ridge thrust in from the left and completely hid the beginning of the gulch.

As I shot across the lower point of the ridge, about to plunge blindly into the gorge, I thought of the possibility of becoming entangled in the hedge-like thickets of dwarfed, gnarled timberline trees. I also realized that I might dash against a cliff or plunge into a deep canyon. Of course I might strike an open way, but certain it was that I could not stop, nor see the beginning of the gorge, nor tell what I should strike when I shot over the ridge.

It was a second of most intense concern as I cleared the ridge blindly to go into what lay below and beyond. It was like leaping into the dark, and with the leap turning on the all-revealing light. As I cleared the ridge, there was just time to pull myself together for a forty-odd-foot leap across one arm of the horseshoe-shaped end of the gorge. In all my wild mountainside coasts on skees, never have I sped as swiftly as when

I made this mad flight. As I shot through the air, I had a glimpse down into the pointed, snow-laden tops of a few tall fir trees that were firmly rooted among the rocks in the bottom of the gorge. Luckily I cleared the gorge and landed in a good place; but so narrowly did I miss the corner of a cliff that my shadow collided with it.

There was no time to bid farewell to fears when the slide started, nor to entertain them while running away from it. Instinct put me to flight; the situation set my wits working at their best, and, once started, I could neither stop nor look back; and so thick and fast did obstructions and dangers rise before me that only dimly and incidentally did I think of the oncoming danger behind.

I came down on the farther side of the gorge, to glance forward like an arrow. There was only an instant to shape my course and direct my flight across the second arm of the gorge, over which I leaped from a high place, sailing far above the snow-mantled trees and boulders in the bottom. My senses were keenly alert, and I remember noticing the shadows of the fir trees on the white snow and hearing while still in the air the brave, cheery notes of a chickadee; then the snowslide on my trail, less than an eighth of a mile behind, plunged into the gorge with a thundering crash. I came back to the snow on the lower side, and went skimming down the slope with the slide only a few seconds behind.

Fortunately most of the fallen masses of trees were buried, though a few broken limbs peeped through the snow to snag or trip me. How I ever dodged my way through the thickly standing tree growths is one feature of the experience that was too swift for recollection. Numerous factors presented themselves which should have done much to dispel mental procrastination and develop decision. There were scores of progressive propositions to decide within a few seconds; should I dodge that tree on the left side and duck under low limbs just beyond, or dodge to the right and scrape that pile of rocks? These, with my speed, required instant decision and action.

With almost uncontrollable rapidity I shot out into a small, nearly level glacier meadow, and had a brief rest from swift decisions and oncoming dangers. How relieved my weary brain felt, with nothing to decide about dodging! As though starved for thought material, I wondered if there were willows buried beneath the snow. Sharp pains in my left hand compelled attention, and showed my left arm drawn tightly against my breast, with fingers and thumb spread to the fullest, and all their muscles tense.

The lower edge of the meadow was almost blockaded with a dense growth of fire-killed trees. Fortunately the easy slope here had so checked my speed that I was able to dodge safely through, but the heavy slide swept across the meadow after me with undiminished speed, and came crashing into the dead trees so close to me that broken limbs were flung flying past as I shot down off a steep moraine less than one hundred feet ahead.

All the way down I had hoped to find a side canyon into which I might dodge. I was going too rapidly to enter the one I had seen. As I coasted off the moraine it flashed through my mind that I had once heard a prospector say it was only a quarter of a mile from Aspen Gulch up to the meadows. Aspen Gulch came in on the right, as the now widening track seemed to indicate.

At the bottom of the moraine I was forced between two trees that stood close together, and a broken limb of one pierced my open coat just beneath the left armhole, and slit the coat to the bottom. My momentum and the resistance of the strong material gave me such a shock that I was flung off my balance, and my left skee smashed against a tree. Two feet of the heel was broken off and the remainder split. I managed to avoid falling, but had to check my speed with my staff for fear of a worse accident.

Battling breakers with a broken oar or racing with a broken skee are struggles of short duration. The slide did not slow down, and so closely did it crowd me that, through the crashing of trees as it struck them down, I could hear the rocks and splintered timbers in its mass grinding together and thudding gainst obstructions over which it swept. These sounds, and flying, broken limbs cried to me "Faster!" and as I started to descend another steep moraine, I threw away my staff and "let go." I simply flashed down the slope, dodged and rounded a cliff, turned awkwardly into Aspen Gulch, and tumbled heels over head—into safety.

Then I picked myself up, to see the slide go by within twenty feet, with great broken trees sticking out of its side, and a snow-cloud dragging above.

---

*"I do not envy those whose introduction to nature
was lush meadows, lakes, and swamps where life abounds."*

SAGEBRUSH, LAVA ROCK, AND RATTLERS

1913
Yakima, Washington

WILLIAM O. DOUGLAS

Supreme Court justice William O. Douglas grew up in Washington State, and was as comfortable outdoors as he was in chambers. He wrote popular books about his wilderness adventures, including Strange Lands and Friendly People, Beyond the High Himalayas, North from Malaya, *and the one from which this account is taken,* Of Men and Mountains.

There is a Russian saying that every devil praises the marshes where he was born. Early associations control the nostalgic urges of every person. For Holmes it was granite rocks and barberry bushes. For others it may be lilacs, sycamores, willows, the checkerboard of wheat lands, or rolling hills. My love is for what many would put down as the dreariest aspects of the dry foothills of the West—sagebrush and lava rock.

This sagebrush (Artemisia tridentata Nutt.) is found throughout the West. It is as American as the New England twang, the Southern drawl, the "You bet" of the West, or "Youse guys" from Brooklyn. It covers the foothills around Yakima. It grows at 8000 feet on Hart Mountain in southern Oregon. It holds the soil in place throughout the western belt from Canada to Mexico. It is the bush that Lewis and Clark called "southern wood." It commonly grows only a foot and a half or two feet high. But in gullies and ravines and other spots that collect water for part of the year, it may grow as high as a man's head. John Scharff, superintendent of the Malheur Bird Refuge in southern Oregon, bragged of the Steens Mountain sagebrush, "It's real timber, boys. This fall my first job is to run some lines and cruise and scale it."

It's tough and wiry; and it makes a quick, hot, pungent fire. In the springtime its tender new leaves make browse for antelope and sheep. Bunchgrass that cures on the stalk, and provides year-round food for stock, grows in its shade. It also furnishes protection and moisture for the myriad of wild flowers that in springtime briefly paint light streaks of blue and yellow and white on desert slopes. And it is in its full glory when spring rains fall.

That's the way I first remember it on the foothills of Yakima at night.

A light, warm rain was falling. The air was permeated with the smell of freshly dampened dust and with the pungent but delicate odor of sage.

The lava rock is part of the great Columbia lava or basalt, which includes some andesite. Layer upon layer of it underlies eastern Washington and Oregon. During the Tertiary period it boiled up from the bowels of the earth. The period of its greatest activity was the Miocene, some 30 million years ago. There were at times centuries between the various flows. This molten rock poured largely out of great fissures, not from volcanoes. It flooded the entire Yakima country, which then was largely a lowland, and covered most of what is now the Cascades. There were at least 28 layers of the hot, liquid rock poured over this country. Their aggregate thickness is over 5000 feet.

This rock retains the heat of the sun throughout the night. For that reason the orchards of Yakima that are surrounded by outcroppings of it are quite free from frosts that kill fruit less favorably located. For that reason also, rattlesnakes are sometimes found curled on lava rock, warming their bellies.

Once a rattler, so positioned, struck at me. I was standing on a steep hillside, shoulder high to a ledge of rimrock. I heard the rattle, and from the corner of my eye I saw him coiled and ready to strike, not more than two feet from my cheek. As he struck I jumped, lost my footing, and rolled 40 or so feet down the ravine. Remembering, I still seem to feel his hissing breath near my ear.

That was carelessness. For we who were raised in the environment of the Columbia lava know the risks of the rattler. All up and down the Ahtanum, Tieton, and Naches were stories of fishermen who were bitten on the fingers or face when they grasped lava ledges above them without first exploring the top. One moves warily through this lava rock country.

The rattlesnake—Wak-puch—is not entirely evil. Unlike other poisonous snakes, he is sufficiently friendly to speak before he strikes, to give notice of his plans. And he much prefers to escape man than to attack him. His attack is only to repel a trespass. This is his domain, his ancestral home. He was here long before man. Hence there is reason why he can speak with authority. Moreover, according to the lore of the Yakimas, he has magical powers. He hears what people say and can avenge insults. To this day the Yakimas are superstitious about killing him. Thus on these earlier explorations of the foothills the rattler added mystery, suspense, and magic to the land of lava rock and sagebrush.

When I walked the foothills of Yakima on wintry nights I would often build a bonfire of sagebrush at the base of an outcropping of rimrock.

There I would sit, my back to the rock, protected from the wind, hoping the warmth of the fire would not awaken a den of rattlers with the false message that an early spring had arrived.

. . . I do not envy those whose introduction to nature was lush meadows, lakes, and swamps where life abounds. The desert hills of Yakima had a poverty that sharpened perception. Even a minute violet quickens the heart when one has walked far or climbed high to find it. Where nature is more bountiful, even the tender bitterroot might go unnoticed. Yet when a lone plant is seen in bloom on scab land between batches of bunchgrass and sage, it can transform the spot as completely as only a whole bank of flowers could do in a more lush environment. It is the old relationship between scarcity and value.

These are botanical lessons of the desert which the foothills of Yakima taught me.

"We propose alliance to Mexico upon the following basis: To make war together; make peace together. . . ."

WORLD WAR I IN THE WEST: THE ZIMMERMANN TELEGRAM

January 19–March 1, 1917
Washington, D.C., and Mexico City

ROBERT LANSING

America had remained neutral since the war in Europe began in August 1914. Then two events shocked the public and President Woodrow Wilson into action. One was resumption of U-boat attacks on American ships after a two-year hiatus. The second was this telegram from German secretary of foreign affairs Arthur Zimmermann to the German minister in Mexico. The telegram quickly changed sentiment in the Western states from isolationism to belligerence.

Fear of aggression from Mexico might seem remote today, but at the time it was a serious concern. The Mexican Revolution (1910–15) began a period of political instability that allowed bandits like the notorious Francisco "Pancho" Villa to become warlords, as rival political factions vied for guerrilla support. When Villa crossed the U.S. border and raided Columbus, New Mexico, in 1916, killing seventeen people, Brigadier General John J. Pershing was ordered into Mexico with 6,000 men to hunt down Villa. President Wilson also ordered the militias of Texas, Arizona, and New Mexico to mobilize along the border. Pershing's troops were still chasing Villa when the Zimmermann telegram was intercepted.

This account is an aide-memoire written by Robert Lansing, Wilson's secretary of state, a few days after the telegram was made public. Lansing had been pushing Wilson to join the Allies for a long time.

NUMBER 1. STRICTLY SECRET. DECODE YOURSELF. WE INTEND TO BEGIN UNRESTRICTED U-BOAT WARFARE ON FEBRUARY FIRST. EFFORT WILL BE MADE NOTWITHSTANDING THIS TO KEEP THE UNITED STATES NEUTRAL. IN THE EVENT THAT WE SHOULD NOT BE SUCCESSFUL IN THIS, WE PROPOSE ALLIANCE TO MEXICO UPON THE FOLLOWING BASIS: TO MAKE WAR TOGETHER; MAKE PEACE TOGETHER; GENEROUS FINANCIAL SUPPORT; AND AGREEMENT ON OUR PART THAT MEXICO SHALL RECONQUER THE FORMERLY LOST TERRITORY IN TEXAS, NEW MEXICO, ARIZONA. ARRANGEMENT OF DETAILS TO BE LEFT TO YOUR HONOR. YOU SHOULD DISCLOSE THE FOREGOING TO THE PRESIDENT [OF MEXICO] IN STRICT SECRECY AS SOON AS OUTBREAK OF WAR WITH THE UNITED STATES IS CERTAIN AND ADD THE PROPOSAL [THAT HE SHALL] INVITE JAPAN TO IMMEDIATE SPONTANEOUS CONCUR-RENT EFFORT AND AT THE SAME TIME USE HIS GOOD OFFICES BETWEEN US AND JAPAN. PLEASE CALL THE PRESIDENT'S ATTENTION TO THE FACT THAT THE RUTHLESS EMPLOYMENT OF OUR U-BOATS OFFERS THE PROSPECT OF FORCING ENGLAND IN A FEW MONTHS TO [MAKE] PEACE. ACKNOWLEDGE RECEIPT. ZIMMERMANN.

. . . The President two or three times during the recital of the fore-going exclaimed, "Good Lord!"

. . . I told the President that I thought it would be unwise for the Department to give out the telegram officially at this time as it would be charged that it was done to influence opinion on the bill for arming merchant vessels, but I thought it might indirectly be made public after we had confirmed [its authenticity]. To this the President agreed.

. . . A little before four [in the] afternoon [of the next day] the President telephoned saying that he thought it was wise to give out the telegram for the morning papers and that he believed that it would be advisable for me to summon Senator Hitchcock, who had charge of the Arming Bill, to the Department and show him the message. I again sug-gested that the message be made public indirectly, that then when we were asked about it we could say that we knew of it and knew that it was authentic. I said that I could do this through a representative of the Associated Press. . . . With this plan the President agreed.

. . . At about six that evening a correspondent [E. M. Hood] of the Associated Press came to my house by appointment and I gave him a paraphrase of the telegram binding him to secrecy as to where he obtained it.

The next morning, [Thursday] March first, the message was published in the papers and created a profound sensation throughout the country. Its effect on Congress was very marked. After a day given over to patriotic speeches the House by a vote of four hundred and three to thirteen passed the Arming Bill.

. . . When the Associated Press report containing the text of the Zimmermann telegram was printed in the morning papers of March first, it was read with conflicting emotions by the people. Amazement and incredulity were general. It was hard for the public to believe that the German Secretary of Foreign Affairs had been so indiscreet as to send a message of this sort through the United States, even though in cipher, where it was liable to fall into the hands of the American authorities. Yet the publishing of the text of the telegram in hundreds of papers was a challenge to the Imperial Government to declare its falsity. The pro-German press unhesitatingly asserted that the government had been imposed upon by some clever forger, presumably in the pay of the Allies, or else had itself manufactured the dispatch in order to influence favorable action on the Armed Ship Bill. . . . [But] when Zimmermann on Saturday, March third, frankly admitted to a German news agency in Berlin the authenticity of the message and made excuses for sending it, the charge of falsification collapsed.

The people of the Eastern States had been clamoring with increasing vehemence for war against Germany because of the submarine outrages, but the Middle West and Pacific States had not responded to that spirit. The people of those sections were as individuals less affected by the German lawlessness on the Atlantic than those of the East. The Zimmermann telegram, however, opened their eyes to the real character and purposes of the Berlin Government. The proposed alliance with Mexico and possibly with Japan, if it materialized, would affect the entire West. It needed but some disclosure of this sort to transform popular indifference into intense hostility to Germany, to convert pacifism and a desire for continued inaction into demands for war.

Thus the Zimmermann telegram resulted in unifying public sentiment throughout the United States against Germany, in putting the people solidly behind the government and in making war inevitable, if not popular, because the German Government's sinister intent toward the United States could no longer be doubted. The "cold-blooded proposition" of Germany's Secretary of Foreign Affairs in one day accomplished a change in sentiment and public opinion which would otherwise have required months to accomplish. From the time that the telegram was published, or at least from the time that its authenticity was admitted by its author, the United States' entry into the war was assured, since it could no longer be doubted that it was desired by the American people from Maine to California and from Michigan to Texas.

Pershing's troops were withdrawn from Mexico to fight overseas. Mexico never did form an alliance with Germany. Japan joined America's side.

"Now the affair could no longer be kept off the front page...."

RICH MAN, POOR MAN, BEGGARMAN, THIEF: THE TEAPOT DOME SCANDAL

1921–1928
Teapot Dome, Wyoming,
Los Angeles, and Washington, D.C.

SENATOR THOMAS WALSH

The Teapot Dome scandal is the most complicated corruption scandal in the history of the United States. By comparison, Watergate was just a misunderstanding. But at its center was a simple scheme: A cabinet secretary accepted a bribe to arrange cheap leases of valuable oil fields. (The name came from the Wyoming site of one of the fields.)

Teapot Dome had it all: huge corporations, co-conspirators who cheated each other, secret codes, documents with signatures "mysteriously" torn off, one of the most powerful figures in Hollywood acting as bagman, a senator who pleaded his Fifth Amendment right against self-incrimination, more money than most people could imagine even in the bubble years of Wall Street, and a last-minute confession.

It started with two old friends, one who was rich, and one who wanted to be. Edward Doheny and Albert Fall had met when both were prospectors in the southwest. By 1922, Doheny controlled various interests including an oil company. Fall, had not done well in business; but he had become Warren G. Harding's secretary of the Interior.

Each had something the other wanted. So Fall arranged for some U.S. Navy *oil reserves to come under the control of the Interior Department, then, in return for a $100,000 "loan," leased those fields to Doheny.*

Doheny also helped Fall make a similar arrangement with another business-man, Harry Sinclair.

Eyewitness Thomas Walsh, a Democratic senator from Montana, headed the committee investigating the scandal.

In the spring of 1922 rumors circulated that a lease had been or was about to be made of Naval Reserve No. 3 in the state of Wyoming,—popularly known, from its local designation, as the Teapot Dome.

. . . Failing to get any definite or reliable information at the departments, upon diligent inquiry, Senator Kendrick of Wyoming introduced a resolution calling on the secretary of the interior for information as to the existence of the lease.

A [response] was transmitted, disclosing that a lease of the entire Reserve No. 3 was made two weeks before, to the Mammoth Oil Company, organized by Harry Sinclair, a spectacular oil operator. . . .

A letter from Secretary Fall to the President in justification of the lease of the Teapot Dome and of leases of limited areas on the other reserves was by him sent to the Senate. . . .

No one seemed willing to assume any wrong in or even to criticize the acts of the new administration, buttressed by that 7 million majority [in the 1920 election] and guided by the "best minds. . . ."

Misstatements of fact in the letter to the President were not infrequent, but more persuasive with me was the total disregard of the plain provisions of the law, and the utterly untenable arguments made to sustain the action that was taken. . . . He fell back on some vague authority arising from the general scheme of our government. . . .

In his letter to the President, [Fall called] himself the guardian of important military secrets of the government in connection with the leases which he would, under no circumstances, reveal, plainly intimating that those who were trying to pry into the affair were lacking in loyalty. He recalled, to me at least, that cynical saying of Dr. Johnson that patriotism is the last refuge of a scoundrel.

In the interim, stories had reached me . . . of Fall's sudden rise from financial embarrassment, if not impecuniosity, to comparative affluence. I then secured subpoenas for witnesses, who told the story of Fall's having paid $91,500 for a ranch in New Mexico—the initial payment of $10,000 having been made in bills taken from a black tin box—of his subsequent purchase of other lands costing $33,000 more, of the installation of a hydroelectric plant at a cost of from $40,000 to $50,000, and of other expenditures in the aggregate approximating $200,000.

It was up to Fall to tell where the money came from. His son-in-law did not appear according to promise. Fall did not. It was reported in a vague way that he was ill—now in Chicago, now in New York. Reporters were unable to locate him, for they were now on the job. In fact he came to Chicago, went from there to New York, thence to Atlantic City, and to Washington, where he told the Committee that he had borrowed $100,000 with which to purchase the ranch from Edward B. McLean, owner and editor of the *Washington Post*. Fall speedily betook himself as McLean's guest at Palm Beach, Florida.

A month had gone by since the damaging evidence had been heard. An honest man would have hastened to take the stand to refute the inferences to which it naturally gave rise and the doubts that it must inevitably have raised. Had such a man been desperately ill he would have told the story on the stand and not sought refuge from cross-examination by sending a letter from his hotel in the city in which the Committee was sitting.

Moreover, the knowing ones smiled incredulously at the idea of Ned McLean's having such a sum of money at hand to loan, though rich in property, or of his loaning it if he had it.

Forthwith that gentleman [McLean] began to exhibit a feverish anxiety lest he be called as a witness, singularly divining what was coming. He communicated by wire with the Committee; he sent lawyers to represent to it and to me that he was ill, that his wife was ill; that it would be dangerous for him to tempt the rigorous climate of Washington at that season of the year; that he had loaned $100,000 to Fall in November or December 1922, and knew nothing about the facts otherwise. . . . He begged not to be called to Washington. . . .

In the discussion Senator Smoot suggested that I go to Palm Beach and take his testimony.

I made the trip in the expectation that he would say that he had made the loan, intending to interrogate him as to the source from which the money was derived. I proposed to trace it to its source, either to his own private funds, kept in his own private accounts or to some account earmarked in a manner that would permit following it to some other origin. I suspected that in some way it came from Sinclair and that I could follow it through various banking transactions to that source.

I was dumbfounded when McLean frankly admitted that he never did loan the money to Fall, adding that he gave Fall his checks for that sum, which were returned a few days later and destroyed without being cashed, the recipient asserting that he had arranged to secure the necessary elsewhere.

Now the affair could no longer be kept off the front page. . . . The climax was reached when . . . Doheny voluntarily appeared to tell that on November 30, 1921, he had loaned $100,000 to Fall without security, moved by old friendship and commiseration for his business misfortunes, negotiations between them then pending eventuating in the contract awarded to Doheny . . . through which he secured, without competition, a contract giving him a preference right to a lease of a large part of Naval Reserve No. 1, to be followed by the lease of the whole of it. . . .

Fall, forced by the Committee to come before it, after pleading inability on account of illness, took refuge under his constitutional immunity, a broken man.

Fall was convicted in his trial, sentenced to a year in prison, and fined $100,000. Doheny and Sinclair were acquitted. (Sinclair was later jailed for contempt of the Senate and for hiring private detectives to shadow the jurors.) The Supreme Court ruled in 1927 that the oil fields had to be returned to the government.

Notable supporting players in the scandal included Will Hays, the former chairman of the Republican National Committee, who facilitated the transactions. (Walsh called him a "bagman.") Just before the scandal broke, Hays moved to Los Angeles, having been hired by the film studios to establish moral standards for the movie business.

Walsh became a national figure. He died in 1933 en route to starting his job as President Franklin Roosevelt's first attorney general.

"We had no great men, but the whole bunch of us put together amounted to something that was very nearly great."

FRESNO

c. 1915–1921

WILLIAM SAROYAN

Fresno County, in California's 25,000-square-mile Central Valley, produces more agricultural products than any other county in the United States. The thousands of farms and groves in the region have been marketing their national brands through cooperatives such as Sun-Maid, Sunkist, and Blue Diamond since the turn of the century.

William Saroyan, a native of the city of Fresno, became a favorite of readers all over the country in 1934 with the publication of his first book of stories, The Daring Young Man on the Flying Trapeze. *He later won the Pulitzer Prize for his play* The Time of Your Life.

A man could walk four or five miles in any direction from the heart of our city and see our streets dwindle to land and weeds. In many places the land would be vineyard and orchard land, but in most places it would be desert land, the weeds would be the strong dry weeds of desert. In this land there would be the living things that had had their being in the quietness of deserts for centuries. There would be snakes and horned-toads, prairie-dogs and jack-rabbits. In the sky over this land would be buzzards and hawks, and the hot sun. And everywhere in the desert would be the marks of wagons that had made lonely roads.

Two miles from the heart of our city a man could come to the desert and feel the loneliness of a desolate area, a place lost in the earth, far from the solace of human thought. Standing at the edge of our city, a man could feel that we had made this place of streets and dwellings in the stillness and loneliness of the desert, and that we had done a brave thing. We had come to this dry area that was without history, and we had paused in it and built our houses and we were slowly creating the legend of our life. We were digging for water and we were leading streams through the dry land. We were planting and ploughing and standing in the midst of the garden we were making.

. . . We had no great men, but the whole bunch of us put together amounted to something that was very nearly great.

. . . Our enterprise wasn't on a vast scale. It wasn't even on a medium-sized scale. There was nothing slick about anything. Our enterprise was neither scientific nor inhuman, as the enterprise of a growing city ought to be. . . . But in time a genius appeared among us and he said that we would change the history of the world. He said that we would do it with raisins.

He said that we would change the eating habits of man.

Nobody thought he was crazy because he wore spectacles and looked important. He appeared to be what our people liked to call an educated man, and any man who had had an education, any man who had gone through a university and read books, must be an important man. He had statistics and the statistical method of proving a point. He proved mathematically that he would be able to do everything he said he was going to do. What our valley needed, he said, was a system whereby the raisin would be established as a necessary part of the national diet, and he said that he had evolved this system and that it was available for our valley.

He made eloquent speeches in our Civic Auditorium and in the public halls of the small towns around our city. He said after we got America accustomed to eating raisins, we would begin to teach Europe and Asia and maybe Australia to eat raisins, our valley would become the richest valley in the whole world. China! he said. He shouted the exact number of Chinese in China. It was a stupendous figure, and the farmers in the Civic Auditorium didn't know whether to applaud or protest. He said that if he could get every living Chinaman to place one raisin, only one mind you, in every pot of rice he cooked, why, then, we could dispose of all our raisins at a good price and everybody in our valley would have money in the bank, and would be able to purchase all the indispensable conveniences of modern life, bathtubs, carpet-sweepers, house electricity, and automobiles.

Rice, he said. That's all they eat. But we can teach them to drop one raisin in every pot of rice they cook.

Raisins had a good taste, he said. People liked to eat raisins. People were so fond of eating raisins that they would be glad to pay money for them. The trouble was that people had gotten out of the habit of eating raisins. It was because grocers all over the country hadn't been carrying raisins for years, or if they had been carrying them, the raisins hadn't been packed in attractive packages.

All we needed, he said, was a raisin association with an executive department and a central packing and distributing plant. He would do the rest. He would have an attractive package designed, and he would create a patented trade-name for our raisins. He would place full-page advertisements in *The Saturday Evening Post* and other national periodicals. He would organize a great sales force. He would do everything. If our farmers would join this raisin association of his, he would do everything, and our city would grow to be one of the liveliest cities in California. Our valley would grow to be one of the richest agricultural centers of the world. He used big words like co-operation, mass production, modern efficiency, modern psychology, modern advertising, and modern distribution, and the farmers who couldn't understand what he was talking about felt that he was very wise and that they must join the raisin association and help make raisins famous.

He was an orator. He was a statistician. He was a genius. I forget his name. Our whole valley has forgotten his name, but in his day he made something of a stir.

The editor of the *Morning Republican* studied this man's proposal and found it sound, and the editor of the *Evening Herald* said that it was a good thing, and our mayor was in favor of it, and there was excitement all over our valley. Farmers from all over our valley came to town in surreys and buggies. They gathered in small and large groups in front of our public buildings, and they talked about this idea of making the raisins famous.

It sounded all right.

The basic purpose of the raisin association was to gather together all the raisins of our valley, and after creating a demand for them through national advertising, to offer them for sale at a price that would pay for all the operating expenses of the association and leave a small margin for the farmers themselves. Well, the association was established and it was called the Sun-Maid Raisin Association. A six-story Sun-Maid Raisin Building was erected, and an enormous packing and distributing plant was erected. It contained the finest of modern machinery. These machines cleaned the raisins and took the stems from them. The whole plant was a picture of order and efficiency.

Every Thursday in those days I went down to Knapp's on Broadway and got a dozen copies of *The Saturday Evening Post*. The magazine was very thick and heavy. I used to carry a dozen of them in a sack slung over my shoulder. By the time I had walked a block my shoulder would be sore. I do not know why I ever wanted to bother about selling *The Saturday Evening Post,* but I suppose it was partly because I knew Benjamin Franklin had founded it, and partly because I liked to take a copy of the magazine home and look at the advertisements. For a while I even got in the habit of reading the stories of George Agnew Chamberlain. One Thursday evening I had a copy of *The Saturday Evening Post* spread before me on our living-room table. I was turning the pages and looking at the things that were being advertised. On one page I read the words, Have you had your iron today? It was a full-page advertisement of our Raisin Association. The advertisement explained in impeccable English that raisins contained iron and that wise people were eating a five-cent package of raisins every afternoon. Raisins banished fatigue, the advertisement said. At the bottom of the page was the name of our Association, its street address, and the name of our city. We were no longer lost in the wilderness, because the name of our city was printed in *The Saturday Evening Post*.

These advertisements began to appear regularly in *The Saturday Evening Post*. It was marvelous. People were hearing about us. It was very expensive to have a full-page advertisement in the *Post,* but people were being taught to eat raisins, and that was the important thing.

For a while people actually did eat raisins. Instead of spending a nickel for a bottle of Coca-Cola or for a bar of candy, people were buying small packages of raisins. The price of raisins began to move upward, and after several years, when all of America was enjoying prosperity, the price of raisins became so high that a man with ten acres of vineyard was considered a man of considerable means, and as a matter of fact he was. Some farmers who had only ten acres were buying brand-new automobiles and driving them around.

Everybody in our city was proud of the Raisin Association. Everything looked fine, values were up, and a man had to pay a lot of money for a little bit of desert.

Then something happened.

It wasn't the fault of our Raisin Association. It just happened. People stopped eating raisins. Maybe it was because there was no longer as much prosperity as there had been, or maybe it was because people had simply become tired of eating raisins. There are other things people can buy for a nickel and eat. At any rate, people stopped eating raisins. Our advertisements kept appearing in *The Saturday Evening Post* and we kept asking the people of America if they had had their iron, but it wasn't doing any good. We had more raisins in our Sun-Maid warehouse than we could ever sell, even to the Chinese, even if they were to drop three raisins in every pot of rice they cooked. The price of raisins began to drop. The great executives of the Association began to worry. They began to think up new ways to use raisins. They hired chemists who invented a raisin syrup. It was supposed to be at least as good as maple syrup, but it wasn't. Not by a long shot. It didn't taste like syrup at all. It simply had a syrupy texture. That's all. But the executives of our Association were desperate and they wanted to dispose of our surplus raisins. They were ready to fool themselves, if necessary, into believing that our valley would grow prosperous through the manufacture and distribution of raisin syrup, and for a while they believed this. But people who were buying the syrup didn't believe it. The price of raisins kept on going down. It got so low it looked as if we had made a mistake by pausing in the desert and building our city in the first place.

Then we found out that it was the same all over the country. Prices were low everywhere. No matter how efficient we were, or how cleverly we wrote our advertisements, or how attractive we made our packages of raisins, we couldn't hope for anything higher than the price we were getting. The six-story building looked sad, the excitement died away, and the packing house became a useless ornament in the landscape. Its machinery became junk, and we knew a great American idea had failed. We hadn't changed the taste of man. Bread was still preferable to raisins. We hadn't taught the Chinese to drop a raisin in their pots of cooking rice. They were satisfied to have the rice without the raisins.

And so we began to eat the raisins ourselves. It was amazing how we learned to eat raisins. We had talked so much about them we had forgotten that they were good to eat. We learned to cook raisins. They were good stewed, they had a fine taste with bread. All over the valley people were eating raisins. People couldn't buy raisins because they were a luxury, and so we had to eat them ourselves although they were no luxury to us.

"Only a few chronic fanners persisted."

"MANUFACTURED WEATHER": THE INVENTION OF AIR CONDITIONING

1922
Newark, New Jersey, and New York City

WILLIS CARRIER

Does air conditioning really rank with Lewis and Clark, or Silicon Valley?

We take it for granted today, but air conditioning made mass settlement of the West possible. Imagine Dallas or Pheonix without it. Life magazine named it one of the hundred most important inventions of the twentieth century.

And while it will never be glamorous, its history is closely tied to the growth of the most glamorous industry of all, show business. Before the era of $100 million films, Hollywood's biggest financial problem was getting customers inside a stuffy theater on a summer day. Eyewitness Willis Carrier, who created the system that is still used today, was counting on theater owners to place enough orders to boost his struggling company.

Here he recalls the first demonstration of a first working model to an audience of engineers at the company's plant in Newark, and an early test at a movie theater. The key customer in the theater audience was Paramount's Adolph Zukor.

When the day of the unveiling arrived, we had turned the machine over but we had not run it under load conditions. We did not have steam in our factory for the turbine, so we borrowed it from our next-door neighbor. By the time the steam reached us it was sufficient to run the machine when idling, but not to run it with the cooling load. By noon we had checked the steam line and fixed a leak. We started up the machine, using it to chill the water for our air conditioning system. When the guests arrived, our offices were cool and comfortable—and it was a hot day.

[Then] I heard [a] long, loud, rumbling, slowly diminishing b-r-r-r. I visualized the rotor of the compressor tearing itself to pieces. Beads of perspiration came out on my forehead and my hands were soaking wet. But I kept right on talking, trying to act as if nothing had happened. Irvine, sitting near the back, casually left the room with an air of calmness I knew he did not feel. He soon came back and signaled to me that all was okay. Later he told me the cause of the noise. In arranging the space for the boxing matches, one of our men pulled a large metal dining table across a rough concrete floor. No sound effects man could have done any better in imitating the disintegration of a rotative machine.

. . . Typical of show business, the opening of the Rivoli was widely advertised and its air conditioning system heralded along Broadway. Long before the doors opened, people lined up at the box office—curious about "cool comfort" as offered by the managers. It was like a World Series crowd waiting for bleacher seats. They were not only curious, but skeptical—all of the women and some of the men had fans—a standard accessory of that day. . . .

Among the spectators was Adolph Zukor. I recall how quiet and reserved he was when he walked in and took a seat in the balcony. Zukor may have come from California, but he was there to be shown!

Final adjustments delayed us in starting up the machine, so that the doors opened before the air conditioning system was turned on. The people poured in, filled all the seats, and stood seven deep in the back of the theater. We had more than we had bargained for and were plenty worried. From the wings we watched in dismay as two thousand fans fluttered. We felt that Mr. Zukor was watching the people instead of the picture—and saw all those waving fans!

It takes time to pull down the temperature in a quickly filled theater on a hot day, and a still longer time for a packed house. Gradually, almost imperceptibly, the fans dropped into laps as the effects of the air conditioning system became evident. Only a few chronic fanners persisted, but soon they, too, ceased fanning. We had stopped them "cold" and breathed a great sigh of relief.

We then went into the lobby and waited for Mr. Zukor to come downstairs. When he saw us, he did not wait for us to ask his opinion. He said tersely, "Yes, the people are going to like it."

The contract Zukor signed with Carrier was just the company's sixteenth. By 1930 it had outfitted 300 theaters, astounding distributors by making movies more popular in summer than in winter.

"He was on a harrow when he had a vision...."

PHILO FARNSWORTH IMAGINES TELEVISION

1922–1928

Rigby, Idaho, and San Francisco, California

EMMA "PEM" FARNSWORTH

Basic electricity was still a novelty in rural America when Idaho farmboy Philo Farnsworth began to conduct home experiments based on plans he found in hobbyist magazines. The idea that fascinated him most was television. His sister Agnes recalled, "Walking up and down the long beet rows in Idaho, thinning beets, we would dream about all these things we were going to have. First was an inside bathroom. Then Philo told us that we would sit in our home and talk on the telephone and see the people we were talking to. He said we were going to see people from as far away as Salt Lake, maybe further. He didn't call it television at that time. It was just something where we would be able to see people at a great distance."

A primitive form of television had been patented in 1884, but it had many limitations. Modern television became possible with the invention in 1897 of the cathode ray tube, which can aim a beam of electronics at a fluorescent screen to produce an image. Farnsworth, reading about early theories for using the tube, began to develop his own.

Eyewitness Pem Farnsworth was Philo's wife. Her account comes from Jeff Kisseloff's oral history of television, The Box.

Phil had read about mechanical television, but he felt that the mechanical disks were not only clumsy but possibly dangerous to operate at the speeds they'd have to be run. He figured he could train electrons to do what the mechanical system was doing. That was just after World War I when he was thirteen.

The summer after he turned fourteen [1922] he was on a harrow when he had a vision about television. He had read that you could manipulate electrons in a vacuum, and he had been thinking about how to make these electrons cover a picture. At one point he turned and saw all the fine lines on the field he had gone over with the harrow, and he said to himself, "I can just magnetically deflect those electrons across the screen in the same way you plow a field, line after line." That's the way he did it, and that's the way it is done today.

. . . When Philo was fifteen, he explained his theories about television to [his science teacher Justin Tolman] and drew him a picture of his "image dissector" camera tube. Mr. Tolman told him, "I don't understand all that you told me, but I'm sure if you keep working on it, you'll get it."

Eventually, Phil lost contact with Mr. Tolman. In 1936 during the patent interference with RCA, our patent attorney found Mr. Tolman in Salt Lake. He went out to take his deposition, and Mr. Tolman was able to describe what Philo had drawn for him. It proved to RCA that Phil had made this invention at that time.

. . . He had very deep blue eyes with a twinkle in them. He was charming, but I was only a sophomore in high school. . . . He had been going with a young lady and I guess he was talking to her about marriage, but when he told her about his ideas for television, she said, "I would never marry a dreamer. The man that I marry has got to be going somewhere."

That turned him off cold about revealing his plans.

He was even careful about what he would say to me about television. Then one day we went on a horseback ride up Provo Canyon to a place called Bridal Veil Falls. We came over a high cliff, and there was a huge rock in the center that parted the stream in two and created misty falls that resembled a bridal veil. It was actually very romantic. When he first told me, it was a fairy tale. I had a hard time understanding it, but I had such faith in Phil that if he said he could fly to the moon, I would have believed him.

He talked a lot about what television would do. He foresaw everything that was going to happen. He saw that television would allow people to learn about each other. He felt that if you could learn how other people live world problems would be settled around the conference table instead of bloody battlefields. He thought that everyone in the world could be educated through television, and that it could also be used for entertainment and sporting and news events.

I remember asking him, "How are you going to get the signal over the ocean?"

He said, "We'll get it there. We'll have to replay it with captive balloons," which is the same concept as the space satellite.

[In San Francisco,] My brother Cliff came to live with us. He took a lesson in glassblowing from the head of the glassblowing department at U.C. Berkeley. Very quickly, he could do things that no one else had done before, and it was Cliff who made the first workable television tubes.

Phil was doing a lot of experiments on a dining room table. When George and Les would bring friends in to see, he would shut the blinds. When they'd go, we would open the blinds. This was during Prohibition, and I guess it looked very suspicious because one day two very large policemen came to the door. One of them said, "We've had a report that you're operating a still here."

I said, "Just a minute, I'll go get my husband."

George had been in the back winding deflection coils and had his hands all covered with shellac. He beat a retreat out the back door because he didn't want to be caught in that situation, but two more big policemen came and said, "Oh, no you don't buddy."

Phil invited them in and explained what we were doing. Then the ones who came in from the front called the ones in back and said, "It's okay, they don't have a still. It's something crazy they call vision or something."

. . . Very few people thought Phil could do it. He spoke to the heads of the electrical departments at Berkeley and Stanford. Both gave him the same advice he was given at BYU: "You are just attempting the impossible." Well, he knew he could do it, so he didn't listen to them, but Phil needed help so badly that I learned to do a lot of things. They taught me how to use the precision welder. I made components to go in the tubes. I did his drawings in his books from his sketches. There were tense moments, but Phil's attitude was, "Well, if one way doesn't work, I'll invent a way around it," and that's what he did.

. . . On August 30, 1927, he got a fuzzy image of a horizontal line— or so he thought, but he was afraid it was just interference, so he took it all apart and tried it again on September 7, 1927.

That morning we went over to the lab around eight as usual. Phil said, "Will you go in and finish making drawings of the sketches I left on my desk, and we'll call you when we're ready." They did. Cliff was in the next room at the transmitter with a picture of a line on a slide. Phil called to him and said, "Turn it at right angles, Cliff." They could see the line move, so they knew they had it.

There was stunned silence in the room for a little bit because we couldn't believe what we were seeing. We were all exhilarated. Phil was outwardly fairly calm, but he was also very, very excited. There was no celebration. It was just get back to work, "We need a two-dimensional picture before we can show the backer."

They did one thing, though. Les Gorrell used to come in and slap Phil on the back and say, "Hi, Phil, you got the damn thing to work yet?" So, George and Phil concocted a wire to send to Les that said, "The damn thing works."

. . . One day we saw something that looked like smoke coming on the picture tube. It turned out that Cliff had tried to step in front of the viewing area but the lights were too hot. Instead, he blew some smoke past the viewing area, and that was the first two-dimensional picture we saw.

Then we started sending still pictures and cartoons. We had the first Mickey Mouse Disney film, Steamboat Willie. We also had short bits of film from Hollywood that we did experiments with. We made a loop of Mary Pickford combing her hair in The Taming of the Shrew.

She came to the lab. United Artists had gotten a little concerned about what television might do to their business, so Mary Pickford, Douglas Fairbanks, and Robert Fairbanks, who was Douglas's brother and business manager, and the producer Joseph Schenck all came to take a look.

We had had a good picture before then, but something happened, and it wasn't nearly as good as it had been, so they went home not very worried.

We didn't show the backers anything until 1928. By then we were showing geometrical forms. One of the backers was a man by the name of James J. Fagan. Whenever he saw George Everson, he would say, "When are we gonna see some money in Phil's gadget?" So when they came in May 1928, Phil was ready for them.

That day he called to Phil, "Farnsworth, when are we gonna see some money in this gadget?" As an answer, Phil put in a slide with a dollar sign on it and showed it to him on the television.

Farnsworth's homespun efforts set him against a powerful adversary, Radio Corporation of America owner David Sarnoff, who was investing millions in the development of television at his New York laboratory. Sarnoff later tried to poach Farnsworth's research, but Farnsworth fought back and won several important patents. To put Farnsworth's work in perspective: The year he began thinking about television, only about 5,000 hobbyists even had radios.

"The gale was in our faces,
the temperature was thirty below. . . ."

THE SERUM DRIVE

January 1925
Nome, Alaska

LEONHARD SEPPALA

It was midwinter in Nome, in the far west of Alaska on the edge of the Bering Strait, when the town's doctor realized a child was suffering from diphtheria, a

*highly contagious infection that can kill in days. Diphtheria antitoxin existed,
but the nearest supply was in Anchorage, more than 1,000 miles away. The serum
couldn't be flown to Nome; Anchorage had just two planes, both of which had
been disassembled for the winter. And the only railroad from Anchorage stopped
almost 700 miles short of Nome.*

*The child died. Soon other children were showing symptoms of the disease,
and authorities contacted eyewitness Leonhard Seppala, the preeminent trail driver in Alaska.*

The Chairman of the Board of Health came to me asking if I would
go out over the trail and bring back the diphtheria serum which was
essential if we were to combat the disease. More children were being
affected every day.

I told the Commissioner that I should be glad to go if the authorities
felt there was no better team. He added that they hoped to use airplanes, but if the airplanes failed word would be sent to me at once so
that we should have time to make the run to Nulato in short mail-trip
drives, hardening the dogs up gradually.

I was told to be ready to start at a moment's notice, and with these
instructions I went back to Little Creek to await developments. There
had been very little snow that winter and I had not driven as much as
usual, so I immediately set to work exercising the dogs and getting them
into condition. Every time the telephone rang the dogs would hear it in
the kennels and all tune up in an expectant howl, but as the hours passed
it looked as if they might not be needed after all.

Then one morning about six o'clock there was a long persistent
ringing in the cabin, and the whole kennel responded in husky chorus.
They must have had their eyes on the cabin hopefully, for when I
appeared, dressed for the trail, there broke loose in the kennel such
excitement as I have never seen equalled, except perhaps at the time of
the Sweepstakes.

The Commissioner had asked me to get off without delay. I singled
the dogs out one by one; naturally not one wanted to be left behind.
Twenty were chosen. I planned to drop some of them off along the way,
to be cared for at Eskimo igloos until the return trip, when we could
substitute the fresh dogs for the tired ones. Also, if any of them showed
any signs of weakness or sore feet, they would have a chance to rest up
and be in good condition for the home stretch. I intended to leave
twelve dogs by the way, arriving in Nulato with a team of eight. I should
hardly need more, as I was told the package containing the serum was
very light. With fresh reinforcement on the way back I should be able to
drive day and night.

Thus I picked out the twenty best dogs, though at the time all were on their best behavior, raising their paws politely and pleading to be taken. A dog named Fox was left as leader for the cull team, which was to continue hauling supplies during our absence and was composed of dogs too slow to be of much use in a fast run.

The people of Nome gave us a great send-off. They knew it was a long, hazardous trip, and they realized what a word of encouragement would mean. The first day we made about thirty-three miles, and from then on the team warmed up to the work and averaged fifty miles and over every day. We passed two villages where there were government schools for Eskimo children, and I told the teachers about the epidemic, advising them to close the school, to keep the children in quarantine, and away from people passing from Nome.

We were lucky in having favorable weather, and the trails were at their best. According to plan, some of the dogs were left along the way to be cared for while the rest of us pushed on. On the third day we arrived at Isaac's Point, where we stopped with an Eskimo family, having covered a hundred and thirty miles since leaving Nome.

The next day we started out for Shaktolik, a native village on the south side of the Bay. It was late by the time we set out over the ice of Norton Bay. We could see it was blowing hard out on the Bay, and with the north wind at our backs we were sure to make good time. The team would deserve a good rest at the end of the day, and surely I should welcome it as well as the dogs.

Having crossed the ice, and being just in sight of our destination for the day, we scented another dog team and struck out with a great spurt. As we came up I could see that the driver was busy refereeing a dog fight. With a word of greeting to the man, I was about to pass by when he called to me. In the wind, and with my parka hood up over my ears, I got only three words: "serum—turn back."

I thought I must have misunderstood, but when I looked back over my shoulder I saw the other driver waving his arm. I called to Togo to "gee," but he couldn't. The other dogs were still on the spurt, and I had to run about a mile further on before I could slow the team down and turn them.

We came to a stretch of hard snow, where I was able to get the dogs under control. Though they hated to, they followed Togo. When we reached the other team a package was tossed into my sled and the stranger handed me a paper which proved to be the instructions accompanying the serum.

The [other] driver explained that after I had passed out of telephone communication the epidemic had increased so alarmingly that the officials had decided to speed the serum by short relays running night and day. Thus I had reached the serum after traveling only a hundred and seventy miles, instead of the three hundred for which I had originally planned.

We had had a hard day, covering forty-three miles with the wind at our backs. But the return was even harder. The gale was in our faces, the temperature was thirty below, and we had the forty-three miles to do over again in the dark. There was nothing for it but to face the music.

The dogs did their best, and I drove as if we were in a race. The ice of Norton Sound is notoriously treacherous: it has a habit of shifting and breaking up, so that before travelers know it they have gone for miles on a loose ice-cake with open water on all sides, slowly but surely being blown out into the Bering Sea.

In spite of these unpleasant prospects, we managed to reach Isaac's Point, and after a drive of nearly ninety miles the team were grateful for a brief rest in a comfortable kennel. They were wild for their rations of salmon and seal blubber.

After they were fed I went into the igloo and read over the instructions. They called for the serum to be warmed up at each station. Accordingly I pulled the sled inside, and undid the fur and canvas wrapped around the package. I found the serum was sealed up in paper cartons, and as I saw nothing about breaking the seals I instructed the Eskimo to make the igloo good and hot and left the package exposed to the heat. As I looked it over and felt of it I was convinced that if it was a liquid it must have been frozen in the severe cold, though we had protected it as well as possible. I doubted if the heat could penetrate the paper cartons, but I had taken off the last wrapping which I was authorized to touch.

When I had allowed as much time as we could spare I came out to the dogs and began putting them back on the line. An old Eskimo stood by as we hitched up, and observing the increase in the wind he cautioned me: "Maybe ice not much good. Maybe breaking off and go out. Old trail plenty no good. Maybe you go more closer shore." I thanked him and followed his suggestion, taking a trail further in. At that, we came within a few feet of open water, as the trail over which we had traveled only the day before had broken off and drifted far out into Bering Sea.

During the afternoon we pulled into Cheenik Village, where another driver was waiting with his relay team. We had traveled in all three hundred and forty miles in the interest of the serum. No other relay made more than fifty-three miles. After delivering the package to the driver at Cheenik, a tired driver and tired dogs all had a good rest until the next day, when we drove to Solomon and then on into Nome. When we arrived there the whole town seemed to be out to meet us. It was like the winner's reception after a Sweepstakes race.

News of the diphtheria had found its way to the outside papers, and in the States the teams were being followed from day to day by the press. They had become heroes while they were peacefully going on their way, totally unconscious that they were headliners in the press. The last relay team landed the serum in Nome at six o'clock on the morning of the second of February, 1925. It was frozen, as I had suspected, but the Surgeon General in Washington advised using it just the same.

There was plenty of scandal connected with the drive, and there were many rumors as to various individuals commercializing it. The chief thing which disturbed me was that Togo's records were given to Balto, a scrub dog, who was pushed into the limelight and made immortal.

It was almost more than I could bear when the "newspaper" dog Balto received a statue for his "glorious achievements," decked out in Togo's colors, and with the claim that he had taken Amundsen to Point Barrow and part way to the Pole—when he had never been two hundred miles north of Nome! By giving him Togo's records he was established as "the greatest racing leader in Alaska," when he was never in a winning team! I know, because I owned and raised Balto, as well as Togo.

The Serum Drive was Togo's last long run. In that drive he had worked his hardest and best. I appreciated this, and tried to take the best possible care of the old dog. Togo, in his sixteenth year, seemed content to rest on his laurels. He even posed without fuss for a photograph with his cups and trophies, perhaps imagining himself as he was in the old days. It seemed best to leave him where he could be pensioned and enjoy a well-earned rest. But it was a sad parting on a cold gray March morning when Togo raised a small paw to my knee as if questioning why he was not going along with me. For the first time in twelve years I hit the trail without Togo.

As he recounts, Seppala was already on the trail when authorities realized that only a relay of dog sled teams racing all day and all night had a chance of getting back to Nome in time. Twenty men answered the call for drivers, and the logistics of the plan were telegraphed along the trail. Moments after the special train carrying the twenty-pound package of serum reached Nenana, the first driver, "Wild Bill" Shannon, headed into the night with a team of ten dogs. The temperature was thirty degrees below zero.

By the time they were done, Seppala and his dogs had travelled 268 miles. His portion of the relay was by far the longest, but it was not the only extraordinary effort. One driver took the place of his two lead dogs when they froze to death.

Normally, the trip would have taken twenty days. The final driver, Gunnar Kasson, arrived in Nome five days and seven and a half hours after the relay began. Five children were already dead. Twenty-nine more were ill. But the serum stopped the epidemic.

Since 1973, an annual dogsled race called the Iditarod ("distant place") has commemorated the serum drive.

"Aimee's empty chair stood on the platform beneath a full-length portrait of her."

THE APPEARANCE AND DISAPPEARANCE OF SISTER AIMEE

1926
Los Angeles

STANLEY WALKER

Aimee Semple McPherson brought religion to Hollywood, and Hollywood to religion. Many colorful evangelists have followed her, but none have topped her gift for showmanship and scandal.

Eyewitness Stanley Walker was a reporter for, and later editor of, the New York Herald-Tribune. *This account comes from his book about the 1920s and '30s,* Mrs. Astor's Horse.

Aimee Semple McPherson is the most successful Evangelist of her time, far surpassing Billy Sunday, the Rev. J. Frank Norris and the late Fundamentalist bellwether, the Rev. Dr. John Roach Straton. To her thousands of followers at Angelus Temple in Los Angeles and the branch "lighthouses" she is "God's Little Girl," who can do no wrong. By putting some sex appeal in the old-fashioned revival brand of salvation, embellishing it all with colored lights, brass bands and the Hollywood tone, she keeps her flock in a constant state of excited admiration. She has sex appeal. Once a reporter for the *New York Times,* a journal which ordinarily ignores sex, rushed into his office after an interview with Aimee and announced:

"My soul may belong to Adolph S. Ochs, but my body belongs to Aimee Semple McPherson."

Much of the woman's life, as well as her religion, has been directed by sex impulses. During the 1920's America became familiar with her

red-gold hair, luminous brown eyes, large sensuous mouth and carefully cut wide-sleeved dresses. Her voice effects were those of an accomplished actress; she was, and is, the Duse of the Mourners' Bench.

Aimee was born October 9, 1890, on a farm near Ingersoll,
Ontario, Canada. Her mother, Mrs. Minnie Kennedy, had been a
Salvation Army lassie before her marriage. . . . At the age of seventeen
she became aware of inner forces which were to propel her toward both
success and scandal. As she describes it: "A vigorous, young evangelist
came to the little town, and his name was Robert Semple. He had curly
brown hair and a beautiful face, and he upset me." This Semple, a former
boilermaker, conducted his revival in camp-meeting style before a con-
gregation which was given to talking in unknown tongues, moaning,
groaning and foaming at the mouth. Aimee was converted, and a few
weeks later she and Semple were married.

For two years the couple traveled. Semple did the preaching and
Aimee helped with boosting. They managed to make a living. On a trip
to China, where many souls were waiting to be saved, Semple died in
ward in a Hong Kong hospital. A month later Aimee became the mother
of a daughter, Roberta Semple. The widow arrived in San Francisco with
a layette for the baby and $65 in cash, the proceeds of a collection she
had taken up among the passengers. Thenceforth, whenever she needed
money, she took up a collection. By September, 1921, she had built the
Angelus Temple at a cost of a half a million dollars. She owned several
houses and a radio station, and was said to possess a personal fortune of
more than $600,000.

After the China adventure Aimee went to New York where "Ma"
Kennedy had rejoined the Salvation Army. At a meeting she became
acquainted with Harold McPherson, a wholesome young grocery sales-
man. They were married, and in 1915 their son, Rolph McPherson, was
born. The couple set out on an evangelical tour; one night in 1916
Aimee took the baby in her arms, Roberta by the hand, and left
McPherson. Calling herself "Sister McPherson," she left the children
with "Ma" and fared forth with a second-hand automobile and a moth-
eaten tent to preach the gospel. By 1918 she had arrived in Los Angeles
with $100 in cash, an automobile as good as new, and the philosophy of
what was to become famous as the Four Square Gospel, which is a belief
in four things: Divine Healing, Baptism of the Holy Spirit, the
Premillennial Coming of the Lord, and Repentance of Sin.

The first plank in this far from startling creed was the most important at first. Southern California, which is said to have more neurotics,
schizophrenics and assorted invalids than any spot in the world, was
ideal for her talents. By creating a state of emotional exaltation and mass

hysteria she performed many "cures." One testimonial . . . came from Mrs. J. A. Nicholson of Los Angeles, who wrote: "I had a cancer under the arm and also back of my shoulders. It was so bad I couldn't raise my arm. Not only that but I had dropsy, heart trouble, tumor and a rupture. Six months ago yesterday I was prayed for on this platform by Sister Alford (one of Aimee's troupe of 'angels') and was healed instantly. The cancer is all melted now. I wasn't able to be up only part of the time and now I can do all my own work."

One of these cancer "cures" led Aimee into difficulties. A Mrs. Catharine McAdams believed that Sister Aimee had cured her of cancer. She gave Aimee real estate valued at $16,000 and made a will leaving to the evangelist most of her $30,000 estate. Then the woman died of cancer. The will was set aside by the Superior Court as "having been made under a morbid delusion." But such setbacks were few. Attendants are proud of the Five Hundred Room at the Temple, the walls of which are lined with crutches, braces, wheelchairs and other proofs of the power of faith healing.

Aimee had sense enough to know that she couldn't depend entirely on faith healing. She set about to appeal to the moderately well-to-do. She soft-pedaled the horrors of hell, frowned on noisy converts, disapproved of attacks of the "jerks," and introduced pleasant entertainment features. She did not accept a salary, but one collection a month was set aside for her personal use, in addition to birthday "offerings" and special donations.

The great temple was dedicated in 1923. It is set in Echo Park, a large oblong plot landscaped with a small lake, willows, palm trees and cypresses. The auditorium, designed by Aimee, is a large white building topped with a round dome and two radio masts. The round side of the building is decorated with eight stained-glass windows, flanked by Corinthian columns. The inside of the dome is painted blue. The Temple has 5,300 upholstered opera chairs, first and second balconies, carpeted aisles and an organ eighty feet high. A wide platform is broken up into tiers to accommodate the silver band, the choir, a group of ministers and workers, and whatever stage effects may have been planned. Back of the pulpit is a mural depicting the coming of the Lord. Colored curtains conceal the baptismal font, where, on Tuesday nights, from fifty to 150 converts are baptized at a time. The Corridor of Angels, on the upper mezzanine, is a show spot. It is decorated with flowers, sixty mirrors, deep carpets, lamps of alabaster, wicker furniture, and curtained windows, each presided over by a guardian angel. A real lifeboat stands at the entrance to the church. In it are placed food, clothing, and gifts for the poor.

The radio station KSFG and the watch tower occupy the top floor. Platoons of church members, working in two-hour shifts, offer prayers day and night in the tower. Aimee likes stunning allegorical effects. In June, 1929, she preached on "Eternity Bound on the F. S. & H. G. Railway." Dressed in her favorite white gown, short skirt and flowing sleeves, with a railroad conductor's cap on her head and waving a lighted lantern, she invited the flock to board "the Father, Son and Holy Ghost Limited for Gloryland." Back of her were two miniature rail roads lighted up. One heaven-bound train went upward, the other, hell-bound, took the winding decline. The upbound train made stops at Calvary Junction, Jordan's Banks, Mount Zion's Upper Room, the Heavenly Fields, and at last rolled into Grand Central Terminal. The other choo-choo paused at Jazzville, Procrastination Town, Earthbound Possessions, and then plunged into the pit of hell, while red flame shot up and burned brightly.

. . . All this work, effective though it was, never would have made Aimee an international figure if it had not been for an extremely peculiar adventure in 1926. On May 18 of that year Aimee, accompanied by her secretary, Emma Schaeffer, drove to Venice Beach, Santa Monica, for a swim. She sent Emma on some errands, and then, clad in a green bathing suit, she stepped into the surf and disappeared. What had happened? At first it was believed she had been drowned. "Ma" Kennedy went to the Temple and announced "Sister McPherson is with Jesus. Pray for her." Great lamentations went up. Bands of converts stormed the altar. For seventeen days and nights crowds watched at the beach. Some wept, while others knelt and prayed or sang hymns. One man said he had seen her image walking on the water. "Ma" rushed truckloads of coffee and picnic dinners to the beach for the mourners. Ed Harrison, a professional deep sea diver, was drowned while searching for the missing soul-saver. Robert Browning, a young follower of Aimee, swam far out crying, "I am going after her," and did not come back alive. Aviators flew low over the water. Sticks of dynamite were exploded in the seaweed. It was no use.

On June 4 "Ma" called the watchers from the beach and announced plans for a memorial service to be held June 20. More than 11,000 persons crowded into the Temple to contribute to a memorial collection. Estimates on the amount taken in range from $15,000 to $40,000. Aimee's empty chair stood on the platform beneath a full-length portrait of her.

The rest of the world was not so credulous. Gossip was going around about Aimee and the radio operator at the Temple, a tall, sharp-featured young man named Kenneth G. Ormiston. Testimony later was brought out that in 1925 Aimee had at intervals occupied a room at the Ambassador Hotel and had been visited by Ormiston. After Aimee's disappearance newspaper men began searching for a man and a woman in a blue sedan bearing Ormiston's license plates.

A curious situation developed. It seems that on May 4, two weeks before the vanishing act, a man giving the name "George McIntyre," later identified by witnesses as Ormiston, rented a furnished cottage in Carmel for a period of three months. He said he and his wife would move in on the night of May 18 or early on the the 19th. For ten days "Mr. and Mrs. McIntyre" lived in seclusion. A neighbor observed a green bathing suit hung out to dry. H. C. Benedict, owner of the cottage, was introduced to "Mrs. McIntyre," who, he said, looked exactly like Aimee Semple McPherson. Handwritten grocery lists were later found outside the cottage and identified by experts as having been written by her.

On May 27 Ormiston appeared briefly at Venice Beach, apparently to stop rumors that he and Aimee had vanished together: He identified himself to a local detective and accompanied him to Los Angeles for further questioning. At a police station the questioning became hot; Ormiston offered a polite excuse for leaving the room, and disappeared. By the morning of May 29 the Carmel cottage was deserted. Benedict, the owner, received a note with a rent check from a "McIntyre" which had been posted at Las Salinas. It said he and his wife had been called to New York by the illness of his wife's mother. A couple, later identified as Ormiston and Aimee, registered at a hotel in San Luis Obispo as "Mr. and Mrs. Frank Gibson." On the 29th the couple was stopped by a Santa Barbara reporter who thought he recognized them, but "Gibson" convinced the reporter that he was mistaken. About June 1 Aimee was seen in Tucson, Arizona. On June 22 an automobile resembling Ormiston's was seen on the outskirts of Agua Prieta. On the morning of June 23 Aimee staggered into Agua Prieta from the desert, babbling that she had been kidnapped and held for ransom. She was taken to a hospital in Douglas, Arizona, where she told a story of having been lured from the beach to pray for a sick baby, then chloroformed and held captive in a shack in Mexicali by two men and a woman. Her shoes were unscuffed and her gingham dress fairly fresh.

The District Attorney and the newspapers doubted her story. It seemed impossible for a woman to dive into the ocean and come up in the desert. Nevertheless, her followers believed her, and welcomed her back home with ceremonies described as "more detailed and lavish than those which attended the visits of President Wilson, King Albert of Belgium or former President Taft." She was carried through the streets of Los Angeles in a rose-decked wicker chair.

The Grand Jury began an investigation into the disappearance, an inquiry which lasted from July until late in September. It was finally decided to hold Aimee, "Ma," Ormiston and Mrs. Lorraine Weisman-Sielaff for trial on charges of criminal conspiracy to obstruct justice, and procuring false witnesses. Mrs. Weisman-Sielaff had said that Aimee and "Ma" had offered her $5,000 to swear that she had been the woman at Carmel. Ormiston, meanwhile, couldn't be found. He checked out of a hotel in New York just a step ahead of investigators, leaving behind a trunk containing a collection of Aimee's finery.

The District Attorney was troubled by the mysterious disappearance of important evidence. His case was getting weaker all the time. Ormiston finally was found in Harrisburg, Pa., and went voluntarily to Los Angeles. He said the "Miss X" of the Carmel cottage was not Aimee but a trained nurse from Seattle. On top of this Mrs. Weisman-Sielaff recanted her testimony. The case went up in smoke.

The hearings boomed business at the Temple. More than 1,000 converts had been taken into the church in less than a year. When the charges against her were dropped, she set out on a country-wide revival tour.

After Aimee died in 1944, from an overdose of sleeping powders, her son continued to preach her "Four Square Gospel."

"You ain't heard nothin' yet."

TALKIES

1925–1927
New York and Hollywood

GEORGE GROVES

Thomas Edison, who invented both motion pictures and the phonograph, first synchronized a movie with a sound recording in 1889. But the technology wasn't refined enough to allow for real sound movies until the 1920s.

Eyewitness George Groves, a young engineer at Bell Labs in New York, helped build the first working system. His account comes from an American Film Institute oral history prepared by Irene Kahn Atkins, whose father, Gus Kahn, wrote songs for several movies in the early sound years.

Warner Brothers were given credit for inventing sound for motion pictures, and they did to the extent that they were the first to make a commercially acceptable sound system and equip theaters and, in conjunction with the Western Electric Company, be able to distribute product all over the country with sound.

. . . Now, it so happened during [1925–1927], that a great invention was being developed in the Bell Labs, and that was the change from acoustic recording of phonograph records, where you just played into a horn, and had a stylus driven by acoustical power, to electrical recording. . . . They had [also] invented, along with electrical recording of phonograph records, a means of synchronizing a record, as it played, with a motion picture.

. . . And they staged a demonstration of their system, to Sam Warner. He was tremendously impressed, and convinced his brothers that they should go ahead and do something about it. Simultaneously with the development of the Bell Labs, there were other developments going on. . . . However, all of these different systems were deficient in fidelity and lack of power to fill an auditorium when they played the product.

So in the Bell Laboratories, they developed amplifiers and loudspeakers to fill an auditorium. And, in course of time, Warner Brothers took over the development and exploitation of the system, under contract with Western Electric Company, and did experimental work in the Vitagraph Studios in Brooklyn. It was there that I think the first experimental job that I know of, that happened when I was there—I was transferred over to Warner Brothers with the equipment when this deal went through—was to record Lee Duncan, the owner of Rin Tin Tin, directing his dog from the sidelines. It was a pretty crude demonstration, but nevertheless it worked, and you could hear him talk.

. . . When Warner Brothers became convinced that the thing was a practical device, and decided to put a big program on, and show it, they took over the Manhattan Opera House on 35th street in New York, and converted it into a studio.

The seats were all taken out, the stage was extended over the whole auditorium, we moved in bag and baggage. The boxes were made into recording rooms. Dressing rooms were used as machine rooms and repair shops. And the only convenient place where a mixer could sit was in the Masonic Shrine room on the sixth floor of the building, in front of the building. So all the microphone lines from the stage were run up through the ventilating system to the Shrine room, and brought out through the grille where the ventilating air normally came out, and the mixer panel fastened onto that grille. That's where I sat, and spent a lot of my time, recording the first Vitaphone programs. Anytime there was a change of set-up or a slight case of trouble, I had to go down six flights in an elevator, then up the stage, get back up, and go back upstairs. And did a lot of running. I kept in good condition.

. . . At that time, the speed of commercial records was 78 revolutions per minute, rpm. In order to accommodate ten minutes of playing time, which was the running time of a thousand feet [one reel] of film at 90 feet a minute, they had to reduce the speed of the turntable to 33⅓. Otherwise it would have been an enormous thing to run a half an hour. So the whole system was designed to run on a turntable that ran at 33⅓, which, interestingly enough, has remained the standard speed for LPs to this day.

. . . We finally put on the Vitaphone program in New York, on August 6, 1926. Of course it was a great success. And along with that, we had some rather ambitious short subjects with Metropolitan Opera stars.

. . . We stayed there in New York until April, 1927, when Warner Brothers decided to move the whole crew and installation to Hollywood. There we made a few short subjects, but the main object of the changeover was the decision to put talking sequences, or singing sequences, rather, in addition to the score, in *The Jazz Singer*. As I remember, *The Jazz Singer* had been shot as a silent picture.

One thing that has impressed me during the passing of time is that nobody thought at that time of putting talking sequences in. Everything we did, somebody was singing, either an opera or a vaudeville act of some kind. The only talking thing that ever happened, in the early days, was a speech by Will Hays [an industry lobbyist], which was made for the opening of Vitaphone. . . . That was a talking thing, but somehow or other it never seemed to dawn on anybody that they should talk in motion pictures.

When we recorded *The Jazz Singer,* at one moment in the picture Al Jolson sat down to play the piano and sing a song for his mother, after he had been on the stage as a singer, much to the annoyance of his father, who was a cantor in the church and wanted his son to follow in his footsteps. Jolson sat down at the piano, and before he sang, he said something to the effect of "Mama, you ain't heard nothin' yet." This speech has been quoted as being very prophetic, and quoted many, many times. And it seemed to take everybody by surprise. "By golly! He talked." After that, it was decided to put talking sequences in pictures.

Groves later went west to work with Warner Brothers, where he helped make hundreds of movies, including the famous Busby Berkeley extravaganzas and My Fair Lady.

". . . The country had been so wonderful that by
comparison what I had done looked very poor to me . . ."

TAOS

1929
New Mexico

GEORGIA O'KEEFFE

In 1898, two artists, Bert Phillips and Ernest Blumenschein, set out on horseback
from Denver to Mexico City, planning to sketch the landscape they passed. When
they reached Taos, New Mexico, they were so struck by its beauty that they sold
their horses and settled there, forming the Taos Art Colony, which soon attracted
artists from around the world.

Painter Georgia O'Keeffe, the artist most closely identified with Taos, found
her lifelong inspiration while visiting her friend Mabel Dodge Luhan, a New York
socialite who had moved there in 1917.

That first summer I spent in New Mexico I was a little surprised that
there were so few flowers. There was no rain so the flowers didn't come.
Bones were easy to find so I began collecting bones. When I was returning East I was bothered about my work—the country had been so wonderful that by comparison what I had done with it looked very poor to
me—although I knew it had been one of my best painting years. I had to
go home—what could I take with me of the country to keep me working on it? I had collected many bones and finally decided that the best
thing I could do was to take with me a barrel of bones—so I took a barrel of bones. . . .

When I arrived at Lake George I painted a horse's skull. After that
came a cow's skull on blue. In my Amarillo days cows had been so much
a part of the country I couldn't think of it without them. As I was working I thought of the city men I had been seeing in the East. They talked
so often of writing the Great American Novel—the Great American
Play—the Great American Poetry. I was not sure that they aspired to the
Great American Painting. Cézanne was so much in the air that I think the
Great American Painting didn't even seem a possible dream. I knew the
middle of the country—knew quite a bit of the South—I knew the cattle country—and I knew that our country was lush and rich. I had
driven across the country many times. I was quite excited over our
country and I knew that at that time almost any one of those great minds
would have been living in Europe if it had been possible for them. They

didn't even want to live in New York—how was the Great American thing going to happen? So as I painted along on my cow's skull on blue [her painting *Cow's Skull—Red, White and Blue,* 1931] I thought to myself, "I'll make it an American painting. They will not think it great with the red stripes down the sides—Red, White and Blue—but they will notice it."

. . . I saw the crosses so often—and often in unexpected places— like a thin dark veil of the Catholic Church spread over the New Mexico landscape. One evening while I was living in Taos we walked back of the morada toward a cross in the hills. I was told that it was a Penitante cross but that meant little to me at the time. The cross was large enough to crucify a mass, with two small crosses—one on either side. It was in the late light and the cross stood out—dark against the evening sky. If I turned a little to the left, away from the cross, I saw the Taos moun- tain—a beautiful shape. I painted the cross against the mountain although I never saw it that way [*Black Cross, New Mexico,* 1929]. I painted it with a red sky and I painted it with a blue sky and stars.

I painted a light cross that I often saw on the road near Alcalde. I looked for it recently but it is not there. I also painted a cross I saw at sunset against the hills near Cameron—hills that look small until you see telephone poles like toothpicks going up and down and you know they are high. The hills are grey—all the same size and shape with once in a while a hot-colored brown hill. That cross was big and strong, put together with wooden pegs. For me, painting the crosses was a way of painting the country.

Luhan's salon also attracted and influenced D. H. Lawrence, painters Stuart Davis and John Marin, and photographers Paul Strand and Ansel Adams.

O'Keeffe moved permanently to New Mexico in 1946.

*"Our work was varied but shared a fresh approach
that stirred the wrath of the salonists. . . ."*

ANSEL ADAMS AND THE *f/64* GROUP

1932
San Francisco

ANSEL ADAMS

*In 1933, Ansel Adams wrote fellow photographer Paul Strand, "I have opened a
small gallery. . . . I am trying to bring things to San Francisco that should have
come many years ago. Despite a certain sneering attitude in the East about
California I can truthfully say to you that I would rather live here and work here
than in any other American city I have seen—and I have seen most of them. There
is a vitality and a purpose, and a magnificent landscape (Hollywood, etc., has
ruined the reputation of all California). There are some of the good qualities of
New York here, and few of the bad ones. It was refreshing to me to get back to it,
even after weeks in New Mexico." Adams eventually gave up his gallery to pursue
photography full time. The "straight" style that he and some of his contemporaries
desired, so familiar to us today, was a departure from tradition. In this account
from his memoirs he recalls the important gathering of young photographers that
comprised what was called the "f/64 group."*

One evening in 1932 there was a remarkable collection of sympati-
cos gathered at the Berkeley home of Willard Van Dyke, a University of
California student and photographer: Van Dyke, Imogen Cunningham,
Edward Weston, Henry Swift, Sonya Noskowiak, John Paul Edwards,
and myself. I presented, with extroverted enthusiasm, my new sense of
direction in photography. The response was immediate, striking powerful sparks of accord from the others, some of whom had already
embarked on the same journey.

We agreed with missionary zeal to a group effort to stem the tides
of oppressive pictorialism and to define what we felt creative photography to be. Perhaps most importantly, our efforts provided moral support for each other. . . .

On another evening at Willard's, we bantered about what we should
call ourselves. The young photographer Preston Holder was present that
night, and he suggested we call ourselves "US 256," the designation of a
very small lens aperture many of us used to achieve greater sharpness
and depth. Afraid that people would confuse us with a highway, I followed his line of thought, picked up a pencil, and drew a curving *f/64*.

The graphics were beautiful and the symbol was apt—*f*/64 was the new aperture marking system identical to the old system number US 256.

Group *f*/64 became synonymous with the renewed interest in the philosophy of straight photography: that is, photographs that looked like photographs, not imitations of other art forms. The simple, straight print is a fact of life—the natural and predominant style for most of photography's history—but in 1932 it had few active proponents.

The members of Group *f*/64 decided that our first goal would be to prepare a visual manifesto. Our work was varied but shared a fresh approach that stirred the wrath of the salonists, perplexed many in our local art world, and delighted a few pioneers including Lloyd Rollins, director of the M. H. de Young Memorial Museum in San Francisco. Lloyd had come to one of our gatherings at Willard's where we had a small display of the group's work. After looking at our photographs, he immediately offered us an exhibition. This was an important event for each of us; for me it was my third major museum exhibition. I had had a solo show in 1931 at the Smithsonian Institution, and both Edward and I had already had exhibits at the de Young earlier in 1932. For this exhibition the seven members of Group *f*/64 invited four others to show with us: Preston Holder, Consuela Kanaga, Alma Lavenson, and Brett Weston, knowing that they represented the same photographic philosophy. The exhibition dates were November 15 through December 31, 1932. There were a total of eighty photographs in the show, from four to ten prints per photographer, with prices that now seem ridiculous: Edward charged fifteen dollars per print and the rest of us charged ten.

At the exhibit we handed out a written manifesto to accompany the visual one. I was one of the authors and feel that it explains quite clearly what we were about.

GROUP *f*/64 MANIFESTO

. . . The chief object of the Group is to present in frequent shows what it considers the best contemporary photography of the West; in addition to the showing of the work of its members, it will include prints from other photographers who evidence tendencies in their work similar to that of the Group. . . .

Our exhibition and accompanying statement created considerable attention and invigorating discussion, much of it negative. The de Young Museum received many letters of protest, mostly from artists and gallery people, complaining that valuable space at a public museum had been given to photography which was not Art! Concerned, Rollins requested the opinion of the board of trustees of the museum, who supported him by saying, "You are our director; if you think exhibits of photography are appropriate for the museum, by all means present them." Rollins telephoned me to describe the meeting and his great relief at its outcome. I have wondered what might have been the effect on the progress of West Coast photography if the Group $f/64$ exhibit had been rejected by the de Young.

"... The occupants of the tower itself ... were still there."

ORIGINS:
THE GALLINA TOWERS

1933
New Mexico

FRANK C. HIBBEN

The Anasazi (Navajo for "Old Ones") were the predecessors of many southwestern Indian peoples. They were culturally diverse, as are their descendants, who include the Hopi, Zuni, and Navajo.

These towers, built about A.D. *1100, were explored in 1933, around the time that the new field of anthropology was popularizing the study of southwest Indian cultures.*

Eyewitness Frank Hibben, an archaeologist who became well-known for hosting nature programs on television with his wife, wrote this account for the Saturday Evening Post.

We saw the first tower as we came through a narrow place in the Gallina Canyon where the wagon hubs almost scraped the walls on either side. Beyond these narrows, the sandstone walls opened up in a basin, possibly a mile long and two hundred or three hundred yards wide.

Outlined against the dazzling sky, as we viewed it from the floor of the canyon below, the tower looked medieval. . . .

Even as we looked at this first tower at the head of the basin, we saw another and another. . . . They looked like castles along the rimrock.

. . . Energetically we set to work. We set up camp in the colorful basin and spent the next several weeks in an extensive survey by foot and by horse. . . . What had at first appeared to be a small cluster of stone towers in one isolated canyon soon turned out to be but one of a whole series of towns or villages made up of these towers. In this one section alone, we located more than five hundred of the stone towers, spreading over an area of some thirty-five by fifty miles.

It was a riddle of the first magnitude. . . .

. . . The first of the Gallina towers was perfectly typical, as we found later on. The story was multiplied only in detail by the other towers that we excavated. Originally, apparently, that edifice had been twenty-five or thirty feet high. The walls were built of sandstone blocks roughly square in shape. These walls were put up with adobe mortar in the form of a double wall with rubble in between, forming a wall about six feet thick at the base. In plan, the towers are generally square, though some of them have rounded corners, so as to appear almost circular.

. . . As we carefully shoveled accumulated dust and fallen masonry from the interior of the first tower . . . the first edge of a painted design appeared on the plaster wall that covered the stone on the inside. Plants and birds and flowers, interposed with pennant-like flags, appeared one after another.

The interior of this first tower was some twenty by twenty feet. The floor was covered with massive slabs of carefully fitted sandstone, so as to form a pavement. Around the edges of this one room was a series of benches of stone and adobe which were hollow, so as to form bins for storage. The bins were carefully capped with other slabs of sandstone, and some of them were sealed with mortar. . . . The bins were full of intimate things—buckskin bags full of ceremonial face powder, shell ornaments, painted prayer sticks of wood and feathers, good-luck pieces, buckskin clothing, feather robes, extra arrows of cane and flint, ceremonial masks and horns.

But these things that had been left so casually there were not the most interesting things in the tower. What fairly made us gasp as we carefully uncovered them was the occupants of the tower itself. They were still there, and their story was with them.

In all, scattered about the tower in positions and attitudes, were sixteen people. These people we got to know very intimately. We even named some of them. There was little "Itchy Fingers," and "Big Bruiser" and "Bold Titania," the woman warrior, and others.

Every place in the Gallina tower there was evidence that this fortification had been attacked, the occupants killed and the whole place burned, either during the attack or just afterward.

As the defenders buckled before the onslaught of still other unknowns, the towers were fired with fire arrows, and the wooden timbers of its roof and the wooden ladders and other combustibles of the interior had started to burn. The roof timbers had burned through, and the whole roof had collapsed, along with the flagstone parts of the upper walls. The few defenders on the parapet doubtless had fallen in with the roof. The remarkable dryness of the Southwestern climate, together with the charring action of the fire, had perfectly preserved the bodies and the evidence with them. They were better preserved than many Egyptian mummies.

Here was the body of a woman sprawled backward over one of the storage bins. She had been crushed by falling stones from the top of the wall, but her body was remarkably preserved; even to a look of intense agony on her somewhat flattened face! Studded in her breast and stomach were the charred ends of sixteen arrows of cane with flint heads. She still clutched in left hand a bow, even with a part of the string still on one end. It was a short bow, powerful looking, of oak wood, and yet the body was undoubtedly that of a woman.

In the center of the floor of the tower, where they had apparently fallen when struck from the roof, were two men, one crosswise on top of the other. In the hands of one were three bows, two of oak and one of juniper wood, and in his other hand was a bundle of twenty-seven arrows. Evidently, this man had been passing the ammunition when he was struck down. The other, too, was a warrior, and he had met the same harsh end. A stone ax with a jagged edge was imbedded in his skull over his left eye, clear to the middle of the blade, and still stuck there.

. . . In the ventilating shaft behind the fire pit was the most pathetic of them all. A young boy, fifteen or sixteen years old, with his hair in long, slender braids, had crawled into the small aperture as far as he could. Apparently he was still living when the burning roof fell, for only the lower part of his body was burned. One arrow had struck him in the hip from behind, and the half-charred flesh was sucked in around the shaft as it penetrated. You could almost read on the dead and mummified face the look of terror and fear it still held, centuries after the boy had crowded himself into the hole, trying to escape the heat. . . .

———————————————

". . . One of the most powerful clubs in the United States, the old-boy network of the University of Texas. . . ."

THE TAIL WAGS THE DOG

1933
Washington, D.C.

WILLIAM S. WHITE

As long as pioneers have lived on the Western frontier, they have complained that governments back east failed to give them a fair shake. But toward the middle of the twentieth century, political reality began to belie that complaint. Now national politicians must kowtow to Western voters. For instance, in presidential elections California controls 54 votes of the 538 in the electoral college, and Texas has 32. The only eastern state that comes close is New York, with 33.

This power shift was signalled decades ago by the Texans in Washington. Texans have been Speaker of the House of Representatives for thirty of the sixty-five or so years since Franklin Roosevelt's New Deal. John Nance Garner, who had been Speaker under Herbert Hoover, parlayed that role into the vice presidency under FDR in 1932. His protégé Sam Rayburn became Speaker a few years later, and held that position at various times over the next two decades, spanning the terms of Roosevelt, Harry Truman, and Dwight Eisenhower. And Jim Wright was Speaker for part of the Reagan and Bush administrations.

As well, Texans enjoyed strength in the Senate. Lyndon Johnson, who started his political career as secretary to a congressman, became the Democratic whip in 1951, minority leader in 1953, and majority leader in 1955. Of course he then became John F. Kennedy's vice president and served as president himself.

This concentration of influence during a period of heavy government spending—prompted by the New Deal, World War II, the cold war, and the space program—greatly benefited Texas.

Eyewitness William White, a New York Times *reporter and a native Texan, had an insider's view of the story from Garner to Johnson.*

Jack Garner could be, for all his bluff and engaging qualities, as savage and pitiless an adversary as William T. Sherman ever was in his march through Georgia down to the sea. I met Garner when he was Speaker of the House during Hoover's first term. I was freshly up from Texas, reporting for the AP [Associated Press]. He was in a cluttered little hideaway office in the Capitol, with Mrs. Garner in attendance upon him, as always. He never cared for any Johnny-come-lately and this was immediately made clear to me. In fact Garner told me that if I ever

275

wanted any news about him or his office I could go ask one of his two old Texas cronies in the Washington press corps, Bascom Timmons and Mark Goodwin. This was the insult deadly to any journalist, new boy or not, and I got up from my chair and said, "Mr. Speaker, with all respect, I will like hell go to any other reporters for news. You can keep your damn news, sir."

He grinned, his white eyebrows dancing up and down, and said to Mrs. Garner: "Looks like we've got a buck here." Whereupon his manner totally changed and he went to a cabinet and took out two hotel glasses and a bottle of bourbon whiskey. He filled both glasses almost to the brim—no water here—handed one to me, and said, "Son, let's strike a blow for liberty." This was at about ten in the morning, early for me but about midday for old Garner. He habitually got up before five in the morning and worked his way through a bottle of whiskey before nightfall, with no perceptible effect on his speech or deportment. He only got redder and redder in the face as the day went on. He also chewed upon a great quantity of cigars. These habits he gave up on the occasion of his ninetieth birthday in his home town in Uvalde, Texas. "Got to thinking they might be bad for my health," he told a birthday caller, Lyndon B. Johnson. It was Garner, as head of the Democratic party in the House of Representatives, who more than any other man managed to convince the nation that President Hoover, who was quite powerless against a worldwide economic storm he never made, had somehow consciously set in motion himself the hurricane that swept through the lives of the people. . . .

I first went East—the great beckoning light to all provincial newspapermen of my era—only months after Franklin D. Roosevelt had been inaugurated in 1933 and was assaulting the Great Depression with innumerable recovery and relief bills that a frightened Congress was passing on the double, sometimes using a rolled-up newspaper on the House floor as the surrogate for a bill not yet actually printed.

At that time, Johnson was nominally "secretary" to a rich, relaxed, and somewhat playboyish congressman, Richard Kleberg, a member of the King Ranch dynasty of Texas, whose federal salary would, I suppose, have paid part of his club bills. The nominal "secretary," however, was the congressman-in-fact most of the time. And with the matchless mixture of audacity, persistence, compassion, and a kind of cold gambler's calculation that would become his lifelong persona, Lyndon Johnson was cajoling, extracting, and emotionally extorting for the needy in Kleberg's district prodigious sums from federal bureaucrats who winced automatically when the telephone rang and Johnson's drawling Texas voice loudly announced that "Congressman Kleberg's office" was calling.

I had been sent to Washington by the AP as what was called a "regional correspondent," meaning that I was to look out mainly for news of Texas and vicinity; but my territory, though disappointingly limited in geography, was from the first pretty wide in scope. For Texans were very big in all of Congress, and Garner, of course, held the vice presidency. My Texas connections soon led me, journalistically, far beyond the limits of the Rio Grande and the Red River alike. As I have said, I met Garner early on, along with Johnson and Sam Rayburn, who would later be Speaker of the House but who even then, in the autumn of 1933, was a powerhouse as chairman of the committee through which he and Roosevelt set out to bring the more brash and monopolistic of public utilities and Wall Street barons to their knees.

Rayburn, Johnson, and to a lesser degree even old Garner, tight-fisted though he was personally, were more or less in the [moderate] school of reform, being careful of the baby while gladly throwing out the bath water—the bath water being too much ancient privilege in too few hands. I suppose I can say that in a small way I became a minor-league Boswell of this confederation of fundamentalist Protestant southerners and Irish Catholic Yankees, even before that confederation ever knew itself to be one. This was an Austin-to-Boston arrangement nearly three decades before John Kennedy and Lyndon Johnson made the big one in the 1960 presidential election.

If you don't "know somebody in Washington," whether you are a reporter or a lobbyist, or for that matter a newly arrived president fresh from some statehouse boys' school and innocent of the Federal City's (sometimes real but more often fancied) unique wickedness, you would be about as well off to stay in, say, Toledo, Ohio. I myself was fresh from a counterpart of Toledo, but I did not remain that way very long. For, long before leaving Texas, I had been inaugurated, without putting in any kind of application and without knowing even what was going on, into one of the most powerful clubs in the United States, the old-boy network made up of alumni of the University of Texas. Whatever the shortcomings of that institution, it was then, as it is now, immensely muscular in the political affairs not only of that state but also of Washington. As a reporter and correspondent in Texas, and earlier as an undergraduate, I had had little patience with that club and certainly had never sought its assistance or followed any of its subtle directives in my work. Nevertheless, for reasons I do not understand, since I was an extremely free thinker in those days, somehow the truly old boys of the old-boy network had decided that I would do. It is conceivable, I guess, that this was because I was innately simpatico with so many lawyers, who practice a profession that occupies a special place in Texas.

Again, it may simply have been because the old-boy network rather likes mavericks. Too, I was by this time pretty well known in Texas journalism and, in the context of Texas, had been successful at it—and success is never undervalued by the old-boy network. For whatever reason, metaphorical letters-of-credit on my behalf had somehow gone up to Washington before ever I set foot in it, not only to such Texans as Garner and Rayburn but also to non-Texas friends of theirs who were among the movers and shakers in public life.

So I cannot truthfully say that I arrived in the capital like a character from Horatio Alger. When I first met Lyndon Johnson and set up with him a lasting entente cordiale that survived many strongly stated political and ideological differences and endured mainly on simple personal friendship, I was actually (and ironically, considering where he was headed) a more established figure than he was. Partly through him, but in fact more because of others senior to him, I soon "knew somebody in Washington," and no mistake about it.

Johnson's boss, Congressman Kleberg, was about to lose some of his Texas patronage appointments (though characteristically Kleberg himself was unaware of this looming threat) because old John Garner was preparing to lay claim to all the patronage of Texas. Garner was simply bored, as vice presidents are sure to be once they have looked around, and I doubt that he cared much of a damn about the patronage business except that he thought it might give him something to get his teeth into. But to Johnson, or so he told me, this was a classic example of that "arrogance of power" of which he himself was much later to be accused, as president of the United States. It was a shameless raid upon the property of innocent Texas congressmen, and was being conducted by a Texan, at that.

I myself did not look upon this as exactly a storied atrocity in political warfare. But as a reporter I did see in it substantial news interest to the people of Texas, my journalistic constituents. My piece turned out, however, to mean a good deal more than that to me.

First of all, it made the national wires of the AP, which had been more or less closed to me since I had moved north as a regional man. Secondly, it caused old Garner to draw back from an unpleasant uproar in his home state and elsewhere. Finally, it was a Washington Secret (meaning no secret at all) that this cocky and successful attack upon the most powerful Democratic politician in Washington short of Roosevelt had been pulled off by a congressional secretary named Lyndon Johnson.

The matter came to the ever-attuned ear of FDR himself, whose affection for Garner had at no point been overwhelming, and FDR marked that young fellow Johnson down as a man to be watched.

Johnson, in short, became a Roosevelt protege before ever he won his first elective office. . . .

". . . The most vicious, felonious, and reprehensible campaign ever conducted. . . ."

"THE CAMPAIGN OF THE CENTURY"

1934
California

DOUGLAS CHURCHILL

The 1934 race for governor of California, wrote historian Greg Mitchell, "showed candidates the way from the smoke-filled room to Madison Avenue. Media experts, making unprecedented use of film, radio, direct mail, opinion polls, and national fund-raising, devised the most astonishing (and visually clever) smear campaign ever directed against a major candidate. . . . The New York Times previewed the 1992 race for president under this heading: TELEVISION IS THE CAMPAIGN. *It was the riotous campaign for governor of California that pointed political campaigns down this path."*

The target of the smear campaign was muckraking novelist Upton Sinclair, already famous for The Jungle. *To cure the ills of the Great Depression, Sinclair proposed a welfare scheme called EPIC—"End Poverty in California"—and ran on that platform in the Democratic primary for governor. He shocked the professional politicians by winning enough votes for nomination. Democratic party leaders, including President Franklin Roosevelt, were perplexed by his candidacy, and kept their distance.*

Mitchell called what followed "the campaign of the century." Eyewitness Douglas Churchill reported for the New York Times.

When California was threatened with its favorite bugaboo, liberalism, in 1934, the horror of the cinema knew no bounds. Moscow's most formidable ally, Sinclair, was pitted against a staunch defender and respector of property rights, Frank Merriam. Merriam was a man that Hollywood normally would hate. An ex-Iowan who lived in Long Beach, a bluenose, one who viewed the giddy goings-on of the studio people with distaste, he had nothing in common with the industry. But he became a great champion of liberal living in the eyes of the populace, for he was the only man who stood between them and an iniquitous state income tax proposed by Sinclair. It was this single factor on which the campaign was conducted, but the public never knew it.

Aided by liberal contributions from outside the industry, the cinema swelled the war chest by compelling every studio employee to surrender a day's pay to the campaign fund of Merriam. This money was spent like water but principally for making motion pictures. Had Sinclair been one-tenth the villain or fool he was painted, the psychopathic officers would have had him years ago if the Department of Justice had not nabbed him first.

A more practical man than Sinclair would have lived the rest of his life in ease, for he could have sued the entire city of Hollywood for libel and collected. It probably was the most vicious, felonious, and reprehensible campaign ever conducted against a political candidate.

Short films running five hundred to one thousand feet [five to ten mintues] were made which the industry would not dared have shown unless it had had supreme contempt for the intelligence of its patrons, a contempt that appears justified, for political leaders attribute Sinclair's defeat to the splendid work on the part of the screen.

Hysteria gripped the state. The Epic boys who were backing Sinclair strove valiantly to offset the attacks but the power of visual argument was too much for them. Tax collectors grabbing homes, fertile fields turning to deserts, unsullied womanhood ravished, Stalin making a tour of inspection of his new province—all these things would happen if Sinclair were elected (and passed the income tax law).

Thus Hollywood helped to defeat Sinclair. . . .

Along with Hollywood's efforts, print ads devised by the political marketing consultants misrepresented Sinclair's views, and misquoted lines from his books. "Sure those quotations were irrelevant," a consultant admitted twenty-five years later. "But we had one objective: to keep him from becoming Governor. But because he was a good man, we were sorry we had to do it that way."

Modern advertising techniques first appeared in Western politics because the population was constantly growing and owed little to political patronage. As well, some states required popular referendums on important issues, to avoid cronyism. Mass marketing was later imitated around the country as patronage machines lost influence.

Actually, the question of who really won the 1934 election is up for debate. One of the first laws Merriam passed was an income tax. And EPIC, along with other Utopian movements and pension schemes that appeared at the time, foreshadowed a variety of New Deal programs, such as Social Security.

"At four o'clock they were still singing in our camp. . . ."

BOHEMIAN GROVE

July 31, 1934
Sonoma County, California

HAROLD ICKES

*If seeing the most powerful men in America drunk and in drag sounds appealing,
try to get an invitation to Bohemian Grove. For more than a century, San
Francisco's Bohemian Club—currently about 2,000 members strong—has held
retreats north of the city, where members and guests put on short plays and throw
parties.*

*But Bohemian Grove serves another purpose. It brings together big money and
big politics, and has led to some worthwhile endeavors. For example, when Ernest
Lawrence needed cash to build an atom-smashing cyclotron, the president of the
University of California at Berkeley took him up to the Grove to introduce him
to rich friends. Lawrence got the money he needed, and the first cyclotron was
built in 1933.*

*As a self-proclaimed "curmudgeon," eyewitness Harold Ickes wouldn't have fit
naturally into the hearty clubbishness of the Bohemian Grove. But as secretary of
the interior, responsible for spending hundreds of millions of dollars on projects
like Boulder Dam, he was made to feel very welcome.*

I had accepted an invitation to spend Saturday night at Bohemian
Grove about seventy-five miles north of San Francisco. . . . I had heard
of the Bohemian Club, but knew little about it. I was invited to the
Grove last year, but, of course, could not accept. Apparently it has quite
a large membership. The club owns some 1,500 acres of redwood forest
beautifully located. The members go to the Grove for three weeks every
summer. The encampment closes on a Saturday night and that night they
have what is called their "High Jinx." This silly name led me to believe it
was a roisterous, drinking occasion. I will not deny that I found a good
deal of drinking; in fact, there was a lot of it, but there was much more
besides.

There are a number of small camps in the Grove, but they are well
hidden and well managed. The members live in cabins, but there is sanitary sewage, hot and cold running water and gas for both light and
cooking. The food was excellent. There is a general bar for the camp and
each particular subcamp has a bar of its own.

The camp grounds have been laid out beautifully. There is one pond at the end of which is a big stone impressionist figure of an owl before which the light always burns. But the thing that made the greatest impression on me was the play that night. The theater is an open-air one in a natural opening, surrounded by towering sequoias. The stage is at the foot of a sharp hill. The hill is covered with trees and undergrowth and the proscenium arch of the stage consists of two giant sequoias with intermingled tops. It was one of the most impressive and magnificent settings I have ever seen. The play that night was a serious one, the theme being the conversion of the old Irish Druids by St. Patrick. It had been written by the late Professor James Stephens, an Englishman, who had been a member of the English faculty at the University of California. All the parts were taken by the members of the Bohemian Club and the acting could not have been better if it had been done by professionals; in fact, I doubt whether it would have been so well done. It was very impressive to see the actors carrying torches and following the trails down the hillside. The costuming and the lighting were very well done. I was told that the lighting for that one play cost $25,000, and certainly it would have been difficult to improve upon it.

After the play there was a very good time had throughout the camp. Members visited various camps and everyone was expected to drink long and often. I met Eugene Meyer, Chairman of the Federal Reserve Board under President Hoover, and now publisher of the *Washington Post*. Mr. Hoover himself had been there the day before. Amon Carter, of Fort Worth, Texas, was there, as was Assistant Secretary of the Treasury Robert. Jim Farley had been there the week before. I also met Mr. Giannini, president of the Bank of America, and Arthur Reynolds, former president of the Continental-Illinois National Bank of Chicago, who is now working for Giannini. There were many other well-known men there, some of whom I met and some of whom I did not meet.

Those in charge of me started to visit the various camps, but I soon begged off and went back to Woof Camp where I was quartered. I explained that I was leaving early in the morning, and about twelve-thirty I went to bed. I got very little sleep because the festivities continued practically all night. I know that at four o'clock they were still singing in our camp.

*"If there was a heaven to which I would go permanently,
I hoped it would look like this."*

"THE RANCH": HEARST AND SAN SIMEON

1934

ADELA ROGERS ST. JOHNS

Today when people think of William Randolph Hearst they picture Charles Foster Kane, filmmaker Orson Welles's version: a multimillionaire who championed the common man and found a way to make that philosophy pay. It wasn't far from the truth.

Charlie Chaplin, a committed socialist and an unlikely but close friend of Hearst, once wrote, "If I were asked what personality in my life has made the deepest impression on me, I would say the late William Randolph Hearst. I should explain that the impression was not always a pleasant one—although he had commendable qualities. It was the enigma of his personality that fascinated me, his boyishness, his shrewdness, his kindness, his ruthlessness, his immense power and wealth, and above all his genuine naturalness. In worldly values, he was the freest man I have ever known."

Hearst's father, George, made millions in mining in the 1800s. He also acquired, as an unexpected payment for a bad debt, the San Francisco Examiner. Shortly after William dropped out of Harvard in 1885, he persuaded his father to let him run the paper. He showed little respect for tradition or propriety, making the paper a mass circulation success by lowering prices, introducing color comics and a magazine section, and emphasizing sensational stories.

In 1895 he invaded Joseph Pulitzer's territory, New York City, by acquiring the New York Morning Journal. In 1898 their competition for ever more sensational stories about Spain's mistreatment of Cubans pushed public sentiment toward war with Spain. (When artist Frederick Remington arrived in Cuba ahead of the troops, he wired back to New York that there was no fighting. Hearst wired back: "Please remain. You furnish the pictures and I'll furnish the war.")

His holdings were always in flux, but at his peak he controlled about 28 major newspapers, 2 wire services, 18 magazines, 8 radio stations, and 2 movie companies.

Hearst lived in a grandiose fantasy castle at San Simeon, a 240,000-acre ranch on the California coast. Construction on the residence began in 1919 and continued past his death. The many buildings included a huge collection of art, along with Etruscan tombs, Egyptian mummies, a zoo, a Spanish monastery, and whole rooms of European castles that had been shipped to America stone by stone and reassembled for Hearst. Hearst's longtime mistress, actress Marion Davies, once said to Chaplin, "The whole place is crazy. Look at it! The creation of mad Otto . . . and he'll go on building and adding to it till the day he dies. Then what use will it be?"

Journalist Adela Rogers St. Johns, as she mentions, was the daughter of Earl Rogers, one of the country's best-known criminal lawyers. She became a close friend of her longtime boss, and visited San Simeon several times.

As Earl Rogers' daughter, I had been able to get anyplace I wanted to go. . . . AWE was something I had never felt. My father had taken me to Mr. Hearst to get me a job, and Mr. Hearst had been real great to me. . . . Nevertheless at the thought of this ride alone with him I shook with the worst case of stage fright I was ever to know. In our many years together I was to learn how shy he was with strangers, how much more often he listened than spoke, how kind his responses were, but I did not know this then.

One thing I had known because his mother, Phoebe Apperson Hearst, had explained it to my grandmother, Adela Andrus Rogers. No one ever quoted Mr. Hearst without mimicking that unique high light voice. The small trumpet squeak of an elephant is a surprise. . . .

He picked me up and we went along quietly beside the Pacific Ocean, in the late afternoon light, . . . Mr. Hearst far in one corner of the big luxurious limousine, me in the other.

As we swung in from the sea toward Oxnard and the stretch of hills and fruitful valley, we were still silent. . . . So I spoke. "I don't know whether I could be happy away from the sea. I think I got booted out of Bryn Mawr because I couldn't bear to stay away—"

He turned to look at me with a smile. He said, "I never thought of that as an alibi for my getting booted out of Harvard. I thought it was natural villainy. . . ."

On the terrace of one of the white-stucco three-story "cottages" that were the only houses then finished, Mr. Hearst bowed and told me a courteous good night and thanked me for my company.

A maid was waiting in my room, the blaze of a wood fire in the huge fireplace was at the moment more important than art treasures and the light gleaming from behind silken shades, and silver sconces gave the peaceful and comforting effect of candlelight. The maid brought a tray of sandwiches, fruit and cake, milk and hot chocolate, and I thought to myself, This is a life I shall be glad to have known. . . .

The fog had fled before the sun when I woke up, in the daylight the room was the richest and most ornate I had ever seen. Exquisite statuettes, priceless brocade hangings, inlaid furniture, the ceiling had been brought from a palace of Richelieu's, the Renaissance decor was deep and rich in color. . . .

My fire was lighted again, I put on a robe and rang, and asked the maid who came—there was twenty-four-hour service of all kinds—for coffee. With a pleasant smile she said I would have to go up to the Castle for that. This was almost the only thing I found difficult about the Ranch. . . . I once asked Marion Davies about this incongruous bit amid the luxury, the meticulous service, and extravagant indulgence by which guests were surrounded. She said W.R. did not approve of breakfast in bed. If people did not get up and get dressed they might frowst away hours that could better be spent outdoors. He thought, Marion said, that the wonderful walk through morning dew and freshness with the sparkle of the sea below and mountain air blowing from above the Sierras was a good way to start the day. I'm sure it was but at the time I thought I could have appreciated it more with one cup of coffee under my riding britches or my tennis skirt.

On that visit the Castle, La Cuesta Encantada, or Enchanted Hill, was far from completed. . . . For this reason William Randolph Hearst's architect was in residence.

In this setting and company Miss Julia Morgan had to be a double-take of unexpectedness. For she was a small, skinny, self-effacing lady whose iron will was fem incognita and sotto voce. Her graying hair was held in a small knob at the back of her head by bone pins, her gray tweed tailored suit was inches too long, and she used no make-up at all. . . . She had designed the unforgettable Tower of Jewels for the 1915 San Francisco World's Fair and she designed and built the Hearst Ranch and everything that had to do with it as long as Mr. Hearst was building it.

As I stood in the window of my own bedroom that morning I said a prayer which I didn't believe in to a God I was convinced didn't exist to the effect that IF there was a heaven to which I would go permanently I hoped it would look like this. . . .

Just then the door opened and to my surprise in came a friend of mine from New York. Helena Young was the wife of a well-known jurist and with her, help us all, was the lady of the Castle. I had never before met Mrs. Hearst and I was astonished at her youth and sparkling handsomeness. She had on a pink Irish linen morning dress, no lady had ever heard of slacks or shorts much less worn them. Mrs. Hearst's hair was dark and worn in an elaborate crown.

Helena bounced as usual, we said the usual things about my trip up, what a lovely morning, then Helena said, "You know Marion Davies, don't you?"

I said, "Yes, I know her." I thought I might as well fall off a tightrope as choke on my own bated breath, so I said, "Mr. Hearst introduced me to her." I hoped this implied that I hadn't invented Marion Davies. It wasn't me who elevated her to the left hand of the throne. Nevertheless she was my friend, so I said, "I like her a lot."

All right, I thought, I will now be ordered to the Tower and nobody will find me for years. I will probably be beheaded, it seems to me my chances of survival are not very good at this moment.

Helena said reassuringly, "Millicent is just curious."

Mrs. Hearst smiled at me and said, "What does she call him?"

I said, "She calls him W.R."

"And what does he call her?"

"He calls her Marion," and you know at this very moment I can hear him calling, "Mare—eee—on, where's Mare—eee—on?" To the day of his death he wanted to know every minute where she was.

Then we talked about the yacht at the pier below and Mrs. Hearst told me why her husband had given up politics. In the beginning he had thought it was his duty to offer to serve his country in government. Then, he found the people didn't want him. Now, we have the Rockefellers and the Kennedys but when Mr. Hearst ran for governor we were against great wealth for candidates, we were still committed to the log cabin. So there was no obligation to continue. He wouldn't quit, she said, just because Congress bored him—as everything might except his newspapers. And the Ranch.

Mrs. Hearst said she didn't like the West. Not even the Ranch.

. . . Just last summer [1965] I went to Southampton to talk to Mrs. Hearst and she said again quite simply that one of the things that had kept her and Mr. Hearst apart so much was that he loved the West, and she was an Easterner. So she kept the Eastern houses and estates and apartments going and he stayed at San Simeon. Of all places on earth the spot he loved the best.

On that summer day in the glorious house at Southampton when he had been dead for fifteen years, Mrs. Hearst told me about her first date with young William Randolph Hearst. Even then, this East-West angle came up.

At that time she was Millicent Willson and she and her sister Anita were favorites on the New York musical comedy stage. Not in the chorus as Marion Davies and her sister Rene were—the Willson girls were featured singers and dancers, both had some talent and a lot of beauty. An old-timer told me they had what is called class.

"When he asked me to go out with him," Mrs. Hearst said, "my mother was against it. We were carefully supervised in those days and I recall she said, 'Who is he? Some young fellow from out West some-where, isn't he?' She insisted Anita had to come or I couldn't go. Well, he took us down to the *Journal,* the *New York Journal,* we'd hardly heard of it, and he showed us over it, all over it. I hadn't the foggiest notion what we were doing, walking miles on rough boards in thin, high-heeled evening slippers, and I thought my feet would kill me. Of course this wasn't our idea of a good time. We wanted to go to Sherry's or Bustanoby's. More than that Anita kept whispering to me, 'We're going to get thrown out of here, Milly, the way he behaves you'd think he owned it.' It wasn't until our next trip that I found out he did—own it, I mean. I told Anita and at first she wouldn't believe me. She said, 'He's like all Westerners. All big brag strutting around as though they owned the earth.' But—" Mrs. Hearst stopped to smile, but whether at me or that long-ago young Westerner talking so big I couldn't tell. "I guess I must have fallen in love with him at once, he asked me to marry him two weeks later and I said yes right away. . . ."

The Hearst family gave the castle compound to the state of California in 1958. It is now a tourist attraction.

". . . A vast wall of new gray-white concrete, curved in a beautiful bow. . . ."

BOULDER DAM

1935
Nevada–Arizona border

BRUCE BLIVEN AND EDMUND WILSON

Marc Reisner, author of Cadillac Desert, *declares that in the West "everything depends on the manipulation of water—on capturing it behind dams, storing it, and rerouting it in concrete rivers over distances of hundreds of miles. Were it not for a century and a half of messianic effort towards that end, the West as we know it would not exist." He calls Boulder Dam (later renamed Hoover Dam) "perhaps the most significant structure that has ever been built in the United States."*

For years, politics stood in the way of it. There was general agreement that a dam would level the flow of the Colorado River, which was prone to flooding and drought. But only California needed all that water. And if California got it, the sparsely populated states in the region—Wyoming, Arizona, Nevada, New

Mexico, Colorado, and Utah—would lose their legal claims to the river's flow, permanently limiting their growth. The smaller states used leverage in Congress to negotiate the Colorado River Compact, which divided the river's flow among the seven states. That agreement, Reisner notes, has been called "a western equivalent of the Constitution."

The politics were important, but the engineering was astounding. Eyewitnesses Edmund Wilson and Bruce Bliven reported on the dam's contruction for the New Republic. *Wilson visited in 1931, when work had just begun, Bliven in 1935, when some of the harsh conditions Wilson reported had been improved.*

WILSON

It was a gesture of Mr. Hoover, wishing to seem to do something about unemployment, to start work on Boulder Dam at once and before any proper facilities had yet been provided for living there. Boulder City, nine miles away, was supposed to be a model camp, but it would take a long time to complete it. In the meantime, the main part of the crew were to do the best they could in the desert. The married men had wretched shacks in what came to be known as Rag City; the single ones the river camp.

The Reclamation Service engineers had been there before the men. They had been there when there was nothing, and they remember it as a "hell-hole," where you "got goofy with the heat." But though these engineers have their own complaints against the government as an employer, they are at least in the service of the government, and as one of them now declares, "It's having a little responsibility that makes all the difference." Boulder Dam, with all its hardships and dangers, makes a challenge one can take pride in meeting: it is the biggest project of the kind that the United States has ever undertaken. And the men felt this pride, too, at first. The government had stipulated in its contract with the companies that ex-service men should be given the preference, and when the men who have been working there started in, they evidently had something of the army spirit. The trouble was that as time went on, they found out that they were not really working for the United States, but for a group of construction companies.

The situation at Boulder Dam is peculiar. The idea originally was that the government should put through the whole project; but it was later, characteristically, decided by Mr. Hoover's administration that it should be handed over to private business, the government only regaining control at the end of a construction job which is supposed to take at least six years. Secretary [of the Interior Ray] Wilbur signed a contract with a combination of six Western companies, associated as "Six Companies, Incorporated," who had offered a bid of $49,890,995—$5,000,000 less than that of any of their competitors. He had Boulder Dam rechristened Hoover Dam, which nobody can remember to call it.

Mr. Wilbur, by an unfortunate chance, arranged this contract just eight days before the going into effect of the Davis bill, which was to regulate wages on government projects. The companies were all nonunion, and the only stipulations in regard to labor that Mr. Wilbur was able to make, beyond the clause about ex-service men, were that Mongolians should not be employed; and that 80 per cent of the men should be housed in Boulder City—and the latter of these was suspended when it was decided to start operations before Boulder City was built. The result was that there was nothing to restrain the companies from resorting automatically and immediately to that systematic skimping, petty swindling and frank indifference to the fate of their employees which are necessary to provide officers with salaries and stockholders with profits. In the first place, the men at the river camp had no means of refreshing themselves: spending all day in the tunnel with shovels and drills, so hot that they always work naked, they could not even get a shower or a cold drink. The only water they had for drinking or washing was the water of the Colorado River, which, full of silt from the decomposing tufa, is always an opaque yellow like coffee with too much cream; and this, with no water-coolers, would get tepid or hot in the tanks. As the weather became hotter and hotter, the water began making people sick. Nor were there any facilities for cooling the barracks. The nights were so suffocating and uncomfortable that one welcomed the diversion of work. And for the shift that got its rest in the daytime, with the sun glaring through the windows and heating the shack like an oven, sleep, if they managed to get any, became a heavy sweating coma. When they got up to go to work, they would find their drills so hot that they had to cool them off before they could take them in their hands.

At Black Canyon, during the last days of July, the thermometer had never dropped below 79, and at times it had been 128 in the shade. The lowest maximum was 104, and thereafter it got steadily worse: it was always at least 100 at night.

The work on the dam is dangerous. The casualty company which is insuring the Six Companies has estimated at 200 the number of lives that is likely to be lost during the course of the first year; and the companies seemed to have done very little in the way of safety precautions. According to the government's own report, there have already been twenty-six men killed since May—including two drowned, two hit by falling rocks, three blown up in explosions and thirteen who died from the heat. When a man would collapse from the heat, the other men—half-stunned by the sun themselves and with no way of giving him relief—could only stand around him and watch him gasp out his life. For till lately they have had nothing at the river camp but a small first-aid station, and there was bound to be a long delay in getting an ambulance from Boulder City. The government has declared that the laws of the state are not valid on the reservation which has been set aside for the dam, and it is evident that the Six Companies have taken advantage of this to ignore the safety laws of Nevada. They had, for example, been sending men back into the tunnels fifteen or twenty minutes after the blasts, though it is usual to allow an hour for the nitroglycerin fumes to evaporate. The Nevada laws insist upon ventilation in tunnels, safety men at the headings and change rooms where the men can dry themselves before going out into the air, but none of these has been supplied. The river camp itself is precariously propped on the broken-stone talus at the bottom of the cliff, where freshly loosened boulders sometimes come hurtling through the mess-room window; and the men have been looking forward rather anxiously to the beginning of the cloudburst season, which they fear may undermine and upset the wooden stilts on which the dormitories are perched, and send the whole outfit down into the river.

BLIVEN

. . . They have built vast tunnels through the canyon walls, paralleling the course of the mighty stream; they have turned the water out of its bed; in that dry bed they have constructed by far the largest dam on earth, six hundred feet through at the base and towering almost two thirds as high as the Empire State Building. Upstream from that dam is now accumulating a lake which will take ten years to fill. It will then be 115 miles long, 8 miles wide at its widest point, and it will contain enough water to cover all of New York State to a depth of one foot. If by some miracle of nature the river itself were to disappear from the face of the earth, its mighty current would continue to sweep onward at the normal volume for two years before this lake would be exhausted.

What you see as you come around [a] hairpin turn is a vast wall of new gray-white concrete, curved in a beautiful bow with its arch upstream for strength. Just beyond it are four concrete towers which look "modern" because they are functional—two on either side of the dam, close inshore—the intake towers through which will pass the water for the hydroelectric plant. That plant will lie nestled against the downstream side of the dam, a U-shaped structure which in fact will be twenty stories high but will, I should say, look like a pygmy beside the flank of that incredible man-made mountain. At present, the floor of the canyon below the dam is the usual appalling litter that goes with big construction—temporary roads, wooden scaffolding, a tangle of power cables. Even from our height, a little below the top of the dam itself, the workers moving about amid their rubbish heaps seem incredibly small and weak; the mind refuses to grasp the fact that these tiny dolls and others like them have actually turned aside the river, built that vast cliff of concrete, chiseled and blasted out all these roads, many of them cut into the very face of the cliff, bored the mighty tunnels through which the entire river is now racing silently, far below our feet in the bowels of the hill.

Abstractedly, as we see huge cages move out on cables strung across the canyon, and then descend 700 feet with their massive cargoes, we hear the Voice of Explanation in our ears: The purposes of Boulder Dam are flood control, irrigation, silt control, water supply and electricity. The new aqueduct, many miles downstream, will carry one billion gallons of water per day to Los Angeles, a distance of 239 miles, over desert and through mountains, lifting it a quarter of a mile, by means of pumping stations, in the process. Still farther downstream, a new irrigation canal will carry water to 1,000,000 acres and ultimately to 500,000 more. In addition, flood danger will be eliminated from another vast area. The dam, when completed, will have a maximum electric capacity four times that of Niagara, three times that of Muscle Shoals, two and one-half times that of the great Russian dam which was once called Dnieprostroy. The sale of electricity and water should pay the expense of construction within about fifty years (the aqueduct will cost some $60,000,000 more than the dam itself, and is next only to the Panama Canal among the great projects of the modern world).

The dam is by far the largest single piece of masonry ever attempted. It weighs 6,000,000 tons, and if this were poured in a cube, it would cover a square block and rise higher than the Empire State Building. Because of the heat engendered in pouring, the dam would take a hundred years to cool, if left to itself. To hasten the process, more than 500 miles of tubing have been built into the structure, through which ice water circulates from a plant capable of turning out 1,000 tons of ice every twenty-four hours. . . .

The dam was completed in 1936, two years ahead of schedule. The water stored behind it created the world's largest reservoir, Lake Mead, which measures 115 miles across.

Other dams soon followed, including the Imperial Valley Dam, the Parker Dam, and the Glen Canyon Dam.

"If you would like to have your heart broken, just come out here."

BOOM AND BUST

June–July 1936
Oklahoma, Colorado, Kansas,
South Dakota, and North Dakota

ERNIE PYLE

The economies of Texas and Oklahoma changed practically overnight around the beginning of the twentieth century, with the discovery of huge oil fields. The first Oklahoma oil strike was made in 1897 at Bartlesville. The first Texas strike came in 1901 at Beaumont. Oil quickly became the most lucrative commodity in those states.

While the oil business boomed, the farmers went bust. The first two decades of the century had been good times for farmers: production rose, and the agricultural wholesale price index almost tripled. Then the depression came. An overabundance of crops, combined with a collapse of the financial markets, drove prices to all-time lows. By 1932, farm receipts had fallen to one-third the 1918 figure. Forced farm sales from bankruptcies, foreclosures, and tax seizures quadrupled. And to add to the indignity of the farmers, a long, severe drought hit the region in 1936, creating dust storms so large they traveled on westerly winds all the way to the east coast. More than 150,000 square miles of land stretching from Texas to Canada became a desert.

Scripps-Howard reporter Ernie Pyle, whose compassionate World War II reporting would later make him one of the most beloved men in America, saw both the highs and lows as he traveled through the West in 1936.

OKLAHOMA CITY

It is late at night. You are coming into Oklahoma City for the first time in your life. You know by your map and your speedometer that you're not far away now. You're tired and bleary after a long day pounding the roads.

You see the reflection of light in the dark sky ahead. That's it. That's

Oklahoma City. It looks good. The road comes down out of complete flatness, and begins to wind a little. The glare in the sky vanishes around a bend, and reappears again at the next curve.

You top a little rise, and the fog of lights divides slowly into individualities. You see tall buildings all lighted up, still far away. You think what a big place Oklahoma City is, with lots of big office buildings—and lots of people working this late at night, too. Why, it looks like the New York skyline at night, only the buildings all seem about the same height. The tops make a ledge of light across the sky.

You think along like that, with the frogs croaking alongside the road and the motor purring through the night, and you getting closer and closer all the time. And then suddenly it hits you, right between the eyes. Those aren't buildings all lighted up. They're oil derricks! Oil derricks right in the city!

I recommend that moment of realization, and the next ten minutes of amazed staring, as one of the most thrilling sights in industrial America. You just come here and see it for the first time at night, and if it doesn't enchant and bewilder and captivate you, then I'll sit on the statehouse steps and drink every barrel of oil produced in Oklahoma City in the next twenty-four hours. That would be a hundred and twenty-five thousand barrels.

You drive on in among the oil derricks. They engulf you. They're all around. There are hundreds of them. They're as thick as trees. Some aren't twenty paces apart. Some are right on the highway, like a filling station. A string of bright lights goes to the top of each one. And down below, on the ground, everything is brightly lighted.

First the sight, and then the sound. In among them, there is a steady, heavy din. The whole field is alive with work. You hear deep, regular poundings; and a throbbing, rumbling circular sound, like a grinding; and the clank of steel tubes and the whirr of great pulleys, and the shooting off of steam. You see muddy autos dashing about, and men at work, and white plumes of steam, and the glare of flame in boilers. Immense activity, and it is nearly midnight. The fiendish boring for oil never stops with the sun.

You drive on and on. People's houses are all around the derricks—or, rather, the derricks are wedged in between houses, on open lots, on filling-station aprons.

You're in the suburbs of Oklahoma City, and pretty soon you see a sign that says CITY LIMITS, OKLAHOMA CITY. You keep driving on, and still you're amidst the oil wells. And you stay amidst them clear into town. They're all over the golf course. There is one on the side lawn of the state capitol. There's one up against the governor's mansion. The bases of some derricks are set flush against the sides of beautiful homes.

Three months ago, there were only two oil wells in the northern part of Oklahoma City. Today there are at least three hundred, and new derricks are going up almost by the hour. Residential sections are being gutted. People are wild for oil. It's one of the big oil booms of petroleum history.

Many people are shocked by this glaring display of commercialism. Rearing an oil field right in the heart of a city, ruining homes and fine residential sections—where is the sanctity of the home? Putting oil wells on the capitol grounds—where is the dignity of the state? Greedy, greedy Oklahoma. Is nothing sacred?

Personally, I get a big wallop out of it. My vote is yes. Put up a thousand more derricks. What if it does waste irrecoverable reserves of oil? Grind a thousand more holes in the ground. Who cares for the heartbreaks and the empty tomorrows? Tear down the statehouse. Throw up more silvery steel shafts. Fire up the black boilers. Drill in the gushers, boys. Cheat the poor folks. Ruin the homes. Squander gas. Throw away fortunes. Who cares? It's fun. Everybody's having fun, even the losers. It's a fever. Spread out your hands and catch the sparkling spray. Let oil reign unrefined. Let's all get rich. Boy, hand me that lease, before it's too late. God, it's exciting. It's a boom. It's a mania. It's great. . . .

COLORADO AND KANSAS

If you would like to have your heart broken, just come out here. This is the dust-storm country. It is the saddest land I have ever seen.

Coming in here from Colorado Springs, a one-day drive, you pass through both the sandstorm and the dust-storm regions. Eastern Colorado is a mild form of desert, and hence rather sandy. When the wind blows there, you have a sandstorm. As you get into Kansas, the soil becomes richer and softer, and when it gets dry and powdery, and when the wind blows, you have a dust storm.

We were still in Colorado. Far behind, old Pikes Peak lifted its snowy sides into the heavens. Far ahead to the east were faint, hazy clouds of sand. The approach to a sandstorm is a dark and chilling experience.

The yellow sand haze ahead grew heavier and darker, making the atmosphere a queer yellow, the way it is sometimes just before a cyclone. To the right were rolling, foreboding rain clouds, dust mixing with them. And over to the left, over where the wind came from, were pillars of sand—giant yellow columns, miles away, rising from the horizon clear up into the sky, like smoke from a burning town. It was frightening, and sickening.

The wind howled. It came at least forty miles an hour, across the prairie from the north. It was hard to steer the car. The roar of the wind was louder than your voice. The sand film grew steadily thicker around us. It darkened the atmosphere, and a little film settled on the inside rim of the windshield.

The country was slightly rolling. In the valleys it was better. But on the rises, the sand-laden wind cut across the highway like a horizontal waterfall. The sand was not drifting, or floating, or hanging in the air— it was shooting south, in thick veins, like air full of thrown baseballs.

Cars we met had their lights on, and we wondered if it was really that bad ahead. It was. We went into the darkness as an airplane flies into fog. The air was black with sand. You could not see from one telephone pole to the next. There wasn't any sky. The tiny rocks smashed and pounded against the car windows. The wind was vicious, and the car was light on its wheels, and inclined to weave. You couldn't hear the motor at all.

It didn't last long, no more than a mile or two. And then we popped out into rain. The air was washed clear. It was like coming out suddenly into fresh air on the windward side of a forest fire.

We came into Kansas. It had been raining for twelve hours. The earth was wet, and we were thus spared the spectacle of a Kansas dust storm. But because the air was clear, we could better see the terrific desolation that is western Kansas. We could not have seen it if the air had been filled with dust.

A few miles from the village of Lakin I stopped, shoved open the door, and stood on the running board, holding on to the car, as the cold wind rushed and roared, and looked around. The land is as flat as a billiard table. The horizon is far, far away. I looked clear around the rim, as you do sometimes from a ship at sea, just following the horizon around. And I saw not a solitary thing but bare earth, and a few lonely, empty farmhouses.

You might truthfully say there is nothing left of western Kansas. As far as the eye could see, there was nothing. There was not a tree, or a blade of grass, or a dog or a cow, or a human being—nothing whatever, nothing at all but gray raw earth and a few far houses and barns, sticking up from the dark gray sea like white cattle skeletons on the desert. There was nobody in the houses. The humans had given up, and gone. It was death, if I have ever seen death.

Today, because of the rain, the ground held firm, and would not give itself up to the wind. But yesterday it did, and tomorrow, after the bright sun, it will again. The air will gradually fill with the earthy powder, and people in its path will scarcely be able to breathe, and houses will be closed. And the soil will blow away from around the roots of things, and pile like snowdrifts against the barns, and fly on the wind south toward Mexico, and leave nothing at all.

As I drove along I thought of all the smart-aleck jokes about President Roosevelt's hundred-mile-wide belt of trees. [On Roosevelt's orders, more than two hundred million trees were planted from North Dakota to Oklahoma.] I thought of the sneers about the college professors trying to improve the earth. I wonder if any of the criticizers have ever seen a country that has died. A belt of trees, or a belt of soybeans, or a belt of billiard cues stuck in the ground—anything that might faintly halt the march of the destroying wind across the face of our earth—seems to me worth trying.

RAPID CITY, SOUTH DAKOTA

The grasshopper is to the Dakotas about the same thing as a hurricane is to Miami or a tidal wave is to Galveston.

The grasshopper opens and closes every conversation. He holds second place only to the great drought itself. You can't say the grasshoppers destroyed everything the drought left; rather, the two galloped down through the sun-parched summer nose and nose, and it would be hard to say whether the last blade of grass died of thirst or was gnawed by a hopper.

I'd always imagined the aftermath looked like World War pictures of a French woods after a heavy shelling, with only the stumps of the trees still standing. But that's not the case. A cornfield after grasshoppers get through with it looks like a freshly plowed field, just after the soil is turned and is all black and rich-looking, with no vegetation at all.

They not only strip the blades; they eat the stalk, and burrow down into the ground and nibble away the roots. They leave nothing on the surface whatever. They do the same with grain and grass and vegetables.

I wanted to take a picture of a hopper-devastated cornfield, but I didn't want a bare field, because you couldn't prove there had been any corn there. I wanted a field that had leafless cornstalks still standing like sticks, and I drove for a full half day through South Dakota before I could find a field that had even the stumps of cornstalks left. There is only one cornfield in about every hundred and fifty miles that hasn't simply disappeared from the face of the earth.

My trip through this withering land of misery swings to a close, and I am glad. The world of drought finally becomes an immersion that levels the senses.

You arrive at a point where you no longer look and say, "My God, this is awful!" You gradually become accustomed to dried field and burned pasture; it stretches into a dull, continuous fact.

Day upon day of driving through this ruined country gradually becomes a sameness that ceases to admit a perspective. You come to accept it as a vast land that is dry and bare, and was that way yesterday and will be tomorrow, and was that way a hundred miles back and will be a hundred miles ahead.

The story is the same everywhere, the farmers say the same thing, the fields look the same—it becomes like the drone of a bee, and after a while you hardly notice it at all. . . .

"Next year the hunger will come again. . . ."

THE MIGRANTS

1936
California

JOHN STEINBECK

The Grapes of Wrath, *for which Steinbeck won the Pulitzer Prize in 1938, was Steinbeck's fourth attempt to write about California's migrant farmworkers. The first was a series of articles written for the* San Francisco News *in 1936, which Steinbeck used to research and organize his ideas. He then started a novel called* The Oklahomans *(most of the workers at the time were escaping the Dust Bowl). It was never finished and has never been found. He tried again with a satire called* L'Affaire Lettuceberg, *which he described as "a vicious book, a mean book." Shortly after his publisher announced it, Steinbeck decided to destroy it. As he explained, "My whole work drive has been aimed at making people understand each other and then I write this book the aim of which is to cause hatred through partial understanding. My father would have called it a smart-alec book. It was full of tricks to make people ridiculous." Finally, he wrote* The Grapes of Wrath.

Steinbeck was convinced the Oklahomans would change California: "Their coming here now is going to change things almost as much as did the coming of the first American settlers. . . . The Californian doesn't know what he wants. The Oklahoman knows exactly what he wants. He wants a piece of land. And he goes after it and gets it."

This account is drawn from the first series of newspaper articles Steinbeck wrote in 1936, and which he updated a few weeks before he started writing The Grapes of Wrath. *The articles were originally accompanied by photographs from Dorothea Lange (see page 301).*

To the casual traveler on the great highways the movements of the migrants are mysterious if they are seen at all, for suddenly the roads will be filled with open rattletrap cars loaded with children and with dirty bedding, with fire-blackened cooking utensils. The boxcars and gondolas on the railroad lines will be filled with men. And then, just as suddenly, they will have disappeared from the main routes. On side roads and near rivers where there is little travel the squalid, filthy squatters' camp will have been set up, and the orchards will be filled with pickers and cutters and driers.

The unique nature of California agriculture requires that these migrants exist, and requires that they move about. Peaches and grapes, hops and cotton cannot be harvested by a resident population of laborers. For example, a large peach orchard which requires the work of twenty men the year round will need as many as 2000 for the brief time of picking and packing. And if the migration of the 2000 should not occur, if it should be delayed even a week, the crop will rot and be lost.

Thus, in California we find a curious attitude toward a group that makes our agriculture successful. The migrants are needed, and they are hated. Arriving in a district they find the dislike always meted out by the resident to the foreigner, the outlander. This hatred of the stranger occurs in the whole range of human history, from the most primitive village farm to our own highly organized industrial farming. The migrants are hated for the following reasons, that they are ignorant and dirty people, that they are carriers of disease, that they increase the necessity for police and the tax bill for schooling in a community, and that if they are allowed to organize they can, simply by refusing to work, wipe out the season's crops. They are never received into a community nor into the life of a community. Wanderers in fact, they are never allowed to feel at home in the communities that demand their services.

Let us see what kind of people they are, where they come from, and the routes of their wanderings. In the past they have been of several races, encouraged to come and often imported as cheap labor; Chinese in the early period, then Filipinos, Japanese, and Mexicans. These were foreigners, and as such they were ostracized and segregated and herded about.

If they attempted to organize they were deported or arrested, and having no advocates they were never able to get a hearing for their problems. But in recent years the foreign migrants have begun to organize, and at this danger signal they have been deported in great numbers, for there was a new reservoir from which a great quantity of cheap labor could be obtained.

The drought in the Middle West has driven the agricultural populations of Oklahoma, Nebraska, and parts of Kansas and Texas westward. Their lands are destroyed and they can never go back to them.

Thousands of them are crossing the borders in ancient rattling automobiles, destitute and hungry and homeless, ready to accept any pay so that they may eat and feed their children. And this is a new thing in migrant labor, for the foreign workers were usually imported without their children and everything that remains of their old life with them.

They arrive in California usually having used up every resource to get here, even to the selling of the poor blankets and utensils and tools on the way to buy gasoline. They arrive bewildered and beaten and usually in a state of semi-starvation, with only one necessity to face immediately, and that is to find work at any wage in order that the family may eat.

And there is only one field in California that can receive them. Ineligible for relief, they must become migratory field workers.

Because the old kind of laborers, Mexicans and Filipinos, are being deported and repatriated very rapidly, while on the other hand the river [of] dust-bowl refugees increases all the time, it is this new kind of migrant that we must largely consider.

The earlier foreign migrants have invariably been drawn from a peon class. This is not the case with the new migrants.

They are small farmers who have lost their farms, or farm hands who lived with the family in the old American way. They are men who have worked hard on their own farms and have felt the pride of possessing and living in close touch with the land.

They are resourceful and intelligent Americans who have gone through the hell of the drought, have seen their lands wither and die and the topsoil blow away; and this, to a man who has owned his land, is a curious and terrible pain.

And then they have made the crossing and have seen often the death of their children on the way. Their cars have broken down and been repaired with the ingenuity of the land man. Often they patched the worn-out tires every few miles. They have weathered the thing, and they can weather much more for their blood is strong.

They are descendants of men who crossed into the Middle West, who won their lands by fighting, who cultivated the prairies and stayed with them until they went back to desert.

And because of their tradition and their training, they are not migrants by nature. They are gypsies by force of circumstance.

In their heads, as they move wearily from harvest to harvest, there is one urge and one overwhelming need, to acquire a little land again, and to settle on it and stop their wandering. One has only to go into the squatters' camps where the families live on the ground and have no homes, no beds, and no equipment; and one has only to look at the strong purposeful faces, often filled with pain and more often, when they see the corporation-held idle lands, filled with anger, to know that this new race is here to stay and that heed must be taken of it.

. . . There is another difference between their [old] life and the new. They have come from little farm districts where democracy was not only possible, but inevitable, where popular government, whether practiced in the Grange, in church organization, or in local government, was the responsibility of every man. And they have come into the country where, because of the movement necessary to make a living, they are not allowed any vote whatever, but are rather considered a properly underprivileged class.

Let us see the fields that require the impact of their labor and the districts to which they must travel. As one little boy in a squatters' camp said, "When they need us they call us migrants, and when we've picked their crop, we're bums and we got to get out."

. . . The squatters' camps are located all over California. Let us see what a typical one is like. It is located on the banks of a river, near an irrigation ditch or on a side road where a spring of water is available. From a distance it looks like a city dump, and well it may, for the city dumps are the sources of material of which it is built. You can see a litter of dirty rags and scrap iron, of houses built of weeds, of flattened cans or of paper. It is only on close approach that it can be seen that these are homes.

Here is a house built by a family who have tried to maintain a neatness. The house is about ten feet by ten feet, and it is built completely of corrugated paper. The roof is peaked, the walls are tacked to a wooden frame. The dirt floor is swept clean, and along the irrigation ditch or in the muddy river the wife of the family scrubs clothes without soap and tries to rinse out the mud in muddy water. The spirit of this family is not quite broken, for the children, three of them, still have clothes, and the family possesses three old quilts and a soggy, lumpy mattress. But the money so needed for food cannot be used for soap nor for clothes.

With the first rain the carefully built house will slop down into a brown, pulpy mush; in a few months the clothes will fray off the children's bodies, while the lack of nourishing food will subject the whole family to pneumonia when the first cold comes.

. . . The spring is rich and green in California this year. In the fields the wild grass is ten inches high, and in the orchards and vineyards the grass is deep and nearly ready to be plowed under to enrich the soil. Already the flowers are starting to bloom.

Very shortly one of the oil companies will be broadcasting the locations of the wild-flower masses. It is a beautiful spring.

———————————

"She had just sold the tires from her car to buy food."

MIGRANT MOTHER

March 1936
Nipomo, California

DOROTHEA LANGE

Photographer Dorothea Lange was hired by the Farm Security Administration, a New Deal agency, to make a record of the FSA's work. One of her photos, of a young mother at a migrant farm camp in California, would become perhaps the most famous image of twentieth-century America.

Lange gave this account to Popular Photography *magazine in 1960.*

It was raining, the camera bags were packed, and I had on the seat beside me in the car the results of my long trip, the box containing all those rolls and packs of exposed film ready to mail back to Washington. It was a time of relief. Sixty-five miles an hour for seven hours would get me home to my family that night, and my eyes were glued to the wet and gleaming highway that stretched out ahead. I felt freed, for I could lift my mind off my job and think of home.

I was on my way and barely saw a crude sign with pointing arrow which flashed by at the side of the road, saying PEA-PICKERS CAMP. But out of the corner of my eye I *did* see it.

I didn't want to stop, and didn't. I didn't want to remember that I had seen it, so I drove on and ignored the summons. Then, accompanied by the rhythmic hum of the windshield wipers, arose an inner argument:

Dorothea, how about that camp back there? What is the situation back there?

Are you going back?

Nobody could ask this of you, now could they?

To turn back certainly is not necessary. Haven't you plenty of negatives already on this subject? Isn't this just one more of the same? Besides, if you take a camera out in this rain, you're just asking for trouble. Now be reasonable, etc., etc., etc.

Having well convinced myself for 20 miles that I could continue on, I did the opposite. Almost without realizing what I was doing I made a U-turn on the empty highway. I went back those 20 miles and turned off the highway at that sign, PEA-PICKERS CAMP.

I was following instinct, not reason; I drove into that wet and soggy camp and parked my car like a homing pigeon.

I saw and approached the hungry and desperate mother, as if drawn by a magnet. I do not remember how I explained my presence or my camera to her but I do remember she asked me no questions. I made five exposures, working closer and closer from the same direction. I did not ask her name or her history She told me her age, that she was 32. She said that they had been living on frozen vegetables from the surrounding fields, and birds that the children killed. She had just sold the tires from her car to buy food. There she sat in that lean-to tent with her children huddled around her, and seemed to know that my pictures might help her, and so she helped me. There was a sort of equality about it.

The pea crop at Nipomo had frozen and there was no work for anybody. But I did not approach the tents and shelters of other stranded pea-pickers. It was not necessary; I knew I had recorded the essence of my assignment.

After returning from the camps, Lange notified a local newspaper editor about the conditions. The federal government sent 20,000 pounds of food to the migrants.

Lange's photos were published across the country, and accompanied newspaper articles that John Steinbeck wrote as a warm-up to The Grapes of Wrath *(see page 297). One of the lesser known exposures, of the mother breastfeeding a child, inspired the powerful and shocking last scene of Steinbeck's novel.*

". . . Texas is so dusty and bad, California is so green and pretty."

OFF TO CALIFORNIA

1937
Pampa, Texas

WOODY GUTHRIE

Songwriter Woody Guthrie was born in Oklahoma in 1912. After a tragic childhood that included bankruptcy, fire, and the early deaths of his sister and mother, he hit the road during the Depression and the Dust Bowl days.
This account comes from his 1943 book, Bound for Glory.

I rolled my sign-painting brushes up inside an old shirt and stuck them down in my rear pants pocket. On the floor of the shack I was reading a letter and thinking to myself. It said:

> ". . . when Texas is so dusty and bad, California is so green
> and pretty. You must be twenty-five by now, Woody. I know I
> can get you a job here in Sonora. Why don't you come? Your
> aunt Laura."

Yes, I'll go, I was thinking. This is a right nice day for hittin' th' road. 'Bout three o'clock in th' afternoon.

I pulled the crooked door shut as best I could, and walked one block south to the main highway leading west. I turned west and walked along a few blocks, across a railroad track, past a carbon-block warehouse. "Good old Pampa. I hit here in 1926. Worked my tail off 'round this here town. But it didn't give me anything. Town had growed up, strung itself all out across these plains. Just a little old low-built cattle town to start with; jumped up big when the oil boom hit. Now eleven years later it had up and died."

A three- or four-ton beer truck blowed its air brakes and I heard the driver talking, "By God! I thought that looked like you, Woody! Where ya heading Amarilla? Hustlin' signs?" We got off to a jumpy start while he was spitting out his window.

"California," I said. "Hustlin' outta this dam dust!"

"Fer piece down th' road, ain't it?"

"Enda this dam highway! Ain't a-lookin' back!"

"Aww, ain'tcha gonna take one more good look at good ol' Pampa?"

I looked out my window and seen it go by. It was just shacks all along this side of town, tired and lonesome-looking, and lots of us wasn't needed here no more. Oil derricks running up to the city limits on three sides; silvery refineries that first smelled good, then bad; and off along the rim of the horizon, the big carbon-black plants throwing smoke worse than ten volcanoes, the fine black powder covering the iron grass and the early green wheat that pushes up just in time to kiss this March wind. Oil cars and stock cars lined up like herds of cattle. Sun so clear and so bright that I felt like I was leaving one of the prettiest and ugliest spots I'd ever seen. "They tell me this town has fell down ta somethin' like sixteen thousan' people," I said.

"She's really goin' with th' dust!" the driver told me. Then we hit another railroad crossing that jarred him into saying, "I seen th' day when there was more folks than that goin' to th' picture shows! She's really shrivelin' up!"

. . . I walked on down the highway bucking into the wind. It got so hard I had to really duck my head and push. Yes. I know this old flat country up here on the caprock plains. Gumbo mud. Hard crust sod. Iron grass for tough cattle and hard-hitting cowboys that work for the ranchers. These old houses that sweep with the country and look like they're crying in the dust. I know who's in there. I know. I've stuck my head in a million. Drove tractors, cleaned plows and harrows, greased discs and pulled the tumbleweeds out from under the machinery. That wind is getting harder. . . . But I thought, somewhere west there's more room. Maybe the west country needs me out there. It's so big and I'm so little. It needs me to help fill it up and I need it to grow up in. I've got to keep bucking this wind, even if it gets colder.

The songs that grew out of Guthrie's itinerant lifestyle, including "So Long, (It's Been Good to Know Yuh)," eventually brought him international fame. He died in 1967, leaving a legacy that has influenced every folk singer since, including Pete Seeger, Bob Dylan, and Woody's son, Arlo. One of his last songs was "This Land Is Your Land."

"Most of these firms were built by people without much education...."

FRED TERMAN'S BOYS

1937
San Francisco Bay Area

DAVID PACKARD

The closely packed collection of high-tech companies in Silicon Valley grew out of the efforts of Stanford engineering professor Fred Terman, who was determined to make Stanford the equal of any eastern university, and to keep graduates in the area.

Eyewitness David Packard, one of his first students, recalls Terman's role in the creation of Hewlett-Packard.

Largely because of [Fred] Terman's classes, the four of us—Hewlett, [Ed] Porter, [Barney] Oliver, and I—became fast friends. It is not a coincidence that a few years later this group would become the management team of Hewlett-Packard. . . . Fred Terman's keen interest in radio engineering induced him to become acquainted with almost all of the pioneers in the industry, many of whom were located in the Palo Alto area. Early wireless work by Stanford graduate Cyril F. Elwell was organized into the Federal Telegraph Company at the beginning of the century. Lee De Forest invented the vacuum tube in Palo Alto in 1908, and Fritz Kolster developed the radio direction finder in the 1920s.

I remember Terman saying something like: "Well, as you can see, most of these successful radio firms were built by people without much education," adding that business opportunities were even greater for someone with a sound theoretical background in the field. That got us thinking, and in our senior year, with Terman's encouragement, Bill Hewlett, Ed Porter, Barney Oliver, and I were making tentative plans to try to do something on our own after graduation. . . . [Two years later] I got together with Bill Hewlett, and at that time we had our first "official" business meeting. The minutes of the meeting, dated August 23, 1937, are headed "tentative organization plans and a tentative work program for a proposed business venture."

. . . During those months Fred Terman had been thinking about how Bill and I might proceed, and in the summer of 1938 he arranged a Stanford fellowship for me. It carried a stipend of $500 a year, but more important, it reunited me with Hewlett. . . .

My bosses at GE gave me their blessing and an unpaid leave of absence, and in August Lu [Lucille Packard] and I drove back to California with a used Sears, Roebuck drill press in the rumble seat. It would be HP's first piece of equipment.

. . . Terman had arranged for me to do the laboratory work on the Varian research project up at Charlie Litton's place, Litton Engineering Laboratories, in Redwood City. He had also arranged for me to get credit for my work at GE so that I could get my EE degree from Stanford with just one year of residence.

. . . Most important, Hewlett was back in town as well. During the interim, he had obtained his master's degree from MIT and upon graduation had exactly one job offer, with Jensen Speaker in Chicago. But Terman came through for him too, putting Bill together with a San Francisco doctor who was interested in developing some medical equipment.

Now that Bill and I were back together, we started putting our plans to work. Bill had found a two-story house on Addison Avenue in Palo Alto, and Lu and I rented the lower floor. Bill, who at the time was still a bachelor, lived in a little building out back. There was also a one-car garage, and that became our workshop.

That garage has been declared a California Historical Landmark. Terman used to say that he knew when HP had orders, because the cars had been moved to the driveway so Hewlett and Packard could work.

Terman became chairman of Stanford's engineering school, and eventually dean of the entire university. He continued to create close ties between the university and industry, long before schools back east accepted the notion of mixing academics with business. Many of the most successful companies of today's Silicon Valley are descendants of firms founded by Terman's protégés.

And here's an interesting footnote to history: Terman really wanted to live in Massachusetts. Although he was the son of a Stanford professor, he had earned his Ph.D. at MIT because, he said, "a serious young engineer had to go back east." Then a severe illness prevented him from taking a teaching position at MIT, and, during a long convalescence back home, he began to teach at Stanford instead.

"They told me that a shell had hit the house of my girl."

WORLD WAR II IN THE WEST:
PEARL HARBOR

December 7, 1941
Hawaii

JOHN GARCIA

The attack on Pearl Harbor claimed 2,403 American lives and left 1,178 wounded. As well, 19 American ships were damaged or sunk and 149 planes lost. The Japanese lost only 29 planes and pilots. Though it is barely remembered today, the Japanese also made surprise attacks on the Philippines, Guam, Midway Island, and Hong Kong, adding to the damage and casualties.

Eyewitness John Garcia was interviewed by reporter and author Studs Terkel for The Good War, *an oral history of World War II.*

I was sixteen years old, employed as a pipe fitter apprentice at Pearl Harbor Navy Yard. On December 7, 1941, oh, around 8:00 A.M., my grandmother woke me. She informed me that the Japanese were bombing Pearl Harbor. I said "They're just practising." She said, no, it was real and the announcer is requesting that all Pearl Harbor workers report to work. I went out on the porch and I could see the anti-aircraft fire up in the sky. I just said, "Oh boy."

I was four miles away. I got out on my motorcycle and took me five, ten minutes to get there. It was a mess.

I was working on the USS *Shaw*. It was on a floating dry dock. It was in flames. I started to go down into the pipe fitter's shop to get my tool-box when another wave of Japanese came in. I got under a set of concrete steps at the dry dock where the battleship *Pennsylvania* was. An officer came by and asked me to go into the *Pennsylvania* and try to get the fires out. A bomb had penetrated the marine deck, and that was three decks below. Under that was the magazines: ammunition, powder, shells. I said, "There ain't a no way I'm gonna go down there." It could blow up any minute. I was young and sixteen, not stupid, not at sixty-two cents an hour. (Laughs.)

A week later, they brought me before a navy court. It was determined that I was not service personnel and could not be ordered. There was no martial law at the time. Because I was sixteen and had gone into the water, the whole thing was dropped.

I was asked by some other officer to go into the water and get sailors out that had been blown off the ships. Some were unconscious, some were dead. So I spent the rest of the day swimming inside the harbour, along with some other Hawaiians. I brought out I don't know how many bodies and how many were alive and how many dead. Another man would put them into ambulances and they'd be gone. We worked all day at that. . . .

The following morning, I went with my tools to the *West Virginia*. It had turned turtle, totally upside down. We found a number of men inside. The *Arizona* was a total washout. Also the *Utah*. There were men in there, too. We spent about a month cutting the superstructure of the *West Virginia*, tilting it back on its hull. About 300 men we cut out of there were still alive by the eighteenth day. It took two weeks to get all the fires out. We worked around the clock for three days. There was so much excitement and confusion. Some of our sailors were shooting five-inch guns at the Japanese planes. You just cannot down a plane with a five-inch shell. They were landing in Honolulu, the unexploded naval shells. They have a ten-mile range. They hurt and killed a lot of people in the city.

When I came back after the third day, they told me that a shell had hit the house of my girl. We had been going together for, oh, about three years. Her house was a few blocks from my place. At the time, they said it was a Japanese bomb. Later we learned it was an American shell. She was killed. She was preparing for church at the time.

"Then navy intelligence agents began contacting people. . . ."

WORLD WAR II IN THE WEST: MANZANAR

1942–1945
Los Angeles and the San Fernando Valley

DR. YOSHIYE TOGASAKI

Two days after the attack on Pearl Harbor, government agents arrested hundreds of Japanese community leaders along the Pacific seaboard, on the pretense that the Japanese Americans were "enemy aliens."

Ten weeks later, still lacking any idea of which individuals might be spies, the government simply decided to round up all the Japanese living along the west coast. Franklin Roosevelt signed a presidential order that forced more than

110,000 to be relocated to inland concentration camps. *Obviously, the motivation was longstanding prejudice against Asians, not national security.*

Eyewitness Yoshiye Togasaki was interviewed by Tom Tiede, author of American Tapestry.

I am a medical doctor. I have spent my life in the care of people. But during World War II it did not matter. When the rumors of the camps could not be ignored, and when Japanese-Americans started being thrown out of work, I went to the president of the Council of Churches of the State of California to ask for his help, and do you know what he said to me? He said that I was just a traitor. He said, "How do I know how to trust you? I don't know you from anything—you're Japanese, so you're not trustworthy." That was the way people thought. There was a hysteria, and we suffered for it.

I have always considered myself American first, Japanese second. I did spend some time in Tokyo as a child, but it was only five months. I am a native of San Francisco. My first home was located where the Geary Theater is now. We had to move later when the great earthquake struck. We were relocated to Post Street, where my father started a grocery business. He later went into the import-export business downtown, where he dealt with things like Japanese foodstuffs and ceramics—setomono, as they used to call it, or dishwear. I had eight brothers and sisters. Two of the sisters became doctors, like me, two became nurses; and my brothers all went into some kind of business.

Everything considered, we all did rather well. When I was a child most white people thought Japanese people should work in the fields or in restaurants or something like that. It was difficult to overcome the discrimination. We could not go to public swimming pools in San Francisco, and they tried to segregate the schools, you know. It was not quite the same discrimination as the blacks in the South experienced, because we were not excluded from most public facilities, but we were definitely set apart. We might have white friends in school, but they did not socialize with us outside of school. We did not date whites, we did not go to parties or dances with them.

They thought of us as inferior, at least many of them did. We were called J-A-P-S. And of course there was the problem that nobody recognized you as a citizen. So we had to struggle that much harder to reach our goals. I certainly had to do my share of struggling to become a doctor. But that was my dream. When I was a young girl my mother used to take in pregnant women so they would get home care while they were having their babies. Then when I was in school I used to accompany Japanese women who had to go to doctors for office visits. The reason I did that was that the women could not speak English, and I acted as an interpreter. I got very close to health care, doing that.

. . . Then navy intelligence agents began contacting people in the Japanese American communities, and I was asked to attend a meeting in the first or second month of 1942. The announcement was made that there would be a curfew. People of Japanese extraction were no longer to be allowed on the streets after dark. They also set a limit on our movements. I didn't pay any attention to it, because I had to travel to see patients, but we were not supposed to go more than three, four, or five miles from our homes, something like that. It was all very frightening, you can imagine. People were losing their jobs, people were being threatened, but there was nothing any of us could do.

Some people wanted to help us. I had doctor friends who said, "Togi, let me know if there is anything I can do." But there wasn't much they could do. One day the army removed all of the Japanese fishermen from Terminal Island, in San Francisco [Bay], and I think they took them to New Mexico. We had no rights. My father was a constitutional scholar, but when he brought that subject up, no one would listen. There were a few Japanese-Americans who demonstrated in the streets on an individual basis, but they were usually arrested. We were helpless. Today you could go to the newspapers, or to the television, to get some support, but that wasn't the way it was in 1942; no one cared.

The announcements were printed on leaflets and posters, and put in store windows and on telephone poles. Everyone had to comply or go to prison. The rule was that everyone was evacuated who was at least one-sixteenth Japanese. I don't know how that determination was made, but that was it. Status didn't matter. You could be very young or old— everyone had to go. Sometimes we were given a few weeks to get ready to leave, sometimes a few days; it was complete upheaval. People had to sell what they could not take with them, or abandon it. The government stepped in to take my father's home on a rather casual basis, and it was then occupied by strangers who were to pay a small rent.

I never received orders to leave. It was inevitable that I would, but, before it happened, I volunteered to go. I knew I would be needed because of my medical background. I took ten girls with me, and we were allowed to go in my car; we did not have to go in trucks and train like most others. I went to Manzanar, which was located on the eastern slopes of the Sierra Nevada Mountains, not too far away from Mount Whitney. That is desert country, very desolate. Death Valley is to the east. The camp was under the control of the military at first, and then it was later turned over to civilians. I got there in the early days; when it reached capacity there were ten thousand people.

It was built from scratch by the military, and so it resembled a military place. They set up a central sanitary facility, a bathhouse and laundry in one building, one side for men and one side for women, and the barracks were constructed around that. The barracks were sectioned off into quarters. There was also a central dining room. And later on a hospital was built. It was cheaply built, very poorly planned, and not a good place for families. Families had no privacy, and they were split apart. I was particularly upset with that aspect of it. A mother and children might be in one place, the father in another, and maybe teen-age daughters would be thrown in with four or five bachelors.

It was also a very dirty place. Manzanar at one time had been a pear orchard, before Los Angeles took over all of the water rights of the area. When that happened, the orchard went dry, and the place became very dusty. The wind would blow from the south, and then it would turn around and blow from the north, and it was a very fine grit that covered everyone and everything. It was in the beds and in the food. We took showers, of course, but that was an unpleasant task. The showers were all open, and you can imagine how the women were embarrassed with that; the people eventually set up a traditional Japanese bath, called a furo; it was unsanitary, but people preferred it to the showers.

I had the responsibility of setting up the medical arrangement. And I tried to do it according to my belief in preventive as well as so-called curing medicine. I wanted to keep people from getting sick, in other words. Avoiding food epidemics, for example, keeping the kitchen utensils clean. I was by myself in this for the first few months, and there were very real problems to confront. We did not have medical equipment at first, and the military did not have many of the medicines we needed. They did not have anything for pregnant women or for the babies we delivered, and we had to do the best we could. The state and federal governments did start sending things as time went on.

There were the usual kinds of diseases. Tuberculosis was a worry, because there was no cure; the antibiotics were not in use until the postwar period. Childhood diseases spread rapidly. Diabetes has always been prevalent among the Japanese. Pneumonia. High blood pressure. All of these things were made worse by the conditions. There was the psychology of it, too. Many of the older people had lived in the United States most of their lives, and the nisei (second-generation Japanese-Americans) were full citizens. They were law-abiding people, they were hard-working, they loved the United States, and now they were treated like traitors; depression is also an illness.

The people did what they could to keep the spirits up. We set up our own leadership, and it was tolerated according to the personality of the government administrator in charge. We also made improvements in the conditions where we could. The food was not to anyone's liking, I recall; it was not Japanese, so the people set up systems where they could bring in things like rice and tofu. Those things were part of our culture. If we didn't have them, then things were even worse than they were. Again, a lot of this depended on the government person in charge of the camp at a given time; we had a few good ones, who understood, and we had at least one who was a very bad apple.

I would say all in all that the government people were mostly fair. They did not seem to be malicious, and it seemed to be a case of just doing their job. You could even disagree with them on some matters. I protested many of the things that went on, for example. On the one hand, everyone understood the things that went on. On the other hand, everyone understood the relative situation; there was a definite line not to cross. The people in charge would not allow any criticism of the United States; they did not want "agitators" or "troublemakers." There was some rioting at Manzanar during one period and the leaders were dealt with quickly. Some of them were taken away to other places, or they would wind up in the stockade in our own camp.

All of Manzanar was a stockade, actually—a prison. We were in jail. There was barbed wire all around, there were great big watch towers in the corners, and there were spotlights turned on during the night. You could not cross the boundaries unless you were authorized on a work detail or something. The guards carried rifles. There was a teen-ager at Manzanar who walked out into the desert one day. He was not running away, he just walked in plain sight. Who in God's name would try to escape in broad daylight? He was mentally deranged. And he got shot. They shot him in the back. So we all knew exactly where we stood.

As soon as they were given the opportunity, young men in the camps rushed to enlist in the army, to "prove" their patriotism. Their unit, the 100th/442nd Regimental Combat Team, won more decorations than any other in U.S. Army history, and earned the nicknames Go For Broke Brigade and Purple Heart Battalion.

The alien exclusion laws that had prevented many of the internees from seeking full citizenship before the war were not repealed until the mid-1950s. In 1988 the U.S. government apologized to the internees and offered reparations. And in 1998, Fred Korematsu, a Japanese American who had fought internment all the way to the U.S. Supreme Court before losing his case, was awarded the Presidential Medal of Freedom, the nation's highest civilian honor.

*"The Japanese area became San Francisco's Harlem
in a matter of months."*

WORLD WAR II IN THE WEST:
CHANGING OF THE GUARD

1942
San Francisco

MAYA ANGELOU

*Before World War II about 64,000 African Americans lived in Los Angeles and
about 20,000 lived in the Bay Area. Those numbers increased more than twentyfold in the next four decades. The first surge was workers for defense plants like the
Kaiser shipyards (see page 314). The trend continued after the war, giving California the largest increase in African American population of any state in that time.*

In this account from I Know Why the Caged Bird Sings, *poet and mem-
oirist Maya Angelou recalls the shift in San Francisco's identity that occurred as
African Americans settled into what had been a Japanese neighborhood before the
removal of the Japanese to concentration camps. She was thirteen at the time.*

In the early months of World War II, San Francisco's Fillmore district, or the Western Addition, experienced a visible revolution. On the
surface it appeared to be totally peaceful and almost a refutation of the
term "revolution." The Yakamoto Sea Food Market quietly became
Sammy's Shoe Shine Parlor and Smoke Shop. Yashigira's Hardware meta-
morphosed into La Salon de Beaute owned by Miss Clorinda Jackson.
The Japanese shops which sold products to Nisei customers were taken
over by enterprising Negro businessmen, and in less than a year became
permanent homes away from home for the newly arrived Southern
Blacks. Where the odors of tempura, raw fish and cha had dominated,
the aroma of chitlings, greens and ham hocks now prevailed.

The Asian population dwindled before my eyes. I was unable to tell
the Japanese from the Chinese and as yet found no real difference in the
national origin of such sounds as Ching and Chan or Moto and Kano.

As the Japanese disappeared, soundlessly and without protest, the
Negroes entered with their loud jukeboxes, their just-released animosities and the relief of escape from Southern bonds. The Japanese area
became San Francisco's Harlem in a matter of months.

A person unaware of all the factors that make up oppression might
have expected sympathy or even support from the Negro newcomers
for the dislodged Japanese. Especially in view of the fact that they (the

Blacks) had themselves undergone concentration-camp living for centuries in slavery's plantations and later in sharecroppers' cabins. But the sensations of common relationship were missing.

The Black newcomer had been recruited on the desiccated farm lands of Georgia and Mississippi by war-plant labor scouts. The chance to live in two- or three-story apartment buildings (which became instant slums), and to earn two- and even three-figured weekly checks, was blinding. For the first time he could think of himself as a Boss, a Spender. He was able to pay other people to work for him, i.e. the dry cleaners, taxi drivers, waitresses, etc. The shipyards and ammunition plants brought to booming life by the war let him know that he was needed and even appreciated. A completely alien yet very pleasant position for him to experience. Who could expect this man to share his new and dizzying importance with concern for a race that he had never known to exist?

Another reason for his indifference to the Japanese removal was more subtle but was more profoundly felt. The Japanese were not whitefolks. Their eyes, language, and customs belied the white skin and proved to their dark successors that since they didn't have to be feared, neither did they have to be considered. All this was decided unconsciously.

No member of my family and none of the family friends ever mentioned the absent Japanese. It was as if they had never owned or lived in the houses we inhabited.

. . . Pride and prejudice stalked in tandem the beautiful hills. Native San Franciscans, possessive of the city, had to cope with an influx, not of awed respecful tourists but of raucous unsophisticated provincials. They were also forced to live with skin-deep guilt brought on by the treatment of their former Nisei schoolmates.

Southern white illiterates brought their biases intact to the West from the hills of Arkansas and the swamps of Georgia. The Black ex-farmers had not left their distrust and fear of whites which history had taught them in distressful lessons. These two groups were obliged to work side by side in the war plants, and their animosities festered and opened like boils on the face of the city.

San Franciscans would have sworn on the Golden Gate Bridge that racism was missing from the heart of their air-conditioned city. But they would have been sadly mistaken.

A story went the rounds about a San Franciscan white matron who refused to sit beside a Negro civilian on the streetcar, even after he made room for her on the seat. Her explanation was that she would not sit beside a draft dodger who was a Negro as well. She added that the least he could do was fight for his country the way her son was fighting on Iwo Jima. The story said that the man pulled his body away from the window to show an armless sleeve. He said quietly and with great dignity, "Then ask your son to look around for my arm, which I left over there."

"Kaiser got the program started only by going to Roosevelt over the heads of both admirals and Navy Department."

WORLD WAR II IN THE WEST: HENRY KAISER'S LIBERTY SHIPS

1942–1945
Richmond, California

JOHN GUNTHER

When the government had to hurriedly strengthen the Pacific fleets at the start of World War II, industrialist Henry Kaiser devised an ambitious plan. Kaiser had already proven he and his company could handle big tasks, having built highways in the Pacific Northwest, the Hoover Dam, and the San Francisco–Oakland Bay Bridge. Now he would build ships, and build them faster than anyone imagined possible. Using new methods and prefabricated parts, his shipyards launched 1,460 ships during the war, including one-quarter of all the cargo ships built. He employed 200,000 workers at his East Bay plants.

Eyewitness John Gunther, perhaps the best known reporter of his day, wrote about Kaiser in his book Inside: U.S.A.

We went out to Richmond, across the bay from San Francisco, on the day that Kaiser's 732nd ship was launched. The first thing I noticed: a chain of cars from the old Sixth Avenue El [elevated train] in New York, which Kaiser used to help move his workers to where they slept and back.

Richmond consists of four yards, built by Kaiser for the U.S. Maritime Commission, on a fee basis in conjunction with other companies. Yards No. 1 and No. 2 were operated by the Permanente Metals Corporation, No. 3 by Kaiser Co., Inc., No. 4 by Kaiser Cargo Co., Inc. For the four together, the peak of wartime employment was 91,000. As of V-J Day the yards had built $1,800,000,000 worth of ships, mostly Liberties and Victories, amounting to about 7,000,000 tons which is 20 per cent of the entire American production of merchant shipping during the war. One fifth of the American merchant navy was, in other words, built by Kaiser in this single area. Count in the Oregon yards, and the proportion goes up to one third.

Kaiser turned out combat ships too; in fact his Vancouver, Washington, yards built fifty baby flattops, small aircraft carriers, in eighteen months. Not only did the Navy say that this could not be done; it fought the project with embittered stubbornness, holding that ships built so fast could not be seaworthy; Kaiser got the program started only by going to Roosevelt over the heads of both admirals and Navy Department. For a time he was delivering carriers at the unprecedented and seemingly impossible rate of one a week.

The Liberties rolled off at Richmond even faster. At peak, a ship could be built in four and one half days, that is the various prefabricated parts and sections were put together in that time, and launchings once reached a rate of thirty-two per month, or one million-dollar ship a day. We visited yard No. 2, and I began dimly to see how the job was done. Part of the secret lay in prefabrication, part in the astute application of new techniques. Take deck houses. These were the toughest problem to solve, because they are the soul and brain of the ship and complex to make. In World War I it took 180 days to build a ship; most of the delay came from deck houses. So a method was contrived to build them in sections—upside down! They proceed down a monstrously large assembly line just like an automobile; then, when finished, they are cut into four huge parts, and each part is carted to the ship on an enormous specially-built eighty-five-ton trailer; finally the deck house is welded together again on the ship itself.

Richmond trained something like three hundred thousand welders out of soda clerks and housewives. Normally it takes two to three months to make a tolerable welder. The Kaiser technique turned them out in ten days, because they were only taught "down-hand" welding, which means welding below the waist, so that the weld itself flows by gravity. To make a good weld overhead takes skill, but practically anybody can do it on the lower level. So forepeaks were built sideways, and the actual sides of ships, cut, shaped and welded to predetermined patterns, were built flat, rather than inside a tall and costly scaffolding. The Kaiser principle was to fit the job to the man, instead of vice versa.

Richmond expanded so fast that a near-by mountain once got in the way. So three million cubic feet of it were moved.

Although Kaiser's conglomerate was once involved in everything from cement to chemicals to building cars—for a time he owned the Jeep brand—little remains of the business today. But the innovative medical plan Kaiser created for his workers and then opened to the public after the war has become the largest health maintenance organization in the state, Kaiser Permanente.

". . . Nobody could tell what the hell they were saying."

WORLD WAR II IN THE WEST:
NAVAJO CODE TALKERS

ANONYMOUS CODE TALKER

Over the course of World War II, code making and code breaking became high-tech endeavors, eventually leading to the first electronic computers; but in the battlefield, cryptography machines weren't practical. A creative officer devised a scheme for field codes: Comanches, Creeks, Choctaws, Menominees, Chippewas, Hopis, and Navajos served as radio officers, speaking in their native languages.

We got to Guadalcanal with our orders to assist by code talking. We were supposed to take our orders to the general, but he was hard to find. He was 'way back of the lines. We were supposed to identify ourselves and turn over our orders. He just sat there and didn't say anything. We went back to the colonel who, I think, was Chief of Staff, and I told him what the deal was.

Finally he sent two guys over to the 1st, two to the 7th, two to the 11th, and two to the 5th regiments. Now we had gotten there about four o'clock in the morning, but we didn't get to talk any until nine o'clock at night. Then we were given permission to talk a little. I called the 7th Marines and before we finished talking, the radio was buzzing, the telephone was ringing, and then runners came to say that the Japs were talking on our frequency and that they had taken over everything, and that nobody could tell what the hell they were saying. The colonel tried to explain that our men [Navajos] were talking.

Well, he didn't know whether to send us back or leave us there. He mumbled, "You guys are more trouble than you're worth." I was sitting there nice and cozy, and now I had to go tell the guys that we wouldn't be using our code—at least for a while, to avoid panic in the ranks.

Then the colonel had an idea. He said he would keep us on one condition: that I could out-race his "white code"—a cylinder-thing that you set a coded message on and send by radio . . . tick, tick, tick. Then the receiver signals he has received the message and gives the roger on it. We both sent messages—with the white cylinder and by voice. Both of us received answers. The race was to see who could decode his answer first.

He said, "Are you ready?"

I said, "I've started already."

"How long will it take you?" I was asked. "Two hours?"

I got the roger on my return message from four units in about four and a half minutes. The other guy was still decoding when I said, "Colonel, when are you going to give up that signal outfit?"

Despite the disbelief they first encountered, their work proved invaluable. For instance, news that marines had raised the flag on Iwo Jima's Mt. Suribachi was first conveyed to commanders on nearby battleships in Navajo by code talkers.

"The B-17 could take a punch like no other aircraft ever built."

WORLD WAR II IN THE WEST: THE BOEING B-17

1943
England and Germany

ANDY ROONEY

A combination of geographical necessity, daring businessmen, and good weather concentrated the nation's airplane industry in the West. Local barnstormers such as Allan Lockheed of southern California and William Boeing of Seattle had founded companies to build planes, and the first aeronautical engineering graduate from the Massachusetts Institute of Technology, Donald Douglas, also opened his factory on the West Coast.

When World War II came, the rush to build planes led to vast changes in Western cities like Los Angeles and Seattle. In 1935, when Seattle's Boeing Company built the first B-17 prototype, it employed 839 workers. In 1943, it employed 78,400 workers, who assembled 250 planes each month. The housing shortage was so severe that residents were pressed to take in boarders. The value of the city's production rose from $70 million to almost $6 billion.

Of all the planes in that war, the B-17, known as the Flying Fortress because of the thirteen machine guns that poked out from its sides, may be the most legendary. It wasn't the fastest bomber, but it could fly even after heavy damage, a boon to its crews. It was so important to the war effort that Boeing's design was also built at the Douglas and Lockheed plants in southern California, to speed production and reduce the chance of an enemy attack halting work. In all, 12,731 B-17s were built.

Eyewitness Andy Rooney, now best known as a commentator for CBS News, served as a reporter for the armed forces newspaper, Stars and Stripes. *This account comes from his memoir of those years,* My War.

The B-17 did more than any other airplane to win the war. The B-17—like the great troop and cargo carrier, the DC-3, Dakota—was not statistically exceptional. It wasn't fast, it wasn't maneuverable. It didn't carry the heaviest bomb load. What it was, was almost indestructible. Thousands of times during the three years B-17s dropped bombs in Europe, they were riddled with flak (Fliegerabwehrkanonen) and 50mm machine-gun bullets from Focke Wulfe 190s and Messerschmitt 109s. With three engines gone, with hydraulic systems drained of fluid, with wounded crewmen onboard, the aircraft, time after time, hauled everyone back home to safety. If airplanes had human qualities, the B-17s would be called valiant.

The people who flew the B-24 Liberators were fiercely loyal to their aircraft and always argued that it was the better of the two. I don't like further angering them here now but it wasn't. The B-24 was never the bomber the B-17 was. The B-24 people argued speed, ease of handling, and bomb load, and if all you looked at were these characteristics, the B-24 was the better airplane. If you had to go to Berlin or Schweinfurt, take a B-17 and your chances of getting home were vastly improved. The B-17 could take a punch like no other aircraft ever built.

. . . I don't know whose idea it was but someone decided the reporters covering the Eighth Air Force ought to go on a mission themselves. It probably grew out of that uneasy feeling we all had that we were watching too many young men our age die while we were writing stories about them and then going back to London for dinner.

. . . There were eight of us: Walter Cronkite, United Press; Homer Bigart, *New York Herald Tribune;* Paul Manning, MBS (Mutual Broadcasting System); Jack Denton Scott, *YANK* magazine; Gladwin Hill, the Associated Press; Bill Wade, International News Service; Bob Post, the *New York Times;* and myself. We were sent to some kind of training camp for a week and we learned a little about parachutes, life rafts, and the .50-caliber machine gun. There was some talk of learning to pack a parachute and several demonstration classes were held but, in the belief that there was no chance that someone who couldn't make a bed would ever learn how to pack a parachute, I did not attend.

. . . On the day of the mission, two of the eight reporters who were to have gone on the raid came up lame and decided they weren't well enough to go. Listen, it happens. The thought crossed my mind that I didn't feel too well myself.

You got in a B-17 through the waist opening on the right side. There was no door because the machine guns were permanently installed and their muzzles protruded enough to give the gunner full range up, down, forward, and backward when he was aiming at an attacking Luftwaffe fighter plane. (It was simple enough, but I never got thoroughly easy with the direction of an approaching enemy fighter. When someone yelled "Bogey! Eleven o'clock high!" meaning there was an Me-109 or an FW-190 bearing in from that direction, I was slow to know where to look. It was not a situation in which visualizing a clock came readily to my mind.)

There was no access from the left side of the plane because the gunner's opening didn't go down to the floor. The open sides made the B-17 slower than it otherwise would have been—and colder, too. Cold was a bitter factor on many missions when men were wounded. It was colder than traveling at eighty miles an hour in a convertible with the top down in below-zero weather, with the added inconvenience of having people shooting at you from the ground and from other aircraft.

To get forward on the B-17, you went from the midsection through the bomb bay, walking on a narrow steel (or perhaps aluminum) beam with the bombs hanging on either side below you. It was easy to get snagged on something as you came through the bomb bay wearing all your equipment because it was narrow and there were wires and jagged spurs of electrical connectors protruding from it on all sides that grabbed at you.

We were given flak jackets, but there was a difference of opinion about the advisability of wearing one. Being lead-lined canvas, they were heavy and bulky and I already had my parachute. The 'chute alone was more than I was comfortable carrying and it was cumbersome. I'd been given the choice between wearing it on my chest and wearing it on my back and I'd chosen to wear it on my chest. That way, I knew where it was.

I made the decision to stand on my flak jacket instead of wearing it for several faulty reasons. I felt that if we had to bail out, my chances would be better if I didn't have to get it off first and, second, I had this natural apprehension about being castrated by a flak burst underneath the aircraft.

The cockpit, half a level up, was immediately ahead of the bomb bay. The top-turret gunner was behind the cockpit, and to get to the nose area you bent down and went under the pilot and the copilot and past the radioman's position. Among other discomforts, I felt claustrophobic.

The nose, from the bombardier up front to the navigator, who was actually under the pilot, was about twelve feet long.

As I sat, considering my circumstance, on the small, makeshift seat behind the bombardier and opposite the navigator, Casey revved the engines to give the propellers enough spin to pull us out off the hardstand and onto the runway.

. . . There were a lot of hard things to do onboard a B-17. I was nervous about everything because I didn't know how to do anything. I was uneasy with my oxygen connections and considered the possibility that I'd be asphyxiated in flight because I didn't know how to work a valve on my tank. You begin to need oxygen anywhere above 12,000 feet and we were going to be in the air at 24,000 feet for five hours. Had I known what I was about to go through, I might have thrown pride to the wind and climbed out.

The trip over the Channel was dull. When we started in over France I was impressed with the regularity of the patterns of the small farms. I thought of myself as going to a war zone and was mildly surprised to see farmers working their fields with horsedrawn plows. It seemed strange that anyone was doing anything so normal as farming.

There were fifty-three bombers in our formation, a relatively small group. No fighter cover. We were ten minutes from Wilhelmshaven when we encountered the first bursts of flak from perimeter antiaircraft artillery. Looking forward over the bombardier's head, I could see the mushroomlike puffs of smoke that marked the shells exploding around the lead planes. When a shell burst, it sent thousands of bulletlike shards of metal in every direction. It was more like a shotgun than a rifle because it released a lethal spray of deadly missiles. Whether you were hit or not was a matter of luck. Direct hits, when the shell actually hit and exploded inside a plane, were relatively rare and, of course, always fatal.

We dropped our bombs—I never saw them hit—and the pilot, Bill Casey, wheeled Banshee around and the bombers regrouped and headed home. Some of the B-17s had been hit and were unable to stay with the formation. They were in the most trouble. Like the old wildebeests in the African herd trying to outrun the lions, it was the bombers that dropped back, with one or two engines knocked out, that were most vulnerable to being shot down by the ME-109s and FW-190s. The raid was before our own fighter planes, the P-51s and P-47s, were flying cover for the bombers.

It was on the way out from the target that we took direct fire from the Luftwaffe, which by now had about 100 planes in the air attacking our relatively small formation of fifty-three bombers. They had stayed clear of the target area because they were as vulnerable to their own antiaircraft shells as we were, but once we'd left the target, the German fighter planes dove through our riddled formation and swished through it head-on with guns firing. I couldn't see anything but a flash of glistening metal in the sunlight because they were flying at 450 mph and we were flying at 250 in the other direction. That was 700 mph, and at that speed the gunners had a hard time sighting the approaching Jerries far enough in advance to aim and get a burst off.

Several B-17s around us were hit. Three in the formation went down. The long, slow, death spiral of a bomber with its crew on board is a terrible thing to see. It was worse for the crew because they knew all thirty men as friends. Ten 'chutes came from one, three emerged from the second. The third exploded into fragments in the air leaving behind nothing but a small cloud of dirty smoke, and it was impossible to tell the parts of machinery from the bodies of men as they all tumbled toward earth. I don't know what happens inside the brain but I was no longer nervous.

Suddenly there was an explosion six feet in front of me in Banshee's nose compartment where the bombardier sat hunched over his bombsight. A shell or fragment of one had clipped off the tip of the plastic nose of Banshee, leaving a jagged hole not much bigger than a man's fist. The Intelligence reports later said that, for the first time, the Germans were using parachute bombs. These were explosives equipped with parachutes that were shot up 25,000 feet by artillery. When the parachute opened, the explosive package was designed to drift down and explode in the middle of one of the bomber formations. I never saw one and I don't know for sure what hit us, but at 200 miles an hour, four miles above the earth, it's a viciously cold gale that rushes in a hole that big. It was the bombardier's first mission and, in a moment of panic, he tore off his gloves and tried to stuff them in the gaping hole. Within minutes his hands had frozen and chips of flesh broke off his fingers as they caught on the jagged edges of the plastic.

I had taken as many steps forward as my oxygen tubes allowed but there wasn't anything I could have done even if I'd known how. I looked over at the navigator, Lt. Bill Owens, and saw that he was slumped over his desk, unconscious, with his oxygen mask supply line dangling free where it had been cut.

"Casey," I called to the pilot. "Bill's out. I think he's lost his oxygen."

Casey had his hands full flying evasive action trying to give the German fighter planes a moving target. He didn't hesitate though.

"There are four oxygen bottles up here behind me," he said matter-of-factly. "Take some deep breaths, take your mask off, and get back up here and grab a bottle for him."

It was unsettling to be pressed into service doing a real job. I felt inadequate. They'd forgotten I was a reporter.

I expected I'd collapse after ten seconds without oxygen but it doesn't happen quite that way or so fast and the bottles were very close. With my parachute dangling from me, I made the trip back up the narrow passage behind the pilot and copilot. Casey saw me out of the corner of his eye but never said a word. He just wanted to make sure I'd done it.

I took the oxygen tank and another mask and tried to remember a few things I'd been taught about how to use one. I was afraid Owens would be dead before I could hook him into the emergency supply. I didn't know. I took off his useless mask, fitted him with the emergency one, and turned on the valve in the air bottle. Within minutes he was conscious again. He looked over at me. I don't know whether he realized what I'd done or not. It was as if he'd awakened from a nap. Owens got the bombardier quieted down and then went back to his position with some maps across from me. (The copilot that day was also named Owens. He wrote to me in 1994 with kind words about my going on the raid but with a complaint about a negative comment I'd made on *60 Minutes* about people who keep trailers or mobile homes in their driveways. He now sells them.)

All I could see from my place at the rear of the nose of the plane was straight ahead and a little to either side. My back was up against the metal sheath of the aircraft before it became Plexiglas a few feet forward. The only reason I knew we were being attacked from the side was the sound of .50-caliber machine-gun fire from the two waist gunners and from the gunner in the top-turret bubble, above and behind the pilot's cockpit.

It was a grim and silent trip back across the English Channel. Not a lot of fun, and it was not clear to any of us that we'd hit much of anything with our bombs. No one spoke on the intercom of seeing the B-17s on our wing go down but everyone must have been thinking about it.

. . . The six correspondents who went out that day were to meet after the raid at Molesworth, where facilities had been set up for us to write our stories and transmit them back to London. Five of us straggled into the temporary pressroom at intervals over a period of half an hour, and then the word came that we had dreaded. There would never be more than five of us. Bob Post, the friendly and able young reporter for the *New York Times*, was missing. Bob was thirty-two, a Harvard graduate with a bright future ahead of him at the *Times*. Others in the formation reported seeing parachutes open before his B-24 crashed into the ground, but Bob was never heard from again.

While Boeing was making Seattle a wartime boomtown, the production of all those B-17s had a dark side. They were needed because 8,007 of them were lost. The statistics reveal the story: Each crew member was officially expected to fly twenty-five missions, but losses were so heavy that the actual life expectancy was just twenty missions, and only a quarter of the men completed the official requirement. The Eighth Air Force, stationed in Britain, lost more than 40,000 men.

THE ZOOT SUIT RIOT

June 3—7, 1943
Los Angeles

AL WAXMAN

Before the Mexican Revolution (1910—15), only about 50,000 of California's 2,500,000 residents were persons of Mexican descent. But the revolution, and the practice of hiring Mexican labor on California's farms, mushroomed the population. By 1945, Los Angeles was second only to Mexico City in Mexican population.

The city didn't welcome the newcomers. The situation turned violent when Los Angeles became a base for thousands of servicemen during the war. The Zoot Suit Riot, sparked by a fight between some sailors and a group of Mexican Americans, lasted five days. (Its name came from a baggy, dressy outfit, not unlike a tuxedo worn several sizes too large. In Los Angeles, "zoot-suiter" was also code for "Mexican," because it was fashionable among Mexican American teenagers.)

Eyewitness Al Waxman was editor of L.A.'s Eastside Journal.

At Twelfth and Central I came upon a scene that will long live in my memory. Police were swinging clubs and servicemen were fighting with civilians. Wholesale arrests were being made by the officers.

Four boys came out of a pool hall. They were wearing the zoot-suits that have become the symbol of a fighting flag. Police ordered them into arrest cars. One refused. He asked: "Why am I being arrested?" The police officer answered with three swift blows of the night-stick across the boy's head and he went down. As he sprawled, he was kicked in the face. Police had difficulty loading his body into the vehicle because he was one-legged and wore a wooden limb. Maybe the officer didn't know he was attacking a cripple.

At the next corner a Mexican mother cried out, "Don't take my boy, he did nothing. He's only fifteen years old. Don't take him." She was struck across the jaw with a night-stick and almost dropped the two and a half year old baby that was clinging in her arms. . . .

Rushing back to the east side to make sure that things were quiet here, I came upon a band of servicemen making a systematic tour of East First Street. They had just come out of a cocktail bar where four men were nursing bruises. Three autos loaded with Los Angeles policemen were on the scene but the soldiers were not molested. Farther down the street the men stopped a streetcar, forcing the motorman to open the door and proceeded to inspect the clothing of the male passengers. "We're looking for zoot-suits to burn," they shouted. Again the police did not interfere. . . . Half a block away I pleaded with the men of the local police sub-station to put a stop to these activities. "It is a matter for the military police," they said.

The complacency of the police was shared by many civilians. One Los Angeles County supervisor told reporters, "All that is needed to end lawlessness is more of the same action as is being exercised by the servicemen." The Los Angeles County District Attorney called the wearing of a zoot suit "subversive." The City Council made wearing it a misdemeanor.

"I had talked about writing a song about Highway 40, but Cynthia suggested, 'Get Your Kicks on Route 66.'"

GET YOUR KICKS ON ROUTE 66

1946
Chicago to Los Angeles

BOBBY TROUP AND CYNTHIA TROUP

Oklahoma booster Cyrus Avery got it in his head that the state needed more roads, and by 1925 he had convinced the government to build a highway from Chicago to Los Angeles, passing through Joplin, Missouri; Oklahoma City; Gallup, New Mexico; Flagstaff, Arizona; and on to the West Coast. It wasn't strictly east-west or north-south, but Avery had successfully argued that it followed the tradition of the old trade routes—a promoter's understandable exaggeration.

The highway almost received the unmelodic name "Route 60 North," but to Avery that sounded more like an extension road than a major highway. He exhausted and annoyed highway officials until the road received a more important name. One of them wrote, "Personally, I think that more time has been spent on this matter than it deserves. I do not feel that it makes one bit of difference to the States along the route from Chicago to Los Angeles whether it is Route No. 60 or 62 or any other number. . . ."

That bureaucrat wasn't counting on the trip songwriter Bobby Troup made with his wife, Cynthia, in 1946.

The Troups related this account to Susan Croce Kelly, co-author with Quinta Scott of Route 66: The Highway and Its People.

I had written one hit before the war, and I was determined to go to Hollywood and see if I could make it as a songwriter. . . .

We left Harrisburg. My mother was in tears. We drove the Pennsylvania Turnpike and then hit 66. We saw the stalactites at Meramec Caverns. We stopped at the Will Rogers Memorial, in Claremore. We ran into a snowstorm outside Amarillo: it was about eleven or twelve at night and absolutely blinding. I was really frightened. Then I stopped for a haircut in one western town. In some places, there was a lot of traffic, and in some other places, not any. I'd never seen a desert before, so that was fascinating. I had talked about writing a song about Highway 40, but Cynthia suggested, "Get Your Kicks on Route 66." I said that was a cute title. I finished the song with a map after we got to Los Angeles. I wasn't aware of what a great lyric I had written. I do remember it was possibly the worst road I'd ever taken in my life.

. . . One of the big disappointments of my writing career was when I heard that a TV show was in the works about Route 66. My publisher called and said they would probably use my song as a theme. But they didn't. They got Nelson Riddle to do the music, which was probably smarter for them because it was their piece and they didn't have to pay royalties, but I was disappointed.

CYNTHIA TROUP

What I really can't believe is that he doesn't have Albuquerque in the song. . . . I know we took ten days to drive across the country—it took ten days! I'd never do that again. We tried to be tourists. We stayed with friends in Ohio before we started, and in Saint Louis we stopped somewhere to see Louis Armstrong. After Saint Louis we just drove, and then we'd stay in a motel. We stopped at some caverns. Then we did Will Rogers. Where is that? They have a glass thing, remember, with the clothes he had on when the plane crashed. I mean, really! After Chicago there was no nice place or we would have stayed at it. We were spending money like we had it.

Bobby took my picture standing in the Painted Desert. I remember that by then I wanted to get to Los Angeles. I think we went off the highway and went to Las Vegas and stood up high on something concrete and looked down at Boulder Dam. It seems to me it was just a long road with cheap motels and restaurants. I wonder how we even knew where to go. . . .

*"Susie, your dad was the greatest gangster
that ever lived."*

GANGSTER'S DAUGHTER

1947
Las Vegas

SUSAN BERMAN

*By any natural law, Las Vegas shouldn't exist. People just don't build cities in the
middle of the desert. But it draws tens of millions of visitors each year, and is currently the fastest-growing city in the country. How did that happen?*

*In 1931, the state repealed its antigambling laws, giving people a way to kill
time while they waited a few weeks to establish residency so they could file for a
fast divorce. Then construction began on the Boulder Dam just south of the town.
Hundreds of men living away from their families had plenty of money to spend
and needed somewhere to spend it. What has always happened at times like that
happened again, and to the gambling was added a booming trade in prostitution.*

*In 1940, mobster Bugsy Siegel, who had headed west a few years earlier to
establish a mob base in Los Angeles, smelled an opportunity in Las Vegas. It took
Siegel four years to put a deal together, and another year to build his famous
Flamingo casino, but he stuck to his dream and convinced his partners back east
that Las Vegas meant big money.*

*Like many dreamers, Siegel was lousy with the details. The Flamingo lost
money, so about a year after Siegel opened it his partners killed him. Just twenty minutes after he was shot at his Beverly Hills home two men walked into the
Flamingo, called a staff meeting, and introduced themselves as the new management. Those men, Moe Sedway and Gus Greenbaum, were among the many
"uncles" who helped raise the author of this account, Susan Berman, daughter of
their mob partner Davie Berman.*

It was 1957, and I was twelve. They said it was the largest funeral
Las Vegas had ever seen—there were thousands of mourners. The pall-
bearers were men I had known: Gus Greenbaum, whose throat would
later be slashed in Phoenix; Willie "Ice Pick" Alderman, who would die
on Terminal Island while serving time in a mob extortion rap; Joe
Rosenberg, one of my father's partners, who was known as his mouth-
piece; Nick the Greek, the famed odds-maker. Squat Jewish men surrounded Uncle Chickie and me at the funeral, saying, "We don't expect
trouble." My father, Davie Berman, 54, lay in an open casket while a
rabbi intoned, "It is a sad day for all of Las Vegas. Davie Berman, one of

our original pioneers who made this city bloom, is dead. There will never be anyone like him. Davie Berman had a vision. He saw a boomtown where others had just seen desert. He was Mr. Las Vegas. Davie Berman, beloved by all of Las Vegas, beloved husband and beloved father, is gone."

Hundreds of mourners held me and kissed me. One man I didn't know grabbed me and said, "Susie, your dad was the greatest gangster that ever lived. You can hold your head up high." Then there was just the Kaddish, uttered by all, most of them crying. It sounded louder than any floor-show orchestra I had ever heard.

. . . In 1944, the year before I was born, my father made the biggest move of his career: He went to Las Vegas to help run it for Meyer Lansky and the mob. After a long and dangerous career spanning every mob venture from the 1920s through the 1940s, he was rewarded with a big piece of the action in what he envisioned as a mob jackpot town.

He went to Las Vegas to front for his East Coast associates—Lansky, Frank Costello, Lucky Luciano, and Joe Adonis. None of them wanted to live in this desert boomtown, but they needed a few men they could trust to run the business for them. My father was one of those men.

He had first visited Las Vegas in 1940 with his friend Bugsy Siegel. Siegel was an original member of the Bugs and Meyer gang, partners with Lansky in a group that started Murder, Inc., and founded the Jewish component of organized crime. Siegel was from the Lower East Side in New York. He had begun his career by bootlegging, organizing the transport of liquor from the New York City docks to the underworld warehouses during Prohibition. He had been sent to California in 1930 by Lucky Luciano to open up the West Coast for the mob. He was to set up a centralized horse-betting system, direct narcotics to the United States from Mexico, and look for new ways to invest syndicate money on the West Coast.

After World War II, my father came back to stake his claim. He brought a suitcase with $1 million—money he had raised from his associates in Minneapolis and St. Paul and in northern Minnesota. With the blessings of his East Coast backers and his promise that they would get 25 percent of everything, he bought his first club downtown, the El Cortez. There was no strip yet. He brought his best friend, Willie Alderman, with him from Minneapolis, joined old friend Moe Sedway, who had come from New York, and met a new partner put in by Siegel, Gus Greenbaum from Phoenix.

Meyer Lansky and Frank Costello had already staked their claims, and they were taking in partners. Before my father left Minneapolis, he had to square my Uncle Chickie's debts. But even with Chickie's debts paid, Chickie wasn't safe in Minneapolis. He had angered too many people this time, so Davie took his brother to Las Vegas with him.

Once he got to Las Vegas, he negotiated with the owner of the El Cortez and got approval to buy. Then he flew to Omaha to meet with Lansky to get official syndicate permission to close the deal and head the new group at the El Cortez. Lansky was in Omaha trying to get dog racing legalized. He was going to Las Vegas every month, complaining of the heat; he didn't want to live there and was delighted to have trusted lieutenants like my father run the city for him. At that time, Lansky and Frank Costello had the whole country. Lucky Luciano was facing deportation to Italy, and there were shifting territories and new opportunities. Lansky asked my father for $160,000 up front and gave his permission.

Back in Las Vegas, Chickie and Davie shared a room at the El Cortez during the negotiating. Finally, all that remained were the signatures and payments. Davie went upstairs to get the money he had asked Chickie to guard. When he got upstairs, Chickie and the suitcase were gone. He feared the worst.

He called everyone he knew to find Chickie. Moe Sedway sent all his boys, and they scoured the town. They finally found Chickie in a small downtown joint. He had lost the $1 million in a high rollers crap game. My father probably would have destroyed anyone else for such a transgression, but Chickie was his brother, and he loved him. Chickie threatened to kill himself if Davie never spoke to him again. My father just looked at him, punched his fist into the wall, peeled off a few bills, and said, "Go to Miami till all this dies down."

Then my father flew back to the Midwest, where he raised another $1 million and promised to make good on the first million. He hurried back to Las Vegas to the El Cortez. Early in 1945, Davie closed the deal; he was in big action in Las Vegas, and he was exultant. The owners included Ben Siegel, Moe Sedway, Gus Greenbaum, Dave Berman, Charles Berman, Meyer Lansky, and Willie Alderman.

. . . When I was two months old, my mother brought me out to Las Vegas on the train. It was the middle of a sweltering July, and she was dressed in a white linen suit and big-brimmed hat, and she had me clothed in a white silk dress. She got off the train and handed me to my father with a look of shock on her face. She uttered the words every midwestern wife would say: "Where is the town?" There was nothing to see but sagebrush, cactus, and the carcasses of prairie dogs. She had expected something more like Los Angeles. . . .

My mother had barely been out of St. Paul, except for a few trips with my father. Las Vegas had a population of about 16,000 and consisted of just two areas—the raggedy downtown, called "Glitter Gulch," where my father had his clubs, and a small residential area. Many people lived in trailers and cinder-block houses, there was a large Indian reservation on the outskirts of town, and most of the town's blacks lived on the west side under a cement structure called "the cement curtain."

It was a cowboy town. Men with deep sunburns and sweaty underarms walked the streets in silver spurs. . . .

The strip was just a two-lane highway then; lizards and snakes decorated the landscape. Most of the action was at the downtown gambling clubs, but the Western Union office always held some drama. There, cast-off spouses hoped for a second chance; divorce and marriage were second only to gambling as a town attraction. Entrances to the town in each direction were lined with wedding chapels.

. . . The "town" was firmly established only in my father's mind. With ardent resolve, he told her how it was going to be the jewel of the desert—with luxury hotels everywhere, sophisticated entertainers, patrons from around the world. He stood on the railroad platform in his tailored suit, pointed at the cowboys hanging around the depot, and vowed, "Gladys, honey, this is only the backdrop."

"The memories die hard."

THE BLACKLIST

1947–1967
Hollywood

RING LARDNER, JR., HOWARD KOCH, PAUL JARRICO, EDWARD DMYTRYK, AND JEFF COREY

From the late 1940s to the mid-1960s, hundreds of film and television artists were blacklisted—prevented from working because of alleged Communist beliefs. Certainly some of them had been members of the Communist party, which was not uncommon in the 1930s, given the appeal of the left-wing politics of the New Deal and the fear of fascism in Europe. And it was not a crime. Nonetheless, after World War II, when America's Soviet allies instantly became the Red menace, a retroactive witch hunt by Congress rounded up many of these artists, whose Communist sympathies, it was often claimed, would lead to insidious propaganda in American movies. In one famous instance, the philosopher Ayn Rand said that the movie Mission to Moscow *was dangerously pro-Communist because the* actors playing Russians smiled, which, she claimed, Russians didn't do in real life.

The first hearings of the House Committee on Un-American Activities (HUAC), in October 1947, were chaired by Representative J. Parnell Thomas (R-New Jersey), propped up by two telephone books and a silk cushion so he could be seen by newsreel and TV cameras. Nineteen alleged Communists were subpoenaed. Ten of them—later known as the Hollywood Ten—testified but refused to discuss their political affiliations or name other party members. They were found in contempt of Congress, and some were sent to prison. All were blacklisted.

Other hearings were held in later years. Over time an understanding developed between the politicians and the Hollywood community: Anyone could be cleared from the blacklist simply by naming others. Some people "named names," as the technique became known. Others refused, claiming that the government had no right to question political beliefs and that implicating others was immoral.

The eyewitnesses assembled here recalled their stories for Griffin Fariello's oral history of the period, Red Scare.

RING LARDNER, JR.

In November of 1947, the real heads of Hollywood, not the studio heads in California but the bankers in New York who ran the companies, held a meeting at the Waldorf Astoria Hotel in New York. They decided to institute a blacklist. They made a public announcement that they wouldn't hire any of us until we had purged ourselves of contempt. They would refuse to hire anybody else who took the same position or who refused to answer any questions before the committee. Five of the ten of us were not working at the time, and the five who were under contract were told that their contracts were abrogated. I was working for Twentieth Century-Fox at the time, and Darryl Zanuck, the head of the studio, first said that he wasn't going to fire anyone unless he was ordered to do so by his board of directors. His board of directors then met and ordered him to do so. It was only about five or six weeks after the hearings, and I had just started on a new assignment. They told me to leave the premises, and I did.

I later had a suit against them for breach of contract, which we finally settled out of court for very little. I had been getting two thousand dollars a week, and the settlement was for ten thousand dollars, a good part of which went to the lawyers.

During the two and a half years between the hearing and when we went to prison, we were all able to get some kind of under-the-table work. Not under our own names, of course, and for less money, about one-fifth of what we'd been getting before. I had several such jobs. I once worked under my own name when I went over to Switzerland and worked on a script for a Swiss company. They borrowed Cornell Wilde from Twentieth Century-Fox to star in this picture. Fox wanted to be sure the picture was going to be good enough for Cornell Wilde, and they were reassured by the producer, who told them he was hiring me. That persuaded Fox to lend Cornell Wilde. They figured they weren't releasing the picture so they weren't breaking the blacklist.

We decided that just two cases, John Howard Lawson's and Dalton Trumbo's, would go to trial. The rest of us would abide by the judicial decision in those cases, because it would cost too much money to fight through all separate trials. We hoped to win this case in the courts and thus immobilize the committee. On the basis of previous Supreme Court decisions, we thought we had a pretty good chance. But things were moving very fast to the Right in those days, starting with the end of the war in '45. By the time our case got to the Supreme Court in the spring of '49, it didn't look so good. The cases had been tried and appealed, with the judgment of the lower court being upheld by the appellate court. In May 1950, the Supreme Court refused to review the case. In other words, they wouldn't decide it one way or the other, and the decision of the appellate court was upheld.

As soon as the Supreme Court ruled, Lawson and Trumbo turned themselves in and proceeded to prison. Their sentences were a year in prison and a thousand-dollar fine. The rest of us had to go to Washington for perfunctory trials. The judges put off sentencing us for a week. While we were waiting for a decision, the Korean War broke out. That didn't help the situation. We had three different judges, one of whom decided it wasn't worth a full year's sentence, and sentenced two of the men, Edward Dmytryk and Herbert Biberman, to six months. The rest of us got a year. It all just took a matter of minutes. We went immediately to the Washington federal jail and then were sent to various places from there.

Lester Cole and I both ended up in Danbury, Connecticut. It's much better to be in federal prison than any of the state or local jails; they're on a higher level. They're cleaner and the food is better. Danbury had a farm and grew vegetables and raised chickens.

Parnell Thomas beat us to prison. [The former chairman of HUAC had been convicted of embezzlement in 1949 and sentenced to three years in prison.] He was already at Danbury when we arrived. He was in charge of the chicken yard, and Lester Cole, who also had a job outside the prison walls, passed him one day and said, "I see you're still shoveling chicken shit."

. . . By the time we came out of prison in 1951, the whole situation had gotten worse. Senator McCarthy had come onto the scene in the meantime, and the Rosenberg case had been tried. The hysteria was much greater. Then it really clamped down in Hollywood. There was a lot of self-censorship on the content of pictures. People just did not dare to come up with ideas that were progressive or might be frowned on. It was very difficult to get any sub rosa work for the first several years. So I left Hollywood after six months of that and transferred to Mexico and then to Connecticut. I have never lived in California since.

HOWARD KOCH

My chief sin was *Mission to Moscow,* which was made at the request of President Roosevelt for Warner Brothers. I had first turned down the assignment because I had done about four scripts in a row and I wanted to come East and see my father. I didn't want another assignment. Then Jack and Harry Warner called me up and said, "You can't turn us down." I said, "Why not?" And they told me they'd just had lunch with President Roosevelt and he had Davies's book on the table, and had said, "You want to do something important for the war effort, so we understand Russia better? Make a picture of this book," and he handed him the book. . . .

Ayn Rand attacked the movie. She said on the stand that it was obviously Communist because it was the first favorable view of the Soviet Union. . . .

Warners was glad to get all the credit for it, in the beginning, before the Inquisition set in. Then Jack Warner disavowed the film and me, saying that I'd put Communist propaganda in his films. He was up against the wall. He was scared because Warners had made the most progressive pictures in Hollywood in that period, and he didn't want them to come down on him.

PAUL JARRICO

It was a watershed event in Hollywood—the hearings and the blacklisting and the informing. The memories die hard, though the people involved are dying. We're talking about thirty years ago. Close to forty years ago for people who were called in '51, and more for the Ten who were called in '47. There are only two of them left. One of them is Ring Lardner, who's a good friend. The other is Eddie Dmytryk, who became an informer after going to prison in order to be able to continue working, who was a friend but no longer is.

I was named by Martin Berkeley and Richard Collins, among others.

I was named fourteen times. I didn't know all the people who named me! (Laughs.) But I did have a fairly high profile and I was fairly well known as a radical in Hollywood, so it was not too surprising.

Richard Collins was more than a friend; he was a collaborator. We collaborated on a couple of pictures together. When he became an informer he seemed to go out of his way to name people who had befriended him, people who'd helped him, and people who'd loaned him money. And in my case, he not only said I was a member of the Party, which was true, he implied I was a foreign agent, which was not true: he said that I would refuse to defend the United States in a conflict with the Soviet Union and was just a real unpatriotic type, and—I mean the whole formulation of "would you fight for your country" and so on. I already had. He hadn't! (Laughs.)

You know, he really went out of his way in his betrayal. It was very well known that in our collaboration I had more or less carried him, and somebody once said that his going out of his way to nail me was a kind of declaration of independence. And I said, "Yes, he wanted to stand on his own two knees!"

EDWARD DMYTRYK

I don't feel sorry for the blacklisted ones. I knew why I was black-listed. I knew how to get off the blacklist, and I did eventually. So did others, including those who testified without the public ever knowing about it. The ones that never got off are the graylisted ones. . . . There were hundreds of people in that category. You know what they did? They probably donated a few bucks to the Spanish War Relief or something, or they signed some petition. . . . Most of them were never members of the Party. . . . Their lives were ruined.

I gave them nineteen [names] or something, I've forgotten, that was all I knew. Of all the people I named, I think there was one person they didn't already know. . . . The purpose of naming names was that they wanted to make sure that I really meant it when I said I was getting out of the Party. If you don't name names, you're still protecting them, whether you're actually a Communist or not.

The idea that it would be a matter of conscience not to name names never entered my mind. I could live with it. I can see how someone else would feel that way, but in a sense, it all comes from fear—you don't want to be called a renegade. In other words, I think I was more coura-geous than they were.

Sure, there's room for the stand that says, "Look, I can't name names because my conscience won't let me do it, and I don't give a damn what

I'm called." There's room for that, and you know where the room is? It depends on how you can support your family. Arthur Miller had no danger of going broke, he had Broadway. Lillian Hellman had no danger of going broke, she had Broadway and the novel. But for Lee Cobb, acting was his only work. For Bud Bridges, acting was his only work. There were a whole lot of people like that.

I was the only one of the Ten that was a director. The rest could try to work under the counter selling scripts—even at low prices. All it meant was that they had to get back down to where they used to be. I'm sure that Trumbo got one-tenth of what he would've gotten if he hadn't been in that trouble. But even with one-tenth of what he got—as long as he didn't keep his ranch up in the valley, which he didn't, he sold it and lived simply—he could live. I couldn't. I couldn't direct a film quietly. I couldn't go out on a set where there were reporters and all these people and say, "My name is Joe Brown, I'm directing this picture." It was my only work. The only work I had done my whole life. My only out would have been to go to England and work, which I could have done, but I would have considered that a defeat."

JEFF COREY

I remember hearing the 1947 hearings, the Hollywood Ten. I knew those guys and I trembled, I had the shakes. I knew it was going to be bad. And coincident with that, I had the best period of my career. I did *Abe Lincoln in Illinois* at the Actors Lab and got wonderful reviews and a lot of attention. I did *Home of the Brave* and did one film after another. But I knew that it would catch up with us. And it did in 1951. I was blacklisted twelve years. I think I was the first one to go back to work.

I was first named by Marc Lawrence, who said I'd been at meetings at a time when I was actually a combat photographer on the U.S.S. *Yorktown,* but that's irrelevant. You took the Fifth Amendment or you didn't. . . .

Then Lee Cobb named me. I respected him and we were friends and we were fond of each other. It's a pity Lee did what he did. . . .

Years later, I worked with his daughter Julie. . . . She said he rarely talked about the blacklist, but one time he said, "Julie, you have no idea how anxiety-making it is to have every arm of the government zero in on you," and I told her, "Julie, you have no idea how exhilarating it is to tell every arm of the government they're behaving poorly and to go fuck themselves." And she looked at me as though, Jesus, she never thought of that.

The blacklist began to weaken in 1961, when Kirk Douglas, star and producer of the movie Spartacus, *gave a screen credit to Dalton Trumbo, one of the Hollywood Ten. (Trumbo had already surprised the film establishment by winning an Academy Award for a script sold under a pseudonym.) A few years later the blacklist was eliminated completely.*

"There are no rules for our kind of show, so we'll make up our own."

I LOVE LUCY

August 15, 1951
Hollywood

LUCILLE BALL

"At the time," actress Lucille Ball recalls, referring to the early 1950s, "television was regarded as the enemy by Hollywood." But it seemed to be the only place she and her husband, Desi Arnaz, could work together.

CBS knew they were getting a great comic actress in the deal. They didn't realize that in Desi they were also getting one of the great television innovators. If they had, they might have struck a very different bargain.

When I was going into my fourth month of pregnancy, CBS suddenly gave Desi the green light: they would finance a pilot for a domestic television show featuring the two of us as a married couple. A show that might go on the air that fall.

. . . "You've got a month to put one together," [said agent Don Sharpe]. "They want the pilot by February fifteenth."

For ten years, Desi and I had been trying to become co-stars and parents; now our dearest goals were being realized much too fast. We suddenly felt unprepared for either and began to have second thoughts.

At that time, television was regarded as the enemy by Hollywood. So terrified was Hollywood of this medium, movie people were afraid to make even guest appearances. If I undertook a weekly television show and it flopped, I might never work in movies again.

It would mean each of us would have to give up our respective radio programs, and Desi would have to cancel all his band engagements. It was a tremendous gamble; it had to be an all-or-nothing commitment.

But this was the first real chance Desi and I would have to work together, something we'd both been longing for, for years.

We continued to wrestle with the decision, trying to look at things from every angle. Then one night Carole Lombard appeared to me in a dream. She was wearing one of those slinky bias-cut gowns of the thirties, waving a long black cigarette holder in her hand. "Go on, kid," she advised me airily. "Give it a whirl."

The next day I told Don Sharpe, "We'll do it. Desi and I want to work together more than anything else in the world."

We called my radio writers on *My Favorite Husband* and together dreamed up a set of television characters. Originally, we were Lucy and Larry Lopez; it wasn't until we started our first shows that we became the Ricardos. Desi would be a Cuban bandleader who worked in New York City; I would play a housewife with burning stage ambitions.

. . . A week later our agent phoned to say, "Philip Morris wants to sponsor you!" We were on our way.

However, in the next few weeks the deal twisted and changed and almost blew up. The sponsor had a second demand: they not only wanted a weekly show, they also wanted it done live in New York. In 1951, a show done live on the West Coast appeared on the East Coast in fuzzy kinescope—with the image about as sharp as a piece of cheesecloth.

We refused to move to New York. Desi suggested that we *film* the show, live, in front of an audience. The network people screamed. A filmed show cost twice as much as a live one. The sponsor wouldn't put up more money and neither would CBS. So Desi made a canny offer: In return for a $1,000 weekly salary cut for us, we were given complete ownership of the show; originally, CBS had owned half of it. CBS also agreed to advance the enormous sums of money needed to film production, with Desi as producer.

All Desi had ever managed was a sixteen-piece Latin band. Now he had to rent a studio and equipment and find actors, cameramen, stagehands, cutters, film editors, writers, and scripts for thirty-nine weekly shows.

When the deal was finally set, it was late March. We had to start filming by August 15 to be on the air by October. We could rehearse and film a half-hour show in a week, but cutting, editing, and scoring would take another five weeks at least.

. . . Lucy Ricardo's nutty predicaments arose from an earnest desire to please. And there was something touching about her stage ambitions. As we were discussing her with our writers, Desi spoke up. "She tries so hard . . . she can't dance and she can't sing . . . she's earnest and pathetic. . . . Oh, I love that Lucy!" And so the title of the show was born.

. . . I had always known that Desi was a great showman, but many were surprised to learn he was a genius with keen instincts for comedy and plot. He has a quick, brilliant mind; he can instantly find the flaw in any story line; and he has inherent good taste and an intuitive knowledge of what will and will not play. He is a great producer, a great director. He never stays on too long or allows anybody else to.

When we had the characters of Lucy and Ricky clear in our minds, Jess Oppenheimer suggested that we add another man and wife—an older couple in a lower income bracket. The writers could then pit couple against couple, and the men against the women. I had known Bill Frawley since my RKO starlet days as a great natural comic; we all agreed upon him for Fred Mertz. We then started thinking about a TV wife for Bill.

We considered a number of actresses, and then one day Desi heard about a fine actress from the Broadway stage named Vivian Vance. . . . As far as I was concerned, it was Kismet. Viv and I were extraordinarily compatible. We both believe wholeheartedly in what we call "an enchanted sense of play," and use it liberally in our show. It's a happy frame of mind, the light touch, skipping into things instead of plodding. It's looking at things from a child's point of view and believing. The only way I can play a funny scene is to believe it. Then I can convincingly eat like a dog under a table, freeze to death beneath burning-hot klieg lights, or bake a loaf of bread ten feet long.

We had no way of knowing how comical she and Bill would be together. Vivian was actually much younger than Bill. Up until then, she'd usually been cast in glamorous "other woman" parts. But she went along gamely with Ethel Mertz's dowdy clothes, no false eyelashes or eye makeup, and hair that looked as if she had washed and set it herself. But she drew the line at padding her body to look fatter.

. . . She and Bill scrapped a good deal, and this put a certain amount of real feeling into their stage quarrels. Bill became the hero of all henpecked husbands. He couldn't walk down the street without some man coming up to him and saying, "Boy, Fred, you tell that Ethel off something beautiful!"

So much good luck was involved in the casting. Early in the series, our writers wanted to write a show in which the Mertzes had to sing and dance. We then learned for the first time that both Vivian and Bill had had big musical comedy careers. Vivian had been in *Skylark* with Gertrude Lawrence, and Bill was a well-known vaudeville hoofer.

I had insisted upon having a studio audience; otherwise, I knew, we'd never hit the right tempo. We did the show every Thursday night in front of four hundred people, a cross-section of America. I could visualize our living and working together on the set like a stock company, then filming it like a movie, and at the same time staging it like a Broadway play. "We'll have opening night every week," I chortled.

Desi's first problem was that there were no movie studios in Hollywood with accommodations for an audience. We also wanted a stage large enough to film the show in its natural sequence, with no long delays setting up stage decorations or shifting lights.

Desi hired Academy Award-winning cameraman Karl Freund, whose work I had admired at MGM, and discussed the problems with him. Karl flew to New York for a week to see how television cameras could be moved around without interfering too much with the audience's view of the action. He came back pretty unimpressed. "There are no rules for our kind of show, so we'll make up our own."

Karl Freund hit upon a revolutionary new way of filming a show with three cameras shooting the action simultaneously. One of these cameras is far back, another recording the medium shots, with a third getting the close-ups. The film editor then has three different shots of a particular bit of action. By shifting back and forth between the three, he can get more variety and flexibility than with the one-camera technique.

But moving three huge cameras about the stage between the actors and the audience called for the most complex planning.

First Desi rented an unused movie studio. By tearing down partitions, he joined two giant soundstages. This gave us enough room to build three permanent sets—the Ricardo living room, bedroom, and kitchen—and a fourth set, which was sometimes the New York nightclub where Ricky worked and sometimes an alligator farm or a vineyard in Italy or the French Alps—whatever the script called for. . . . The roving cameras couldn't roll easily on the wooden stage, so a smooth concrete floor was laid down. . . .

While the three rooms slowly took form before our eyes, bleachers for three hundred people were built facing them. The Los Angeles Fire and Health departments threw a mountain of red tape at us when they learned we were inviting a large weekly audience into a movie studio. Desi had to add rest rooms, water fountains, and an expensive sprinkler system. Microphones were installed over the heads of the audience; we wanted our laughs live—some of the canned laughter you hear today came from our *Lucy* show audiences.

. . . It took me a long time to recover physically from Lucie's birth, but I had no time to pamper myself. Six weeks after she arrived, I walked on the *Lucy* set to start filming the series.

Rehearsals got under way to the pounding of hammers and buzzing of saws; the set was only half built and a whole wall of the soundstage was still missing when we started. Desi was so nervous that he memorized everybody's lines and moved his own lips as they spoke; he also kept flicking his eyes around the stage watching the progress of the three cameras. He soon got over this, but proved to be the fastest learner of dialogue.

We rehearsed the first show twelve hours a day. Then on Friday evening, August 15, 1951, the bleachers filled up by eight o'clock and Desi explained to the audience that they would be seeing a brand-new kind of television show. He stepped behind the curtain and we all took our places.

Sitting in the bleachers that first night were a lot of anxious rooters: DeDe and Desi's mother, Dolores; our writers; Andrew Hickox; and a raft of Philip Morris representatives and CBS officials. To launch the series, the network had paid out $300,000. They hoped it would last long enough to pay back that advance.

We were lucky all the way. The first four shows put us among the top ten on television. Arthur Godfrey, one of the giants, preceded us and urged his watchers to stay tuned to *I Love Lucy*. Our twentieth show made us number one on the air and there we stayed for three wild, incredible years.

I Love Lucy has been called the most popular television show of all time. Such national devotion to one show can never happen again; there are too many shows, on many more channels, now. But in 1951–1952, our show changed the Monday night habits of America. Between nine and nine-thirty, taxis disappeared from the streets of New York. Marshall Fields department store in Chicago hung up a sign: "We Love Lucy too, so from now on we will be open Thursday nights instead of Monday." Telephone calls across the nation dropped sharply during that half hour, as well as the water flush rate, as whole families sat glued to their seats.

. . . During our first season someone told Desi that our show had a hit rating of 70. He looked worried, thinking that a "grade" of 70 was barely passing. "You're kidding," he said, not realizing that a rating of 70 was indeed phenomenal.

Three-camera shooting required new editing equipment and techniques, which Desi also helped devise. He bet that all the extra effort was worthwhile because he and Lucy had the rights to sell reruns, which the networks considered almost worthless. His business acumen led to the purchase of the show's shooting stages, turning RKO Studios into Desilu Studios, where other television shows copied the I Love Lucy *innovations.*

*"We intend to buy old car or truck, pack gear,
and drive to Frisco."*

GOING ON THE ROAD

1951

JACK KEROUAC

*In early 1954 this editor's father received an unexpected visit at his literary
agency from a disheveled man wearing a dirty winter coat. The man, apparently
a writer judging from the large manuscript, bound with laundry rope, stacked
beside him in the doorway, held out a label torn from a phonograph record titled
"Kerouac"—cut by some musician friends, it was later learned. Jack Kerouac,
already the author of one relatively traditional novel, had written a stream-of-
consciousness tome—the one tied with rope—that his editor had rejected. The
editor had suggested he come here. Could he leave the manuscript?*

*Much of what was in that stack of paper was unintelligible. But then, about
a hundred pages in, came a section called "On the Road."*

*Kerouac's compulsion to find spiritual enlightment on the way west came
from a long tradition of seekers, but made the experience seem utterly new, and
prompted a new generation—dubbed the beat generation—to follow his path,
which led directly to the hippies and the counterculture of the sixties. This letter
to Neal Cassady, Kerouac's best friend and the protagonist of many of his novels,
was written just before Kerouac took the trip that led to his classic work.*

Neal, a word or two about my plans. Joan and I have decided to get
fulltime jobs till March to save several hundred bucks. In March, if I get
a Guggenheim (decided around last week) we will at once buy an old
panel truck, load gear, and take off for 3 wonderful lazy years perhaps in
provincial Mexico (cheaper than Mexcity.) Texcoco, 30 miles away, 24¢
bus into town that I rode, pissing from the back, with Jeff, under shadow of the snowtopt volcanoes; 1¢ buys waterglass of raw tequila. Can
live there off $400 or $500 a year. Guggenheim is $2500 or even 3
grand;—however, not to depend on such a dream of possibilities, if we
don't get this dough, we intend to buy old car or truck, pack gear, and
drive to Frisco; where we work till I get $1000 from Harcourt if ever
they publish me again, if not we will work & live in Frisco, saving best
we can, for eventual date in Mexico. This being case, when you get here,
I hope you have car so I can get driver's license with you (also few
lessons for sharpup). If only you weren't so hung up and could yourself
save a few Texcoco's worth of years and come with us, or with the wife

& kids . . . if we ever run out of $ together we could ride bus to Texas border and in few months rake up at construction or oilfield work and come back to year of life with kicks & wives. I wish in fact you could do this with all my heart, as with Joan I will be completely happy, but with you, I would also be completely befriended and need nothing; we'd live on same street and meet in dusty alley and go down to teafields to see Jose and hang around sun. Nights, write. I'd have me wife, and me near friend nearby, and you too. $500 a year I say. No foolishness like La Vie Parisienne, but purchase of eggs from country Indians, strict haggling purchases of bread and tortilla mix and pinto beans & cheese; buy bottles water; etc. go to big city for connection as smalltown too obvious, and take great care as Bill did with odor as I say big city is hour away in car, 1 and a half in old bus. Texcoco, which you never saw, is south of Mexcity; it is hot and fine, same altitude but somehow drowsier and finer; crazy Gregors all over; Mambo in little doorway joints. It is a town with one square in middle surrounded by crumbling Spanish masonry; 3 old beautiful churches with lovely bells; fiestas almost every day and attendant fireworks; no fancy Americans like at Oaxaca and Taxco and such. We'd hang on to every cent, give the Mexes no quarter, let them get sullen at the cheap Americans and stand side by side in defense, and make friends in the end when they saw we was poor too. Comes another Mex revolution, we stands them off with our Burroughsian arsenal bought cheap on Madero St. and dash to big city in car for safety shooting and pissing as we go; whole Mex army follows hi on weed; now no worries any more. Just sit on roof hi enjoying hot dry sun and sound of kids yelling and have us wives & American talk of our own as well as exotic kicks and regular old honest Indian kicks. Become Indians . . . I personally play mambo in local catband, because of this we get close to them and go to town. Wow. How's about it? Hurry to N.Y. so we can plan and all take off in big flying boat '32 Chandler across crazy land. Bring juke, bop records, mambo records and dixieland records; typewriters, clothes, toasters, percolators, etc.

Until I see you . . . let me know when . . . I got to work now on script so I can pay Uncle Sam his bloody tax & landlord's bloody old rent & all the bloody shits together.

"I laughed till the tears ran down my cheeks."

TRIPPING

1953−1954
Los Angeles

ALDOUS HUXLEY

The psychedelic sixties were greatly inspired by Aldous Huxley, the stiff, socially inept British author of Brave New World. *Huxley, fascinated by the use of peyote and other hallucinogenics by the Indians of the Southwest, wanted to try the drugs for himself. Coming from a family of scientists, he brought an analytical approach to the idea. He solicited a psychiatrist to act as supervisor, and bought a dictaphone to record the experiences. The only worry came from the supervising psychiatrist, Dr. Humphry Osmond, who said, "I did not relish the possibility, however remote, of being the man who drove Aldous Huxley mad."*

This account comes from Huxley's influential book about his mescaline and LSD trips, The Doors of Perception.

One bright May morning, I swallowed four-tenths of a gram of mescalin dissolved in half a glass of water and sat down to wait for the results. . . .

. . . Confronted by a chair which looked like the Last Judgment—or, to be more accurate, by a Last Judgment which, after a long time and with considerable difficulty, I recognized as a chair—I found myself all at once on the brink of panic. This, I suddenly felt, was going too far. Too far, even though the going was into intenser beauty, deeper significance. The fear, as I analyze it in retrospect, was of being overwhelmed, of disintegrating under a pressure of reality greater than a mind, accustomed to living most of the time in a cosy world of symbols, could possibly bear. The literature of religious experience abounds in references to the pains and terrors overwhelming those who have come, too suddenly, face to face with some manifestation of the Mysterium tremendum. In theological language, this fear is due to the incompatibility between man's egoism and the divine purity, between man's self-aggravated separateness and the infinity of God. . . . Anything other than the burning brightness of unmitigated Reality—anything!

. . . None too soon, I was steered away from the disquieting splendors of my garden chair. Drooping in green parabolas from the hedge, the ivy fronds shone with a kind of glassy, jade-like radiance. A moment later a clump of Red Hot Pokers, in full bloom, had exploded into my field of vision. So passionately alive that they seemed to be standing on the very brink of utterance, the flowers strained up yards into the blue. I looked down at the leaves and discovered a cavernous intricacy of the most delicate green lights and shadows, pulsing with undecipherable mystery.

. . . We walked out into the street. A large pale blue automobile was standing at the curb. At the sight of it, I was suddenly overcome by enormous merriment. What complacency, what an absurd self-satisfaction beamed from those bulging surfaces of glossiest enamel! Man had created the thing in his own image—or rather in the image of his favorite character in fiction. I laughed till the tears ran down my cheeks.

We reentered the house. A meal had been prepared. Somebody who was not yet identical with myself, fell to with ravenous appetite. From a considerable distance and without much interest, I looked on.

When the meal had been eaten, we got into the car and went for a drive. The effects of the mescalin were already on the decline: but the flowers in the gardens still trembled on the brink of being supernatural, the pepper trees and carobs along the side streets still manifestly belonged to some sacred grove. Eden alternated with Dodona [the oldest oracle in Greece]. Yggdrasil [in Norse mythology, the great ash tree that supported the universe] with the mystic Rose. And then, abruptly we were at an intersection, waiting to cross Sunset Boulevard. Before us the cars were rolling by in a steady stream—thousands of them, all bright and shiny like an advertiser's dream and each more ludicrous than the last. Once again I was convulsed with laughter.

The Red Sea of traffic parted at last, and we crossed into another oasis of trees and lawns and roses. In a few minutes we had climbed to a vantage point in the hills, and there was the city spread out beneath us. We drove on, and so long as we remained in the hills, with view succeeding distant view, significance was at its everyday level, well below transfiguration point. The magic began to work again only when we turned down into a new suburb and were gliding between two rows of houses. Here, in spite of the peculiar hideousness of the architecture, there were renewals of transcendental otherness, hints of the morning's heaven. Brick chimneys and green composition roofs glowed in the sunshine, like fragments of the New Jerusalem. And all at once I saw what Guardi had seen and (with what incomparable skill) had so often rendered in his paintings—a stucco wall with a shadow slanting across it, blank but unforgettably beautiful, empty but charged with all the meaning and the mystery of existence. The revelation dawned and was gone again within a fraction of a second.

. . . An hour later, with ten more miles and the visit to the World's

Biggest Drug Store safely behind us, we were back at home, and I had returned to that reassuring but profoundly unsatisfactory state known as "being in one's right mind."

Huxley started with mescaline, then moved on to LSD, which was a new and rare drug. Created by in1938, it had been practically ignored for five years until a pharmaceutical researcher, Dr. Albert Hofmann, accidentally absorbed some through his skin, and took the first LSD trip on record.

At the time, LSD wasn't a controlled substance. Huxley's wife, Laura, later wrote: "Now, in 1967, when LSD has become a household word, I realize how lucky those of us were who ten years ago approached LSD before it had either the demoniacal or the paradisiacal vibrations it has now—when it had no echoes of gurus and heroes, doctors or delinquents. We went into the experience not knowing what would happen. . . . LSD—those three now-famous letters were free of association with scientific righteousness and beatnik conformity, with earthly paradise and parental loving concern—also free from closed-mindedness, obscurantism, and bigotry. The unconscious identification with those ideas, feelings, and fears inevitably occurs now, with disastrous consequences."

Dr. Hofmann's research attracted the attention of the Central Intelligence Agency, which thought LSD might be a good mind-control drug. The CIA sponsored LSD research at several universities, but all it did was create the subversion it was trying to prevent. As Harvard professor and LSD guru Timothy Leary said many years later, "I wouldn't be here now without the foresight of the CIA scientists." Another important LSD supporter in the 1960s, writer Ken Kesey, first took LSD when he agreed to be a subject in a CIA-sponsored experiment because he needed cash.

By the way, the title of Huxley's book came from a line of William Blake—"If the doors of perception were cleansed, every thing would appear to man as it is, infinite"—and inspired the name of Jim Morrison's rock band, The Doors.

" 'My roots are New York,' O'Malley told
Mayor Robert Wagner."

BASEBALL MOVES WEST

1953–1957
New York

ROGER KAHN

The industrial efforts of World War II had turned Los Angeles and the Bay Area into sprawling, diverse, metropolitan centers, but New Yorkers remained smug that their town was the center of the world. Then in 1957 the Brooklyn Dodgers and the New York Giants moved to California.

Eyewitness Roger Kahn covered baseball as a reporter for the New York Herald-Tribune. *He later wrote* The Boys of Summer *and the book from which this account comes,* The Era.

O'Malley took me into his confidence that March [1953]. "Did you ever ask yourself," he began in the modest Florida office where he worked, "why in an electronic age we play our games in a horse-and-buggy park?"

I had never asked myself anything like that. Ebbets Field was a Brooklyn fixture, like the Soldiers and Sailors Monument at Grand Army Plaza and the Cyclone roller coaster at Coney Island.

"The aisles are too narrow," O'Malley said. The stairs are too steep. Poles obstruct the views. We can't park enough cars. We need twice as many seats. The bathrooms smell. The girders holding up the whole thing are rusting away."

He puffed his cigar, looking unhappy, then brightened. "Imagine a new park. Seventy thousand seats just like the Yankees have. No poles. You can cantilever construction now. Escalators take the fans to their seats. Plenty of parking. Restaurants and train stations right in the park. Then, to end worries about rain, we put a dome over everything."

After a while I said, "Walter, as far as I know, grass won't grow under a dome."

"We can get agronomy people to work on that, or maybe we can find a substitute for grass." His face was beaming; he was serious.

. . . After [architect Raymond] Loewy built a model, people made dismissive jokes about O'Malley's Pleasure Dome. Walter was the wrong man to dismiss.

. . . The Dodgers reached their mountaintop in 1953. . . . Francis Sugrue of the *Herald Tribune* described victory night in Brooklyn. "The Fourth of July, New Year's Eve, St. Patrick's Day, V-E Day, and Bastille Day, all in one. Add to that a touch of Mardi Gras. The minute Pee Wee Reese threw out Elston Howard for the last out at first base, Brooklyn police headquarters sent out an alert for all to be on the lookout for Dodger fans. As this edition went to press, there were no fatalities." Brooklyn had won its first World Series.

. . . Walter O'Malley summoned the press a few days later. He had commissioned "Buckminster Fuller of Princeton" to design the new Dodger Stadium as a geodesic dome.

A sportswriter asked how to spell the word.

"Dome," Buzzie Bavasi said. "D-o-m-e."

"Are you gonna give Podres a raise?" someone else asked.

"We're here to talk about the geodesic dome," O'Malley said. *Nobody took him or Bucky Fuller seriously.*

. . . Dick Young insisted O'Malley told him he wanted to leave Ebbets Field "because the area is getting full of blacks and spics." O'Malley denied having said any such thing.

"Oh, yeah," Young parried when I pressed him. "O'Malley also said the trouble with Brooklyn was that the place had too many blacks and spics *and Jews.*"

Certainly O'Malley was most comfortable with his Roman Catholic cadre, Bavasi and Fresco Thompson. Jackie Robinson disquieted O'Malley, not just because Robinson was Rickey's man but also because he was a challenging, defiant black. Walter liked blacks docile. He preferred Pullman porters to Jackie Robinson.

. . . O'Malley was aware of everyone's ethnicity. It is excessive to accuse him of bigotry, but he did harbor stereotypes. Brooklyn blacks were moving southward out of Bedford-Stuyvesant toward Eastern Parkway and Crown Heights. Ebbets Field stood in the path of the black advance. This became another reason he wanted to move.

. . . "By 1957 we had a terrible situation at the Polo Grounds" [New York Giants owner] Chub Feeney remembers. "The park was deteriorating. People were afraid of the neighborhood. At the very least, we needed three million dollars as a minimum to break even and we weren't getting it. We offered Jackie [Robinson] fifty thousand dollars to play for us, although we knew he wasn't in great shape. We were hoping desperately to boost attendance with Robinson. We were drawing only six hundred fifty thousand a year in a metropolitan area of twelve million. . . .

"We owned the Minneapolis Millers in the American Association," Feeney says. "By June of 1957, Horace and I were finishing arrangements to move the team there. Then Horace's phone rang. Walter O'Malley said, 'Why not move to California with me?'"

No one [had] paid appropriate attention in 1955 when O'Malley sold Ebbets Field for three million dollars to a real estate developer named Marvin Kratter. He also sold ballparks the Dodgers owned in Fort Worth and Montreal for one million dollars each. "That five million dollars," he said, "is the money that will, one way or another, go into our new Brooklyn ballpark." But he also invested some of the money by acquiring the Los Angeles franchise in the Pacific Coast League from the Chicago Cubs. He now owned territorial rights to Los Angeles. He was ready to play his special game: stroke and tomahawk.

"My roots are New York," O'Malley told Mayor Robert Wagner at City Hall on June 2, 1957. "People in Los Angeles want the Dodgers to move. They've made flattering offers. I am in no way committed."

"What do you want?" Wagner asked.

"Air rights over the Long Island Railroad station at Atlantic Avenue and Flatbush Avenue in downtown Brooklyn. The Dodgers don't want anything else. We'll pay for a new ballpark by ourselves."

Wagner was a pleasant person, part Tammany hack, part liberal reformer, and totally overmatched in negotiating with O'Malley. Robert Moses, New York's commissioner of parks, was the principal city player. Through a series of appointments Moses controlled not only parks, but highways and urban projects as well. Urbanologists regard Moses as "the single most powerful figure in twentieth-century New York City government." Moses put hard questions to O'Malley.

"You aren't suggesting, sir, that four or five million dollars is enough to build the domed stadium you propose?"

O'Malley conceded that the cost would be higher. "The Brooklyn Dodgers are prepared to sell a bond issue to citizens of Brooklyn, backed by the full faith and credit of our franchise. I have no doubt, Mr. Moses, none whatsoever, about our ability to finance ourselves."

Further, O'Malley said, he was negotiating with Mathew Fox of Skiatron, Inc., "to put our games on subscription TV." The technology involved a coin box on television sets. Fans would have to put two quarters into the box to unscramble pictures of Dodger games. "These receipts will help pay for the new ballpark."

Moses looked incredulous. "Engineers and electronic experts," O'Malley said, "tell me coin box television is no problem at all."

"As a matter of fact," Moses said, "I just don't want to see a baseball field in downtown Brooklyn at all. The streets will never handle all the cars."

O'Malley said that his plans for the domed stadium, over the Long Island Railroad station, included such good access that most people would come to the park by train.

"You are in error, Mr. O'Malley. If I let you build your domed stadium, your ballgames will create a China Wall of traffic in Brooklyn. No one will be able to pass."

"Where would you prefer that we relocate?" O'Malley said.

"I have a lovely parcel of land in Flushing Meadow, at the old World's Fair site in Queens."

O'Malley looked steadily at Robert Moses. "If my team is forced to play in the borough of Queens, they will no longer be the Brooklyn Dodgers."

Next day the front page of the *Herald Tribune* announced that a new aquarium was being dedicated in Coney Island and that Margaret Truman, wife of Clifton Daniel, Jr., assistant managing editor of the *New York Times,* had given birth to a son. A headline in columns four and five, more prescient than the copyeditor knew, described the meeting among O'Malley, Wagner, and Moses as "a scoreless tie."

In September the Los Angeles City Council voted to offer the Dodgers 307 acres in Chavez Ravine in exchange for a small parcel of land at the Los Angeles minor league park called Wrigley Field.

The last ballgame at Ebbets Field occurred on September 24, 1957. The Dodgers defeated Branch Rickey's Pittsburgh Pirates, 2 to 0.

Gladys Goodding, the organist, played sad songs for the crowd, 6,702 fans in—as O'Malley said—"a borough of fully two million." Goodding played in order:

"Am I Blue?"
"What Can I Say, Dear, After I've Said I'm Sorry?"
"Thanks for the Memory!"
"When I Grow Too Old to Dream"
"When the Blue of the Night Meets the Gold of the Day"
"Auld Lang Syne"

. . . The Era was done. . . . The new [Los Angeles] ballpark, Dodger Stadium, opened on April 10, 1962. O'Malley met the cost, $22 million, with a low-interest (two percent) loan from the Union Oil Company, which in exchange won exclusive rights to advertise within the ballpark. Dodger home attendance began to surpass three million late in the 1970s.

Some find irony in the fact that O'Malley's son, Peter, led opposition to the Giants moving from San Francisco to St. Petersburg, Florida, after the 1992 season. But the O'Malleys are businesspeople, expedients. It seemed good business for Walter to move West at the end of the Era. It seemed bad business to Peter O'Malley for the Dodgers to lose a profitable intra-California rivalry a generation later.

"Aerospace and California were made not just for but by each other."

BLUE SKY DREAM

1957–1976
Valley of Heart's Delight, California

DAVID BEERS

In 1957, when Russia launched the first man-made satellite, reporter David Beers was a newborn in Ohio. Soon afterward, his father, an engineer, received a call from Lockheed Corporation's missiles and space division in California. Sputnik had scared America into the space race; could the senior Beers help develop America's response? Aviation, already an important industry on the West Coast, was about to become aerospace, creating missiles and rockets and high-tech supersonic planes.

In this piece written for The Atlantic Monthly—*which later became the basis of his book* Blue Sky Dream—*Beers recalls the rise and fall of the aerospace industry and the culture it bred. He also introduces a neighbor, another son of a Lockheed engineer, whose rebellious nature played a crucial role in the transition of the area from the quaint and parochial Valley of Heart's Delight to the metropolis of the digital age, Silicon Valley.*

Aerospace and California were made not just for but by each other. World War I-era airplane makers came west for the test-flight weather and also because East Coast money was dubious that there would be much of an aviation industry. *Los Angeles Times* publisher Harry Chandler and other Southern California empire builders were not. They invested in aero-entrepreneurs like Donald Douglas, Glenn Martin, and the Loughheed [later changed to "Lockheed"] brothers; and they wrangled millions to make the California Institute of Technology in Pasadena a national science and aviation center in time for World War II. By 1940 half of all U.S. airframe factories were in Southern California. By the end of World War II the state was a mesh of military bases, university labs, and aeronautical R&D and production sites—a Pentagon-dependent economy.

Lockheed had long been aviation's Team Ferrari. Lockheeds were those sleek monoplanes preferred by Lindbergh and Earhart; the silvery Electra that carries away Ingrid Bergman in *Casablanca*; the catamaran-like P-38 superfighter of World War II; the original Air Force jet, conceived and built in a legendary 143 days by the company's "Skunk Works" team in Burbank. Now, at the dawn of the 1960s, Lockheed was hiring en masse for a new division flush with contracts to create not only the nation's first satellites but, under the guidance of its own former Nazi, Wolfgang Noggerath, the first ballistic missile to be launched from beneath the sea.

"The most beautiful missiles ever fired," one admiral pronounced the nuclear-tipped Polaris AlX, having witnessed its successful submarine test on a summer day in 1960. Beautiful to a professional lover of the bomb, you say, but beautiful as well to me, a boy who later would thumbtack a color photograph of that launch to the wall of my new bedroom in the Valley of Heart's Delight. In those early years my father brought home publicity pictures of Lockheed products: stubby-winged jets and fire-swathed rockets and satellites that hung in space like tinfoil dragonflies. My favorite was the Polaris, smooth and white and perfect, frozen above the convulsed ocean surface it had just burst through. Lockheed always photographed its missiles headed up, never killing-end down. As a child I didn't wonder what the Polaris was for; that it was so obviously the future exploding out of the sea seemed reason enough to create it.

Lockheed's missiles and space division methodically stamped its design onto the Valley of Heart's Delight, working closely with the politicians to put schools and hospitals in place, laying out the grid of high-speed expressways that within a few years delivered more than 25,000 workers to its gates. No local firm employed nearly as many, though others, like Varian (radar) and Hewlett-Packard (most early sales were to the military), helped create a synergy with nearby Stanford and military sites. Expressways connected to freeways. Up and down California the missiles and space business was growing 20 percent a year, filling up subdivisions like ours with Rockedyne families, McDonnell Douglas families, Northrop families, Motorola, Hughes, Westinghouse, TRW, Rockwell, and Jet Propulsion Laboratory families, feeding the state's root economy: real-estate speculation. Offered millions to sell out to developers, the orchard families could no longer afford to fill with blossoms the Valley of Heart's Delight. In time, we stopped calling it that. After a while more, everyone called it Silicon Valley.

The key development in the aerospace industry, however, was not to be found in its esoteric products but in the very way it brought them into being. The idea, refined during the space buildup of the 1960s, was systems engineering, and it cut directly against America's favorite myth about how it created technology. The old catechism taught that the light bulb, the automobile, the airplane—almost every American history-changing machine—had sprung from a lonely visionary tinkering against a mass of naysayers. First, individual triumph. Then, via the marketplace, national progress. But the mobilization of scientists and engineers for World War II, and then for the Cold War, made that creation story seem as quaint as the RCA dog. From here on, survival dictated that our technological fate would be commanded into being from above. A blue-sky goal would be set—an atom bomb, a space station, the most beautiful missile—and the nation's very will would be invested, a monolith of our best minds put to it and given a deadline. Rather than growing organically from the single "Eureka!," machines that mattered would now begin at the end, with the first step being the official imagining of a complete system that could, say, level a dozen cities instantly or get a couple of men in and out of space alive.

Systems engineering, therefore, sought a grand unified theory for bureaucracy. Building a machine of systems meant constructing a system of humans. How, for example, to order tasks so that when someone changed the shape of a nose cone in Anaheim, all other contractors and subcontractors, all over the country, changed their designs accordingly? . . .

By 1963 the missiles and space business, with 700,000 employees, was vying with the auto industry as the country's top employer. Placed in charge of the future, aerospace met no serious challenge to its position until after it had delivered, as promised, a man to the moon. Yet almost at that same moment, the icons of blue-sky culture seemed to lose their mojo powers. Environmentalists, utterly unmoved by the sleek loveliness of the SST, painted it loud and rude, shot it down. The B-70 superbomber program crashed in Congress as the antiwar movement challenged the notion that the Pentagon, or any state authority, should be the revered and unchallenged steward of a people's imagination.

At the close of the Sixties, weapons spending slowed, coinciding with a cyclical slump in commercial-jet sales, and there were mass aerospace layoffs, particularly in California. Some of my father's peers went from designing satellites to perfecting alloy backpack frames. (Surely Dad hadn't been a compatriot of Neil Armstrong's only to make camping gear!) I remember, while watching the Jetsons suburbanize the Milky Way on TV, reading newspaper stories about out-of-work Lockheed men killing themselves. The year 1970 was "the gloomiest year in decades," concluded *Aviation Week and Space Technology*. The magazine blamed barbarians: "the mounting assault on technology by a strange coalition of political opportunists, disgruntled youth, ecologists, and advocates of the social welfare state."

The real challenge to the primacy of blue-sky culture, however, would eventually come from within its own family rooms, most brazenly in the person of Steve Wozniak, a Lockheed child whose father worked with mine. A half-dozen years older than I, Wozniak was disgruntled not with technology but with authority's claim on the word. (Note that "technology" was then perfectly synonymous with "state-sponsored aerospace" as *Aviation Week* used the term.) Young Steve of Sunnyvale planted shrill sound devices behind the classroom TV, made sirens blare in driver's ed. "The teachers always said, 'We know Wozniak did this, but he's too bright to catch.' I never got caught," he recalled in an interview. One quarter shy of a degree, he spurned college and sold electronic "blue boxes" that illegally jimmied into long-distance phone networks. He started Dial-A-Joke from his apartment and around the same time, in the late 1970s, invented, of course, the monolith-subverting Apple computer.

My family found alien what Wozniak and his tribe caused around us, the rush to personalize the microchip and get it to the marketplace. Blue-sky technology was built in secret for the state; its incomprehensibility was part of its appeal. But now suddenly everyone was a "start-up" schemer, racing to be the first to invent some new peripheral or interface, gadgets too "friendly" to too many "users" to hold any mystique for us. Little computer-jammed labs above strip malls, instant assembly lines staffed with illegal brown people, workaholic ponytailed geniuses hopping from employer to employer—it was so un-Lockheed.

"He had some some peculiar ideas
about how to motivate people."

SILICON COMES TO SILICON VALLEY

GORDON MOORE

The vacuum tube, a bulky, fragile device, was the basis of early electronics. Vacuum tube computers were the size of a room and had less power than today's laptops. And replacing tubes was almost a full-time job.

Transistors changed all that. Invented in 1947 by William Shockley, John Bardeen, and Walter Brattain, the transistor was a small crystal. Like a vacuum tube, it controlled the flow of electrical current; but it wouldn't blow out easily, and it was small enough for hundreds or thousands to be used in a single device. Today, millions of transistors, so tiny they can be seen only with the most powerful microscopes, are combined on a single computer chip. The material used to make transistors is the silicon in Silicon Valley.

William Shockley was recruited by Stanford dean Fred Terman (see page 305) to establish a company in the Palo Alto area. John Bardeen recalls, "[Shockley] searched the world to assemble the outstanding group that became the nucleus of Silicon Valley. Along with outstanding talent came independent minds. . . ."

One of those independent minds, Gordon Moore, recalls the early days, when eight young, ambitious scientists were ready to change the world—if only they could convince the world that it needed changing.

Dr. Shockley thought that he could make an inexpensive transistor and set up the company to pursue that goal. We were each working on our individual various parts of the project, trying to make this come to pass, while we were all learning about semiconductors and the processes that had to be developed to make it into a real business. This was a very interesting operation.

Dr. Shockley was a very competent scientist, very competitive by nature. And while he had fantastic physical intuition about what was going to go in the materials, and what the physics was going to be of the structures we were building, he had some some peculiar ideas about how to motivate people. So we got into some peculiar problems in those early days, eventually ending up with his suggesting that everyone in the company take a lie detector test to see who was responsible for some rather minor thing that had occurred in the operation.

Based on that and a few other things, a group of us decided that this wasn't going to work out the way it was organized, and actually went around Dr. Shockley to Arnold Beckman, who was the source of the money behind the operation, to see if we could come up with a different organization that kind of put Bill aside, maybe get him a professorship at Stanford or something, so he could be a technical consultant to the company but would no longer be responsible for running it.

After a few meetings with Dr. Beckman, where we thought we were making some progress, Dr. Beckman became convinced that such a move would destroy Shockley's career. Of course by that time Shockley had won a Nobel prize for his original invention of the transistor, and it was rather presumptuous for a group of young scientists to think we could push him aside and run things our way.

But we felt we had burned our bridges so badly that we couldn't stick around any longer after that decision on Dr. Beckman's part, so we decided that we were going to have to leave and look for jobs. And one of the members of the group wrote to a friend of his father's, and said, there are a group of us here who like to work together, do you think there's a company that would like to hire the group of us so we could stay together? And that friend of his father's happened to work for one of the New York investment banking firms, and the friend and a junior partner in the firm came out to visit with us, to see what we were really interested in, and suggested that maybe we didn't want to find a company to work for, what we might want to do is set up our own company.

So we said OK, what does that involve? That way we wouldn't have to move or anything, we'd be able to stay right where we were; we liked living in the area.

So they set out to find us funding to see if we could set up our own company, with an objective different than what Shockley's objective had become by that time. And we literally sat down with the *Wall Street Journal* and went through all of the companies on the New York Stock Exchange to identify those that we thought might be interested in a semiconductor operation.

We identified some 32 companies as I recall that we thought were likely prospects, and the investment bankers went out and talked to all 32 companies and all 32 turned the idea down. And then quite by accident they ran into Sherman Fairchild, who really was a technology buff. He loved new technology. He had originally set up a company to do aerial surveying, and had to make both an airplane compay and a camera company to have everything he needed to do the aerial surveying. His apartment was full of all the latest electronic gadgets.

Anyhow, he introduced the investment bankers to the chairman of

Fairchild Camera and Instrument, and they took a look at the group and decided to risk a modest investment to see if we could do anything. So we got caught up with Fairchild and that was the formation of Fairchild semiconductor.

The Shockley mutineers became known as the Fairchild Eight. Left to pursue their own ideas, they did brilliant work at Fairchild, then split again, forming companies like Intel.

Transistors sent electronics in a new direction. So what maintained the momentum of the West Coast electronics industry? The transistor had been invented at Bell Labs in New York. The most logical customers were East Coast firms, such as AT&T and IBM. And established West Coast companies like Hewlett-Packard didn't pursue the new technology. As with the vacuum tube (see page 222), the transistor became the basis of a Western phenomenon as a result of determination, such as Fred Terman's desire to bring Shockley west in the first place, and whimsy, such as the desire of the Fairchild Eight to stick together and stay on the West Coast.

William Shockley did eventually become a Stanford professor, as his employees had suggested years earlier. His reputation as an electronics engineer was overshadowed by the racist sociological views that became his obsession.

"They surrounded Ike with anti-statehood people."

ALASKAN STATEHOOD

1935–1959
Anchorage and Washington, D.C.

ROBERT ATWOOD

What makes a state? After all the grand theories, it often came down to a backroom political deal. One of the most important parts of the 1787 Constitutional Convention in Philadelphia was the negotiation of the Northwest Ordinance, which set standards of population for territories to become states. But its antislavery provisions led to problems that prompted the Missouri Compromise (1820) and the Compromise of 1850, and eventually led to the secession of the southern states in 1860 and '61. The case of Alaska was no exception to the realpolitik of statehood.

Robert Atwood, who was a player in the behind-the-scenes action, was publisher of the Anchorage Times. *An Illinois native, he moved north to the home state of his wife in 1932, and bought the paper three years later. At the time,*

Alaska was considered just a poor relation of Washington State, and was governed as a federal territory. "Washington [D.C.] controlled the land and the resources in it, on it, over it, the water, the air—everything was in federal hands," Atwood recalled. "We couldn't even cut a Christmas tree here without getting permission from Washington. We used to go out and sneak around, of course, and bootleg our Christmas trees."

In this account, drawn from an interview given to Tom Tiede for the book American Tapestry, *Atwood describes the fight to secure equal status with the "lower 48."*

I think the idea of statehood began seriously during World War II. We realized then that something had to happen. I said before that the federal government controlled everything at the time I arrived, but it got much worse during the Second World War. When the military came up here to defend this area from the Japanese, we were placed under a situation that was very close to being military rule. The commanding general here had the authority to exclude any of us from Alaska if he wanted; he controlled travel; he controlled what supplies we could bring in. The government even censored our mail. And when we went to Seattle, we had to be accepted into the United States. They treated us like foreigners. And this burned us all up.

I made myself a hero once during all of this. I had flown to Seattle, where I was expected to produce identification to prove I was a citizen before I could leave the airport. When I went to the window, however, I said I did not have any identification. That was not true, but I was trying to make a point. Well, they didn't know what to do with me, so they pleaded with me to produce something—anything—as identification. So I pulled out a permit that I had which allowed me to leave trash at the Anchorage garbage dump. When they let me through on that, I wrote a story about it, printed it on the front page of my newspaper, and from then on lots of people who went to Seattle took along garbage-dump ID to get through the silly gate.

When the war ended, the talk of statehood began to get serious. It was a gradual thing at first and it was not favored by everyone, but in my case I was persuaded for a couple of reasons. One, I wanted the people in Alaska to get the national respect they deserved, and, two, I argued about it with Ernest Gruening over a period of time and I came to agree with him completely. Gruening was the territorial governor, and a great man in my book, and he was a strong champion of statehood. He said that it would bring about development; he said it would guarantee a progressive future for Alaska; and he said it would also help the people break away from the grip of the canned salmon industry.

The salmon industry was the most powerful private entity in the territory. And the people who controlled it also controlled all of the economics in the territory, as well as the politics. I think the industry employed fifteen thousand people directly, or something like that, and most of the people who worked in small business were also beholden. The salmon industry did not want statehood, of course. They did not want to lose any of their power. I remember covering the legislature at the close of the war, and there was no doubt Gruening was right. I saw how the salmon industry manipulated the legislators; I saw how it got exactly what it wanted; and from then on I was sold on statehood. We had to have it.

That put me at odds with a lot of people. All of my friends in the establishment supported the salmon industry and opposed statehood. My father-in-law, the man who lent me the money to buy the newspaper, his bank did a lot of business with the salmon industry. So I was a maverick. And I admit I proceeded cautiously at first. But I did start selling people on the idea, and as I did I got bolder and bolder, and louder and louder, and soon a bandwagon started to form in the territory. I got pretty quick support from newspapers like *The Ketchikan Chronicle*. Bill Baker over there jumped right in. My wife [Evangeline] also made up her mind for statehood, and that was a great personal help. Things had started, we were on our way.

It took quite a while to get anywhere, of course. Because, there was this powerful opposition. The salmon industry said statehood would hurt business (because the state would then control fisheries), and people were afraid of losing their jobs. *The Juneau Empire* was opposed. *The News Miner* in Fairbanks was opposed; *The Sitka Sentinel* was opposed. Most of the little newspapers in the territory were also opposed, because they were so close to the fishermen and the canneries. We had lots of bad words on the subject. Many politicians condemned it, because that's what they were told to do by the salmon people. Everyone argued about it. Some people didn't know who or what to believe. And, naturally, we didn't have any help from Washington.

I don't think Washington cared about it one way or another at first. Alaska did not have a lot of political influence there. We had one delegate to Congress, but he was not allowed to vote. So we had to go to Washington to generate interest. Gruening appointed a statehood committee, and the members of the committee elected me as chairman, and one of my principal duties was to go to Washington as many as five times a year to lobby and to peddle the idea of statehood in the House and the Senate. I had to attend hearings and buttonhole officials, and all those things. Meanwhile, the salmon industry was doing the same thing; the industry hired a lot of lawyers and spent big money in Washington to fight us every step of the way.

I remember the salmon lawyers got to one fellow in particular. He was Senator Hugh Butler of Nebraska. I never really understood his motives, but he didn't like anything about statehood. He ranted and raved for years. I argued with him so many times that we got to be good friends. The canned salmon people also got to Dwight Eisenhower in the White House. They surrounded Ike with anti-statehood people. The secretary of the interior under Eisenhower was anti-statehood, and the Eisenhower appointees who administered the territory were anti-statehood. Harry Truman had supported us when he was in office, but when Eisenhower arrived we found that all of our normal channels for moving around the federal government were abruptly closed.

It got so bad then that I decided I had to see Eisenhower personally. We had gotten the statehood bill introduced years before, but it was not going anywhere under Ike's administration. So I asked for and got an appointment. But, technically, it was not to discuss statehood. I was put on the schedule because I was an out-of-town newspaper publisher. When I went to the White House I was delivered to Jim Hagerty, who was Ike's press secretary, and he said to me, "Now, Bob, I know why you're in Washington, but your meeting with the president is just a courtesy call." He said I was only there to pay my respects, period, and that I would not be permitted to say anything about anything unless the president mentioned it first.

Then we went in to the Oval Office. And the three of us were sitting there. I was facing Ike, and Hagerty was at the side, staring at me. He was there to make sure I behaved myself. Well, we started talking. I had known Ike from before, actually. He had been to Alaska, and we had dinner together then, and we had lots to talk about. He started recollecting everything about Alaska, what he'd done on his visits, and that sort of thing. And all of a sudden, out of the blue, he said, "You know, Bob, about this statehood thing. I'm really for that, but I just can't get out front on it." Well, I looked at Hagerty, and he looked at me, and everyone sort of relaxed. I guess we spent the next twenty or thirty minutes talking about statehood.

I came out of the meeting all fired up. That was the first time Ike had mentioned statehood favorably since he was elected. He said that one of the reasons that he was not taking an active role for statehood was that the military had designs in the territory. They were looking around for missile and defense installations and they did not want to have to deal with a state government. So that was the hangup. The federal government needed the unencumbered use of some of the territorial land. I immediately contacted Senator Butler. I also got together with everyone else who had anything to do with the statehood issue. I said that if we could resolve the problem with the military, then Eisenhower would no longer stand in the way of statehood.

It took a long time to resolve the problem. We had a lot of meetings with a lot of people, and out of this came the so-called Yukon-Porcupine Line agreement. It stated that the new state could not select any of its lands north of the Yukon and Porcupine rivers without special permission from the federal government. That area was where Eisenhower and the military were wheeling and dealing with the defense installations. Well, it satisfied Ike, and after that he became gung-ho for statehood. Then a new secretary of the interior was appointed, who was for our cause, and who incidentally was a newspaperman from Nebraska. A lot of other influential people got aboard, and, after fifteen very long years of trying, that's the way we got statehood.

"He is a weird combination of menace, obscenity, elegance and genuine distrust of everything that moves."

HELL'S ANGELS

1965
Bass Lake, California

HUNTER S. THOMPSON

Like a pack of bikers overtaking a car on the highway, outlaw motorcycle clubs appeared out of nowhere after World War II. Hunter S. Thompson, one of the first journalists to get close to the best-known club, the Hell's Angels, said, "There were thousands of veterans in 1945 who flatly rejected the idea of going back to their prewar pattern. They didn't want order, but privacy—and time to figure things out. It was a nervous, downhill feeling, a mean kind of angst that always comes out of wars . . . a compressed sense of time on the outer limits of fatalism. They wanted more action, and one of the ways to look for it was on a big motorcycle. By 1947 the state was alive with bikes. . . ."

Motorcycle registrations jumped, in less than twenty years, from fewer than 200,000 to more than 1.5 million. Because the California climate and long stretches of highway were perfect for motorcycles, it had about a quarter of all the registered riders.

In 1947, 3,000 bikers showed up for what had previously been a small July

Fourth motorcycle race in a sleepy California town. The town's seven-man police force couldn't control them. The bikers raced through town, got drunk, began to brawl, and terrorized the residents. The riot caught the attention of movie producer Stanley Kramer, who used it as the basis of The Wild One, starring Marlon Brando and Lee Marvin. The movie didn't start the outlaw club phenomenon, as many have claimed, but it certainly influenced the bikers and would-be bikers, who were happy to think of themselves, Thompson said, as "modern Robin Hoods . . . virile, inarticulate brutes whose good instincts got warped somewhere in the struggle for self-expression and who spent the rest of their violent lives seeking revenge on a world that done them wrong when they were young and defenseless."

The Hell's Angels grew out of those early clubs. They were founded in Fontana, east of Los Angeles in San Bernardino County, in 1950. By 1965, when Thompson wrote this account, the club was centered in Oakland.

This account of a trip to a weekend gathering of bikers comes from Thompson's book Hell's Angels, which established his place as a favorite writer of his generation.

Somewhere around two in the afternoon I reached the smooth pavement of Highway 41, just south of Bass Lake. I was flipping the radio dial for bulletins when I passed a hot dog stand and saw two outlaw bikes parked conspicuously beside the road. I made a U-turn, parked beside the bikes and found Gut and Buzzard brooding over the restraining order. Buzzard, formerly of Berdoo, is a Hell's Angel straight out of Central Casting. He is a weird combination of menace, obscenity, elegance and genuine distrust of everything that moves. He turns his back on photographers and thinks all journalists are agents of the Main Cop, who lives in a penthouse on the other side of some bottomless moat that no Hell's Angel will ever cross except as a prisoner—and then only to have his hands chopped off as a lesson to the others. There is a beautiful consistency about Buzzard; he is a porcupine among men, with his quills always flared. If he won a new car with a raffle ticket bought in his name by some momentary girl friend, he would recognize it at once as a trick to con him out of a license fee. He would denounce the girl as a hired slut, beat up the raffle sponsor, and trade off the car for five hundred Seconals and a gold-handled cattle prod.

I enjoy Buzzard, but I have never met anyone outside the Angels who thought he deserved anything better than twelve hours of the bastinado. One morning when Murray was doing his research for the Post article I assured him it would be safe to go over to Barger's house in Oakland for an interview. Then I went back to sleep. Several hours later the phone rang, and it was Murray, yelling with rage. He'd been talking quietly with Barger, he said, when suddenly he was confronted by a wild-eyed psychotic who shook a knotty cane under his nose and shouted, "Who the fuck are you?" The assailant's description didn't fit any Angel I'd ever met, so I called Sonny and asked what had happened. "Aw hell, it was just Buzzard," he said with a laugh. "You know how he is."

Indeed. Anyone who has ever met Buzzard knows how he is.

. . . My first encounter with Buzzard was at the hot dog stand just out of Bass Lake. He and Gut were sitting at a patio table, pondering the five-page legal document they'd been handed moments earlier. "They have a roadblock down by Coarsegold," said Gut. "Everybody who comes through gets one of these—and they take your picture when they give it to you."

"That dirty sonofabitch," said Buzzard.

"Who?" I asked.

"Lynch, that bastard. [Attorney General Thomas Lynch.] This is his work. I'd like to get my hands on that cheap-ass punk." He suddenly shoved the document across the table. "Here, you read this. Can you tell me what it means? Hell no, you can't! Nobody could make sense of this shit!"

The thing was titled: ORDER TO SHOW CAUSE WHY PRELIMINARY INJUNCTION SHOULD NOT ISSUE AND TEMPORARY RESTRAINING ORDER MADE. It named as plaintiff "The People of the State of California," and as defendants "John Does 1 through 500, Jane Does 1 through 500, individually and as associated under the name and style of HELL'S ANGELS OR ONE PERCENTERS, or COFFIN CHEATERS, or SATAN'S SLAVES, or IRON HORSEMEN, or BLACK AND BLUE, or PURPLE AND PINK, or RED AND YELLOW, unincorporated associations."

The intent of the order was clear, but the specific language was as vague and archaic as the list of defendants, which must have been taken from some yellowed newspaper clipping dating from the late fifties. What it amounted to was a temporary injunction. . . . To Buzzard's vast amusement, I couldn't explain what the document meant. (Nor, several weeks later, could a San Francisco lawyer who tried to interpret it for me.) As it turned out, the Madera County police couldn't explain it either, but their roadside translation was relatively clear: at the first sign of trouble, everybody on a motorcycle would be clapped in jail and denied bond.

Gut seemed more depressed than angry at this turn of events. "Just because I have a beard," he muttered, "they want to put me in jail. What's this country coming to?" I was trying to think of an answer when a Highway Patrol car drove up to within ten feet of where we were sitting. I hastily wrapped the court order around the can of beer I was drinking.

The two cops just sat there and stared at us, a shotgun mounted in front of them on the dashboard. A high-pitched dispatcher's voice crackled urgently from their radio, telling of various Hell's Angels movements:

"No arrests reported in Fresno . . . group of twenty stopped at road-block west of Bass Lake . . ."

I made a point of talking to my tape recorder, hoping the sight of it would keep them from shooting all three of us if the radio suddenly ordered them to "take appropriate action." Gut slumped in his wooden chair, sipping an Orange Crush and staring off at the sky. Buzzard seemed to quiver with rage, but he kept himself under control. The surface resemblance between the two was striking: both tall, lean, dressed for the road, but neither looking particularly scraggy—beards trimmed, medium-long hair, and neither with any sign of weaponry or weird extras. Without the Hell's Angels' insignia they wouldn't have attracted any more attention than a couple of touring hipsters from L.A.

. . . The three of us were still sitting there, talking aimlessly, when the patrol car suddenly jumped backward, made a tight circle in the parking lot and zoomed off down the highway. I quickly finished my beer and was packing up the tape recorder when there was a tremendous sound all around us. Seconds later, a phalanx of motorcycles came roaring over the hill from the west. Both Gut and Buzzard rushed toward the highway, waving and shouting happily. The road was dense with bikes. The hot dog stand was on the crest of a hill above Bass Lake; it was the last geographic barrier between the Angels and their destination. The police, in their wisdom, had managed to pile up at least a hundred bikes at the roadblock—where the restraining orders were ceremoniously handed out—and then release them all at once. So instead of arriving in quiet knots, the outlaws crested the hill in a great body . . . howling, hooting, waving bandanas and presenting the citizens with a really terrifying spectacle. The discipline of the highway had broken down entirely; now it was madness. The sight of Gut and Buzzard cheering beside the road caused Little Jesus to fling his hands in the air and utter triumphant screams. His bike veered off to the right and nearly collided with Charger Charley the Child Molester. An Angel I had never seen came by on an orange three-wheeler, kicking his feet straight out like a rodeo rider. Andy from Oakland who has no driver's license, came by with his wife sitting in front of him on the gas tank, ready to grab the handlebars at the first sight of the fuzz. The noise was like a landslide, or a wing of bombers passing over. Even knowing the Angels, I couldn't quite handle what I was seeing. It was like Genghis Khan, Morgan's Raiders, The Wild One and the Rape of Nanking all at once. Both Gut and Buzzard leaped on their bikes and roared off to join the pack.

. . . The outlaws weren't exceeding the speed limit, but they were gearing down noisily and zooming four abreast through the curves, yelling and waving at people beside the road . . . doing everything possible to inject the maximum degree of civic trauma into their arrival. If I had been a citizen of Bass Lake at the time I would have gone home and loaded every gun I owned.

In 1969, at a Woodstock-style rock festival held in nearby Altamont, the Angels were hired as security, perhaps to prevent them from causing trouble. Bad decision. During the concert they stabbed a man to death. The outcry that followed contributed to the decline of the club over the next few years.

"We had overheard the sirens outside,
all the calling, hollering, and screaming. . . ."

WATTS

August 11–16, 1965
Los Angeles

"MEL" AND ELDRIDGE CLEAVER

During World War II and in the decades that followed, the African American population of California increased twentyfold. In certain Bay Area cities, like Oakland and Richmond, African Americans became the major influence in government and business. But that didn't happen in Los Angeles because of the all-encompassing boundaries of the metropolitan city. Los Angeles became an extreme example of the ethnic divisions affecting the whole country.

Until the Los Angeles police were videotaped while beating motorist Rodney King in 1990 (see page 448), this riot in Watts was the most dramatic event in the black community's postwar history. It began when a white policeman stopped a black driver, and turned into a week of violence and looting. In all, 34 people were killed and more than 1,000 injured. Damage was estimated at $200 million.

The riot contrasted with the nonviolent efforts led by civil rights activists like Dr. Martin Luther King, Jr., whose Selma-to-Montgomery march had occurred the previous March. But it was not an isolated incident. Two years later similar riots broke out across the country, during what came to be called "the long, hot summer."

The pseudonymous eyewitness "Mel" was interviewed by sociologist Paul Bullock. Eldridge Cleaver, who went on to become minister of information for the

"MEL"

We were all in the house watching television, and . . . we heard over the news that there was a riot in Watts, that peoples were burning up and looting. We had overheard the sirens outside, all the calling, hollering, and screaming, and peoples hollering "Whitey, kill Whitey," and all this different stuff, so my girl friend's mother wouldn't let me out of the house. My girl friend's sister's boy friend was over, so myself and him and his brother, we tried to get out the house; we tried to sneak out the house. We finally sneaked out after everyone had went to bed that night.

So, across over on Imperial and Central, over a gas station called United gas station, there was a liquor store called Rocket. Peoples started running from the project, from across Imperial over, getting, just taking what they want, anything, all kinds of liquor, just from the store. This upset my mind, you know; I never seen anything like this. But at first I was really frightened, because I had heard about riots in other countries, but never a riot in America. Never had I realized what a riot really was. So I went in the store, and I was panicky. Everybody was knocking down, peoples grabbing stuff, grabbing wine, bottles, beer; stuff was all over the floor; people were just taking what they want.

Little kids was all out on the streets. Peoples were shooting guns, and the sky was just black, like the world was going to come to an end. People was running out, and there was this one lady, she was hollering, "Stop, you peoples don't know what you're doin'," and all this different stuff. It was in the afternoon, and people were coming from work, I guess. They was white people, Caucasian people coming from work, and they would have to take this route to get to Bellflower or South Gate, down Central and Avalon. And this was just horrible because colored peoples over there they just took advantage of them. They even detoured the buses through the projects, and why they do this, I do not know, because I was giving it up. They was just telling them, "Come on, you can do anything you want" . . . and it was horrible; I just didn't think stuff like that would exist, and I heard of wars and all this. . . .

People was turnin' over people's cars. . . . They ran over to the gas station, on Imperial; they took over the man's gas station, United. They started takin' gas out of the pump, putting 'em in Coca-Cola bottles, and beer bottles, and anything they could, big jugs, and scratchin' a match, and puttin' it to it, and throwin' it to a car, and blowin' it up, taking alcohol and making cocktail bombs out of 'em, whatever you want to call 'em, and just catch a car on fire in a matter of seconds. . . .

I saw cars with kids, this is what made me want to stop, because I saw little kids, seven or eight years old, Caucasian kids, in the cars flying down the street. Their fathers, their mothers, were driving; they had big holes in their heads, and all the windows were broken out of their cars. Peoples were hollering: every time a car would come by, everybody would jump over the fence and run at it, and it would look like a torch or something, like someone putting you in a room and just throwin' down on you with bottles, and bricks, and cans, anything they had, sticks. I saw one boy run after a car and had a big two by four in his hand, and the man came out, he was shooting a gun. He was just starting to shoot; the boy, he hit him across the head with the two by four and five or six other ones just beat him to death, beat him so bad, they beat all the clothes off of him. He was beaten badly. They tore all his clothes off him, the skin all off his back, all off the side of his face. It was just horrible.

I will be truthful with you. About two or three days after the thing happened, everybody was getting what they could get; I figure, well, I might as well get all what I could get. So people started talking about they coming down 103rd; they was burning up 103rd. They said the whole 103rd was on fire. This I could not believe. They said they was running into the pawn shop, getting guns, rifles, and machetes, all this other thing; so myself and a friend of mine and my brother-in-law we went to walking down 103rd; we saw these peoples running with suits in their hands; I never owned a suit in my life, and this just excited me. And when I got there, everybody was running with stuff, tape recorders, and record players; people were—even little kids—pushing washing machines down the street. And the first thing I saw was a stamp machine, a government stamp machine, and I thought about all the dimes that was in that stamp machine, and I pulled the stamp machine off the wall in the liquor store. And by the time I tore it off, all the dimes fell on the floor, there wasn't any dimes left because everybody else beat me to these dimes. Everybody pushed me out of the way, so I didn't get but maybe thirty, forty cents worth of dimes. So I saw a chance to get me a couple record players; I took those and then went over to Shop Rite market and got a little stuff.

. . . It was just horrible. If I could do it all over again, I don't think I would do anything, because after I looked at the television and looked at everything, looked at how the smoke was smoking, it looked like the world was coming to an end; I was sitting out in my front yard wondering what tomorrow was going to hold. And that Saturday, that whole weekend, people just took what they want; they just ran all the white peoples away from Watts as far as they could; just tore it up. Just drank it; wine, the winos had so much wine till they couldn't drink: the dope addicts had so much dope, they couldn't smoke it all. They couldn't take it all. The hypes had all they could have, and it was just a free for all, for everybody. And at the time, myself, I didn't have enough because I was scared. I was really scared.

ELDRIDGE CLEAVER

As we left the Mess Hall Sunday morning and milled around in the prison yard, after four days of abortive uprising in Watts, a group of low riders [street toughs] from Watts assembled on the basketball court. They were wearing jubilant, triumphant smiles, animated by a vicarious spirit by which they, too, were in the thick of the uprising taking place hundreds of miles away to the south in the Watts ghetto.

"Man," said one, "what they doing out there? Break it down for me, Baby."

They slapped each other's outstretched palms in a cool salute and burst out laughing with joy.

"Home boy, them Brothers is taking care of Business!" shrieked another ecstatically.

Then one low rider, stepping into the center of the circle formed by the others, reared back on his legs and swaggered, hunching his belt up with his forearms as he'd seen James Cagney and George Raft do in too many gangster movies. I joined the circle. Sensing a creative moment in the offing, we all got very quiet, very still, and others passing by joined the circle and did likewise.

"Baby," he said, "they walking in fours and kicking in doors; dropping Reds and busting heads; drinking wine and committing crime, shooting and looting; high-siding and low-riding, setting fires and slashing tires; turning over cars and burning down bars; making [Police Chief William] Parker mad and making me glad; putting an end to that "go slow" crap and putting sweet Watts on the map—my black ass is in Folsom this morning but my black heart is in Watts!" Tears of joy were rolling from his eyes.

It was a cleansing, revolutionary laugh we all shared, something we have not often had occasion for.

Watts was a place of shame. We used to use Watts as an epithet in much the same way as city boys used "country" as a term of derision. To deride one as a "lame," who did not know what was happening (a rustic bumpkin), the "in-crowd" of the time from L.A. would bring a cat down by saying that he had just left Watts, that he ought to go back to Watts until he had learned what was happening, or that he had just stolen enough money to move out of Watts and was already trying to play a cool part. But now, blacks are seen in Folsom saying, "I'm from Watts, Baby!"—whether true or no, but I think their meaning is clear. Confession: I, too, have participated in this game, saying, I'm from Watts. In fact, I did live there for a time, and I'm proud of it, the tired lamentations of Whitney Young, Roy Wilkins, and The Preacher [Martin Luther King, Jr.] notwithstanding.

A commission was formed to determine the cause of the riot. Its findings, which included a call for better relations between the black community and the police, were not much different from conclusions of the commission that investigated the Rodney King riots in 1992—a sign that little had been done in the meantime.

"The First Great Psychedelic Age begins. . ."

THE GRATEFUL DEAD

1966–1967
San Francisco

ROCK SCULLY

As the Beat Generation turned into the psychedelic sixties, a folk-rock band, the Grateful Dead, became the hub of the music and social scene. The Dead hung out with writers Neal Cassady and Alan Ginsberg and played at Ken Kesey's Acid Tests. They gave free concerts in San Francisco during 1967's "Summer of Love." They played at Woodstock in 1969.

The band's musical and spiritual center was Jerry Garcia, who started out as a Bay Area banjo prodigy with a taste for Beat literature and the bohemian lifestyle. After a short stint in the army—he enlisted, but was dishonorably discharged within months—he began playing in coffeehouses. There he met Ron "Pigpen" McKernan, a keyboardist, and Bob Weir, a guitarist, and the three formed a band, Mother McCree's Uptown Jug Champions. The group evolved through different rosters and names, eventually including bassist Phil Lesh, drummers Bill Kreutzmann and Mickey Hart, and poet Robert Hunter as a lyricist.

Defying the vagaries of popular culture and the hard facts of medical science, the Dead survived through several musical fads and potent combinations of controlled substances, becoming the most popular touring band of the 1980s and

1990s. *They were the single biggest entertainment draw in the country, playing long, ad-libbed concerts to crowds of "Deadheads," many of whom followed them from city to city.*

This account, by longtime Dead manager Rock Scully, comes from his memoir Living with the Dead, *written with music reporter David Dalton.*

By fall of 1966 we're back from Lagunitas and nearly the whole band has moved into 710 [Ashbury]. It is at this moment—take note, ye Deadbase scribes!—that the First Great Psychedelic Age begins. Not the Broadway Age of Aquarius with show tunes, but the Merry Prankster, rock 'n' roll, Haight-Ashbury version. If there ever is a Haight-Ashbury theme park—and I'm betting there will be—it'll have 710 as its epicenter. Deadland! It will always be 1967, the streets filled with Hell's Angels, hippie chicks, patchouli, communes, and antiwar demonstrations. Everywhere, like little Latin Santa Clauses, there'll be Jerry Garcia impersonators in black T-shirts and motorcycle boots, smoking joints and dispensing Cheech and Chong-like koans. And outside the gates of Deadland, the evil empire of the UnDead: the uncool, unhip, unhigh ones of the straight world.

At 710 we have the whole house to ourselves, but everybody is still piled on top of everybody else. There isn't a nook, cranny, or ratty armchair that someone hasn't claimed for a bed. The front room downstairs is an office during the day and a bedroom at night. Weir sleeps there in the bay window, stretched out in an easy chair. Bob Matthews, who is also helping with our sound, is in the other one. These chairs don't recline so you have to stretch out stiff as a dead gunslinger to get any sleep. Rifkin is still in 710A in the basement, someone is crashing in the bay window upstairs, Pigpen's room is right behind the kitchen. Garcia's is the room at the top of the stairs, mine is the closet next to it. Up in the attic is Neal Cassady. He has a hammock slung from the rafters and a couple of planks laid down so you can walk without falling between the floor joists. Plus there's the various people just crashing here and there. There'd be Sue Swanson and Connie sleeping on the floor and Gary Jackson, one of the early high tech guitar guys, under the kitchen table.

"Uh, they're fumigating my house, man, okay if I just crash?" You wake up in the morning never knowing what is going to happen. Some freak shoving a bottle of water in your face more often than not dosed with LSD, and away you go, with no way to claim your day.

Even with the whole house finally to ourselves we can't fit everybody into 710 Ashbury, so Lesh and Kreutzmann live in another house up the street. And we have no sooner settled in than we are on the verge of losing the place. Because in the early days, before they begin to hassle us about dope, it is the sanitary conditions they nail us for. The tidy police are on their way and the place is a disaster area. The kitchen is a shambles. The freezer's been so permanently ice-bound that the latch that closes it no longer works. The old restaurant stove is so encased with grease and grime it looks like a rusty Balkan freighter in dry dock. The bathroom is a Sargasso Sea of moldy towels and dirty clothes, the bedroom's strewn with empty Spaghetti-O cans, wine bottles, and stale donuts. Old carpets and crumbling plaster, glass everywhere from broken windows (when someone forgot their key), and the ceiling is caving in from the attic. Nothing in the place has been upgraded for a hundred years. It still has working gas jets. It is so far offcode finding infractions will be easy. We are sitting ducks.

I am yelling at Garcia and Pigpen to get the place cleaned up before the Health Department gets here. I'm pleading with them, cajoling them, threatening them with total doom (like our parents would). "If we get busted we're gonna lose the house, and if we lose the house we won't have any place to live and then . . ." Out of the corner of my eye I see Jerry, leaning on the bannister, eyeing me intently. It isn't that he has any intention of *doing* anything, he's just spellbound by my jeremiad. He's got an idea.

"Say, maaan," says Jerry, "why don't we just tell them the truth?"

"Which is?"

"We're time-traveling gunslingers from the planet Zircon and our transporter beam ran out of, you know, aludium fozdex, so we're stuck here. . . ."

Meanwhile out on the porch my girlfriend Tangerine is trying to tell the Health Department guys that the reason the place is such a mess is because we're, uh, renovating.

. . . A key gig is the long-planned Acid Test Graduation Ceremony. [Ken] Kesey has been in Mexico much of the year, a fugitive from the FBI and the San Francisco police after faking his suicide. He obviously isn't going to be able to attend any kind of Acid Test in the flesh. The moment he walks onstage there are going to be a dozen guys in shiny black shoes and white socks just waiting to nab him. Still, it is a tempting scenario for a Prankster: to tweak their noses in plain view of a thousand freaks high on acid. How to pull it off: Kesey gets this wild idea. He will be there and he will *not* be there. A sort of lysergic transubstantiation. The perfect McLuhanesque fake-out. And where better to pull off his Houdini hoax than at San Francisco State College—Acid U. itself! Plans are laid. Word goes out, handbills get passed, posters go up. It's going to be the social event of the season!

Now he makes plans to get back into the States. A typical over-the-top Ken Kesey movie. Drunk cowboy singer Jim Englund Jr., out of Las Vegas, has been boozing it up in Mexico all night, gets rolled outside the cantina (hence no I.D.) and comes across the border early in the morning. Kesey rents a horse, douses himself with gin, ingesting quite a bit of it along the way, and comes weaving across the Brownsville bridge, playing his souvenir guitar and singing old Gene Autry songs. Dressed up as foolish as a dude rancher—cowboy hat, buckskin jacket, shiny red dude boots—and stinking of booze. The customs guys don't even ask him to get off his horse, they just wave him on through. He is obviously American, and you don't need a driver's license to ride horseback. He just rolls off on the other side, gives a kid a few bucks to take the horse back, gets on a Greyhound to Salt Lake City, and then flies into San Francisco airport right under the noses of the carabinieri.

Meanwhile, we begin setting up the Trips Festival in the Commons at San Francisco State. A big cavernous cafeteria. We take all the tables and pile them up, fold the chairs and stack them in a corner, put up big screens, hang banners, and build a mini-tower in the middle of the floor. An industrial-strength Acid Test.

Everyone jamming, hammering, cabling, constant soldering going on. We get a bunch of big square boxes and pile them up and put TVs on top of them. Live cameras placed around the room. There's one on the band and one showing people dancing and another one right at the door so you can see who's coming in. Strobes, liquid lights, plus there are the slides playing all over the walls. The Dead set up in the corner right on the inside of the big glass doors as you walk in. No stage, we just set up on the floor.

Even the narcs have dressed up for the occasion in their Ironsides-goes-to-the-hippie-club outfits. But where's the Cat in the Hat? The instructions are: Bring a portable radio with you. You can't get in without one. The emcee then tells everybody to tune into KSFS, the San Francisco State station, and when you tune in—there's Kesey! He's broadcasting from some unknown location—only a couple of buildings away—but it's as if he's in the room. The Shadow knows! He is calling the shots like your favorite zonked-out sports broadcaster, walking around the Olympics and doing a running commentary on all the events. "If you'll just proceed to stage right you'll find Mr. Neal Cassady juggling his world-renowned hammer. . . . If you are wondering what all that equipment is in the center of the floor, so am I. The TVs were donated by Owsley Stanley."

The long, strange trip ended in August 1995 when Jerry Garcia died, felled by years of overdosing everything from high-grade heroin to candy bars. This editor was living next to the Polo Fields in San Francisco's Golden Gate Park on the day Garcia died, and saw the neighborhood fill up with people from all over the Bay Area who arrived for a spontaneous memorial where the band had played at the first "Be-In" of the sixties. The group disbanded soon after.

"...There is this illusion of abundance here...."

HIPPIES

1967
San Francisco

ALEX FORMAN

Forman moved to San Francisco in 1966, just as the wave of counterculture was peaking. He still lives there and works in a holistic health clinic.

This account comes from an interview he gave to Joan and Robert Morrison for their oral history of the sixties, From Camelot to Kent State.

When I came to San Francisco, the city was just exploding with this counterculture movement. I thought, "This is it!" It was like paradise there. Everybody was in love with life and in love with their fellow human beings to the point where they were just sharing in incredible ways with everybody. Taking people in off the street and letting them stay in their homes, breaking free of conventional morality. You could walk down almost any street in Haight-Ashbury where I was living, and someone would smile at you and just go, "Hey, it's beautiful, isn't it?" It was like people were high on the street and willing to share that energy. It was a very special time.

It was a whole other vision of what was possible. Rents were cheap and people were living in big communal groups, and we didn't have to work very hard. There was a sense that you didn't need very much, and that people who worked hard were just trapped into trying to acquire more and more possessions. People should just begin more to enjoy life, play music, dance, experience nature. We were going to raise our kids communally and all that stuff, and such attitudes would flourish even more. I thought this was the new world beginning right here—an alternative society—and this was where I wanted to be. So I stayed.

The first human Be-In was in January of '67 in Golden Gate Park.

That was a very high moment. People went and just kind of experienced. A lot of people were on LSD or peyote or marijuana. They played music, shared food, played drums, did American Indian chanting. You know, tie-dyed clothes, the whole thing. It all seems very trite now, but at the time it was all new. People were coming from all over the world to research it, to experience it. People from Czechoslovakia, Australia, Finland. It was a real phenomenon.

For a while I worked with a group in the Haight called the Diggers, who had a kind of a primitive communism view that was just "share all the wealth." The Diggers set up a free store, and people could just come in and take whatever they needed, and we fed people for free in the park. At one point I realized the absurdity of that when these people from the neighborhood, these older black women, came into the free store and said, "How much do these clothes cost in here?"

We said, "Oh, it's all free. You just take what you need, and then if you have extra, you give."

They said, "What do you mean, you just take what you need?"

"Well, you just take what you need, that's all."

They said, "Really?"

So they came back with these big boxes and they started just taking tons of stuff off the racks.

We said, "What are you doing?"

They said, "Well, you said take what you need."

We said, "Yeah, well, you don't need all those clothes for yourself."

They said, "No, but we need the money, so we're going to take the clothes and sell them."

They were in real scarcity, you know, they needed money, and here we were saying just take what you need for your own personal, immediate needs. But for them, that wasn't reality. Their reality was, "How are we going to get some money, and here's these foolish white people just letting us take whatever we need. Well, we need it all. We don't have anything."

That was the illusion of the whole hippie ethos, that there was this abundance. I think the hippie movement started in California—and was most powerful here—because there is this illusion of abundance here. Fruits were falling from the trees, rent was cheap, there were places to stay, the weather was tolerable even in the winter, there was a community of people who were into sharing. But there wasn't an abundance. There was an abundance at a certain time for certain people.

In early 1967, people would just give things away. On every street corner, there would be somebody giving things away, free food, a free place to stay. Then in the summer of '67 was the Summer of Love.

People started storming in by the thousands, and within three months there were people begging, "Do you have free food?" In other words, so many came that the surplus changed to scarcity. It got very ugly very fast. People got into really bad drugs like speed and heroin. There were ripoffs, violence, guns being drawn, people really malnourished, hepatitis, people living on the street with no place to stay.

I quickly saw then that the counterculture wasn't going to make it. It wasn't going to work. It was an illusion. And meanwhile the war was going on. It became more and more clear that you couldn't just set up little islands of peace and love in the middle of the Vietnam War.

"My parents' . . . only concern was that their children would not become hippies."

LIKE A ROLLING STONE

1967
San Francisco

BEN FONG-TORRES

Ben Fong-Torres's real family name was Fong, and both his parents were wholly Chinese. His father changed the name so he could immigrate with the false identity of a Filipino. For Ben and his siblings, like so many other children of immigrants, the question of culture was just as muddled. After facing a hundred years of discrimination in America, Asians had finally won all the rights of citizenship in the 1950s, but Ben Fong-Torres's generation was so American it faced a conflict at home. When Ben became a reporter for a new rock-'n'-roll magazine called Rolling Stone, *he had a hard time explaining himself to his parents.*

The reporter and radio personality wrote this account in his memoir, The Rice Room.

Unshackled from the corporate world, I dressed more casually than I even had in college. There, taking my role as an editor too seriously, I often showed up at the newspaper office in a white shirt and narrow tie. With my horn-rimmed glasses and short hair, I looked like some engineering student who'd stumbled into the wrong place.

Now, I took to blue work shirts and jeans. I switched to rimless glasses. I grew a moustache and I let my hair grow, leaving it unwashed for days at a time.

Still, like my siblings, I would manage to make my way over to Hayward and to the Bamboo Hut to work a few hours or an entire day on the occasional weekend. With [sister] Shirley married and in Texas, [brother] Burton took over most of the chores, while [brother] Barry and I made guest appearances.

When I showed up one Sunday that summer, my parents were not happy to see me. They did not mince words, and as soon as my mother saw me, she cried out: "*Ai-ya! Nay kawyeong!*" This has no direct English translation, but roughly meant, "You look like *that?*"

"Why so long?" she asked, indicating my hair and looking ashamed for me. "It looks not good." She didn't press the issue, but when she went into the kitchen, she told my father, and he came out to the dining room for a look.

It was the middle of the afternoon, and there were no customers.

"You look like a *girl,*" he snapped.

That's all it took. I turned, gave poor Burton a pat on the shoulder—he'd be working alone again—and drove back to San Francisco.

A few days later, Barry heard about the blowup and called. He, too, had grown a moustache, but he kept his hair at early Beatles length, with sideburns. He was a probation officer and subject to office policies.

"You should tell them it's a job requirement," he said, laughing.

"How do you say 'job requirement' in Chinese?" I asked. It was a rhetorical question. In Chinese, there are no requirements. You just showed up and worked.

"I know," said Barry. "I'll bring them some pictures of some *real* freaks. That should calm them down."

When I next visited home for my mother's birthday in August, the subject of hair-length was left undiscussed. But, then, so was almost every subject. We were incapable of talking about politics, the war, civil rights, or what young people were thinking. My parents, as far as I knew, didn't care. Their only concern was that their children would not become hippies.

When I joined *Rolling Stone,* I told them only that I was working at a newspaper in San Francisco that covered music. There was no easy way—and no point, really—telling them more. My parents tended to judge people on surface appearances. That's how they had treated Shirley's dates; how they responded to various friends of ours; and why Barry and I rarely talked about our dates. When Barry mentioned that he liked Kate, and that she was not Chinese, Mom had told him, "Please, don't. Sarah already upset us so much."

They meant well. Sure, they had their own concerns about *seet-meen,* the dreaded loss of face; they wanted us to be more Chinese, even if it meant being less American. But they were also concerned for us. They, too, knew about racism and knew that life would be easier for their sons and daughters if they weren't involved in interracial marriages.

I wished I could have engaged them in a real conversation about my feelings. I understand your concerns, I would have said. But I can't let your worries about how people in Chinatown look at you dictate how I live my life.

Here I am, in a profession few, if any, Asians have cracked, and race had absolutely nothing to do with my getting the job. That was true of my jobs at the phone company magazine, at the radio station, and in college.

Here I am, an editor at a magazine chronicling not only music but the massive social and cultural revolutions that are irrevocably changing our world. At the heart of the movement is an ideal, of a more just and equal society in which one recognizes differences in cultures, but doesn't discriminate because of those differences.

And here I am, writing about some of the most creative forces of our time, many of them rhythm and blues artists I have loved since first turning on Top 40 radio ten years ago.

This is who I am, and you're asking that I go out with only Chinese? I'm sorry, but I can't do that. And it's not because I need to rebel against you, to do the opposite of what you want. In an ideal world, I would love a woman who happened to be Chinese, and we'd all be happy. In reality, the women I'm seeing are people you wouldn't want to meet. They're good women, too. It's just too bad they've got that one thing wrong with them.

Once, I used the pages of *East West* [a weekly English-language tabloid for the city's Chinese community] to tear into my fellow Chinese—specifically, Chinese a generation older than me—for their racist ways. Somewhere in America, there were Chinese kids who did kowtow to their parents in the matters of professions and relationships. That kind of submission, I said, fostered perpetual racism and other biases. That was the kind of thinking, I wrote, that had to be wiped out "among people of all colors."

Seeing my raw anger in print, I was relieved that my parents couldn't read English. Barry could, and sent me a note from Hawaii, where he was spending a weekend with Kate. "Continue socking it to them," he said.

"You have to spend time with people, that's all."

CESAR CHAVEZ AND LA CAUSA

1968
Delano, California

PETER MATTHIESSEN

Farmworkers had been specifically excluded from the minimum wage laws passed during the New Deal. And their working conditions were inhumane, best illustrated by el cortito, "the short one," a short-handled hoe that forced the workers to bend to the ground, and often left them crippled for life. The overseers used it so they could know at a glance who was resting.

Union organizers had made only small gains with the workers despite years of trying. Then one of them met Cesar Chavez, a skeptical, second-generation farmworker. Chavez joined "La Causa" and went on to head it.

In Delano, named for the town where the union was headquartered, John Gregory Dunne wrote, "It was Robert Kennedy who legitimized Chavez. Prior to 1966, when the U.S. Senate Subcommittee on Migratory Labor held hearings in the [San Joaquin] Valley, no Democrat would touch the Chavez movement. . . . But he was persuaded to attend the hearings in March 1966 by one of his aides, Peter Edelman, acting in concert with a handful of union officials alive to the drama in Delano. Even while flying to California, Kennedy was reluctant to get involved, demanding of his staff, 'Why am I going?' He finally showed up at the hearings a day late. The effect was electric, a perfect meeting of complementary mystiques. Kennedy—ruthless, arrogant, a predator in the corridors of power. And Chavez—nonviolent, Christian, mystical, not without a moral imperative of his own. For the next two years, it was almost impossible to think of Chavez except in conjunction with Robert Kennedy. The Kennedys sponged up ideas, and implicit in Chavez was the inexorable strength of an idea whose time had come. Kennedy's real concern for the farmworkers helped soften his image as a self-serving keeper of his brother's flame and in turn plugged Chavez into the power outlets of Washington and New York. For the first time Chavez became fashionable, a national figure registering on the nation's moral thermometer. Robert Kennedy and Cesar Chavez—the names seemed wired into the same circuitry, the one a spokesman, the other a symbol for the constituency of the dispossessed."

This account by Peter Matthiessen was written shortly after Chavez led a successful nationwide boycott of grapes. It comes from the book he titled after the barrio where Chavez grew up: Sal Si Puedes—*"get out if you can."*

The man who has threatened California has an Indian's bow nose and lank black hair, with sad eyes and an open smile that is shy and friendly; at moments he is beautiful, like a dark seraph. He is five feet six inches tall, and since his twenty-five-day fast the previous winter, has weighed no more than one hundred and fifty pounds. Yet the word "slight" does not properly describe him. There is an effect of being centered in himself so that no energy is wasted, an effect of density; at the same time, he walks as lightly as a fox. One feels immediately that this man does not stumble, and that to get where he is going he will walk all day.

. . . In the days that followed, I was able to piece together the story of how Chavez became an organizer. Chavez, who described most of it himself, picketed the cotton fields at Corcoran for the National Agricultural Workers Union in 1946, when he was nineteen, and watched the union fail. Subsequently he would mutter about the frustrations of the poor to his wife, Helen, and his brother Richard, but he saw no way to put his outrage into action until 1952. That year he and Richard lived across the street from each other in San Jose, and worked together in the apricot groves. The Los Angeles headquarters of Saul Alinsky's Community Service Organization wanted to set up a chapter there, and among the names given to the CSO organizer by the parish priest, Father Donald McDonnell, was that of Cesar Chavez.

"I came home from work and this gringo wanted to see me. In those days when a gringo wanted to see you, it was something special; we never heard anything from whites unless it was the police. So anyway, Helen says, 'Oh no, it must be something good for Mexicans—money and a better job and things!'" Chavez's expression conveyed what he had thought about promises of something good for Mexicans. "You see, Stanford University had people nosing around, writing all kinds of screwy reports about how Mexicans eat and sleep, you know, and a lot of dirty kind of stuff, and Berkeley had its guys down there, and San Jose State—all the private colleges; they were interested in the worst barrio, the toughest slum, and they all picked Sal Si Puedes."

"What?"

"Sal—"

"'Escape If You Can'?"

"Yah. That's what that barrio was called, because it was every man for himself, and not too many could get out of it, except to prison. Anyway, we were sick and tired of these people coming around asking stupid questions. I said to hell with him. Well, he came that day again and said he would come back in the evening, so when I got home I went across the street to Richard's house, and in a little while this old car pulled up and this gringo knocked on my door, and Helen told him I was working late or something. As soon as he left I came back and said, 'What happened?' and she said, 'He's coming tomorrow,' and I said, 'Well, I'm not going to be here tomorrow either.' So I came home from work and just dumped my lunch pail and my sweater and went over to Richard's house, and the same thing happened again. Helen said he was coming back tomorrow, and I said I wouldn't see him, and she said, 'Well, this time you tell him that, because I'm not going to lie to him any more.'

"So he came and talked to me. I was very closed, I didn't say a thing. I just let him talk. I'd say 'Yes' and nod my head, but half the time I was plotting how to get him. Still, there were certain things that struck me. One of them was how much I didn't like him even though he was sincere. I couldn't admit how sincere he was, and I was bothered by not being able to look at it. And the other thing was, he wore kind of rumpled clothes, and his car was very poor. And his flawless pronunciation of the Mexican language—that really impressed me. It's minor, I know, but I was impressed.

"Well, he wanted a meeting as soon as possible, and I said, 'How many people do you want?' and he said, 'Oh, four or five,' and I said, 'How about twenty?' 'Gee, that'd be great!' I had my little plan, you see. So I invited some of the rough guys in the barrio, and I bought some beer and told them how to handle it: when I switched my cigarette from my left hand to my right, they could start getting nasty."

The memory of his own behavior made Chavez frown. "These damn people used to talk about forty- or fifty-year patterns, and how did we eat our beans and tortillas, and whether we'd like to live in a two-bedroom house instead of a slum room, things like that. They try to make us real different, you know, because it spices up their studies when they do that. I thought this guy meant to snoop like all the rest. We didn't have anything else in our experience to go by; we were being pushed around by all these studies. So we were going to be nasty, and then he'd leave, and we'd be even. But I knew all the time that this gringo had really impressed me, and that I was being dishonest.

"So he came in and sat down and began to talk about farm workers, and then he took on the police and the politicians, not rabble-rousing either, but saying the truth. He knew the problems as well as we did; he wasn't confused about the problems like so many people who want to help the poor. He talked about the CSO and then the famous Bloody Christmas case a few years before, when some drunken cops beat up some Mexican prisoners down in L.A. I didn't know what the CSO was or who this guy Fred Ross was, but I knew about the Bloody Christmas case, and so did everybody in that room; some cops had actually been sent to jail for brutality, and it turned out that this miracle was thanks to the CSO.

"By this time a couple of guys began to get a little drunk, you know, and started to press me for some action. But I couldn't give the signal, because the gringo wasn't a phony.

"I mean, how could I—I couldn't do it, that's all. So some of them got nasty and I jumped in and said, 'Listen, the deal's off. If you want to stay here and drink, then drink, but if you can't keep your mouth shut, then get out.' They said I had chickened out, so I took them outside and explained. There were a couple of guys that still wanted to get this gringo, but anyway, the meeting continued, and he put everything very plainly. He did such a good job of explaining how poor people could build power that I could even taste it, I could feel it. I thought, Gee, it's like digging a hole; there's nothing complicated about it!" Sixteen years later, as he recalled this moment, there was still a note of discovery in Chavez's voice.

"You see, Fred was already an organizer when Alinsky hired him. I guess some of his theories came from Alinsky, but I learned everything from Fred. It was Fred who developed this technique of house meetings—Alinsky never used them.

"Anyway, I walked out with him to his car and thanked him for coming, and then I kind of wanted to know—well, what next? He said, 'Well, I have another meeting, and I don't suppose you'd like to come?' I said, 'Oh yes, I would.' I told the others I'd be right back, and I got in his car and went with him, and that was it.

"That first meeting . . . I'd never been in a group before, and I didn't know a thing. Somebody asked for a motion, and I didn't know what the hell they were talking about. I tried to get answers from my friends, and none of us knew. We were just a bunch of pachucos—you know, long hair and pegged pants. But Fred wanted to get the pachucos involved—no one had really done this—and he knew how to handle the difficulties that came up, and he didn't take for granted a lot of little things that other people take for granted when they're working with the poor. He had learned, you know. Finally I said, 'What about the farm workers?' and he said that the CSO could be a base for organizing farm workers, and it was a good prediction, not exactly as he envisioned it, but it came about."

Chavez laughed. "I was his constant companion. I used to get home from work between five and five-thirty, and he'd say, 'I'll pick you up at six-thirty, give you a little time to clean up and eat,' and I'd say, 'No, I don't want to clean up and eat, pick me up at five-thirty!' So he would be waiting when I got home from work, and I'd just drop my lunch pail and rush right out. I was observing how he did things, how he talked to people and how patient he was, and I began to learn. A lot of people worked with him, but few learned what I learned. I think the reason was that I had more need to learn than anybody else. I really had to learn. So I'd pay attention to the smallest detail, and it became sort of a—well, I'd use the word 'game' if it didn't throw a wrong light on it. It wasn't a job, and at the same time it was very, very important, trying to understand these things and then apply them."

Chavez first joined the CSO as a volunteer in a voter-registration drive: the organization of Mexican-American bloc voting was the first lesson in his understanding of a power base. "Most of the volunteers were college people, or had good jobs—very few were farm workers. I had a part-time job in a lumberyard. Voter registration depended on as many evenings as you could give, and soon so many people stopped showing up that we had to find a new chairman every day. Finally I was the only one who went with Fred every night, so he made me chairman.

"So here I am in charge, and where do I start? I can't go to the middle class, or even the aspiring middle class, for my deputy registrars; I have to go to my friends in Sal Si Puedes. So I round up about sixteen guys"—at the memory he began to smile—"and not one of them can qualify as a deputy registrar, not one. They can't even vote! Every damn one of these guys had a felony!" He laughed. "Well, they could still knock on doors, you know. . . . You have to spend time with people, that's all. If a man's interested, it makes no difference if he can read or write; he is a man."

" . . . We could see thick lines of police with gas masks already on."

STATE OF EMERGENCY AT "THE PEOPLE'S REPUBLIC OF BERKELEY"

May 1969
Berkeley, California

TOM HAYDEN

In the early 1960s the civil rights movement gained support from college students around the country, leading to the "Mississippi Summer" of 1964, when hundreds of young civil rights workers, many of them students, helped in a voter registration drive in that southern state.

Jack Weinberg, who had dropped out of a University of California at Berkeley doctoral program to devote his full energies to the civil rights effort, remembered people saying, "In the fall when the students return, things are really going to happen."

They were right. What happened at Berkeley was the Free Speech Movement, a protest against the university's refusal to allow social or political activism on campus. That action wasn't a surprise, because the school's charter required that it be apolitical; but when the school ruled that a sidewalk on the edge of campus, traditionally used for organizing, was now considered to be on school property, and therefore off-limits for organizers, the conflict began.

Students decided that they now wanted to be able to exercise free speech everywhere on campus—or, as some of them later said, they at least wanted to start negotiating from that position, so they could have their sidewalk back. But the university stiffened, so the students responded in kind. Loud demonstrations and sit-ins climaxed in a takeover of the school's central administration building in December. Over 750 protesters were arrested, the largest mass arrest in the state's history.

A student strike followed, and after a short shutdown of the university the faculty asked the administration to accept the demands of the protesters. It was an important activist victory. (And it gave the world Weinberg's famous line, which summed up most of the sixties: "Never trust anyone over thirty.")

"In the worried calculations of the establishment," wrote protester-turned-politician Hayden, "Berkeley occupied the same sinister, conspiratorial, and central role which, in their view, Havana played in the Third World. . . . From the free-speech movement forward, [it] continually set an example for movements across the country. To be in Berkeley was to feel yourself at the center of history being made."

In the late sixties, when civil rights activism turned to anti–Vietnam War protests, the mood at Berkeley, as at other campuses, became increasingly violent. In 1968, Hayden, seeking refuge from the riots that occurred at student protests during that summer's Democratic National Convention in Chicago, and awaiting trial for his alleged role in inciting those riots, visited Berkeley. He had a busman's holiday: Protests began when the university denied academic credit to students who had taken a course taught by Eldridge Cleaver, the Minister of Propaganda for the Black Panther party.

In February 1969, Ronald Reagan, then governor of California, declared a "state of extreme emergency" at Berkeley, and called in the National Guard.

The bloodiest 1969 confrontation, a precursor of Kent State and Jackson State one year later, took place over "People's Park," an acre of neglected vacant land belonging to the university just south of campus and one block from Telegraph. The university, it was believed, was quietly planning to transform the lot into a colorless mall, hoping to pressure away the legions of hippies, teenage runaways, sidewalk jewelers, and tarot readers, not to mention revolutionary leafleteers who dominated the once-respectable south-campus area. Instead one day, a group of quite gentle street people took up shovels and began making a community park out of the littered and unused lot. Their act caught on, and over several weekends a growing number labored, hammered, and planted grass until a charming, green, little gathering place came into existence, with plenty of benches for relaxing, and swings and building blocks for kids. Tambourines and flutes played into the night as the builders took pride in their creation. Stew Albert and Judy Clavir, two of the most political Yippies, drew me into this creation of "turf." I helped a little with the manual labor, enjoying this refreshing respite from the usual wars with the system. Many political radicals viewed the park project as a hippie cop-out from serious revolutionary work, and a lively debate developed over where the life-style component fit into one's agenda. This inquiry was cut short rather quickly, however, since the university looked with growing distress at this unauthorized urban beautification project. They would not tolerate it, and we would not abandon the gardens and saplings just planted. To head off an irrational confrontation, several city officials and faculty leaders proposed negotiations with the university for a change of ownership of the $1.3 million property. The debate over the park drew such national figures as General William Dean, a Korean War commander who pushed a hard line, and Thomas Hoving, director of New York's Metropolitan Museum of Art, who urged creation of the new park. Meanwhile, a handful of local activists posted themselves in the park every night, sensing possible trouble.

With no warning, hard-line elements decided to move against the park, on the night of May 14. Captain Charles Plummer pulled his battle-ready Berkeley police together for a pep talk, declaring that they were "the last stronghold against the Commies, and today we are going to crush them." Just before dawn, Berkeley police officers, backed by a helicopter and 250 highway patrolman, marched into the park, forcing out the young people maintaining the watch. At five A.M., about fifty construction workers, protected by the police, erected an eight-foot-high chain link fence all the way around the block containing the park. Like many Berkeley activists, I was awakened early in the morning with phone calls recounting what happened. By eight A.M., many were standing in cold disbelief around the fence being spiked into the park they had built. Inside the fence, heavily protected Berkeley police lounged and laughed on the children's swings. According to the press, the university explained that the fence was installed "to make sure that the land was recognized as University property."

By noon, at least five thousand people were massed in nearby Sproul Plaza to protest the destruction of the park. Though an exact plan was never discussed, it was clear that the angered crowd would tear the fence down if they reached it. I was scheduled to speak on the steps of Sproul Hall and was wondering what to advise while I listened to student body president Dan Siegel. Dan called out something about the need to "take back the park"—and was drowned out by the impatient throng, who turned his phrase into a chant, and before our eyes began moving in a giant sea toward Telegraph Avenue and the three short blocks to the location of the park. Ahead of them, we could see thick lines of police with gas masks already on. They also held tear-gas launchers and shotguns. As the crowd walked and trotted toward their positions, the police began wafting canisters of gas, trailing a wisp of white smoke, at the front line. The marchers held, covering their eyes, and a few ran forward to pick up the hot canisters and hurl them back toward the police.

From this initial stand-off, there began seventeen consecutive days of street fighting, the longest such battle in American history, finally ending in a solemn and nonviolent march to the park fence by almost thirty thousand people. During those days, scenes of the Vietnam War were replayed on a college campus for the first time. The Alameda County sheriffs carried shotguns loaded, not only with birdshot but with deadly double-O buckshot, never before used against students. About 150 demonstrators were shot and wounded, many in the back. Seventy people were treated for gunshot wounds at local hospitals.

On May 15, the day the fence went up and we marched down Telegraph Avenue, a Berkeley freshman named Steve Carr climbed on the roof of an apartment building overlooking the skirmishes. Now a loan officer at Citibank in San Francisco, he remembered being a Naval ROTC student who was "curious about what was going on." He wanted to get above the tear gas, so he sat on a rooftop and watched. The sheriffs' response to the march had been immediate; they started opening fire on people. But then there was a lull, Carr recalled. A car was burning, but the avenue had quieted down. I was on the avenue, where debris, rocks, and overturned trash cans reflected a growing war zone. I was choking from the gas and yelling that people should move off the avenue, where they were easy targets. The police looked like armed and swaggering astronauts, slowly swiveling in the avenue with weapons pointed only a few feet away. Then Carr saw someone who'd thrown a brick from the rooftop twenty minutes earlier. "I turned and told him not to do it again. Then I felt a tremendous concussion, like a tear-gas canister." The sheriffs had spun and fired across four rooftops. Carr was hit with 125 pieces of birdshot; one pellet was less than a millimeter from his eye; another was lodged against his carotid artery. The individual sitting next to him, Alan Blanchard, was not lucky enough to have turned his head and was instantly blinded. Two roofs over, a twenty-five-year-old carpenter named James Rector was wounded and bleeding. All three waited over forty-five minutes in an apartment before being taken to the hospital, where Rector died twenty-four hours later.

On the day following Rector's death, a funeral march and vigil was met by a National Guard helicopter, which dropped white clouds of misty CS gas over Sproul Plaza. Several hundred faculty members started to boycott the university the next day, calling for the chancellor's resignation and charging that the campus was becoming an "experimental laboratory for the National Guard." The student paper demanded the closing of the university as "not safe for human beings."

On the other hand, Major General Glenn Ames, commander of the state National Guard, defended the helicopter drop of CS gas as "perfectly logical." Ronald Reagan had not yet made his famous statement— "If the students want a bloodbath, let's get it over with"—but the murderous precedent was established. (Reagan's bloodbath comment was made to the Council of California Growers on April 7, 1970—one month before Kent State.)

Steve Carr, whose father was a military officer, spent three days in an intensive care unit at Oak Knoll Naval Hospital, where an American soldier wounded in Vietnam slowly died next to him. He watched the rest of the Berkeley events on television among the war-wounded in the hospital and was released ten days later. He testified at a coroner's inquest and trial that he thought the policies of Ed Meese and the county sheriffs were an "extreme reaction." I went to visit Alan Blanchard shortly after he was shot, fighting off feelings of responsibility for what had happened to him. He was a blond, long-haired young man in his mid-twenties, an aspiring artist. But now he was uncomfortably rotating his head to locate me, trying to adjust to his sudden deprivation. Though still in shock at the sudden and random nature of his loss, he moved me by his acceptance of the life he now faced. I went away still feeling guilty.

> *"Los Angeles is . . . the worst reported*
> *of American cities. . . ."*

EUREKA!

JOHN GREGORY DUNNE

"Honi soit qui Malibu," F. Scott Fitzgerald once wisecracked. The world's obsession with Los Angeles, and with what appears to be an emphasis of style over substance, goes back to the early days of the film business. But who is being superficial? Not the Angelenos, according to author John Gregory Dunne, who moved from New York to California in 1964, and lived there for almost a quarter of a century. Because he and his wife, author Joan Didion, are known as much for their sharp social commentary as for their novels and screenplays, acquaintances "back east" often assume they share the common view of L.A. as "Lotusland": slow and mind-less. But, as usual, Dunne argues to the contrary, convincingly.

. . . Imagine: an Irish Catholic out of Hartford, Connecticut, two generations removed from steerage, with the political outlook of an alderman and social graces polished to a semigloss at the Hartford Golf Club. Imagine a traveler with this passport confronting that capital south of the Tehachapi called El Pueblo de Nuestra Senora la Reina de Los Angeles. My wife, Joan Didion, was a fifth-generation Californian and was in a sense returning home (although her real home was the equally impenetrable flatland of the Central Valley), but to me it was a new world: the new world. I watched Los Angeles television, listened to Los Angeles radio, devoured Los Angeles newspapers trying to find the visa that would provide entry. "Go gargle razor blades," advised a local talk show host pleasantly; it was a benediction that seemed to set the tone of the place. Dawn televised live on the Sunset Strip: A minister of the Lord inquired of a stringy-haired nubile what she liked doing best in the world. An unequivocal answer: "Balling." Another channel, another preacher. This one ascribed the evils of the contemporary liberal ethic to one "J. J. Russo." It was some time before I apprehended that the Italianate "J.J." was in fact Jean-Jacques Rousseau. In a newspaper I read of a man living on the rim of Death Valley who walked alone out into the desert, leaving behind a note that he wanted to "talk to God." God apparently talked back. The man was bitten by a rattlesnake and died.

Fundamentalism, the Deity, the elements—those familiar aides-memoire that titillate the casual visitor to the western shore. I did not need a pony to find the immediate subtext of banality and vulgarity. It took a long time, however, to learn that the real lesson in each of those parables was to quite another point. Los Angeles is the least accessible and therefore the worst reported of American cities. It is not available to the walker in the city. There is no place where the natives gather. Distance obliterates unity and community. This inaccessibility means that the contemporary de Tocqueville on a layover between planes can define Los Angeles only in terms of his own culture shock. A negative moral value is attached to the taco stand, to the unnatural presence of palm trees at Christmas (although the climate of Los Angeles at Christmas exactly duplicates that of Bethlehem), even to the San Andreas fault. Whenever she thought of California, an editor at *The New York Times* once told me, she thought of Capri pants and plastic flowers. She is an intelligent woman and I do not think she meant to embrace the cliche with such absolute credulity; she would have been sincerely pained had I replied that whenever I thought of New York I thought of Halston and Bobby Zarem. (My most endearing memory of this woman is seeing her at a party in New York, as always meticulously pulled together, except that the side seam on her Pucci dress had parted. The parted seam was the sort of social detail that marked her own reportage, which had a feel for texture absent in her a priori invention of a California overrun with plastic greenery.) "I would love to see you play with the idea of California as the only true source of American culture," she wrote my wife and me, fellow conspirators, or so she thought, in her fantasy of the western experience. "I mean, what other state would have pearlized, rainbow-colored plastic shells around its public telephones?"

Notice "plastic," that perfect trigger word, the one word that invariably identifies its user as culturally superior. When I arrived in California in 1964, the catch words and phrases meant to define the place were "smog" and "freeways" and "kook religions," which then spun off alliteratively into "kooky California cults." Still the emigre, I referred to my new country as "Lotusland"; it was a while before I realized that anyone who calls Los Angeles "Lotusland" is a functioning booby. In the years since 1964, only the words have changed. California is a land of "rapacious philodendron" and "squash yellow Datsuns," Marion Knox noted on the Op-Ed page of *The New York Times;* seven months in the Los Angeles bureau of *Time* seemed to Ms. Knox an adventure in Oz. "Angel dust." "The 'in' dry cleaner." "Men in black bathing suits, glossy with Bain de Soleil." (Perhaps a tad of homophobia there, a residual nightmare of Harry's Bar in Bloomingdale's.) "The place of honor at . . . dinner parties," Ms. Knox reported, "is next to the hotshot realtor." I wonder idly whose dinner parties, wonder at what press party do you find the chic hairdresser and the hotshot realtor. I also think I have never read a more poignant illustration of Cecilia Brady's line in *The Last Tycoon:* "We don't go for strangers in Hollywood."

In *Esquire,* Richard Reeves spoke of "ideas with a California twist, or twisted California ideas—drinking vodka, est, credit cards, student revolts, political consultants, skateboards . . ." An absurd catalogue, venial sins, if sins they be at all, some not even Californian in origin. Ivy Lee had the Rockefeller ear before the term "political consultant" was invented, not to mention Edward Bernays and Benjamin Sonnenberg, who were plugged into the sockets of power when normalcy was still an idea to be cultivated. And what is est after all but a virus of psychiatry, a mutation of the search to find one's self, passed west from Vienna via Park Avenue, then carried back again, mutated, on the prevailing winds. (Stone-throwing in glass houses, this kind of exchange, a Ping-Pong game between midgets, est on one coast, Arica on the other, vodka drinking in California, Plato's Retreat in Manhattan, lacquered swimmers on the Malibu, their equally glossy brothers three time zones east in Cherry Grove.) The trigger words meant to define California become a litany, the litany a religion. The chief priests and pharisees attending the Los Angeles bureaus of eastern publications keep the faith free from heresy. A year ago a reporter from *Time* telephoned my wife and said that the magazine was preparing a new cover story on California; he wondered if she had noticed any significant changes in the state since *Time's* last California cover.

Still they come, these amateur anthropologists, the planes disgorging them at LAX, their date books available for dinner with the hotshot realtor. They are bent under the cargo of their preconceived notions. "The only people who live in L.A. are those who can't make it in New York," I once heard a young woman remark at dinner. She was the associate producer of a rock 'n' roll television special and she was scarfing down chicken mole, chiles Jalapenos, guacamole, sour cream, cilantro and tortillas. "You cook New York," she complimented her hostess. "Mexico, actually," her hostess replied evenly, passing her a tortilla and watching her lather sour cream on it as if it were jam. Another dinner party, this for an eastern publisher in town to visit a local author. There were ten at dinner, it was late, we had all drunk too much. "Don't you miss New York?" the publisher asked. "Books. Publishing. Politics. Talk." His tone was sadly expansive. "Evenings like this."

The visitors have opinions, they cherish opinions, their opinions ricochet around the room like tracer fire. The very expression of an opinion seems to certify its worth. Socially acceptable opinion, edged with the most sentimental kind of humanism, condescension in drag. "Why can't you find the little guy doing a good job and give him a pat on the back?" the managing editor of *Life* once asked my wife. Little people, that population west of the Hudson, this butcher, that baker, the candlestick maker, each with a heart as big as all outdoors. Usually there is a scheme to enrich the life of this little person, this cultural dwarf, some effort to bring him closer to the theater or the good new galleries. Mass transit, say. I remember one evening when a writer whose subject was menopausal sexual conduct insisted that mass transit was the only means of giving Southern California that sense of community she thought it so sadly lacked. I did not say that I thought "community" was just another ersatz humanistic cryptogram. Nor did I say that I considered mass transit a punitive concept, an idea that runs counter to the fluidity that is, for better or worse, the bedrock precept of Southern California, a fluidity that is the antithesis of community. She would not have heard me if I had said it, for one purpose of such promiscuous opinionizing is to filter out the disagreeable, to confirm the humanistic consensus.

He who rejects the dictatorship of this consensus is said to lack "input." Actors out from New York tell me they miss the input, novelists with a step deal at Paramount, journalists trying to escape the eastern winter. I inquire often after input, because I am so often told that California (except for San Francisco) is deficient in it, as if it were a vitamin. Input is people, I am told. Ideas. Street life. I question more closely. Input is the pot-au-feu of urban community. I wonder how much input Faulkner had in Oxford, Mississippi, and it occurs to me that scarcity of input might be a benign deficiency. Not everyone agrees. After two weeks in California, a New York publishing figure told Dick Cavett at a party in New York, he felt "brain-damaged." Delphina Ratazi was at that party, and Geraldo Rivera. And Truman Capote, Calvin Klein, Charlotte Ford, George Plimpton, Barbara Allen with Philip Niarchos, Kurt Vonnegut, Carrie Fisher with Desi Arnaz Jr., Joan Hackett and Arnold Schwarzenegger. I do not have much faith in any input I might have picked up at that party.

"Go ahead and make your stand at Wounded Knee."

SIEGE AT WOUNDED KNEE

1973
Wounded Knee, South Dakota

MARY CROW DOG

Wounded Knee is a small village on the Pine Ridge Indian Reservation in south-western South Dakota, famous because the army massacred 200 Sioux there in 1890 for performing a religious ritual (see page 202).

In February 1973, 200 members of a civil rights activist group, the American Indian Movement, took control of Wounded Knee. AIM declared an "Independent Sioux Nation," and demanded a review of all government treaties and the replacement of the tribal leadership.

Mary Crow Dog's account of the 1973 siege comes from her autobiography, Lakota Woman, *written with Richard Erdoes.*

The Oglala elders thought that we all had been wasting our time and energies in Rapid City and Custer when the knife was at our throats at home. And so, finally and inevitably, our caravan started rolling toward Pine Ridge. [Tribal president Dicky] Wilson was expecting us. His heavily armed goons had been reinforced by a number of rednecks with Remingtons and Winchesters on gun racks behind their driver's seats, eager to bag themselves an Injun. The marshals and FBI had come too, with some thirty armored cars equipped with machine guns and rocket launchers. These were called APCs, Armored Personnel Carriers. The tribal office had been sandbagged and a machine gun installed on its roof. The Indians called it "Fort Wilson." Our movements were kept under observation and reported several times a day. Still we came on.

To tell the truth, I had not joined the caravan with the notion that I would perform what some people later called "that great symbolic act." I did not even know that we would wind up at Wounded Knee. Nobody did.

. . . There was still no definite plan for what to do. We had all assumed that we would go to Pine Ridge town, the administrative center of the reservation, the seat of Wilson's and the government's power. We had always thought that the fate of the Oglalas would be settled there. But as the talks progressed it became clear that nobody wanted us to storm Pine Ridge, garrisoned as it was by the goons, the marshals, and the FBI. We did not want to be slaughtered. There had been too many massacred Indians already in our history. But if not Pine Ridge, then what? As I remember, it was the older women like Ellen Moves Camp and Gladys Bissonette who first pronounced the magic words "Wounded Knee," who said, "Go ahead and make your stand at Wounded Knee. If you men won't do it, you can stay here and talk for all eternity and we women will do it."

When I heard the words "Wounded Knee" I became very, very serious. Wounded Knee—*Cankpe Opi* in our language—has a special meaning for our people. There is the long ditch into which the frozen bodies of almost three hundred of our people, mostly women and children, were thrown like so much cordwood. And the bodies are still there in their mass grave, unmarked except for a cement border. Next to the ditch, on a hill, stands the white-painted Catholic church, gleaming in the sunlight, the monument of an alien faith imposed upon the landscape. And below it flows Cankpe Opi Wakpala, the creek along which the women and children were hunted down like animals by Custer's old Seventh, out to avenge themselves for their defeat by butchering the helpless ones. That happened long ago, but no Sioux ever forgot it.

Wounded Knee is part of our family's history. Leonard's great-grandfather, the first Crow Dog, had been one of the leaders of the Ghost Dancers. He and his group had held out in the icy ravines of the Badlands all winter, but when the soldiers came in force to kill all the Ghost Dancers he had surrendered his band to avoid having his people killed. Old accounts describe how Crow Dog simply sat down between the rows of soldiers on one side, and the Indians on the other, all ready and eager to start shooting. He had covered himself with a blanket and was just sitting there. Nobody knew what to make of it. The leaders on both sides were so puzzled that they just did not get around to opening fire. They went to Crow Dog, lifted the blanket, and asked him what he meant to do. He told them that sitting there with the blanket over him was the only thing he could think of to make all the hotheads, white and red, curious enough to forget fighting. Then he persuaded his people to lay down their arms. Thus he saved his people just a few miles away from where Big Foot and his band were massacred. And old Uncle Dick Fool Bull, a relative of both the Crow Dogs and my own family, often described to me how he himself heard the rifle and cannon shots that mowed our people down when he was a little boy camping only two miles away. He had seen the bodies, too, and described to me how he had found the body of a dead baby girl with an American flag beaded on her tiny bonnet.

Before we set out for Wounded Knee, Leonard and Wallace Black Elk prayed for all of us with their pipe. I counted some fifty cars full of people. We went right through Pine Ridge. The half-bloods and goons, the marshals and the government snipers on their rooftop, were watching us, expecting us to stop and start a confrontation, but our caravan drove right by them, leaving them wondering. From Pine Ridge it was only eighteen miles more to our destination. Leonard was in the first car and I was way in the back.

Finally, on February 27, 1973, we stood on the hill where the fate of the old Sioux Nation, Sitting Bull's and Crazy Horse's nation, had been decided, and where we, ourselves, came face to face with our fate. We stood silently, some of us wrapped in our blankets, separated by our personal thoughts and feelings, and yet united, shivering a little with excitement and the chill of a fading winter. You could almost hear our heartbeats.

It was not cold on this next-to-last day of February—not for a South Dakota February anyway. Most of us had not even bothered to wear gloves. I could feel a light wind stirring my hair, blowing it gently about my face. There were a few snowflakes in the air. We all felt the presence of the spirits of those lying close by in the long ditch, wondering whether we were about to join them, wondering when the marshals would arrive. We knew that we would not have to wait long for them to make their appearance.

. . . Suddenly the spell was broken. Everybody got busy. The men were digging trenches and making bunkers, putting up low walls of cinder blocks, establishing a last-resort defense perimeter around the Sacred Heart Church. Those few who had weapons were checking them, mostly small-bore .22s and old hunting rifles. We had only one automatic weapon, an AK-47 that one Oklahoma boy had brought back from Vietnam as a souvenir. Altogether we had twenty-six firearms— not much compared to what the other side would bring up against us. None of us had any illusions that we could take over Wounded Knee unopposed. Our message to the government was: "Come and discuss our demands or kill us!" Somebody called someone on the outside from a telephone inside the trading post. I could hear him yelling proudly again and again, "We hold the Knee!"

The occupiers were besieged by federal marshals until May 8, when AIM surrendered after securing a promise that their complaints would be investigated. Two Indians and one marshall were killed during the fighting.

"This rock was an invitation no passerby could resist."

INDEPENDENCE ROCK

1974
Wyoming

CHARLES KURALT

Independence Rock, a 193-foot slab of granite, rises next to a tributary of the North Platte River in Wyoming. It got its name in the 1800s because emigrants following the Oregon Trail were advised to reach it by Independence Day if they hoped to cross the Sierra Nevada range before winter.

The lauded reporter Charles Kuralt wrote this account for his Dateline America *show on CBS Radio.*

This rock was an invitation no passerby could resist. It bulges up from the desert right beside the Oregon Trail, and it begs to be written upon. And so they wrote upon it, and some of them did such a careful job with hammer and chisel that their names are still plainly visible: "Milo J. Ayer, age 29, 1849." He had heard about gold in California, no doubt. You stand here and look at the neatly carved name of a forty-niner, Milo J. Ayer, and the anonymity of the Gold Rush falls away. You want to know more. Did you make it to California, Milo, and if so, how did you fare with your pick and your pan? Nothing at Independence Rock testifies to that. All it says is "Milo J. Ayer, age 29, 1849."

There are hundreds of other names written large on the big rocks along the Oregon Trail. Each invests the abstract facts of American history, the westward migration, Manifest Destiny, with a fragment of humanity.

These were not just pioneers; these were people, with names: "Jedediah Hines," it says on the steep stone face called Register Cliff. And ages: "J. R. Hornaday, aged 19 yrs., 1 month, 9 days." And hometowns: "Samuel White, Phoenixville, Pennsylvania." "Fox, Cincinnati, Ohio." "Ryan, Indianapolis."

It was graffiti when it was written. But it is history now, very personal and affecting history. The first sixty-nine people plodded these two thousand miles from Missouri to Oregon in 1841. Two hundred people the year after that. A thousand the year after that. In places the Oregon Trail is a lonely wagon track through the sagebrush. But in other places it is Interstate 25, and more people pass along it in an hour than passed in those first three years. It is all so easy for us.

It wasn't easy for them. There is a grave on the average of every eighty yards along the Oregon Trail from Independence, Missouri, to the Continental Divide. Accidents, Indian attacks, cholera, and typhoid accounted for twenty thousand lives along this hellish track in less than thirty years. The graves are mostly unmarked. Only the living left their names in Wyoming.

If you make your way along a rough bank below Register Cliff and push aside some young cottonwoods that have grown up there, your reward is a political sentiment of 1861 carved in a large and enthusiastic script: "Hurrah For Old Abe And The Union!"

That patriot was the only pioneer I could find in a couple of days of perusing the name-bearing rocks who yielded up any of his thoughts. The others put down their names and where they had come from and little else. It was a way of saying, "You see, I have made it this far, all the way from Maryville, Missouri. Think of that!"

Yes, think of that.

"How about the Big Bad Wolf? . . .He's my size."

DISNEYLAND

1961–1974
Anaheim, California

RICHARD STAYTON

In 1955, about thirty years after Walt Disney first drew Mickey Mouse, he opened Disneyland. By then his escapist fantasies were ingrained in American culture.

Journalist and dramatist Richard Stayton recalls visiting "the Happiest Place on Earth" during two very different eras in his and the country's life.

1961

Main Street, USA, beckoned whenever my mother felt homesick. She and my sisters and I would climb into the car, and Dad would steer east out of Lakewood, "Tomorrow's City Today." He almost always took surface streets: My mom was frightened by freeways.

When my dad caught the great California fever of 1960, he packed our family into a Nash Rambler and drove west to seek his fortune. Here Dad thrived in his new job at North American Aviation, but Mom, who had never roamed far from her Indiana town of 5,000, missed her mother, her relatives, the soda fountain, the "picture show," the Methodist Church, and just sitting quietly on the front porch at sunset, listening to crickets and watching the fireflies. Above all, my mother missed the small-town Saturday night ritual of Main Street, of strolling the sidewalk without a destination, waving to friends and neighbors.

Dad kept trying to cure her of the need to return to the "promised land," as he came to call southern Indiana, by "showing us the sights" of Southern California. We cruised Hollywood Boulevard and the Miracle Mile, walked along Olvera Street, and strolled the beaches of Long Beach. We saw Dodgers outfielder Wally Moon pop a home run over the temporary fence of the Coliseum. Yet only one place made my mother truly happy.

For us, Disneyland truly was the "Happiest Place on Earth." The moment we stepped through the gates onto Main Street, we were home. First we'd sit on the benches in the park by City Hall, absorbing the magic. Under the Disney trees my parents grew talkative—a rare event for those shy Midwesterners. Dad would talk about the vintage Model A, which had been his first car, as a Disney replica tooted by. Mom remembered cutting her fur coat into pieces to make me a coonskin cap during the Davy Crockett craze, when every kid longed to be "King of the Wild Frontier."

Then we'd separate according to lands, agreeing to meet later for dinner on Main Street. Disneyland was the only place in the perplexing colossus of Southern California where our parents allowed us to roam without supervision as we always had done back home. Uncle Walt, an old Midwesterner too, had been with us in Indiana through his Sunday night TV show. My parents could rest easy, knowing we were cradled in his protective embrace.

1974

"I'm sorry, but you're too tall to be a dwarf."

I am not prepared for rejection, not after the sacrifices already endured: moving from San Francisco to Los Angeles; giving up drugs and sex, since the two were inevitably connected; then entering the cheapest Orange County barber shop I could find and commanding the alcoholic barber to, "Cut it close, I'm seeking employment as a dwarf in Disneyland."

No, I had to get inside the Magic Kingdom—because I'd had it. This was the summer of 1974, and I'd just barely survived a decade of drugs, Haight-Ashbury communes, bisexuality, political craziness in ultra-hip San Fancisco. I desperately needed to get back, to find sanctuary, to be like I was as a youth, a Boy Scout leader and winner of the coveted God and Country Award. Get back to my Middle American roots, yes, back when I first saw Disney's Snow White and the Seven Dwarfs, yes by God

I was happy then. . . . Besides, this was Impeachment Summer, and from what better location could one watch the Fall of Nixon than from the ramparts of the "Happiest Place on Earth"? Anyway, I'd just spent two years getting a master's in creative writing from San Francisco State, so a job in Disneyland seemed the logical postgraduate study program.

"How about the Big Bad Wolf?" I am totally sincere. "He's my size."

The Disney employment interviewer smiles kindly and says, "I'm afraid all Character positions have been filled." I like her because she didn't find it at all strange that I'd want a job as a dwarf. I like her even more because she didn't check my application, which is nothing but an outrageous series of distortions, lies, and delusions.

"However, there are a few openings in Foods."

"What's that mean?"

"Selling popcorn. Officially, a Fantasyland Utility Man. . . ."

Popcorn Man in Fantasyland . . . What the hell? "I'll take it." We settle a few formalities. . . .

"One more thing. Your hair—it's much too long."

"THIS!" I grip all I can of my butchered locks, a bare finger's worth. I start to rave, but check myself and don't blow my cover.

"The Disneyland Look," she lets me know gently, "is a neat and natural look with no extremes."

"I guess they need their minority."

AFFIRMATIVE ACTION:
BAKKE V. UNIVERSITY OF CALIFORNIA

1975
Berkeley, California

RICHARD RODRIGUEZ

The West has long been a predictor of social trends that eventually become national. Religious freedom was first guaranteed in the 1663 charter of Rhode Island, which was, to the Puritans, the Wild West. The first state to grant women the right to vote was Wyoming, in 1869—actually, it was done while Wyoming was still a territory. The hippies of Haight-Ashbury in the 1960s inspired the youth movement and the environmental movement. Gay rights were first enacted in California.

Some of the reasons are political: When new territories and states established their laws, they could take into account changed social conditions. Some are demographic: The strong Hispanic and Asian influences on American culture were first felt in the West because that was where Hispanics and Asians constituted the greatest portion of the population.

As journalist and essayist Richard Rodriguez recalls, what begins first in the West can end there first. This account comes from one of his memoirs, Hunger of Memory.

I was at Berkeley in 1974 when the romantic sixties came to an end. A more pragmatic time succeeded it. Reporters for *Time* and for CBS informed the nation that a new mood of careerism had seized the campus. . . . Suddenly students in my classes admitted to being ambitious for good grades. Freshmen had already mapped the progress that would lead them to business or law school. (Professional schools were the only places which dispensed diplomas promising jobs.) Students would come to my office to challenge the grade of B they had received. ("Couldn't you please reconsider, Professor Rodriguez? I need an A-minus for my transcript.") They would sit in the back rows of my classes surreptitiously reading biochemistry textbooks, while I lectured on Spenser or Dickens, insisting that the reader of literature is made mindful of his social position and privilege. In such classrooms, before students who were so anxious and uncertain of their social advancement, the enlarging lessons of the humanities seemed an irrelevance. . . .

White students in the seventies frequently complained to me about affirmative action. They said that the reason they couldn't get admitted to business school or the reason their fellowship application had been rejected was the minorities. I tried to sympathize with the convenient complaint. I was on record as being opposed to affirmative action. But I was increasingly annoyed by the fact that the white students who complained about affirmative action never bothered to complain that it was unfair to lower-class whites. What solely concerned them was that affirmative action limited their chances, their plans.

I would tell fellow graduate students about my outrageous good fortune. Smiling at my irony, I would say that I had been invited to join "minority leaders" on trips to distant Third World countries. Or I would mention that I had been awarded a thousand dollars for winning an essay contest I had not even entered. Or I would say that I had been offered a teaching job by an English department. Some listeners smiled back, only to say: "I guess they need their minority." The comment silenced me. It burned. (It was one thing for me to say such a thing; oddly hard to hear someone else say it.) But it was true, I knew.

In the seventies, as more and more Americans spoke out against affirmative action, university presidents were forced to take the defense.

They spoke for the necessity of creating a nonwhite leadership class. But their argument was challenged by a man named Allan Bakke—a man of the new university, a man ambitious for his future, caught in the furious competition for professional school. He suggested a middle-class hero of a sort as he struggled for success and asserted his rights. I supported his claim. I continued to speak out in opposition to affirmative action. I publicly scorned the university presidents' call for a nonwhite leadership class. This defense seemed to me to belong to an earlier time, before World War II, when higher education could ensure positions of social power and prominence. I did not yearn for that older, more exclusive (less open) type of school. I wanted, however, something more from the new middle-class institution than either the decadent romanticism of the sixties or the careerism of the seventies. I wanted students more aware of their differences from persons less advantaged. I wanted university presidents to encourage students to work to improve the condition of disadvantaged Americans. To work, however, not as leaders but in order that the socially disadvantaged could lead their own lives.

My thoughts on the issue were printed. But by the late seventies the debate over affirmative action concerned itself only with the rights of white middle-class students. Opinions came from both sides. One heard from politicians and social activists and editorial writers. Finally, the justices of the Supreme Court rendered their judgment in the case of Bakke v. University of California. (Bakke was admitted to medical school.) But no one wondered if it had ever been possible to make higher education accessible to the genuinely socially disadvantaged.

Allan Bakke sued the University of California twenty years before the federal government began to eliminate affirmative action programs. Ironically, some of the strongest opposition to affirmative action in the West came from a minority group that had once suffered severe discrimination, especially in education: In the 1980s, Asian Americans began to protest that, judged on merit alone, they would be accepted to universities in a greater proportion than their affirmative action quotas allowed. In the late 1990s, those same arguments began to be voiced in the East.

"I bet this kind of shit doesn't happen in Saudi Arabia."

THE PIPELINE

July 1977
Valdez, Alaska

JOE McGINNISS

In 1968, one of the world's largest oil fields was found in Prudhoe Bay, in Alaska's North Slope. A five-year battle between oil companies and environmentalists followed. It ended in 1973, when Congress backed the building of a 789-mile pipeline to carry the oil to the closest ice-free port, Valdez. (If that decision had ever been in doubt, the nation's oil shortage, caused by that year's Arab oil embargo, settled the matter. The oil crisis had sent the economy into a nosedive. Oil self-sufficiency was deemed to be a vital national interest.)

The pipeline was built in just four years. Later it was revealed that the project was completed on time because of shoddy construction work that caused serious environmental damage; but the riches that flowed with the daily arrival of a million barrels of oil swept away concerns, as author Joe McGinniss discovered when he visited Valdez for his book Going to Extremes.

The first oil reached Valdez at 11:02 on a Thursday night. By coming closest to guessing the amount of time required for the oil to travel through the pipeline from Prudhoe Bay—38 days, 12 hours, 56 minutes—a crippled widow from Anchorage won the $30,000 grand prize in the building-fund lottery conducted by St. Patrick's Catholic Church.

. . . Valdez was only about a hundred miles east of Anchorage. The cities were separated, however, by the Chugach Mountains, with peaks as high as 13,000 feet, and by the Columbia Glacier, which was itself a bit larger than Rhode Island. . . . It was an all-day drive from Anchorage, but I could fly in less than an hour, which I did, the day after the oil had arrived.

. . . All the motel rooms in Valdez were taken, but a pipeline public relations man let me sleep in a spare room in his home. It was a modern, prefabricated house, with thick, shaggy carpeting on the floor. There was plenty of hot water, and electricity, and a Farrah Fawcett poster over my bed.

. . . The clouds grew thicker and darker after dinner. Sometime in the night, rain began. By 7:15 the next morning the highest visible point in all of Valdez was the upper floor of the split-level house across the street.

. . . The ARCO Juneau, which would carry the oil from Valdez to a refinery in the state of Washington, had pulled in and docked by the oil tanks. It was the length of six football fields, weighed, when empty, 120,000 tons, and the sides of it were so high that they disappeared into the clouds that hung low over the water.

A plane managed to penetrate the overcast, delivering copies of the *Anchorage Times*. After having ballyhooed the pipeline for a decade, and having proclaimed the arrival of the oil in Valdez to be the greatest event since statehood, the *Times* had not bothered to send any of its reporters to Valdez to cover the event and was relying upon wire service stories instead.

. . . That afternoon, I visited the Valdez Travel Service, which was the busiest travel agency in the state.

The manager was thin, intense, and thirty years old, with a week's growth of beard on his face, a shirt opened halfway to his waist, and a gold chain and medallion around his neck. He answered the telephone and wrote out tickets as he spoke. There were four other people behind the counter, equally busy.

"Last year," he said, "we sent three hundred people just to Hawaii. Second-busiest spot was Tulsa, Oklahoma. I guess people were just going home. We're the only travel service in town and we've got seven thousand construction workers here doing eight weeks on and two off. And they sure as hell don't want to spend those two weeks here."

His two partners in the agency were leaders in the Native business and political community in Anchorage. Through them—because they were Natives—the partnership qualified for a low-interest loan from the Bureau of Indian Affairs. Also through them, and their power in the Native community, the new corporation qualified for a large bank loan in Anchorage. The two sums together had been enough to buy the Valdez Travel Service, and the non-Native had come down to run it.

"Insane, man. It has been totally insane. For the first six months I was too busy to even find a place to live. I slept in the back of the office. No running water. I couldn't have made money any faster if I'd been minting it. We did two million dollars' worth of business the first six months. The same pace this year, too, but now with the line finished, this thing is really going to fade. And, man, I'm fading, too. Fading fast. I'm burned out. And getting out. The place is for sale, and I've got a new manager coming in tomorrow. Some out-of-work actor from L.A. I forget his name, I've got it written down here somewhere. Some guy who was in a movie with Anne Bancroft. I'll be out of here within two weeks. I'm going to Columbia, Maryland. Our little corporation just did a deal with

Morrison Knudsen, the big international construction firm. They've got this mammoth job in Saudi Arabia, building dams, highways, bridges, the whole schmeer. We're going to handle their traffic management. Shipping their people in and out. Man, it's going to make this thing look like nothing but the corner candy store. So much money involved there I'm not even allowed to talk about it. We got it through my same two partners, too. See, these guys are really heavies when it comes to that Native political shit. They told Morrison Knudsen, if you want to get any work on this big natural gas pipeline that's going to come, then maybe you ought to let us work for you in Saudi Arabia. The old quid pro quo, man, know what I mean? Hey, if I'm not making much sense, don't be alarmed. I mean, I've been partying, partying, partying. But that's the whole thing out here these days. If you can latch on to a Native with some clout as a partner, that's just like having your own little oil well all to yourself."

A young woman in a tight dress came into the travel agency. She had two deep scars across her face. Her hands were trembling and there was a look of extreme tension in her eyes.

"I got to see you," she said to the manager. "Right now."

"I'm busy, sweetheart. Can't talk."

"I said I got to see you." It was not just her hands; it was her whole body that was trembling.

"Lunch tomorrow. Meet me at the Sheffield. One o'clock." A phone rang and he answered it. "Oh, hi. Yes, listen, you're all set. Well, almost all set. The good news is, I've got you confirmed out of Seattle. The bad news is, the plane from Anchorage is full. You're on standby. What? No, no, don't worry. You'll get on. Just have faith. Well, no, I can't guarantee it, but you'll get on. There. Does that make you feel better? Does that sound like a guarantee?"

The woman in the tight dress had not moved. She was carrying a large handbag. She reached into the bag and took out a gun. She did not point it at anyone, and she did not say anything. She just stood there, holding it, as if it were a travel brochure, with her whole body trembling.

The manager spotted the gun. "Got to run," he said, over the telephone. "Have a great trip. Bye." He hung up. "Now, Mickey," he said soothingly. "Put that away."

"Lunch tomorrow, bullshit," she said. "I'm really upset. I need to talk to you right now."

"Sure, baby, sure. But not in the office. Remember what I told you about guns in the office? Let's just go outside for a minute or two."

The manager excused himself and stepped out from behind the

counter. He put an arm around the woman's shoulders and guided her carefully toward the door. She put the gun back inside her bag. It was a .357 Magnum, the kind which, if handled correctly, could kill a bear.

The manager was gone for fifteen minutes. When he returned there was perspiration on his forehead and his week's growth of beard seemed shiny with sweat. A phone was ringing. He answered it. "Oh, hi, Joan. Yeah. What you do is, if it's not confirmed—Hey, can you give me a call back? I've got about six people in the office right now. And a lady with a loaded .357 Magnum sitting in my car, waiting for me to buy her a drink."

He hung up. He took a couple of blank ticket forms from a locked metal box that was inside a safe behind the counter. He explained that he was going to have to be out of the office for a while.

"When I first got here," he said, "Mickey was the number-one hooker in town. Then she had a real bad car accident. Got those scars. After that, she wasn't number one. Except with a few of the sickies. So she started running coke, from New York. A thousand per trip she got paid. Once a month. I handle her airline and hotels. She flies to New York with the money and the next day she flies back with the stuff. Except last week something got a little messed up. She left here with twenty thousand in cash, and yesterday she came back empty. Said she lost her purse. In the ladies' room at La Guardia. Hell of an excuse, right? The man she's working for is less than happy. Told her she had three days to come up with the twenty thou. Or else those scars would be the least of her worries. So what does she do? She comes to me. Wants five hundred cash and a one-way ticket to San Francisco. Says she knows a plastic surgeon down there who will fix up her face. With a new face and some phony IDs, she figures no one from here can ever trace her. I think she's got a boyfriend waiting down there with the money, but who knows? She is not, by any means, one of the more stable ladies in Valdez. What I really think is that she's going to kill herself. I think she's going to blow her brains out with that three fifty-seven sometime in the next twenty-four hours. But at least if I give her the ticket and the money I won't have it on my conscience."

He walked toward the door, shaking his head. Three phones were ringing, and there were five customers lined up, waiting, at the counter.

"Wow," he said. "I bet this kind of shit doesn't happen in Saudi Arabia."

———————————————————

"If I were a communist, I would vote for Proposition 13...."

PROPOSITION 13

1978
California

LOU CANNON

Democracy, wrote social critic H. L. Mencken, is the theory that the people know what they want and deserve to get it—good and hard. There's no better example than California's Proposition 13, a public referendum on tax reform that occured in 1978.

Championed by the crusty and obnoxious businessman Howard Jarvis, a political gadfly since the 1930s, "Prop 13" was simply a rollback of property taxes. The price of California real estate had skyrocketed during the 1970s, pushing up property taxes to match the increasing assessments. Prop 13 would lower the tax rate, and limit how much the legislature could increase it each year.

Legislators didn't want the new law, but a special characteristic of Western politics limited their ability to stop it. In 1903, Los Angeles had adopted a charter with a unique idea: To end corruption, certain decisions would be taken out of the hands of elected officials and decided by a referendum. Anyone could put a referendum on the ballot by collecting enough signatures. In 1911, the idea was extended to the whole state.

Journalist and author Lou Cannon, a longtime observer of California and national politics, reported on the impassioned Prop 13 campaign for the Washington Post.

A tax revolt that its backers modestly call "a second American Revolution" has caught fire in California.

"There's no question this is the wave of the future," says Proposition 13's creator, cigar-chomping, fast-talking tax crusader Howard Jarvis, who works as director of an apartment owner's association.

. . . Not since Upton Sinclair's "End Poverty in California" revolt of the 1930s (see page 279), in which hundreds of thousands of Depression-wracked voters tried to alter radically the California constitution and tax structure, has a movement struck such fear into the hearts of California's establishment.

When a politically powerful movement arises in California, it invariably is denounced as "communist." Proposition 13 is no exception. "If I were a communist, I would vote for Proposition 13," says former governor Edmund G. [Pat] Brown, whose son and current governor, Jerry, is risking his own political reputation in opposing the measure. The senior Brown said that communists would favor such a plan because it would destroy local government.

The other rhetoric directed against Proposition 13 has also been heavy-handed. Southern California Edison executive director Howard Allen, the president of the Los Angeles Chamber of Commerce, describes it as a "fraud on the taxpayer that will cause fiscal chaos, massive unemployment and disruption of the economy." Los Angeles Mayor Thomas Bradley, not to be outdone, says Proposition 13 will "hit the city like a neutron bomb, leaving some city facilities standing virtually empty and human services devastated."

All of these cries of alarm are music to the ears of Jarvis, who after spending many years working for right-wing Republican causes, now finds that he is called "subversive" by some of the state's biggest businessmen.

Jarvis, who has made hundreds of speeches up and down the state in behalf of his cause, is a disheveled, shouting speaker of the William Jennings Bryan school. He engages in florid oratory studded with four letter words. He angers and forgives easily, and seems to enjoy hugely the discomfiture he causes local governments and the news media.

"I've been misquoted and I'll be misquoted again," Los Angeles Magazine quoted Jarvis as saying. "I don't give a good goddam Christ, they couldn't cut me up much more than they do. . . ."

Both Gov. Brown and the legislature dallied in the face of the Jarvis threat. . . . But the legislature, supported by Brown, finally responded by passing a tax-relief plan of its own that also will be on the June ballot.

The legislative plan, Proposition 8 on the ballot, would provide about 30 percent relief compared to 50 percent under the Jarvis plan. A typical home valued at $100,000, for instance, presently would be taxed $2,495. The tax relief would be $1,333 under Jarvis and $791 under Proposition 8.

The early polls show Proposition 13 leading. . . .

That impact could be devastating. The San Francisco Board of Supervisors has prepared a contingency budget that calls for the firing of 5,500 city employees, raising bus fares from 25 cents to 75 cents, cutting the funding for the general hospital by 25 percent, cutting library services by 20 percent, and eliminating funds for golf courses, the Human Rights Commission and the Delinquency Prevention Commission.

In Los Angeles, Mayor Bradley says that 8,000 city workers would be fired plus 5,500 more, mostly minority employees under the Comprehensive Employment Training Act. There would be radical cuts, he predicts, in ambulance, street cleaning, brush clearance, recreation and refuse collection services.

This fear has created an odd anti-Proposition 13 coalition of labor and minority groups, which fear that high sales taxes would hurt them, and businesses, which is worried about the potential doubling of bank and corporation taxes.

With all this firepower and a potential $1.5 million advertising campaign lined up to stop Proposition 13, it would appear to have little chance. But there are some who think that former Los Angeles Police Chief Ed Davis, a Republican gubernatorial candidate who is supporting Proposition 13, is right when he forecasts that voters will not settle for the lesser relief provided by the legislature.

As Davis put it in a recent debate: "If you're going to fight a revolution and go to all that trouble, you're not going to settle for some promise from King George that he's going to give you half a loaf. . . ."

Prop 13 passed, with a 2-1 ratio, and choked off about $6 billion of government income, literally overnight. It put money back in the pockets of the taxpayers, but it began decades of neglect of public services.

Prop 13's critics have blamed it for a wide range of ills. Police effectiveness has supposedly declined because of a lack of equipment. The Bay Bridge apparently collapsed during the 1989 Bay Area earthquake because it had not been properly maintained. The California school system crumbled for lack of funds.

Of course, there are those who take the other view. They believe all those services could have been provided if the government didn't waste its other income, or try to protect its own bureacracy at the expense of direct spending.

Either way, no other law has changed California as much. It also led to similar reforms in other states.

Howard Jarvis, successful at last, became a celebrity symbol of angry tax reform, often posing with a large axe for news photographers.

A final thought: If Jarvis's campaign seems selfish, consider the case of Governor Hiram Johnson, who was responsible for introducing referendums on a state level in 1911. His intent—in fact, the basis of his campaign for governor— was to limit the power of the Southern Pacific railroad, which effectively controlled the legislature. That pitted him against the boss of the railroad's political machine: His father.

". . . One by one he would have each of my sons murdered."

AN OFFER HE COULDN'T REFUSE

June 1978
Kansas City and Las Vegas

MIKE DEFEO, BILL OUSELEY,
ALLEN GLICK, AND CARL DeLUNA

Despite its criminal origins, today's Las Vegas is more Disneyland than gangland. Oddly, the transformation of the glitziest city in the world began in a run-down restaurant, a thousand miles from the neon glamour of the Strip.

Nicholas Pileggi, author of Casino, *interviewed eyewitnesses Mike Defeo, deputy director of the Justice Department's Organized Crime Strike Force, and Bill Ouseley, an FBI agent.*

Eyewitness Allen Glick, a key figure in the events, was a Las Vegas casino owner. A few years earlier, impatient to expand his company, he had borrowed millions of dollars from the the mob-controlled Central States Teamster Pension Fund. His account comes from court testimony.

MIKE DEFEO

Until the late 1970s, there had been a hiatus in law enforcement in Las Vegas. There was corruption. There were judges who made things difficult. Paul Laxalt, as both a senator and governor, complained that there were too many FBI and IRS agents in the state. Our wiretaps were leaked. One judge used to unseal grand jury minutes we asked to be sealed. At one point, one of the corrupt cops who worked for [mobster] Tony Spilotro had his sister-in-law working as the chief clerk of the court. All this meant for law enforcement was years and years of frustration. We were beating our heads against the wall.

And then finally, when a break did come, it didn't come out of Vegas but out of the back room of a Kansas City pizzeria.

BILL OUSELEY

We put the bug in there because we were looking for information on [a] murder. Instead, at about ten thirty on the night of June 2, 1978, Carl DeLuna [hit man for Kansas City's Civella crime family] and Nick Civella's brother Corky sat down in the back of this two-tabled sliced-pizza restaurant and they start talking about buying and selling Las Vegas casinos, and about ordering Allen Glick to sell his casinos. They talked about the various groups lined up to buy Glick's casinos and how they wanted the group backed by their man—Joe Agosto at the Tropicana—to take over, and not a Chicago-mob-backed group that included Lefty Rosenthal, Bobby Stella, and Gene Cimorelli. It was like the Rosetta stone for all of our suspicions. No one had ever recorded mob guys talking about buying and selling casinos and who should and should not be permitted to take them over. Still, it was hard for us to believe that "Toughy" DeLuna, in his windbreaker and pizza apron, was negotiating the sale of multimillion dollar Las Vegas casinos. We didn't know for sure until eight days later, on June tenth, when Allen Glick called a press conference in Las Vegas and announced he was planning to step away from [his casino holding company,] the Argent Corporation.

ALLEN GLICK

[A few weeks earlier, Carl DeLuna had] said that he and his partners were finally sick of having to deal with me and having me around and that I could no longer be tolerated. He wanted me to know that everything he said would be the last time I would hear it from him or anyone else because there would be no other opportunity for me to hear it unless I abided by what he said. He informed me that it was their desire to have me sell Argent Corporation immediately and I was to announce that sale as soon as I left [attorney Oscar] Goodman's office that day after the meeting with Mr. DeLuna. He said that he realized that the threats that I received perhaps may not have been taken by me to be as serious as they were given to me. And he says that since I perhaps find my life expendable, he was certain I wouldn't find my children's life expendable. With that he looked down on his piece of paper and he gave me the names and ages of each one of my sons. And he said that if he did not hear within a short period of time that I announced the sale, that one by one he would have each of my sons murdered. . . .

CARL DELUNA
FROM THE WIRE TAP AT THE VILLA CAPRI PIZZERIA

Genius [Allen Glick] wants to make a public announcement. . . . Which, those were my words to him: Do what you got to do, boy. Make your public announcement that you are getting out of this for whatever fuckin' reason you want to pick and get out. I put that in his head. Make a news conference.

[The break] was fortuitous. It was luck. But mostly it was the fact that the Kansas City supervisor, Gary Hart [not the Colorado senator], and his squad knew there was something to be pursued on that wire and they pursued it. If you listen to that wire, even today, it's not all that obvious. These guys didn't talk with footnotes. You hear DeLuna telling Carl Civella about how he was going to get Genius to get out of the Stardust. None of it is all that clear or all that direct. Lots of it is impenetrable. Lazy listeners could have easily missed it.

. . . It was Carl DeLuna who made the case for us in the end. He was an inverted, compulsive note taker. He kept notes on everything. Every twenty-dollar roll of quarters. Every trip. Every gas tank filled. He did it so that he could never be questioned about his expenses, because he would be able to show where the money went. DeLuna's notes and the telephone tap at Spilotro's Gold Rush and later at Allen Dorfman's insurance company in Chicago all confirmed what we knew all along—that there was a strong link between the mob, the Teamsters' Central States pension fund, and Las Vegas—only now we were in a position to maybe do something about it.

Allen Glick was granted immunity in return for his testimony. Carl DeLuna was sentenced to thirty years in prison, and his records helped convict several other mobsters. By the early 1980s, the mob's grip on the city was loosened.

"We were too young to drive ...
but we could give this big machine orders."

THE BIRTH OF THE PERSONAL COMPUTER

1968–1983

Seattle, Washington;
Albuquerque, New Mexico;
Cambridge, Massachussets;
and Palo Alto, California

BILL GATES

When the personal computer was developed in the 1970s, Silicon Valley was already an established fact, a collection of high-tech companies producing sophisticated electronics. Nurtured by strong individuals like Stanford professor Fred Terman (see page 305), the valley had grown from a haven for radio pioneers like Lee De Forest (page 222) to the center of the world's semiconductor industry (page 354). Defense contractors like Lockheed also contributed to the pool of talented engineers (page 350).

Yet almost nobody in the Silicon Valley establishment envisioned the personal computer. At the time, computers were found only at large institutions and corporations. Semiconductor companies focused on making chips for specific uses, from traffic lights to airplane controls. Few people saw the possibilities even as late as 1974, when Intel, the premier semiconductor company, created a chip with enough processing power to run a small stand-alone computer. "I turned down the idea of a home computer at that time," recalled Gordon Moore, cofounder of Intel. "One of our engineers came up with the idea that you could build a computer and you could put it in the home. I kind of asked him what it was good for, and the only application I got back was that the housewife could put her recipes on it. I could imagine my wife sitting there with a computer by the stove! It didn't really look very practical."

To the engineers of Silicon Valley, who had easy access to mainframe computers, the need for a PC wasn't compelling. But to their kids, and to other hobbyists all over the country, it was a dream. Microsoft founder Bill Gates tells the story in The Road Ahead.

I wrote my first software program when I was thirteen years old. It was for playing tic-tac-toe. The computer I was using was huge and cumbersome and slow and absolutely compelling.

Letting a bunch of teenagers loose on a computer was the idea of the Mothers' Club at Lakeside, the private school I attended. The mothers decided that the proceeds from a rummage sale should be used to install a terminal and buy computer time for students. Letting students use a computer in the late 1960s was a pretty amazing choice at the time in Seattle and one I'll always be grateful for.

This computer terminal didn't have a screen. To play, we typed in our moves on a typewriter-style keyboard and then sat around until the results came chug-chugging out of a loud printing device on paper. Then we'd rush over to take a look and see who'd won or decide our next move. A game of tic-tac-toe, which would take thirty seconds with a pencil and paper, might consume most of a lunch period. But who cared? There was just something neat about the machine.

I realized later part of the appeal was that here was an enormous, expensive, grown-up machine and we, the kids, could control it. We were too young to drive or to do any of the other fun-seeming adult activities, but we could give this big machine orders and it would always obey. Computers are great because when you're working with them you get immediate results that let you know if your program works. It's feedback you don't get from many other things. That was the beginning of my fascination with software. The feedback from simple programs is particularly unambiguous. And to this day it still thrills me to know that if I can get the program right it will always work perfectly, every time, just the way I told it to.

As my friends and I gained confidence, we began to mess around with the computer, speeding things up when we could or making the games more difficult. A friend at Lakeside developed a program in BASIC that simulated the play of Monopoly. BASIC (Beginner's All-purpose Symbolic Instruction Code) is, as its name suggests, a relatively easy-to-learn programming language we used to develop increasingly complex programs. He figured out how to make the computer play hundreds of games really fast. We fed it instructions to test out various methods of play. We wanted to discover what strategies won most. And chug-a-chug, chug-a-chug—the computer told us.

Like all kids, we not only fooled around with our toys, we changed them. If you've ever watched a child with a cardboard carton and a box of crayons create a spaceship with cool control panels, or listened to their improvised rules, such as "Red cars can jump all others," then you know that this impulse to make a toy do more is at the heart of innovative childhood play. It is also the essence of creativity.

Of course, in those days we were just goofing around, or so we thought. But the toy we had—well, it turned out to be some toy. A few of us at Lakeside refused to quit playing with it. . . .

The computer we played tic-tac-toe on in 1968 and most computers at that time were mainframes: temperamental monsters that resided in climate-controlled cocoons. After we had used up the money the Mothers' Club had provided, my school friend Paul Allen, with whom I later started Microsoft, and I spent a lot of time trying to get access to computers. They performed modestly by today's standards, but seemed awesome to us because they were big and complicated and cost as much as millions of dollars each. They were connected by phone lines to clackety Teletype terminals so they could be shared by people at different locations.

We rarely got close to the actual mainframes. Computer time was very expensive. When I was in high school, it cost about $40 an hour to access a time-shared computer using a Teletype—for that $40 an hour you got a slice of the computer's precious attention. This seems odd today, when some people have more than one PC and think nothing of leaving them idle for most of the day. Actually, it was possible even then to own your own computer. If you could afford $18,000, Digital Equipment Corporation (DEC) made the PDP-8. Although it was called a "minicomputer," it was large by today's standards. It occupied a rack about two feet square and six feet high and weighed 250 pounds. We had one at our high school for a while, and I fooled around with it a lot. The PDP-8 was very limited compared to the mainframes we could reach by phone; in fact, it had less raw computing power than some wristwatches do today. But it was programmable the same way the big, expensive ones were: by giving it software instructions. Despite its limitations, the PDP-8 inspired us to indulge in the dream that one day millions of individuals could possess their own computers.

With each passing year, I became more certain that computers and computing were destined to be cheap and ubiquitous. I'm sure that one of the reasons I was so determined to help develop the personal computer is that I wanted one for myself.

At that time software, like computer hardware, was expensive. It had to be written specifically for each kind of computer. And each time computer hardware changed, which it did regularly, the software for it pretty much had to be rewritten. Computer manufacturers provided some standard software program building blocks (for example, libraries of mathematical functions) with their machines, but most software was written specifically to solve some business's individual problems. Some software was shared, and a few companies were selling general-purpose software, but there was very little packaged software that you could buy off the shelf.

My parents paid my tuition at Lakeside and gave me money for books, but I had to take care of my own computer-time bills. This is what drove me to the commercial side of the software business. A bunch of us, including Paul Allen, got entry-level software programming jobs. For high school students the pay was extraordinary—about $5,000 each summer, part in cash and the rest in computer time. We also worked out deals with a few companies whereby we could use computers for free if we'd locate problems in their software. One of the programs I wrote was the one that scheduled students in classes. I surreptitiously added a few instructions and found myself nearly the only guy in a class full of girls. As I said before, it was hard to tear myself away from a machine at which I could so unambiguously demonstrate success. I was hooked.

Paul knew a lot more than I did about computer hardware, the machines themselves. One summer day in 1972, when I was sixteen and Paul was nineteen, he showed me a ten-paragraph article buried on page 143 of *Electronics* magazine. It was announcing that a young firm named Intel had released a microprocessor chip called The 8008.

A microprocessor is a simple chip that contains the entire brain of a whole computer. Paul and I realized this first microprocessor was very limited, but he was sure that the chips would get more powerful and computers on a chip would improve very rapidly.

At the time, the computer industry had no idea of building a real computer around a microprocessor. The *Electronics* article, for example, described the 8008 as suitable for "any arithmetic, control, or decision-making system, such as a smart terminal." The writers didn't see that a microprocessor could grow up to be a general-purpose computer. Microprocessors were slow and limited in the amount of information they could handle. None of the languages programmers were familiar with was available for the 8008, which made it nearly impossible to write complex programs for it. Every application had to be programmed with the few dozen simple instructions the chip could understand. The 8008 was condemned to life as a beast of burden, carrying out uncomplicated and unchanging tasks over and over. It was quite popular in elevators and calculators.

To put it another way, a simple microprocessor in an embedded application, such as an elevator's controls, is a single instrument, a drum or a horn, in the hands of an amateur: good for basic rhythm or uncomplicated tunes. A powerful microprocessor with programming languages, however, is like an accomplished orchestra. With the right software, or sheet music, it can play anything.

Paul and I wondered what we could program the 8008 to do. He called up Intel to request a manual. We were a little surprised when they actually sent him one. We both dug into it. I had worked out a version of BASIC, which ran on the limited DEC PDP-8, and was excited at the thought of doing the same for the little Intel chip. But as I studied the 8008's manual, I realized it was futile to try. The 8008 just wasn't sophisticated enough, didn't have enough transistors.

We did, however, figure out a way to use the little chip to power a machine that could analyze the information counted by traffic monitors on city streets. Many municipalities that measured traffic flow did so by stringing a rubber hose over a selected street. When a car crossed the hose, it punched a paper tape inside a metal box at the end of the hose. We saw that we could use the 8008 to process these tapes, to print out graphs and other statistics. We baptized our first company "Traf-O-Data." At the time it sounded like poetry.

I wrote much of the software for the Traf-O-Data machine on cross-state bus trips from Seattle to Pullman, Washington, where Paul was attending college. Our prototype worked well, and we envisioned selling lots of our new machines across the country. We used it to process traffic-volume tapes for a few customers, but no one actually wanted to buy the machines, at least not from a couple of teenagers.

Despite our disappointment, we still believed our future, even if it was not to be in hardware, might have something to do with microprocessors. After I started at Harvard College in 1973, Paul somehow managed to coax his clunky old Chrysler New Yorker cross-country from Washington State and took a job in Boston, programming minicomputers at Honeywell. He drove over to Cambridge a lot so we could continue our long talks about future schemes.

In the spring of 1974, *Electronics* magazine announced Intel's new 8080 chip—ten times the power of the 8008 inside the Traf-O-Data machine. The 8080 was not much larger than the 8008, but it contained 2,700 more transistors. All at once we were looking at the heart of a real computer, and the price was under $200. We attacked the manual. "DEC can't sell any more PDP-8s now," I told Paul. It seemed obvious to us that if a tiny chip could get so much more powerful, the end of big unwieldy machines was coming.

Computer manufacturers, however, didn't see the microprocessor as a threat. They just couldn't imagine a puny chip taking on a "real" computer. Not even the scientists at Intel saw its full potential. To them, the 8080 represented nothing more than an improvement in chip technology. In the short term, the computer establishment was right. The 8080 was just another slight advance. But Paul and I looked past the limits of that new chip and saw a different kind of computer that would be perfect for us, and for everyone—personal, affordable, and adaptable. It was absolutely clear to us that because the new chips were so cheap, they soon would be everywhere.

Computer hardware, which had once been scarce, would soon be readily available, and access to computers would no longer be charged for at a high hourly rate. It seemed to us people would find all kinds of new uses for computing if it was cheap. Then software would be the key to delivering the full potential of these machines. Paul and I speculated that Japanese companies and IBM would likely produce most of the hardware. We believed we could come up with new and innovative software. And why not? The microprocessor would change the structure of the industry. Maybe there was a place for the two of us.

This kind of talk is what college is all about. You have all kinds of new experiences, and dream crazy dreams. We were young and assumed we had all the time in the world. I enrolled for another year at Harvard and kept thinking about how we could get a software company going. One plan was pretty simple. We sent letters from my dorm room to all the big computer companies, offering to write them a version of BASIC for the new Intel chip. We got no takers. By December, we were pretty discouraged. I was planning to fly home to Seattle for the holidays, and Paul was staying in Boston. On an achingly cold Massachusetts morning a few days before I left, Paul and I were hanging out at the Harvard Square newsstand, and Paul picked up the January issue of *Popular Electronics*. . . . This gave reality to our dreams about the future.

On the magazine's cover was a photograph of a very small computer, not much larger than a toaster oven. It had a name only slightly more dignified than Traf-O-Data: the Altair 8800 ("Altair" was a destination in a *Star Trek* episode). It was being sold for $397 as a kit. When it was assembled, it had no keyboard or display. It had sixteen address switches to direct commands and sixteen lights. You could get the little lights on the front pad to blink, but that was about all. Part of the problem was that the Altair 8800 lacked software. It couldn't be programmed, which made it more a novelty than a tool.

What the Altair did have was an Intel 8080 microprocessor chip as its brain. When we saw that, panic set in. "Oh no! It's happening without us! People are going to go write real software for this chip." I was sure it would happen sooner rather than later, and I wanted to be involved from the beginning. The chance to get in on the first stages of the PC revolution seemed the opportunity of a lifetime, and I seized it.

. . . There was no time to waste. Our first project was to create BASIC for the little computer.

The Altair was built by a small calculator company, MITS, in Albuquerque, New Mexico. Bankrupt by the time the machine was to go on sale, owner Ed Roberts had secured an emergency loan to ship it.

Roberts had told the banker who provided his last-minute loan that he hoped to sell 800 kits in the first year—and he was exaggerating to get the loan. Within a month the company was receiving 250 orders a day. Gates and Allen rushed to create an operating system.

We had to squeeze a lot of capability into the computer's small memory. The typical Altair had about 4,000 characters of memory. Today most personal computers have 4 or 8 million characters of memory. Our task was further complicated because we didn't actually own an Altair, and had never even seen one. That didn't really matter because what we were really interested in was the new Intel 8080 microprocessor chip, and we'd never seen that, either. Undaunted, Paul studied a manual for the chip, then wrote a program that made a big computer at Harvard mimic the little Altair. This was like having a whole orchestra available and using it to play a simple duet, but it worked.

. . . After five weeks, our BASIC was written—and the world's first microcomputer software company was born. In time we named it "Microsoft."

We knew getting a company started would mean sacrifice. But we also realized we had to do it then or forever lose the opportunity to make it in microcomputer software. In the spring of 1975, Paul quit his programming job and I decided to go on leave from Harvard.

I talked it over with my parents, both of whom were pretty savvy about business. They saw how much I wanted to try starting a software company and they were supportive. My plan was to take time off, start the company, and then go back later and finish college. I never really made a conscious decision to forgo a degree. Technically, I'm just on a really long leave. Unlike some students, I loved college. I thought it was fun to sit around and talk with so many smart people my own age. However, I felt the window of opportunity to start a software company might not open again. So I dove into the world of business when I was nineteen years old.

Gates and Allen moved to Albuquerque, New Mexico, to be close to MITS. They lived in a cheap motel, writing software.

From the start, Paul and I funded everything ourselves. Each of us had saved some money. Paul had been well paid at Honeywell, and some of the money I had came from late-night poker games in the dorm. Fortunately, our company didn't require massive funding.

People often ask me to explain Microsoft's success. . . . I think the most important element was our original vision. We glimpsed what lay beyond that Intel 8080 chip, and then acted on it. We asked, What if computing were nearly free? We believed there would be computers everywhere because of cheap computing power and great new software that would take advantage of it.

. . . In the summer of 1980, two IBM emissaries came to Microsoft to discuss a personal computer they might or might not build.

At the time, IBM's position was unchallenged in the realm of hardware, with a more than 80 percent market share of large computers. It had had only modest success with small computers. IBM was used to selling big, expensive machines to big customers. . . . IBM wanted to bring its personal computer to market in less than a year. In order to meet this schedule it had to abandon its traditional course of doing all the hardware and software itself. So IBM had elected to build its PC mainly from off-the-shelf components available to anyone. This made a platform that was fundamentally open, which made it easy to copy.

. . . IBM, with its reputation and its decision to employ an open design that other companies could copy, had a real chance to create a new, broad standard in personal computing. We wanted to be a part of it. So we took on the operating-system challenge. We bought some early work from another Seattle company and hired its top engineer, Tim Paterson. With lots of modifications the system became the Microsoft Disk Operating System, or MS-DOS. Tim became, in effect, the father of MS-DOS.

IBM, our first licensee, called the system PC-DOS; the PC was for personal computer. The IBM Personal Computer hit the market in August 1981 and was a triumph. The company marketed it well and popularized the term "PC." The project had been conceived by Bill Lowe and shepherded to completion by Don Estridge. It is a tribute to the quality of the IBM people involved that they were able to take their personal computer from idea to market in less than a year.

Few remember this now, but the original IBM PC actually shipped with a choice of three operating systems—our PC-DOS, CP/M-86, and the UCSD Pascal P-system. We knew that only one of the three could succeed and become the standard. . . . We saw three ways to get MS-DOS out in front.

First was to make MS-DOS the best product. Second was to help other software companies write MS-DOS-based software. Third was to ensure MS-DOS was inexpensive.

We gave IBM a fabulous deal—a low, one-time fee that granted the company the right to use Microsoft's operating system on as many computers as it could sell. This offered IBM an incentive to push MS-DOS, and to sell it inexpensively. Our strategy worked. IBM sold the UCSD Pascal P-System for about $450, CP/M-86 for about $175, and MS-DOS for about $60.

Our goal was not to make money directly from IBM, but to profit from licensing MS-DOS to computer companies that wanted to offer machines more or less compatible with the IBM PC. IBM could use our software for free, but it did not have an exclusive license or control of future enhancements. This put Microsoft in the business of licensing a software platform to the personal-computer industry. Eventually IBM abandoned the UCSD Pascal P-system and CP/M-86 enhancements.

Consumers bought the IBM PC with confidence, and in 1982, software developers began turning out applications to run on it. Each new customer, and each new application, added to the IBM PC's strength as a potential de facto standard for the industry. Soon most of the new and best software, such as Lotus 1-2-3, was being written for it. . . .

Within three years almost all the competing standards for personal computers disappeared. The only exceptions were Apple's Apple II and Macintosh. Hewlett Packard, DEC, Texas Instruments, and Xerox, despite their technologies, reputations, and customer bases, failed in the personal-computer market in the early 1980s because their machines weren't compatible and didn't offer significant enough improvements over the IBM architecture. . . . Although buyers of a PC might not have articulated it this way, what they were looking for was the hardware that ran the most software, and they wanted the same system the people they knew and worked with had.

It has become popular for certain revisionist historians to conclude that IBM made a mistake working with Intel and Microsoft to create its PC. They argue that IBM should have kept the PC architecture proprietary, and that Intel and Microsoft somehow got the better of IBM. But the revisionists are missing the point. IBM became the central force in the PC industry precisely because it was able to harness an incredible amount of innovative talent and entrepreneurial energy and use it to promote its open architecture. IBM set the standards.

In 1984, just ten years after the debut of the Intel chip that powered the Altair, Apple launched the Macintosh, with the first operating system to use icons and a mouse instead of typewritten commands. Broadening the appeal of computers to consumers who might have otherwise been intimidated, it helped create a mass market for the machines. Microsoft quickly adapted the improved method to the IBM PC with its new system, Windows.

Hailed as a brilliant new vision, the "graphical user interface" (GUI) concept had been developed before Intel made the chip that started the PC revolution. Conceived by Douglas Englelbart at the Stanford Research Center in 1966, GUI and the mouse had been built into the Alto, a computer created in 1973 at the Xerox Corporation's Palo Alto Research Center (PARC). The Alto sported a graphical interface, a mouse, networking, e-mail, and multiple typefaces. But Xerox executives didn't know what to do with it. PARC researchers were continually frustrated by their inability to find company support for their ideas.

Their work gained an unexpected supporter in 1979, when Apple Computer cofounder Steve Jobs visited. The 24-year-old wunderkind, a Silicon Valley native, had recently launched the Apple II computer. (It had been designed by his partner, Steve Wozniak, another Silicon Valley teenager and the son of a Lockheed engineer.) Sold as a complete, assembled machine, rather than a hobbyist's kit like earlier computers, the Apple II had become an instant success. Invited to PARC by Xerox, Jobs saw a graphical user interface for the first time. "I thought it was the best thing I'd ever seen in my life," he recalled. "Within ten minutes it was obvious to me that all computers would work like this some day."

Jobs returned to PARC with his programming staff. "He came back and, I almost said 'asked,' but the truth is, he demanded that his entire programming team get a demo," recalled PARC researcher Adele Goldberg. "The head of the science center asked me to give the demo, because Steve specifically asked for me to give the demo. And I said, No way. I had a big argument with these Xerox executives, telling them that they were about to give away the kitchen sink. And I said that I would only do it if I were ordered to do it, because then of course it would be their responsibility. And that's what they did."

"I looked around and the crowd had tripled."

WHITE NIGHTS, DARK DAYS

May 1979—May 1981
San Francisco

CLEVE JONES

California was a gay mecca long before San Francisco's Castro district became world-famous in the 1970s. Critic Edmund Wilson, visiting San Diego in 1931, offered this comment, surprisingly candid during that closeted era: "There are also the individuals who do not fit in in the conventional communities from which they come and who have heard that life in San Diego is freer and more relaxed. There at last their psychological bents or their particular sexual tastes will be recognized, allowed some latitude." The arrival of World War II and the creation of large military bases sharply increased the gay population in the West, and the men who found themselves in a freer and more relaxed place didn't rush back to their hometowns.

The nation's first large organization for gay men, the Mattachine Society, was organized between 1949 and 1951 in Los Angeles by Henry Hay, often called "the founder of gay liberation in America." The name came from a medieval French theater troupe, Société Mattachine, whose actors played in masks. Chapters were opened in other cities through the 1950s. In 1955, the Daughters of Bilitis, the first lesbian organization, was founded in San Francisco. Its name came from an 1894 collection of Sapphic love poems, Chansons de Bilitis, by Pierre Louÿs. By the 1960s, the gay rights movement was gathering steam, and following the 1969 Stonewall Inn riot in New York's Greenwich Village it was out nationwide. In 1973, psychiatrists stopped classifying homosexuality as a mental illness. In 1975 the first open homosexual received security clearance for government work. In 1977, California passed the first antidiscrimination law.

Also in 1977, San Francisco politician Harvey Milk, a gay rights activist, was elected to the city's Board of Supervisors. His personal transition from activist to city official marked an important moment for gay rights—but it lasted only a moment. On November 27, 1978, an angry former city supervisor, Dan White, assassinated Milk and Mayor George Moscone. That night, 40,000 citizens marched silently from the Castro neighborhood to Civic Center by candlelight.

Later, when Dan White was found guilty of just involuntary manslaughter, the protest march was not as calm. Activist Cleve Jones, best known for creating the AIDS quilt, recalls the "White Night" riots that followed the verdict. He also reveals how the early days of the AIDS epidemic, which followed so closely on Milk's assassination, forced a bitter dilemma upon gays in the city. Having fought against society and the government for the freedom to pursue their lifestyle, should they accept the opinions of public health officials to alter that lifestyle? Or should they risk death to reject what might be just the latest excuse for the government to restrict their freedom?

Jones gave this account to Benjamin Heim Shepard, author of the oral history White Nights and Ascending Shadows.

When the verdict came down, I was sitting in my apartment on Castro Street. . . . My first reaction was that I got violently sick to my stomach. . . . So I went into the bathroom and puked and the phone started ringing. Everybody came to my house because my apartment on Castro had been an organizing center for many of the demonstrations for the last couple of years. So they came over to my house. Someone came running up and said that there were news cameras on Castro Street and that they were looking for me. I went and found Don Martin and Phyllis Lyon. We arrived at the corner of Castro and 18th at about 5 or 5:30, still light out. The thing was that several months prior, I had decided to celebrate Harvey Milk's birthday, May 22nd, on Castro Street. I had permits from the police to close Castro Street, put up a stage and have this enormous party. I had booked Sylvester and other fabulous acts. People were really focused on me. The reporter said, "Well tomorrow is Harvey Milk's birthday and it would take permits to hold this party on Castro Street. Is that when the reaction will be?" and I said, "No, I think the reaction will be swift and it will be tonight."

As I was doing this I was focused on the reporter and answering the questions and looking at the camera and the rest of it. Then when the interview was done, which only was about three minutes, I looked around and the crowd had tripled. What had started as a knot of people standing around me and Don and Phyllis and this camera had tripled. It was now a couple of hundred people. One thing I will never forget was scanning the crowd and seeing someone whose face was so twisted with rage that I didn't even recognize him. It was Chris Perry who was the President of the Gay Democratic Club. Chris, himself, is a very mild-mannered fellow. I couldn't imagine that his face would look so different, so enraged. He had a sign; it said, "AVENGE HARVEY MILK."

Then I told my friends not to let anybody march down Market Street until I got back. I ran back up to my apartment to get my bull-horn. My apartment was packed. People were shoulder to shoulder. All the rooms, the kitchen, the back porch were just packed with people, everybody just white with anger, very, very strange. We got down to Castro Street and there were now about five thousand people. I'm not very good with crowd estimates but a large crowd was blocking traffic.

People were honking their horns. But it was unlike anything I had ever seen before because in the past these gatherings, no matter how political the purpose was, it was always very gay, this odd blend of humor and sarcasm and camp that gay people employ, but this time (laughs) there were no smart remarks, no fancy dress. People were just fucking furious, a very, very different feeling. So we marched.

There was still some light. And we marched on Market Street. All I remember really of this was to keep people from running, to try to slow it down. I figured that the death penalty coalition was already at City Hall and in fact they were and had already set up a sound system. So as the crowd swarmed down Market Street I hopped on the back of a friend's motorcycle and went ahead of them down to City Hall. I met people from the Death Penalty Coalition and said, "Hi, have you got a sound system?" They said yes and they had a generator so they had an independent power source and they had put up the cables going up the stairs but they hadn't secured the front area. So as the marchers arrived, people immediately pressed up onto the stairs right up against the City Hall doors.

At this point the police became really alarmed and sent in a line of officers in riot gear up onto the stairs to try to come between the demonstrators and the building. At this point there still had been no violence, no rocks thrown, only shouting. The police, as they came up onto the stairs, knocked over the generator, knocked over the sound, not intentionally—because of the rush and the chaos and the press of all these people. Actually, I think the generator had to be moved because it was going to fall or something. So the result of all this chaos was that there was no sound system and I really had the only bullhorn.

I was just so confused and angry myself. For the first time, I found myself taking this position that my emotions were taking me one way and my brain taking me the other way. I gave some lame remarks. I don't even remember what I said, something like, "Let's not be violent. Let's not be violent." I'm not a violent person but I felt violent. Then the bullhorn got passed around. Everybody gave basically the same line: We don't want to be violent; Dan White was violent; the police were violent. We're gay people; we don't want to be violent. And none of it was really working 'cause the crowd was just seething. And then finally Amber Hollibaugh, she's currently in New York City doing AIDS work, she's a fabulous glamourous dyke, filmmaker, a wonderful, wonderful woman, she got up. I don't remember anything she said except the one sentence. She said, "I think we oughta do this more often!" (Laughs.) By this time, I was no longer on the stairs. I had worked my way into the crowd and I was just watching in amazement. The crowd went wild.

Then the rocks started flying and the police retreated into the building. I was about maybe ten yards out into the street and I could see people I knew, people who I knew to be just the gentlest souls ripping that ornamental grillwork off the main front and jamming it through the front doors of City Hall. The police retreating back inside. One by one all of the windows were smashed and then I saw this burst of flames. There was one police car parked right next to the City Hall front door. The other police cars were all lined up right on McAllister Street in front of the state building. There had been two dozen, at least, police cars lined up there. So then the first police car burned up by the front door of City Hall and the crowd went nuts, then that glow. It was animal. That's when I started getting really confused, "Holy shit! What is going to happen?!" Then suddenly more breaking glass and you could see that people were getting into the building through basement windows.

. . . I got pushed as far as east of McAllister, Powell Street, I ended up down at Powell and Market. Market Street was trashed down from Powell Street to Van Ness. And I ran into Bill Kraus, who was a wonderful man who died of AIDS early in the epidemic. He was Harry Britt's right-hand man. At one point we were at Market Street in front of the Bank of America. I saw him and we just started laughing at each other. (Emotional laughing.) It was so weird. I said, "Bill, have you ever broken a window?" And he said, "No, have you?" I said, "No. Not since I was a Cub Scout," and we were looking at this bank window. I said, "Well, do you wanna?" And he said, "God, just once in my life I'd like to throw a brick through a bank window." I said, "Go for it Bill. Go for it." He picked up this rock and throws it as hard as he could and it bounced off the window. So I'm falling down on the sidewalk laughing at him and I said, "You nelly thing, you can't even break a window. Let me show you how its done." So I pick up another rock and throw it as hard as I can at the window and it bounces off. So we're both just rolling around on the sidewalk just laughing in the flames and smoke and sirens all around us and we're just laughing at the fact that we're too nelly to break a window with a brick. And then this big butch bulldyke comes running around the corner, picks up one of those big garbage cans and threw the whole thing, smashing the window right in, and then reached in and set the curtains on fire. So we all looked at each other, "Shit, lets get out of here!" (Laughs.)

[In 1981,] I got hired by the Speaker to the Assembly to work as a consultant in the legislature. It was a political appointment. I was the first openly gay staff person hired in legislature. But I was assigned to be the liaison from the Democratic Caucus to the health committee. I began receiving the CDC [Centers for Disease Control] publications, including the *MMWR*, the *Mortality and Morbidity Weekly Report,* so I remember the first report. I remember being puzzled, alarmed. I saved it. Shortly after that there was a wire service report of what the *MMWR* had said, and I clipped that and put it on my bulletin board. I thought it was poppers [ampules of inhalable amyl nitrate, used to enhance orgasm]. I couldn't think of anything else we did that straight people didn't do. Even the specific sex acts were the same.

At some point, I met Bobbi Campbell [an early AIDS sufferer and activist]. I was introduced to him by Hank Wilson. I was just walking down the street and saw Hank in the Twin Peaks bar; he knocked on the window and told me to come in. Bobbi had started writing a column for *The Sentinel* called, "Gay Cancer Journal." He took his shoes and socks off in the bar and showed me the lesions on the bottom of his feet. . . . So we did up a big flyer that explained the little bit we knew. We suggested that people cut down on their drug and alcohol intake and said that it looks like it may well be sexually transmitted but it was terribly hard to give anything definitive. Everybody was terribly suspicious. There were the beginnings of all the conspiracy theories starting to float around, kind of great denial and paranoia. It's hard.

Then I got a call from [Dr.] Marcus Conant [one of the first doctors to focus on AIDS]. Marcus knew of me as an activist although I wasn't an activist back then, but he also wanted access to [Mayor Art] Agnos, who at that time had considerable power in the legislature. We have dinner at the Zuni [restaurant]. There's something about Conant's delivery that I believed what he said. That night he told me that he thought that there was supposed to be a virus, sexually transmitted, similar to hepatitis. Further, he said that there was a potential for a long incubation period. I think in that first conversation he told me about some of the clusters. One was a house on Fire Island where my best friend had stayed and there was a house here in the neighborhood. I did not personally know the people, but I knew who they were. Then there was a cluster in L.A. Then Marcus, I think Marcus has always known how to manipulate me, but he said that he wanted me to meet one of his patients. He took me up to UC [University of California at San Francisco Medical Center] and there was a man named Simon Guzman and that just was terrifying. His body was covered with lesions and he was near death. I think that he died a few weeks later. There was a picture of him sitting by the bed from when he was healthy, and I love Latino men. He was just my type. I was quite shaken by that and I think I knew that night at the Zuni what was going to happen. Marcus's delivery was so matter of fact.

He led me through the bits of evidence that there were. He was jumping to a lot of conclusions but he was basically right. I knew that night.

That night, I left the restaurant and I thought that I would be killed by it, that everybody I knew would be killed by it, that they would find a cure but that it would destroy our community and our movement before. I thought that everything was in jeopardy. It was not at all clear how gay people would respond. Would we stay together? We had political power because we all came to live here. Why was it that we lived here? Was it only for sex? If we couldn't have sex, would we still want to live together? Would we have a community? What about all these things that had been created in less than a decade? The churches, all the social institutions. Would they survive? Would we pull together or would we fall apart?

"I found another oil well!"

WILDCATTER

1982
Havre, Montana

MARY CLEARMAN BLEW

The boom-and-bust cycles of the West haven't disappeared, especially in commodity businesses like oil and gas. Eyewitness Mary Clearman Blew, an award-winning writer, experienced the effects of that common story when she married an oil wildcatter.

"He rode the rollercoaster of oil and gas exploration and production," she wrote, "addicted like a gambler to the upward swoops and adrenaline rushes, landing on his feet when he hit bottom, starting all over again on another of his nine lives. He came to Havre in the early 1970s, broke, to make a new start in drilling gas wells into the shallow Judith River and Eagle formations. He went broke again and lost his rigs, but then he hit a lucky streak, scalping oil field pipe. When I met him, he was rolling in money."

"Hell, I'm the luckiest son of a bitch I know," he told her.

After he spent most of the money he'd had when he met Mary, he bought a ranch. Then, at the same time as his business luck began to run out, he developed a serious lung disease.

In this account from her book All But the Waltz, *Blew describes the summer that the romance of Western life lost its luster.*

How much financial havoc can a man cause when he sets a farming operation into motion and then watches as through a haze of detachment while fields go uncultivated, obligations unmet, notes unrenewed? How many additional difficulties can he bring down around his shoulders as well as his family's when he fails to file his corporation reports? His FICA and W-4 forms? What if he fails to file his income taxes? Answer: more difficulties than I ever dreamed possible.

I lay awake at two, three, four o'clock in the morning while birch twigs brushed against the bedroom window and cast a maze of shadows as complex and random as the maze my life had become. Hundreds of thousands of dollars whirred through my brain on a squirrel-wheel frequency, organizing themselves into columns and disintegrating to form new totals at rising interest rates. What was I to do? What to do, what to do? Every hope for a way out of the maze was as treacherous as false dawn. The bank would foreclose on the farm in lieu of the $450,000 note? Very well, but the bank would report the transaction to the IRS as a forgiven debt. What, I wondered, did the IRS do with people like me who owed income tax on $450,000? Did they have jails with squirrel wheels in them?

By this time I lay awake alone, usually, in the bed in the shadows of birch twigs. In the mornings I rose and dressed, drove Rachel to her sitter, and hammered away at the solutions that had eluded me in the small hours. By confronting every debt and filing every delinquent report, I could still cling to my illusions. *Face it! Fight it! If we can once deal with the finances, we can still live comfortably on my salary, and surely the disease can be slowed, maybe for years—if you don't believe in the diagnosis, we'll find another specialist. We'll go to Seattle or San Francisco and find another course of treatment, and surely, surely we can buy time, we can have years together. You'll see Rachel grow up—*

But Bob was away from home most of the time now, driven by my frantic tirades and his own denial of the disease that was slowly strangling him. Fired with the idea of getting back into the oil business, of another chance of striking it lucky, he went back to his native Kansas for weeks and then months at a stretch, coming home only to try to raise money for the leases he was buying.

"I found another oil well!"

He looks up from the logbook he has unfolded on the dining room table. Another thirty or forty logbooks are stacked around him or strewn on the floor. Cigarette smoke hangs blue over his head.

"See here? Where the line wavers? I don't see how they could have overlooked it. When they perforated, they missed the zone entirely. I can go in there, unplug it and reperforate, maybe run acid, get the well on stream for fifty, sixty barrels a day, initially—"

Sometimes he finds two or three oil wells in an evening.

"—cost?"

His eyes go opaque for an instant, as though my question has traveled on some dim transmission from outer space.

"What? The cost to rework one well? Hell, I don't know, honey, it'd be just one part of my program—twelve wells, say, at fifteen or twenty thousand—Hell, the cost of one well don't make no nevermind. I'll be talking to my old buddy the banker when I go back to Kansas next week. Now, can you see this? This jiggle on the graph? That's another oil-producing zone they missed when they finished this well—"

"Honey, I realize you don't know a goddamn thing about the oil business, but I don't understand why you can't *see* it! Hell, it's right there on the log! And fifty, sixty barrels a day, even at thirteen dollars a barrel—"

He's down to 150 pounds now. His skin has shrunken over his cheekbones, and his nails are cyanosed. Still, he's drawing on some invisible source of energy; his eyes are huge, his voice urgent as he stabs out one cigarette, lights another, and uses it to gesture at his logbook. All he needs to get on his feet again is a few thousand dollars I have in a savings account. Listening to his fevered chatter, I feel drawn into his dream, his certainty that out there somewhere, in the next fold of the graph, the next thousand feet of well pipe, is the ultimate fountainhead of wealth and health. I could drift with him, believe in him . . . *It was the drought, it was the farm crisis that bankrupted us, it wasn't his fault—and he knows the oil business, knows what he's talking about, it's just a matter of giving him his chance—*

But no.

He flies into a rage at my refusal. "You make me want to puke! *Puke! Puke! Puke! Puke! Puke!*"

A week of verbal bludgeoning is more than enough. I hand over the money, and he sets off for Kansas, serene in his knowledge that the next throw of the dice is his.

A month later he calls home, jabbering, ecstatic. His old buddy the banker believes in him.

"It's growing on trees down here! The money's growing on trees!"

We don't hear from him after that. Another spring deepens into another hot summer, and the lawns and evergreens in Havre suffer the stress from curtailed watering. After work I pick Rachel up from her sitter's and play with her in the swing I have hung in the backyard willow.

Rachel has seen so little rain in her life that when a brief deceptive shower fits its way overhead and a few raindrops lash the willow leaves, she asks, "What's that, Mom?"

Swing, swing, every day a bead on a string. Take Rachel to the sitter's and go to work in the mornings, pick her up and come home at night, swing her in the swing and bathe her and feed her and put her to bed. A whiskey and a book and Emmylou Harris for me. Swing, swing, the phone doesn't ring.

"Why don't you divorce him?" one of the attorneys had asked last summer.

This summer I file for divorce.

"Downtown Laredo lay before us, about two miles ahead."

CROSSING

1985
Nuevo Laredo, Mexico, and Laredo, Texas

TED CONOVER

Each month approximately 60,000 illegal aliens, from everywhere in the world, are caught crossing into the U.S. at the Mexican border. In California, illegal aliens comprise about 6 percent of the population. From 1980 to 1990 approximately 1 million of its 5 million immigrants were illegal.

To research his book, Coyotes, *Ted Conover joined a Mexican who was crossing. The title refers to the guides that help people cross.*

. . . One Mexican I had met told me he was ferried across the Rio Grande in the overturned hood of an old car. Others floated across on inner tubes. Expecting a shiny speedboat, hidden under the branches of a weeping willow, I was a bit chagrined when the kids dragged an old inflatable yellow raft in through the door of the shack.

"First, we need to blow it up," explained one. All of us took turns, and I was glad, because the deep breathing helped get rid of some of my nervousness, and finally being able to do something helped alleviate the complete sense of helplessness I'd been feeling. Meanwhile, one of the kids rummaged around the floor of the shack and dusted off a couple of the planks, which I now noticed had been carved into crude paddles. We squeezed the thing out the door, and suddenly were being led quickly toward some trees which Alonso realized must line the banks of the river.

"We're there!" he said excitedly. *"La línea divisoria!"* It was a shock to realize we were so close to the river and a surprise, at least, to see that we were going to cross in broad daylight. We had to negotiate two broken-down barbed-wire fences to reach it, but the kids showed no caution until the river itself was visible.

Then they crouched low, surveying the opposite bank through the trees. Alonso, farther behind, took the opportunity to visit a nearby tree. "My last pee in Mexico," he explained with a grin.

The banks of the river harbored a world different from that of the dusty shacks behind us—one of greenery, cool breezes, and dancing shadows. Somehow, though, the murky waters of the Rio Grande beyond did not exude the epic quality that I had expected after talking with Mexicans for so many weeks. It looked too tame and weedy, too mundane to serve as the great symbol of division between two cultures, two economies. Though apparently deep, it could not have been more than fifty yards across. And the U.S. side, grassy and treeless with a couple of junked cars visible: this was the promised land?

From where we crouched, a steep and muddy slope dropped to the brown water. The three boys negotiated the mud with the raft, looked around again, and then signaled that the way was clear. Alonso and I skittered down the bank to the water line. As the small raft was placed in the river, we were told to take our shoes off—"so that they won't damage the bottom." Alonso, meanwhile, noticed a rapid stream of big bubbles emerging from underneath one side of the raft. One of the kids smiled sheepishly. "We'll have to hurry" was all he said.

Knees to our chins, Alonso and I packed ourselves in between the two paddlers, someone gave a push, and we were off into international waters. As the current was strong, the boys paddled furiously. The tiny raft bobbed and twisted. About halfway across I spotted the trampled spot on the opposite bank for which we were aiming, some twenty yards downstream. The front paddle was slow, and we almost missed the landing spot. Then, all of a sudden, we were there, and Alonso was out— "careful! careful!" hissed a kid, as the raft lurched—and then me, both of us scrambling up the bank barefoot, shoes in hand, heading for a patch of tall grass. It felt like a war movie, guerrillas penetrating enemy lines. "Did you see anybody? Did you see anybody?" I asked Alonso.

"No! Relax!" he said, tightening his laces.

The kids had given us directions to downtown Laredo, and cautiously Alonso led the way, through the grass and shrubs of the floodplain, past larger trees and then a house. Some of the reports on the "flood" of aliens entering the United States had let me to think the path would be well worn, but instead we had to pick our own way, deciding which routes would be least likely to have one of Immigration's motion sensors—devices which detect the vibrations of footsteps and transmit the information to a main computer—and which ones offered the best concealment. Onto pavement, then past two stop signs and a traffic light, a right-hand turn and . . . downtown Laredo lay before us, about two miles ahead.

Strangely opposite emotions swept over Alonso and me as we walked those streets of Laredo. I suddenly felt a great excitement and wave of relief, a joy at being home again after so many weeks, out of the hands of the coyotes, away from Mexican law enforcement, back in a place, I thought, where I could explain myself out of most predicaments I might find myself in. A joy, in other words, at being alive.

Alonso, on the other hand, was now out of the frying pan and into the fire: suddenly an "illegal alien," subject to arrest, almost alone in a foreign land where he didn't know the language. . . . We continued our afternoon walk down the wide, warm, quiet, and paved streets of Laredo. It was probably the poor side of town, but worlds away from the poor side of Nuevo Laredo.

. . . The next day Alonso spent alone, figuring out his course of action. From other Spanish-speaking people he learned that finding work in Laredo was next to impossible. The risk of getting nabbed by Immigration was great. Smugglers' rates for rides away from the border zone were nearly as high as they had been in Nuevo Laredo. The Trailways bus station was hot, but, according to at least two people, the Greyhound station at night was not. This information Alonso shared when we reconvened in a park that afternoon; it was the sort of intelligence, we had agreed that morning, that having me along might make hard to discover. I had spent the day exploring a different side of Laredo. At a fashionable department store, I told Alonso with surprise, I had eaten lunch in a cafeteria where no employee, including the cashier, spoke any English at all.

"Maybe they would give me a job," he said, hopefully.

"I think it's all women down there," I replied.

"I think I'm going to take the bus then," he said after a while.

"To where?"

"Well, maybe Houston. I worked there two years ago. I was on a lawn crew, and I worked for some cement pourers. Here—see?—Larry gave me his phone number."

Alonso showed me the inside cover of a matchbook, where, after a few beers on the last night of work, Larry, the cement boss, had penned his number for Alonso.

"He said he would give me my job back if I wanted. Would you call him for me? Larry said to call collect." Alonso explained that Larry spoke very little Spanish, communicating with his workers via those who spoke some English.

"Okay, sure." Houston, I remembered, was well known for its heavy reliance on undocumented labor in the construction industry. It might be a good tip—and Alonso said Larry might even have a job for me, which would be a good way to be able to stick together for a while.

. . . We boarded the Greyhound around 9:30 P.M. Though there was no sign of Immigration anywhere, Alonso and I boarded separately and took seats a couple of rows apart. You never knew if there might be an inspection along the highway, or in the next town down the road. A couple of minutes later, Alonso quietly got up and walked back to the lavatory. To create the illusion that no one was inside, he would not shut the door. Rather he would stand quietly behind it until the bus had pulled out—just a precaution against a last-minute check.

I heard the station's final call for the bus to Houston, and saw the driver climb in. Right behind him was the Immigration officer. He strode unostentatiously down the aisle, glancing to his left and his right, and asked two people for their papers. Both apparently had them. With my racing pulse and the lump in my throat, one might have thought he was looking for me. But quietly he walked by . . . to the empty back of the bus, to the lavatory. Out of the corner of my eye, I saw him push open the door. . . .

I didn't turn around to watch my friend leave the bus; he did me the favor of not looking over as he followed the officer down the aisle. The bus door groaned shut as they stepped out, and the Greyhound shifted into gear. Alonso was crossing the street to an Immigration van as the coach lumbered out of the station and away to Houston.

"In the middle of a reverie,
I got up from the driver's seat...."

"PEOPLE DO STRANGE THINGS"

1985
Nevada

JAMES CONAWAY

The federal Bureau of Land Management and the U.S. Forest Service administrate 300 million acres of land, almost all of it in the West. That's more than half the land west of the 100th meridian, which runs down the middle of the Dakotas, Nebraska, and Texas. Just under 90 percent of Nevada, for instance, is owned by the federal government.

In 1985, James Conaway, a reporter for the "Style" section of the Washington Post, journeyed through thousands of miles of those public lands. It was a whimsical notion. "It occurred to me that a person could travel this federal kingdom from the Mexican border to Canada and never lose sight of it.... I decided to head west, without a salary or the need for day hits [daily stories], and took a year's leave of absence from Style, knowing I wouldn't return. I told myself that I was obeying the same impulse that had drawn people out of fields and factories a century before; I had to admit that an adolescent urge had become a middle-age preoccupation. I said goodbye to my wife and children, knowing I wouldn't see them for months, and left in a van packed to the windowsills with camping gear, books, a typewriter, and oil company credit cards."

Conaway met many people in the course of that trip, from sheepherders and loggers, to pot growers and environmental activists, but perhaps the most revealing incident occurred when he was alone. He described it in his book about his trip, The Kingdom in the Country.

The West may be a collection of remnants, but they are the most spectacular remnants on earth, full of the past, and of second chances.

Public lands are also an inadvertent refuge for the enduring notion of the West, and consequently for a significant piece of our collective unconscious. For six months I had contemplated the public domain through the windshield, or that narrow gap of window next to my hanging backpack. . . .

Toward the end of the trip, on the edge of Nevada, I began to lose whatever it is that enables the person to distinguish himself from the land. The earth rose and fell before me, under a secondary highway perfectly straight and perfectly empty. In the middle of a reverie, I got up from the driver's seat and walked to the rear of the van. It seemed a logical thing to do, the landscape being deserted and the road a slip of concrete dwindling into mirage. After all, in the greater scheme of things, it made no difference where I drove, or at what velocity, since the country was endless.

I opened the ice chest and grasped the neck of a beer bottle—my first, I should add, in two days. Now, I do not believe in fate, but I do believe that revelation lies in peculiar circumstances, and for some reason this bottle would not budge. An entirely sane person would not have been back there to begin with, but one with at least a glimmer of reason would have, by then, been lunging for the steering wheel. Instead, I wrestled with the bottle.

Months later, a friend would remind me of a passage from Moby-Dick about the mesmerizing quality of the ocean, and its dangers: "There is no life in thee, now, except that rocking life imparted by a gentle rolling ship. . . . But while this sleep, this dream is on ye, move your foot or hand an inch; slip your hold at all; and your identity comes back in horror. . . . And perhaps, at mid-day, in the fairest weather, with one half-throttled shriek you drop through that transparent air into the summer sea, no more to rise for ever."

When finally the bottle relented and came out of the ice chest, I looked up and saw that I was indeed dropping through transparent air: the van had separated from the road. I rushed forward too late, and remember standing in the middle of the floor, gripping the bottle in one hand and the steering wheel in the other, shouting abuse at myself while a culvert materialized out of the glare. We—the van, the bottle, and I— sailed over it and came down with a tremendous crash on the far side. Doors flew open, half a ton of equipment rearranged itself behind me, and hubcaps leaped through the sage like chrome jack rabbits. The van rolled to a halt and I got out and looked back at a column of dust hanging in the air.

Miraculously, I was unhurt, and the van escaped with nothing more than an exploded shock absorber and a bent axle. I drove into a town where a mechanic—the modern medicine man—replaced the shock and straightened the wheel enough for me to drive on. I told him I had swerved to avoid a cow, a lie he recognized as such and listened to with perfect aplomb. He had been in that country long enough to know that people do strange things alone, and that the final justification is surviving.

> "... *Administration officials conceded that the Forest Service was out of control.* ..."

GETTING OUT THE CUT

1987–1995
The Cascadia Mountains and Washington, D.C.

PAUL ROBERTS

James Conaway, author of the preceding account, left Washington, D.C., to trek through the vast federal lands of the West. Reporter Paul Roberts believes the key to understanding those lands—the 300 million acres controlled by the Bureau of Land Management and the U.S. Forest Service—is to be found where Conaway started, Washington.

Roberts, clearly an environmentalist, is no fan of the federal government's administration of its natural resources. (He calls it "the Federal Chain-Saw Massacre.") But what he witnessed could make a political conservative nod in agreement. He reveals that those powerful agencies are like any other bureaucracy: focused on their own survival.

This account comes from a report for Harper's.

Geographically speaking, [the Forest Service] is very much a western agency: national forests are scattered from Alaska to Maine, but 92 percent of the system's acreage lies left of the 100th meridian. This is by and large rugged territory, remnants of the old frontier, which has helped foster the agency's image as a kind of country cousin, a rough-hewn western type who knows birdcalls, likes to sleep on the ground, and chafes at the fancy-pants bean counters in Washington, D.C.

Actually, the Forest Service is among the Beltway's more adept insiders. Although its national office, in a four-story, red-brick edifice one block east of the Mall, is formally charged with administering all 155 national forests, officials there historically have focused on more proximate matters: lobbying congressional budget writers and stopping the undersecretary of agriculture, a White House appointee who oversees the agency, from doing anything rash. Over the decades, the Forest Service has excelled at both tasks, keeping timber-state lawmakers sated with public timber and keeping the hapless undersecretary, as one forestry scientist puts it, "exactly like a mushroom: in the dark, fed nothing but bullshit."

... Moreover, the Forest Service was awarded with an expanding budget: Timber sales required planning and administration, which

433

required budget appropriations; more sales meant larger budget requests. . . . Thus by selling more timber, agency officials could grow their own budgets, staffs, and operations.

. . . The impact of this budgetary back-scratching on national timber policy cannot be understated. Each year, agency officials set themselves an annual timber-sale goal, put in their budget requests, and then worked diligently to ensure that budgeted sales were actually sold. Indeed, to fall short of a sale target meant resuming some of that year's appropriations; worse, it meant not being able to ask for an even higher appropriation the following year. Within the agency, "production" became the watchword. In the field, "getting out the cut" was the key to promotion. . . .

When fires swept the West in 1987, the Forest Service grasped the new benefit of salvage: a way to sell trees and collect receipts without fear of environmentalists or deficit hawks. . . . "And suddenly," says [Robert Wolf, a former Congressional Research Service analyst who helped draft the 1976 salvage provision], "every tree was very sick."

Agency officials everywhere began scouring their forests for anything remotely resembling a dead or dying tree, and between 1988 and 1989 salvage receipts quadrupled, from $32 million to $144 million. . . .

Privately, some administration officials conceded that the Forest Service was out of control on salvage. Yet for nearly a year, the White House maintained publicly that the Forest Service was properly conducting salvage sales and refused to take action. Even Clinton's orders to the Forest Service to behave turned out to be hollow: when environmentalists referred to the memo during a suit against salvage in Montana, Justice Department attorneys pointed out, correctly, that such memos do not carry the force of law.

. . . On July 27, 1995, the day [a new salvage law] was signed, arsonists torched 20,000 acres of the Gila National Forest in New Mexico.

". . . The frenzied screams of grown men and women. . . ."

WEST TEXAS FOOTBALL

1988
Midland, Texas

H. G. BISSINGER

In Texas, high school football is a nearly a religion. Bissinger, a Pulitzer Prize—winning reporter, wrote about it in one of his books, Friday Night Lights.

Tickets for the showdown at Midland High didn't go on sale until Tuesday afternoon, which explained why the first handful of Permian fans started camping outside the gate of Ratliff Stadium Sunday night.

About fifty came together in the darkness. Once the gate was opened, others flooded in and began battening down for the thirty-six-hour vigil. Since many of them had done it before, there was no particular trick to it. Some spent the night in elaborate motor homes as long as railroad cars. Others slept in sleeping bags in the backs of their Suburbans, and others just caught a few winks in lawn chairs. During the day they used umbrellas to shield themselves from the West Texas sun. An Ector County sheriff's deputy was on hand to make sure no fights broke out over who was where in line.

By Tuesday afternoon the line snaked almost the length of the parking lot and 366 fans were in it. One Permian booster, surveying the happy, bleary-eyed skein of people waiting to buy tickets for what, on the surface at least, was just a high school football game, looking out over the parking lot filled on a workday afternoon not only with vehicles but with generators to power television sets and card tables for playing dominoes during the quiet hours before dawn, came to what seemed to be an inarguable conclusion: "Aren't Mojo fans crazy sons of bitches?"

Maybe they were, but the wait paid off. And when Friday night came round on the last day of September, roughly four thousand of them were crammed into the visitor's side for the biggest district showdown of the season.

To those who had fretted after the Marshall game, there was cause to breathe easier now. Mojo was back. The performance the week before against Odessa High, the methodical, relentless carving of Permian's crosstown rival, had proven it. But as soon as the game ended, the not-so-subtle whispers started that the Midland High Bulldogs had the stuff to take Permian.

. . . At the end of practice during the middle of the week, as the final shadows of September crossed over the field and a merciful touch of coolness crept into the wind, Gaines gathered his players around him.

"I guarantee you, men, it will be a sick, sick feeling if we go over there and play poorly," he told them. "We're not that talented. If we go over there and play poorly and lose, it's somethin' you'll remember for a long, long time. Till the day you put your body in the ground, you'll remember it."

. . . Outside the Midland High band, dressed in its purple and gold costumes, played the national anthem. An announcer's voice then came over the public address system, asking the sellout crowd of eleven thousand to rise for the prayer, which everyone eagerly did. At the kickoff, hundreds of purple and gold balloons dreamily floated into the sweet, gorgeous night.

. . . With the score 35-0 by the fourth quarter, the Midland High Bulldogs, sufficiently humbled, might have expected a little letup from Permian, but there was none. . . . Permian scored again to make it 42-0, and some of the starters stood on the benches behind the sidelines, finally able to relax. The win raised their record to four and one overall and a perfect two and zero mark in the district. They were on top now and it didn't seem possible for anyone to catch them. They had their helmets off and they looked like a row of beauty queens. . . . They smiled and laughed and turned to wave at proud parents and proud fans.

All around them the world seemed to be caving in; the way of life that had existed in Odessa for sixty years was badly shaken. Wherever you looked the economic news for this already hard-strapped area was dismal. Echoes persisted of the 1986 crash, when the area had become a scavenger hunt for repossessed Lear jets, Mercedeses, mobile homes, oil rigs, ranches, and two-bedroom houses with walls so thin they seemed translucent. The very day of the game, oil prices, the bread-and-butter benchmark of everyone who lived here, had skidded to $13.25 a barrel, their lowest level since August 1986 and far from that of the halcyon days of 1981 when $35 a barrel oil had made this part of the country a combination of Plato's Retreat and the Barnum and Bailey Circus.

The same day, federal regulators announced they were spending $2.49 billion to rescue six Texas savings and loan institutions that had finally fallen under the weight of the crash in oil prices, and everyone knew that that was just the tip of the iceberg. On the immediate local front, reports showed that rental rates for apartments in Odessa had dropped 10 percent and occupancy rates 8 percent, boding disaster for a market that was woefully overbuilt from the boom. In addition, a news report showed that over the past six years the number of employed workers in Odessa had dropped by 22,400, from 65,200 to 42,800.

But here in Memorial Stadium in Midland, where a near-sellout crowd had gathered to watch a high school football game, none of that seemed to matter. The joyous swells of the band, with no note ever too loud or too off-key, the unflagging faith of the cheerleaders and all those high-octave cheers served up without a trace of self-consciousness, the frenzied screams of grown men and women as the boys on the field rose to dizzying, unheard-of heights. . . .

"I have too many cars in my emotional garage."

ESALEN

1988
Big Sur, California

JONATHAN LIEBERSON

The Esalen Institute is sometimes credited as being the birthplace of the "human potential" movement, which aims to expand one's consciousness. Founded in 1962 by Michael Murphy on 175 acres of his family's estate near Big Sur, and named for a small tribe of local Indians, the institute offers courses that are either enlightening or amusing, depending on your attitude.

This eyewitness, author Jonathan Lieberson, was not enlightened.

Although once one has been exposed to the Esalen catalogue it is difficult to put down, the descriptions in it of courses offered by the institute present some unusual problems of interpretation. One weekend course, entitled "Exorcising the Demon 'Should,' " is described in part as follows: "Within each of us there lives a demon—our own personal critic—whose greatest joy comes from criticizing, denigrating, and destroying every experience we have. This demon, who commands us to be who we aren't in order to satisfy someone we can never satisfy, is the demon that we will seek to exorcise during the weekend." The price is $230, quite a bargain in light of the far greater price paid in similar efforts by Rimbaud or the Marquis de Sade. The promises made by other courses are not as easy to pin down. A course, also carrying the price tag of $230, called "Zen and the Art of Fly Fishing," is described as "a combination of practical instruction, visualization, physical exercise, and guided fantasy"; it argues that "there is a focus and subtlety of movement in fly fishing akin to Eastern meditative disciplines. The possibility always exists of entering the trout's world. In fly fishing, the trout are the teachers," a claim which suggests underwater tutorials, taught by Disney-like professor fishes wearing spectacles.

Pitiless Teutonic rigor is implied in the following course, entitled "Polarity Massage" ($230): "The Esalen mineral baths will be the classroom for exploring and learning by experience the basic concepts of polarity body work through the medium of massage. Emphasis will be on the dynamics of living anatomy and polarity energy balancing methods as implemented in the course of complete, full-body massage." And one course that would seem to require a stern hand if it is not to degenerate into hanky-panky claims to introduce "a new way of seeing the body, using eyes, nose, throat, hands, ears, and hara," the last-named being "an energy center located two fingers below the navel." The course description that sent thought balloons with question marks in them gliding over my head was "Shamanic Healing, Journeying, and the Afterlife Experience: Basic and Intermediate Shamanic Practice" ($680). In it, "with the aid of traditional sonic-driving and dancing methods, the group will engage in archetypical exercises and rituals practiced by North and South American Indian shamans to awaken dormant human capabilities and forgotten connections with the powers of nature. Practice will include shamanic journeys to both the Lower- and Upperworlds for knowledge and power, work with animal and plant powers, divination, clairvoyance, and shamanic methods of healing." In addition, "there will be an introduction to the Ghost Dance method and to shamanic ways of exploring the afterlife experience"; participants are invited to "bring drums and rattles." The faculty conducting these seminars and workshops contains many unusual personalities, including a specialist in "personal applications of video," the founder of the "Gestalt Fool Theater Family of San Francisco," a writer "with earlier careers as homemaker and fiber artist," and someone called "Hareesh," crisply described as "interested in alternative nutritional programs." A tenure-track faculty member is Jezariah Canyon Munyer, who teaches a course entitled "Miracles of Infancy" ($230) with his parents; he is one year old.

Inflamed by expectations of witnessing some of these activities during my visit to Esalen, I was distressed to find that none of them were being currently offered, and that because of the rockslide I was doomed to spend twelve hours in what can only be described as a peculiar mixture of a singles resort and a lunatic asylum. This impression was suggested to me by my first sight of residents at the institute, a wiry, bearded old man out of John Brown's gang jogging painfully down a hillside path in the company of two laughing young women wearing waist-length hair and feather earrings, and it was confirmed by my encounters with others, equally arresting: a tall, head-nodding man who had just been to Findhorn, in Scotland, a "community" where he had been taught to speak with affection to cabbages and roses in order to make them grow, and where, he assured me, astonishing results had occurred; an earnest, bespectacled woman who had vowed never to use the word "I," and who hugged whomever she was with before taking leave; two elderly ladies in jumpsuits, sitting motionlessly and staring pop-eyed at the sea, then vigorously stripping off the suits and surrendering them-selves to the sun; a woman who skipped down a hill singing coloratura exercises in half-voice, and then stopped, took a breath, and erupted into some deafening spectacular high notes; a man who said, "I have too many cars in my emotional garage."

To be fair, there is a sincere side to all this.

Sensualist author Henry Miller, forced by World War II to return to the U.S. from Europe, exiled himself to Big Sur. At the time, Big Sur was home to just a loose collection of loners and seekers, whom Miller admired:

"Since living here in Big Sur I have become more and more aware of this ten-dency in my fellow-American to experiment. Today it is not communities or groups who seek to lead 'the good life' but isolated individuals. . . . We are in the habit of speaking of 'the last frontier,' but wherever there are 'individuals' there will always be new frontiers. . . .

"Everyone who has come here in search of a new way of life has made a com-plete change-about in his daily routine. Nearly every one has come from afar, usually from a big city. It meant abandoning a job and a mode of life which was detestable and insufferable. To what degree each one has found 'new life' can be estimated only by the efforts he or she put forth. Some, I suspect, would have found 'it' even had they remained where they were.

"The most important thing I have witnessed, since coming here, is the trans-formation people have wrought in their own being. Nowhere have I seen individ-uals work so earnestly and assiduously on themselves. . . . The people of this vicinity are striving to live up to the grandeur and nobility which is such an inte-gral part of the setting. . . . There being nothing to improve on in the surround-ings, the tendency is to set about improving oneself."

". . . She suddenly discovered that she was up to her nose in politics."

THE *EXXON VALDEZ*

March–April 1989
Valdez, Alaska

JOHN KEEBLE

Author Joe McGinniss, visiting Valdez when it became the seaport terminus of the Alaska Pipeline in 1977 (see page 399), said the town "had, perhaps, the most beautiful natural setting of any town in Alaska. Mountains—higher and more rugged mountains than in Juneau—curved around it on three sides, broken only by the waters of the fjord. In its pre-pipeline days, Valdez had billed itself as "the Switzerland of Alaska," though one would have been hard-pressed in Switzerland to find its equal.

On March 24, 1989, the oil supertanker Exxon Valdez *left Valdez after being laden with 1.26 million barrels of oil drawn from the pipeline. About 25 miles outside of Valdez, the 987-foot-long ship struck a reef. It ran aground, and had a hole torn in its hull. Millions of gallons of crude oil gushed into Prince William Sound. The ship lost about 11 million gallons of oil, creating a slick that stretched for hundreds of miles and eventually 1,200 miles of coastline. And it occurred when perhaps hundreds of thousands of seabirds were being drawn to the coastline to feed on the seasonal herring hatch.*

Most of the spill's damage was to wildlife. But John Keeble, author of Out of the Channel, *found the story of the spill had a lot to do with people.*

From Marge Tillion I heard another version of what had become the main story told and retold by lower Kenai Peninsula people—the shock felt when Exxon and its contractors came to town, even here, well around the corner from the oil spill's principal effects in Prince William Sound. I sat on a couch in Marge's living room in Homer and she sat across from me on an easy chair. She and her husband are fishers. She is also a fireman and licensed emergency medical technician. Her father-in-law, Gem Tillion, was an old-time Alaska legislator and close associate of former governor Jay Hammond. Marge has dark, short hair and flashing eyes and is deeply tanned by the outdoors. She is articulate and, as Larry had said, formidable.

She'd become involved with the response four days after the oil spill. "My immediate thought was that they were going to need boats to help them," she said. "I made a database by feeding in the lists from fishing organizations." She got up and left the living room, then came back with a three-inch-thick stack of spread sheet-sized computer printouts, set it down on the floor, and ranged through it, looking down at it at times as she spoke and then over at me. The database had grown fast, she said. People began calling to get their boats and equipment on it. For its sheer voluminousness, her database echoed the other lists that were everywhere. Hers included storage tanks, hydroblasters, shovels, five-gallon buckets, people, showers, skiffs, airplanes, and 800 boats.

Right away, she said, she and the other local volunteers arranged to use the high school as a Bird Rescue Center and the junior high swimming pool for the Otter Rescue Center (later moved to Jackolof Bay near Seldovia). The high-school teachers encouraged their students to help with the effort. An Exxon representative called from Valdez to ask if he could get access to her database. She had so many calls that she added five telephone lines to her house, and a fax and photocopy machine. By the first week in April, her house had become the Oil Resource Center, and then she suddenly discovered that she was up to her nose in politics.

The people were calling from the Prince William counties of Valdez and Cordova, warning about inflated prices, housing problems, the press, lawyers, the ruthless takeover of the towns. "I worked for hours begging our mayor not to let them bring [construction and maintenance subcontractor] Veco in," she said. She wanted a local organization to work with Exxon. She remembered what had happened in Valdez when the pipeline came in. "I had the clearest picture of what was going to happen here. But I still wasn't paying close enough attention. I still didn't believe that we wouldn't be able to do something to stop it. I picked up the first two Exxon people at the airport and pleaded with them—'Please don't bring Veco in.' I showed them my database. They assured me all they wanted Veco for was to do the accounting. I worked for two or three weeks without a contract, just to watch them because I had a gut feeling they were not being straight. Sure enough, Veco came in and started up with the accounting. During a storm, I heard Veco was hiring skiffs to go out in heavy seas to pull boom. Suddenly it hit me that somebody might die out there and that if they did I might be liable, too, and I told the Veco people, and they said, 'You shut up. You do what we want you to do, and say what we want you to say.'"

She moved back to the chair and looked at me. "I will not be bought off," she said. "A guy from Exxon blocked off my car one day and said, 'Hey, what do you want? Six, seven thousand a day? We'd pay you.' I said, 'I can't work with you. This is my database and I want control of it.' It was a tough spot. I wanted to take my database out of there, but at the same time if I did I'd set the whole effort back several weeks."

At that time, the Homer and Seldovia volunteers' log boom project was well under way. Marge said that Exxon went back on its word and turned the entire Kenai Peninsula cleanup operation over to Veco. "Everything went bad then," she said. She said that Veco inflated figures, including counting boat people twice—once as a boat crew and once again as cleanup crew—in order to increase the margin on its "cost plus" contract. Marge, like many others, had become distraught and decided to go out with a science crew to "cool out." When she returned she found that Larry Smith and John Mickelson, the Seldovia MAC representative, had secured a million dollars from Exxon, which was to be channeled through the borough to run an independent cleanup crew. It was at first thought to be a replenishable million, that is, a million-dollar balance that would be sustained by Exxon, but as it turned out, by the time the million ran out the entire operation had been taken over by Veco. In Marge's view, this was how Veco took the town over—by gradually encroaching upon agreements and filling in all the gaps until it had control.

In the meantime, an 18-person crew had been hired and put to work. In an echo of some of the Cordova efforts, it picked up between four and five thousand gallons of oil a day. But then they were left out there, awaiting tankerage to take on their oil. When the money ran out, Marge tried—and, but for one boat skipper, failed—to get her crew taken on by Veco. The entire operation was stalled, she said, while the new manager, a real estate agent, took two weeks to develop a company to handle his business. At the same time, oil was appearing in Cook Inlet. When it was reported, it took between two and three weeks to get anybody to look at it. She claimed that the Veco workers went to absorbent pads for cleaning because the crews were always green, and anything else was too complicated for them. She said they hired 40 crew members, flew them to the beach to perform for a film crew. and then when the filming was over, let the entire crew go. "We don't hold it against them that they don't know how to clean beaches," Marge said. "What we do hold against them is that they refuse to use our expertise. They could have benefited from us and at the same time left us all feeling good about oil companies by putting us to work.

"Salmon is my whole income," she said. "They gave us ten thousand for the Cook Inlet Drift Net Closure, and that may be all I'll see. In the meantime I can't leave, I can't get a job, and I can't fish. I've got three kids, and one of them is going to a school in Seattle for dyslexia. The contract for our tender boat makes two-thirds of the payments on the boat, and we've got to find the other third somewhere or lose the boat." Her voice had begun to shake. She paused, and then told me I should get

Larry Smith to show me the bird-burning video. Eventually, I saw it at his house. Rough and grainy, strictly amateur and not attempting to be anything else, a kind of accidental document, the video carries more of the weight of death than any of the professional photographic records I have yet seen.

Marge's disappointment, and her desire to do something, to be engaged, along with similar feelings by others, led to a project sponsored by HARC. A beach cleaning project, it came to be centered at Mars Cove, not far from Gore Point on the southern side of the Kenai Peninsula's heavily oiled area that Exxon had essentially abandoned to the elements. The project proposed to rehabilitate one beach. It would raise all its funding through contributions, apply the strictest methods of accounting, and employ an all-volunteer labor force. Begun in early July, and initially using shovels, buckets, and absorbent pads, the project later used a rock washing machine invented by a young man named Billy Day. The process involved digging up a small section of oiled beach at low tide, running the rocks through a system of high-pressure hoses, vacuuming off the oil from a catch pond, then replacing the rocks The project was begun in late August and ran through September, after the Exxon cleanup operation had pulled out. When the volunteers were done, a small patch of the beach was clean.

"The more I learn about what it means to be a 'downwinder,' the more questions I drown in."

THE CLAN OF ONE-BREASTED WOMEN

1989
Utah

TERRY TEMPEST WILLIAMS

It seems fairly obvious Because the wind blows across America from west to east, a nuclear bomb detonated in the West can spread fallout across the country. Yet, in the 1950s and 1960s, the government detonated nearly 100 atomic bombs above ground in Nevada, sending fallout as far as the east coast. "There were few, if any, Americans in the contiguous 48 states at that time who were not exposed to some level of fallout," Dr. Richard Klausner, director of the National Cancer Institute, recently told the New York Times.

Even supporters of nuclear testing should have thought twice. As author

Rebecca Solnit has observed, "test is something of a misnomer when it comes to nuclear bombs. A test is controlled and contained, a preliminary to the thing itself, and though these nuclear bombs weren't being dropped on cities or strategic centers, they were full-scale explosions in the real world, with all the attendant effects."

Terry Tempest Williams is the author of Refuge, from which this account comes.

I belong to a Clan of One-breasted Women. My mother, my grandmothers, and six aunts have all had mastectomies. Seven are dead. The two who survive have just completed rounds of chemotherapy and radiation.

I've had my own problems: two biopsies for breast cancer and a small tumor between my ribs diagnosed as "a borderline malignancy."

This is my family history.

Most statistics tell us breast cancer is genetic, hereditary, with rising percentages attached to fatty diets, childlessness, or becoming pregnant after thirty. What they don't say is living in Utah may be the greatest hazard of all.

We are a Mormon family with roots in Utah since 1847. The word-of-wisdom, a religious doctrine of health, kept the women in my family aligned with good foods: no coffee, no tea, tobacco, or alcohol. For the most part, these women were finished having their babies by the time they were thirty. And only one faced breast cancer before 1960. Traditionally, as a group of people, Mormons have a low rate of cancer.

Is our family a cultural anomaly? The truth is we didn't think about it. Those who did, usually the men, simply said, "bad genes." The women's attitude was stoic. Cancer was part of life. On February 16, 1971, the eve of my mother's surgery, I accidentally picked up the telephone and overheard her ask my grandmother what she could expect.

"Diane, it is one of the most spiritual experiences you will ever encounter."

I quietly put down the receiver.

Two days later, my father took my three brothers and me to the hospital to visit her. She met us in the lobby in a wheelchair. No bandages were visible. I'll never forget her radiance, the way she held herself in a purple velvet robe and how she gathered us around her.

"Children, I am fine. I want you to know I felt the arms of God around me."

We believed her. My father cried. Our mother, his wife, was thirty-eight years old.

A little over a year after Mother's death, my father and I were having dinner together. He had just returned from St. George, where the Tempest company was completing the natural gas lines that would service southern Utah. He spoke of his love for the country, the sandstone landscape, bare-boned and beautiful. He had just finished hiking the Kolob Trail in Zion National Park. We got caught up in reminiscing, recalling with fondness our walk up Angel's Landing on his fiftieth birthday and the years our family had vacationed there.

Over dessert, I shared a recurring dream of mine. I told my father that for years, as long as I could remember, I saw this flash of light in the night in the desert. That this image had so permeated my being, I could not venture south without seeing it again, on the horizon, illuminating buttes and mesas.

"You did see it," he said.

"Saw what?" I asked, a bit tentative.

"The bomb. The cloud. We were driving home from Riverside, California. You were sitting on your mother's lap. She was pregnant. In fact, I remember the date, September 7, 1957. We had just gotten out of the service. We were driving north, past Las Vegas. It was an hour or so before dawn, when this explosion went off. We not only heard it but felt it. I thought the oil tanker in front of us had blown up. We pulled over and suddenly, rising from the desert floor, we saw it clearly, this golden-stemmed cloud, the mushroom. The sky seemed to vibrate with an eerie pink glow. Within a few minutes, a light ash was raining on the car."

I stared at my father. This was new information to me.

"I thought you knew that," he said. "It was a common occurrence in the fifties."

It was at this moment I realized the deceit I had been living under. Children growing up in the American Southwest, drinking contaminated milk, from contaminated cows, even from the contaminated breasts of their mothers, my mother—members, years later, of the Clan of One-breasted Women.

It is a well-known story in the Desert West, "The Day We Bombed Utah." Or perhaps, "The Years We Bombed Utah." Above-ground atomic testing in Nevada took place from January 27, 1951, through July 11, 1962. Not only were the winds blowing north covering "low use segments of the population" with fallout and leaving sheep dead in their tracks, but the climate was right. The United States in the 1950s was red, white, and blue. The Korean War was raging, McCarthyism was rampant. Ike was it, and the Cold War was hot. If you were against nuclear testing, you were for a Communist regime.

Much has been written about this "American nuclear tragedy." Public health was secondary to national security. The atomic energy commissioner, Thomas Murray, said, "Gentlemen, we must not let anything interfere with this series of tests, nothing."

Again and again, the American public was told by its government, in spite of burns, blisters, and nausea, "It has been found that the tests may be conducted with adequate assurance of safety under conditions prevailing at the bombing reservations." Assuaging public fears was simply a matter of public relations. "Your best action," an Atomic Energy Commission booklet read, "is not to be worried about fallout." A news release typical of the times stated, "We find no basis for concluding that harm to any individual has resulted from radioactive fallout."

On August 30, 1979, during Jimmy Carter's presidency, a suit was filed entitled *Irene Allen v. the United States of America*. Mrs. Allen was the first to be alphabetically listed with twenty-four test cases, representative of nearly twelve hundred plaintiffs seeking compensation from the U.S. government for cancers caused from nuclear testing in Nevada.

Irene Allen lived in Hurricane, Utah. She was the mother of five children and had been widowed twice. Her first husband, with their two oldest boys, had watched the tests from the roof of the local high school. He died of leukemia in 1956. Her second husband died of pancreatic cancer in 1978.

In a town meeting conducted by Utah Senator Orrin Hatch, shortly before the suit was filed, Mrs. Allen said, "I am not blaming the government, I want you to know that, Senator Hatch. But I thought if my testimony could help in any way so this wouldn't happen again to any of the generations coming up after us . . . I am really happy to be here this day to bear testimony of this."

God-fearing people. This is just one story in an anthology of thousands.

On May 10, 1984, Judge Bruce S. Jenkins handed down his opinion. Ten of the plaintiffs were awarded damages. It was the first time a federal court had determined that nuclear tests had been the cause of cancers. For the remaining fourteen test cases, the proof of causation was not sufficient. In spite of the split decision, it was considered a landmark ruling. It was not to remain so for long.

In April 1987, the Tenth Circuit Court of Appeals overturned Judge Jenkins's ruling on the ground that the United States was protected from suit by the legal doctrine of sovereign immunity, a centuries' old idea from England in the days of absolute monarchs.

In January 1988, the Supreme Court refused to review the appeals court decision. To our court system, it does not matter whether the U.S. government is immune. "The King can do no wrong."

In Mormon culture, authority is respected, obedience is revered, and independent thinking is not. I was taught as a young girl not to "make waves" or "rock the boat."

"Just let it go," my mother would say. "You know how you feel, that's what counts."

For many years, I did just that—listened, observed, and quietly formed my own opinion within a culture that rarely asked questions because they had all the answers. But one by one, I watched the women in my family die common, heroic deaths. We sat in waiting rooms hoping for good news, always receiving the bad. I cared for them, bathed their scarred bodies and kept their secrets. I watched beautiful women become bald as Cytoxan, cisplatin, and Adriamycin were injected into their veins. I held their foreheads as they vomited green-black bile, and I shot them with morphine when the pain became inhuman. In the end, I witnessed their last, peaceful breaths, becoming a midwife to the rebirth of their souls.

The price of obedience became too high.

The fear and inability to question authority that ultimately killed rural communities in Utah during atmospheric testing of atomic weapons was the same fear I saw being held in my mother's body. Sheep. Dead sheep. The evidence is buried.

I cannot prove that my mother, Diane Dixon Tempest, or my grandmothers, Lettie Romney Dixon and Kathryn Blackett Tempest, along with my aunts, contracted cancer from nuclear fallout in Utah. But I can't prove they didn't.

My father's memory was correct. The September blast we drove through in 1957 was part of Operation Plumbbob, one of the most intensive series of bomb tests to be initiated. The flash of light in the night in the desert I had always thought was a dream developed into a family nightmare. It took fourteen years, from 1957 to 1971, for cancer to show up in my mother—the same time Howard L. Andrews, an authority on radioactive fallout at the National Institutes of Health, says radiation cancer requires to become evident. The more I learn about what it means to be a "downwinder," the more questions I drown in.

What I do know, however, is that as a Mormon woman of the fifth generation of "Latter-day Saints," I must question everything, even if it means losing my faith, even if it means becoming a member of a border tribe among my own people. Tolerating blind obedience in the name of patriotism or religion ultimately takes our lives.

When the Atomic Energy Commission described the country north of the Nevada Test Site as "virtually uninhabited desert terrain," my family were some of the "virtual uninhabitants."

Part of the fallout was concentrated by dairy cows in milk, harming children worst. Among people who were children during the testing, doctors expect 10,000 to 75,000 cases of thyroid cancer, three-quarters of which cases had yet to be diagnosed by the 1990s. Ten percent may be fatal.

"It was Rodney Glen King who controlled his own destiny."

THE THIN BLUE LINE

April 1992
Simi Valley, California

LINDA DEUTSCH AND ANNETTE HADDAD

On the evening of March 3, 1991, motorist Rodney King was stopped for speeding in Los Angeles. In the course of arresting him, several Los Angeles Police Department officers beat him severely, unaware that they were being videotaped by an eyewitness.

The videotape was broadcast all over the world, causing an international outcry against police brutality and racism. Officers Laurence Powell, Stacey Koon, Theodore Briseno, and Timothy Wind were charged with assault.

Eyewitness Linda Deutsch reported on the trial for the Associated Press. Annette Haddad reported for United Press International.

DEUTSCH

Police officers were obeying society's demand for protection when they clubbed and kicked black motorist Rodney King, a defense lawyer told the jury in closing arguments.

Michael Stone, a former policeman who represents Officer Laurence Powell, recalled a sign he once saw in a police gymnasium: "There are no second-place ribbons in a street fight."

"These officers, these defendants, do not get paid to lose a street fight," Stone said. "They do not get paid to roll around in the dirt with the likes of Rodney Glen King. That's not their job. That's not their duty."

Stone added: "These are not 'Robocops,' ladies and gentlemen."

"They hurt. They feel pain and they die like everyone else," he said. "We leave it to them to take care of the mean streets so we can enjoy our lives with our families."

. . . Although Powell is not claiming he struck King in self-defense, the policeman was protecting himself, Stone said.

"Duty required Officer Powell to react, not to run away, and he was faithful to his charge," Stone said. "Duty did not require Officer Powell to wind up himself on a gurney in a hospital. Duty did not require Officer Powell to wind up on a slab, toes up, in the morgue."

. . . Stone said race is not an issue, and urged jurors to ignore Powell's computer message referring to a separate encounter with a black family as "right out of 'Gorillas in the Mist.' "

Stone said King started the fight when he led police on a high-speed chase then acted strangely when he got out of his car.

"He chose to fight them," Stone said. "Rodney Glen King made the choices and every choice Rodney Glen King made was the wrong one. Whose fault is that? . . . From start to finish, it was Rodney Glen King who controlled his own destiny. . . ."

HADDAD

In a fiery "in your face" final summation in the Los Angeles police brutality trial, the prosecutor singled out Officer Laurence Powell as the man chiefly responsible for beating Rodney King.

Displaying a rarely exhibited passion, Deputy District Attorney Terry White stormed across the courtroom to Powell during his final rebuttal argument, jabbing his finger inches from Powell's face.

"This is the man and look at him," White said. "He laughed, he taunted (King) and he's denying it."

With White's stinging words hanging in the air, Powell's attorney objected and Judge Stanley Weisberg told White to get back to the podium.

Prosecutors have contended that Powell can be heard on a police radio tape laughing about the beating, and that he mocked King in a hospital emergency room after the incident.

Powell claimed the sound prosecutors describe as laughter is merely heavy breathing.

. . . The 81-second video is the prosecution's key piece of evidence and with the exception of Briseno, the three others have sought to downplay its significance, focusing instead on the threat King allegedly presented because of his "bizarre behavior," imposing physical size and criminal background.

Briseno has said his colleagues were wrong and testified they were "out of control" while kicking and clubbing King.

Powell, seen on the tape swinging his steel night stick dozens of times at King, has argued he had no choice because King acted aggressively and continued to resist arrest. At one point in his testimony, Powell said King acted like an animal.

White reserved much of his rebuttal for Powell, whose attorney, Mike Stone, spent five hours on his closing argument, saying Powell was not a "brutal thug."

"They treated (King) like an animal and yet Mike Stone does not want you to call his client a 'thug,'" White said turning to look at Powell over his shoulder.

"All right then, you're not a thug—you were just acting like one, just like you said Rodney King was acting like an animal that night."

. . . White . . . called it a "tragedy" that Koon, Powell and Wind argued they were within their right to beat King as they did.

"For the three of them to come in here and hide behind that badge, it's an embarrassment to every man and woman in law enforcement in this country . . . who go to work every day and follow the law," White said.

"These men and women do their job every day without resorting to the brutality and violence you've seen on this screen over the last six weeks," White told jurors as he pointed to the TV monitor where the video has been shown dozens of times since the trial began. . . .

The officers were found not guilty. Within hours of the reading of the all-white jury's verdict, protests and riots broke out across the country.

In Los Angeles, looting and arson continued for seven days, ending only after the arrival of 9,800 National Guardsmen and 3,300 federal troops, along with officers from the FBI and the border patrol. The riot there was estimated to have caused 55 deaths and more than 2,300 injuries. More than 600 fires were set, and more than 1,100 buildings were damaged.

". . . Can you say that Mr. Weaver
even pointed a gun at anybody?"

GOVERNMENT ON TRIAL

1993
Boise, Idaho

GEORGE LARDNER, JR., AND RICHARD LEIBY

Antigovernment militia groups invoke the shootout at Ruby Ridge as a modern version of the Boston Massacre or the Alamo siege. It wasn't on nearly as grand a scale, occurring only at an isolated mountain cabin. But that's the point, they say.

On August 21, 1992, federal marshals surrounded the cabin of white supremacist Randy Weaver. They wanted to arrest Weaver on a weapons charge. Instead, a shootout began. Deputy U.S. Marshal William Degan and Sammy Weaver, Randy's fourteen-year-old-son, were killed. Randy, his wife, Vicki, and family friend Kevin Harris refused to leave the cabin. With them were the three remaining Weaver children, teenagers Rachel and Sara, and infant Elisheba.

The FBI's Hostage Rescue Team was called in, and team commander Richard Rogers set a shoot-on-sight policy for any armed adult in or near the cabin. When Randy Weaver left the cabin the next day, FBI sniper Lon Horiuchi shot him, but only wounded him. Horiuchi then fired at Kevin Harris. The shot wounded Harris and ricocheted to kill Vicki Weaver, who was standing in the cabin doorway with her baby. On August 31, Weaver and Harris surrendered, and were charged with killing Marshall William Degan.

Lardner and Leiby reported for the Washington Post.

FBI sniper Lon Horiuchi and his boss, Richard Rogers, stepped into the Boise federal courthouse on June 2, 1993, flanked by a squad of husky bodyguards with what spectators thought to be large automatic weapons under their jackets. It was a visible show of force in the midst of a criminal prosecution that was growing weaker by the day.

. . . Rogers, commander of the FBI's elite Hostage Rescue Team, was the first to testify. His squad had been dispatched to deal with the Weavers after Degan was killed. Before Rogers even arrived at the scene on the morning of Aug. 22, 1992, he composed "rules of engagement" for the snipers that amounted to a "shoot on sight" policy for any armed adult seen near the Weaver cabin.

Under questioning, Rogers said he was satisfied from reports received during a hurried flight west that Weaver had "clearly demonstrated that he was willing to shoot at federal officers."

"Well," Weaver's chief defense lawyer, Gerry Spence, asked Rogers, "did you know of anybody then, and do you know of anybody now, as you sit there today, who ever saw Mr. Weaver shoot at anybody?"

Rogers: "No, I do not."

Spence: "Do you know of anybody, as you sit there now today, that can say that Mr. Weaver even pointed a gun at anybody?"

Rogers: "No, I'm not aware of any."

Weaver listened at the defense table. During the brief Aug. 21 gunfight, Weaver himself fired no shots at anyone. The next evening, Horiuchi, without warning, fired two shots from his perch behind a pine tree, wounding Weaver and Harris, and killing Weaver's wife, Vicki.

Horiuchi, a West Point graduate and 10-year FBI veteran, testified next. Since the snipers were told the Weavers usually came out of their house armed, he said, the "rules of engagement" made them fair game.

Spence: "Under your rules of engagement, you could then, and should—if they came out of the house, you could and should use deadly force?"

Horiuchi: "Yes sir, it is true."

What about a warning shot? Spence asked.

"Sir, we do not fire warning shots in the FBI."

Spence: "If you're going to shoot, you shoot to kill, don't you?"

Horiuchi: "Yes, sir."

At another point, Spence asked the sniper if he enjoyed his job. He said he did.

In the jury box, Dorothy Mitchell felt a shudder. "I interpreted his answer to be, 'I enjoy killing,'" she said in a recent interview, "That was hard for me to take. He was just cold-hearted." She and other jurors were struck by the trauma Weaver's children must have suffered, living in the cabin for almost 10 days with their mother's bloody corpse on the kitchen floor.

In this context, Rogers's testimony was equally chilling. "Even after all this horrible stuff happened, he wasn't questioning whether what they did was right," recalled juror Dorothy Hoffman. "He didn't seem to have any conscience, if that's the word."

"He took those [standard FBI rules of deadly force] that are drilled into everybody and basically threw them out the window and wrote his own," said jury foreman Jack Weaver (no relation to Randy Weaver). "I got the sense that if he had to do it all over again, he'd do the same thing."

The five men and seven women sitting in judgment of Weaver and Harris eventually came to wonder whether the right people were on trial. "This is a murder case," Spence thundered in closing. "But the people who committed the murder have not been charged."

In July 1993, a federal jury found Weaver and Harris not guilty of murder. The Justice Department subsequently agreed to pay Weaver compensation of $3.1 million for the killing of his wife and son. The Justice Department's report called the rules of engagement set for the snipers "unconstitutional." And in 1998, FBI sniper Horiuchi was ordered to stand trial for murder.

But was the shootout really an example of organized oppression? Sara Weaver, Randy's daughter, once offered this succinct summary: "I think it came down to the F.B.I.'s ego and my dad's pride," she said. "And they had the bigger guns."

"This is just the first sound of the alarm."

WAITING FOR THE END OF THE WORLD

June 18, 1995
Kingman, Arizona

KIT R. ROANE

The deadliest act of terrorism in the United States occurred in Oklahoma City on April 19, 1995, when Timothy McVeigh detonated a homemade bomb that demolished the Alfred P. Murrah Federal Building.

The date of the blast was significant. McVeigh wanted to commemorate the final showdown between federal agents and members of the Branch Davidian religious cult in Waco, Texas, on the same day in 1993. The Waco incident had begun when authorities tried to raid the heavily defended Branch Davidian compound, hoping to arrest its leader, David Koresh. (The official reason for the raid was concern about the safety of children in the cult.) The agents bungled the raid. Four were killed, as were six Branch Davidians. The agents retreated to a standoff that lasted almost two months. On April 19, 1993, another surprise raid turned the compound into a huge funeral pyre, killing eighty Branch Davidians.

McVeigh and his accomplice in the Oklahoma bombing, Terry Nichols, saw themselves as patriots, defenders of the rights of the individual against big government. Most Americans saw them as losers, men with more ambition than ability, for whom big government was just an object of displaced hatred they felt for people at large. They had each traveled from job to job, city to city, feeling and acting like failures and outsiders wherever they went. The problems they faced weren't the making of big government; their victims weren't big government. McVeigh detonated his bomb on a weekday morning, ensuring that he would do much more than destroy the building and shut down government services. The bomb killed 168 people and left more than 850 injured.

Shortly after the bombing, McVeigh was stopped by a highway patrolman for a traffic violation, and arrested when the patrolman saw he had a gun. He was quickly linked to the bombing, but he refused to discuss his actions. In Kingman, Arizona, where McVeigh lived before the attack, Kit Roane of the New York Times looked for clues to what was going on in McVeigh's mind. A lot of like-minded people were happy to oblige.

James Maxwell Oliphant has waited more than a decade for United Nations occupational forces to come knocking at his door here in the desert scrub of Mohave County. During that time, the 70-year-old Mr. Oliphant, a self-described patriot who proudly displays a Ku Klux Klan business card, has blown off one of his arms practicing with explosives, taken in skinheads who later turned against him and served a spell in prison for conspiring to rob armored cars.

Now his expectations are finally being realized: the first wave of enemies, Mr. Oliphant says, has arrived.

And finding agreement among other residents of Kingman is easy.

Since April, so many Federal investigators have scoured Kingman for clues to the Oklahoma City bombing that at times the town has seemed a place for only two kinds of people: suspects and suspected agents.

Timothy J. McVeigh, already charged with the bombing, spent much of the last two years in and around Kingman, and agents have pushed hard to uncover his connections here, staking out his friends' homes and questioning all those who met him.

To be sure, far from everyone in this community of almost 13,000 people is wary of things Federal. But the number who are is sufficient that rumors of impending assault by mystery helicopters and jackbooted foreign troops under one-world command have circulated for years.

Against that backdrop, the influx of the agents, wearing dark glasses and driving shiny rental cars, has lent this ancestral home of the cowboy comic Andy Devine an air of intrigue, as if it were a Wild West version of East Berlin.

"This is just the first sound of the alarm," said a man peering out from under a floppy leather hat, one of many residents who now either decline to identify themselves altogether or, alternatively, make up names on the spot. "People are going to rise up. There's going to be a war. You can hear about it on AM radio."

Kingman, a mining town 180 miles northwest of Phoenix, was founded in 1880 and has long attracted malcontents, drifters and those dodging the law. Most recently, since the 1970's, it has become a haven for disillusioned Americans hoping to distance themselves from big government.

Now the arrival of the agents has brought the realization that Kingman is not entirely insulated, and a few here have come unhinged. Jim Rosencrans became so irritated with the investigators' presence that he bought a new assault-style rifle and then, when the agents came to search a nearby house trailer, brandished several other guns. He was promptly hauled off to jail.

And David Baker, an auto mechanic who says he once sold Mr. McVeigh a beat-up sedan, rarely leaves his house anymore for fear that agents may be lying in wait to question him.

At the Golden Valley Swap Meet, a weekend flea market where men sell guns alongside broken toasters and counterfeit watches, the presence of Federal agents conspicuously rummaging around has left some vendors so fearful that they ignore actual customers whom they do not know.

But a security guard at the flea market said he was now more worried about some of the vendors than about shoplifters. "Like that guy," motioned the guard, who said his name was Glenn. "He tells everybody he wants to be called Adolf—Adolf Hitler. I tell you, I wouldn't trust any of them."

The agents' presence in Kingman has also led to occasional confusion, not limited to the local citizenry. More than once, agents themselves have rushed off after reporters driving away from one location or another, in the mistaken belief that a possible suspect was fleeing. And during a midnight raid on a house trailer, one agent briefly mistook a reporter for another agent and, before realizing his error, began sharing confidential information.

Adding to the confusion are the residents who happily provide information to reporters and agents alike but juice up their accounts with each succeeding interview.

Jack Gohn, 66, who was once a neighbor of Mr. McVeigh, seems to remember more about him every day. Most recently, after relating his troubles with Alzheimer's disease and his wish to receive a $2 million reward, Mr. Gohn told a reporter that he had seen Mr. McVeigh in the presence of a man who resembled Terry L. Nichols, the other imprisoned bombing suspect. He also provided a name for a man he described as a dead ringer for John Doe No. 2, since identified as a soldier at Fort Riley, Kan., who apparently had no connection to the bombing whatever.

On the other hand, the manager of a local video store where Mr. McVeigh had rented the movie "Blown Away," about a mad bomber, did not tell investigators of the rental for some time, because, he said, they had never asked. And George Boerst, the manager of a photocopy shop where Mr. McVeigh had browsed through paramilitary magazines, did not come forward with that information, instead waiting until a customer's recollection caused inquisitive agents to visit the shop.

One vendor at the Golden Valley Swap Meet said proudly that he lied to the agents just for sport. "I sold McVeigh a .44 Magnum once," said the vendor, adding that his name was John Smith and pausing to see whether the reporter appeared to believe him. "But I didn't tell them that. It's none of their business."

McVeigh was found guilty in a 1997 federal trial. During the sentencing phase, his attorneys asked the jurors to consider a list of "mitigating circumstances," including:

"1. Timothy McVeigh believed deeply in the ideals upon which the United States was founded.

"2. He believed that the Bureau of Alcohol, Tobacco and Firearms and Federal Bureau of Investigation were responsible for the deaths in the Branch Davidian compound at Waco, Tex., in 1993.

"3. He believed that Federal law-enforcement agents murdered Sammy and Vicki Weaver near Ruby Ridge Idaho, in August 1992.

"4. He believed that the increasing use of military-style force and tactics by Federal law enforcement agencies against American citizens was leading to a police state.

"5. His belief that Federal law-enforcement agencies failed to take responsibilities for their actions at Ruby Ridge and Waco, and failed to punish those responsible, added to his growing concerns about the existence of a police state and a loss of constitutional liberties. . . ."

If the lawyers thought they could convince the jury that their client's motivations were reasonable, they were wrong. McVeigh was sentenced to death.

Accomplice Terry Nichols was also found guilty. He received a life sentence. As of 1998, both men face further trials.

"The aliens have done a deal with the U.S. government."

AREA 51

1996
Nevada

RANDALL ROTHENBERG

"If Disney were to create a theme park celebrating American paranoia," critic
Walter Kirn wrote, *"it might want to base the design on central Nevada. . . .
The Great Basin does not just trap precipitation; it is also a sinkhole for curious ideas. . . . Manipulation by distant Mr. Bigs is an obsession here. Almost
90% of Nevada's land is owned and managed by the Federal Government—a
distant imperial power to many locals. . . . Paranoia may be not a pathology
but a rational coping mechanism."*

*The wildest conspiracy theories concern a 1947 incident near Roswell, New
Mexico, where something mysterious fell out of the sky. Was it a weather ballon?
An experimental aircraft? A spy plane? Or was it, as so many people now believe,
a flying saucer flown by extraterrestrials? Retired civil servant Frank Kauffman,
who claims to have been sent by the army to the crash site with eight other men,
says he saw five dead aliens. "They were fairly good-looking people. They didn't
have those big slanted eyes. They had ash-covered skin, were hairless with small
noses and ears."*

*The story usually goes that the aliens and their spaceship were taken to Area
51, the top-secret armed forces base where new technology is developed and tested.
The mysteries of the base attract many believers.*

Journalist Randall Rothenberg visited the region for Esquire.

Chuck Clark is sitting at the end of the Formica bar in the Little
A'Le'Inn, draining a Diet Coke and staring at the bumper stickers
affixed to a beer cooler. NO NEW WORLD ORDER and YEAH, YOU CAN HAVE
MY GUN—BULLETS FIRST! they say—not uncommon sentiments in the
Nevada desert. Chuck, who has come into the Little A'Le'Inn (pronounced "little alien") almost every day since he moved to Rachel two
years ago, pays them no heed. The stickers are as much a part of the
backdrop as the pool table and the video-poker machines at the only
saloon in town.

Chuck came to Rachel, a dusty medley of corrugated-steel trailers
about a hundred miles north of Las Vegas, to complete his book of
astronomical photography. "I wanted a dark-sky place from which I
could shoot the two hundred best objects in the sky," he says. The most

dramatic object he's seen appeared last February, near a black mailbox about twenty miles east of town that has lately become a rendezvous for those who watch the heavens. "It was a yellow-orange ball that rose up vertically and hung motionless for twelve minutes, then started to descend. All along, I thought it was a magnesium illumination flare. But after hovering, it shot horizontally to my right, stopped cold, hovered for three to four seconds, and vanished. It covered four to eight miles in a few seconds—that figures out to nine thousand to fourteen thousand miles per hour. No sound, no sonic boom. I don't know anything in our physics that can do this."

Chuck calmly offers a theory about what he saw. "I don't think it's extraterrestrial technology. I'm of the opinion that it's an interdimensional technology that's been developed right here. Don't get me wrong; I think the Roswell crash did happen, and we did come into possession of an alien craft and some beings. But I think what we're seeing here are craft that our own government has been back-engineering from that vehicle.

"With my own eyes," Chuck concludes, "I know there's something going on they haven't told us." On that point, pretty much every one who comes into the Little A'Le'Inn agrees. During the last seven years, Rachel, Nevada, has become the center of the galaxy for the truest of believers—ufologists, paranormalists, conspiriologists, alien abductees—who are convinced something is going on beyond the mountains that ring this desolate basin. That something—most here believe it involves extraterrestrials, and all assume it involves the government—is a powerful lure; according to some studies, between 560,000 and 3.7 million Americans think they have been shanghaied by flying saucers. So many of them were finding their way to Rachel—and so many more were anticipated, with the hit film *Independence Day* set partly in the area—that earlier this year, the state government, hoping to boost the depressed region's economy, declared Route 375, the road that runs through town, Nevada's official "Extraterrestrial Highway."

. . . Kathleen Ford is typical of the new arrivals. One night a few years ago, to unwind after returning home from her late-night shift as a Las Vegas blackjack dealer, she tuned to a television talk show. The guest was John Lear, the disinherited son of Learjet founder Bill Lear. "And he's saying," Kathleen is recalling, "that the aliens have done a deal with the U.S. government. They give us technology, in exchange for . . . whatever. Maybe the abductions—that's part of the rumor. He says they're on the backslide of evolution and can't reproduce. So they need our body parts to have babies. He showed a film of a craft, which he'd shot near Groom Lake, where he said we were developing the UFO technology."

Groom Lake is a dry lake bed due south of Rachel whose name is one of several near-synonyms—the others include Dreamland and, most famously, Area 51—for a secret installation that lies adjacent to the Nellis Bombing and Gunnery Range, an Air Force combat-training and weapons-testing location, and to the Nevada Test Site, a region in which nuclear weapons are assayed. There is a real facility at Area 51, at which actual aircraft, notably the U-2 spy plane and the stealth bomber, were covertly developed. But the Air Force steadfastly refuses to acknowledge the existence of anything beyond mere "operations" out there, prompting UFO adherents to contend that the government, with or without the help of alien visitors, is building and testing flying saucers at the base.

. . . The Travises . . . arrived in 1988 to take over the Rachel Bar & Grill, which had lost its previous owners about $500 a month, despite being the only such establishment for forty miles.

It was a propitious moment. About a year after the Travises' arrival, a fellow named Robert Lazar, a thirty-year-old self-described physicist who liked to build and blow up bombs in the desert, came forward to say that he had been employed at a secret government base near Area 51, at which he saw nine alien saucers.

Large parts of Lazar's story—for example, his claim to have received degrees from both MIT and Caltech—did not check out. Still, his story spread, by talk radio, television, and, later, the Internet, throughout the worldwide ufology community.

The effect of Lazar's tale was felt almost immediately at the Rachel Bar & Grill, where tourists started wandering in to ask about the objects they'd heard were flying nearby. Sensing an opportunity, the Travises quickly added several motel rooms to their property and in 1990 changed the name of the place to the Little A'Le'Inn. Gradually, their own political views began to incorporate the convictions held by their growing number of visitors. "It's just a theory," says Pat, "but one of the things that have been discussed by a number of people is whether the government will use an alien invasion as the reason we all have to get behind this New World Order."

Glenn Campbell arrived in February 1993. A former computer programmer, he saw himself, somewhat grandiosely, as the modern equivalent of the lawmen who once rode into the West to impose order on the barbarous citizenry. "There was an intellectual challenge there," says Campbell, a bald, mustached man with a crisply erudite manner. "There was so much nonsense floating around. I enjoy being thrown into a wilderness and having to find my way out."

Campbell, who describes himself as a compulsive data collector, began driving and hiking around the territory to find out what he could about Area 51, planning (as many visitors to the region have done) to exploit his discoveries commercially. Very quickly, he ran up against the government's wall of secrecy. As a challenge, he started to lead expeditions to the mountainous vantage points overlooking the Groom Lake military installation. The contest between the citizen investigators and the military drew mainstream media attention, which provoked the military to arrest some trespassers and close several viewing sites. This, in turn, inspired more coverage, notably a live broadcast of CNN's Larry King Show from Rachel in October 1994.

The reports lured even more ufologists to the area. They also attracted the notice of Bob Price, a Nevada state assemblyman who hatched the idea of renaming Route 375 the Extraterrestrial Highway as a way of boosting the region's economy, which locals say had been hurt by reductions in defense spending.

Rachel, in a sense, has become a symbol of the American economy's gradual transition from making things—out here, aircraft and bombs—to marketing symbols: in this case, the bulbous, noseless, big-eyed gray head immortalized by Steven Spielberg in *Close Encounters of the Third Kind* and featured on the bumper stickers, T-shirts, and figurines sold in Rachel.

It is 9:30 p.m. out at the Black Mailbox. A blue curtain has descended on the brushed-suede landscape, and the gnarly yucca trees are fading into mountains some twenty miles distant. Most nights, a revolving band of UFO watchers, some local, some visiting, gather here for the arrival of a space vehicle that appears so frequently it's been dubbed Old Faithful.

Robert Meggers, who has come from the San Francisco Bay Area for his second visit to Rachel in three months, peers into his binoculars at the sky to the south.

"I'm seeing all kinds of orbs and lights out there," says Robert, fifty, who explains that he's been interested in UFOs since he was a child and heard the tale of Barney and Betty Hill, who claimed to have been abducted by aliens near their home in New Hampshire.

"Bob Lazar says they're working on particle-beam weapons here," says Kathleen Ford. "I've got pictures."

The Milky Way begins to shimmer in the east. Jupiter rises above Tikaboo Peak. A rock band named Possum Dixon drives up in a white van. They'd just finished a gig in Vegas and were on their way to a one-night stand in Salt Lake City when their tour manager insisted they detour to Area 51. After a brief consultation with Chuck and Kathleen, they head off toward the mountains, hoping, says their guitarist, to be abducted.

Robert turns his binoculars west. "See those lights?" he says excitedly. Chuck Clark tilts up the brim of his cap and looks through his own scope.

"Those're choppers."

"Oh, goody!" says Kathleen, who claps in anticipation. "If the choppers are up, the saucers'll be right behind."

". . . Catch a cab to Alaska and cover that story."

SEATTLE

1998

EMMETT WATSON

The West has helped define the forward edge of American style and culture for a century, from the creation of Levi's through to the Hollywood lifestyle, the Beach Boys, the hippies, and New Age religion. But in that context the West really meant California.

Now Californians seem to be following a new leader. They drink Seattle coffee while listening to grunge rock and hoping that Microsoft will buy the software programs they're writing so they can get rich and move to the Pacific Northwest. How'd that happen? Only a few decades ago, Seattle was a small city dependent on a few businesses: lumber, shipyards, and the Boeing aircraft plant. When Boeing hit hard times in the 1970s, the whole town felt the effects. The joke was, Will the last person to leave Seattle please turn out the lights?

Emmett Watson, a columnist for the Seattle Times, *is puzzled by the reorientation of America's cultural compass.*

"It's just a hot city," Ancil Payne was saying as the two of us thrashed around on a state-of-the-city theme. Yes, it is hot. Nobody knows quite how it got that way.

Like many of us, Ancil Payne, former head of KING-TV, was around here when the Smith Tower dwarfed every building in town, when a "tolerance policy" made the cops rich and waiters snatched the drink out of your hand at midnight.

You couldn't buy meat on Sunday, you found Velveeta cheese in the gourmet section, the Mariners didn't exist, ditto the Seahawks, and our Huskies couldn't make a first down against a south wind.

When Ancil said "it's just a hot city" he meant in a national sense.

Now people know who we are, even what we are, which is more than we know about ourselves. Long gone is the day (a true story) when a New York bureau of a wire service advised a local news hound, "Catch a cab to Alaska and cover that story."

Dave Beck, the beleaguered Teamster boss, was Seattle's best-known citizen, a fact that embarrassed some of our boosters.

Now we've got billionaires to spare. Bill Gates, the kid from Laurelhurst, is the richest man in the world, being up there at about $44 billion, and Paul Allen, his cohort in computerdom, seems to own half of Seattle.

First Avenue, traditionally a series of taverns and pawn shops, a battling street for gobs fighting during Fleet Week, is getting so gentrified it's downright embarrassing. Where, oh where, are the hookers of yesteryear, when the running joke about the Diller Hotel was that you could "get a diller for a dollar."

Nobody knows really how it happened, how Seattle became a "hot city," but it's all out there. . . .

Nordstrom, a humble little shoe store (Elmer Nordstrom, one of the family patriarchs, used to fit my new school shoes) is now one of the nation's most powerful fashion retailers.

Gordon Bowker and a couple of friends wanted a better cup of coffee, so they began researching. Their first Starbucks was a tiny store at Virginia and Western. Now there are hundreds worldwide.

You wanted a cheap baseball glove? Kids went to Eddie Bauer's, a tiny sports-equipment store between Second and Third on Seneca. Anybody left in America who hasn't heard of Eddie Bauer?

Everybody has a theory as to how it all started. Some say Seattle became a real, recognized city with the introduction, in the late '50s, of digit phone dialing, which enabled efficient long-distance, transcontinental phone calls to Seattle. Or maybe it was the World's Fair or the hydroplane races or the way Mount St. Helens went public. Who knows?

My own favorite reference point came on a clear August day in 1955 when Tex Johnston, the drawling, laconic test pilot, was wringing out a totally new airplane for Boeing.

With 200,000 people on Lake Washington (including the chiefs of all the world's airlines) Tex brought the Dash-80 (the prototype of the Boeing 707) down low, 200 feet above the water. As thousands gasped, he slow-rolled it like a small fighter jet.

"I figgered I had their attention," Tex told me later, "so I did it again."

Tex, who got into all kinds of hot water over that one, had sold the 707. The great first jet (more than 1,000 were sold) became that famous "plane from Seattle," and Tex himself would later drawl, "We have shrunk the world by a factor of two."

And the world came to Seattle. . . .

"For God's sake, man, the world is getting better! Look for something new to do!"

SILICON VALLEY: WHAT'S NEXT

1997

MICHAEL LEWIS

Michael Lewis, author of Liar's Poker, *visited Silicon Valley for the* New York Times Magazine.

There are two parts to this story, and the first, like most things in Silicon Valley, can be dispensed with quickly. It runs something like this: In the 1960's and 70's, the Santa Clara Valley got itself a new name by making silicon chips, personal computers and related goods. . . .

Part 1 of the Silicon Valley story was about men—all of them were men—building machines, building them cheaper, faster, smaller and better. They built them so fast and cheap that they made themselves uninteresting. The world came to take them for granted.

Part 2 is what the world has not yet taken for granted. What has happened in the Valley over the past few years has the locals comparing themselves to Renaissance Florentines. It is, as Doerr puts it, "the single greatest legal creation of wealth in the history of the planet." Actually building machines is today a slightly second-rate occupation: the computer has become a commodity. Factories are messy, workers unnecessary. These days, the thrill is in dreaming up things for the ubiquitous computer to do. Software, in a word. Because change is happening too fast for large corporations to control it, the new game favors the new guys. "The little creepy critters who will eat you in the night," as a man from Xerox described them. The speed of growth of the Internet, in particular, has meant that neither AT&T nor I.B.M. nor Xerox nor even Microsoft can dominate the business. It's the age of the creepy critter.

And so all across Silicon Valley you find these office buildings crammed with little creepy critters who will eat you in the night. They are mainly young men who have just discovered their inner entrepreneur and hope to grab their little billion-dollar slices of the new world. Incubators, these buildings are called. Incubators shelter engineers and computer scientists whose ideas might make a fortune but are too fragile at this point to survive in the free market. Big companies like Xerox have incubator projects; venture-capital firms like the Mayfield Fund have them; even local city councils have taken to turning vacant office space into way stations for new entrepreneurs.

One incubator just off Interstate 280 across from a strip mall in San Jose is a case in point. It was created by the National Aeronautics and Space Agency in 1993. . . .

. . . The message beamed into the renal cortexes of young engineers and computer scientists is simple: Invent something! Start something! For God's sake, man, the world is getting better! Look for something new to do!

That's the message that brought an unlikely 26-year-old Indian named Venkat Krishnamurthy to the NASA Incubator. A few years ago, Krishnamurthy had gone looking for something new to do. As 1 of 30 students chosen from a pool of 600 overqualified applicants to join the Stanford Ph.D. program in computer science, Krishnamurthy was obliged to seek out a problem that would interest a professor who would, in turn, take him under his wing.

On the third floor of the university's Gates Building, he stumbled across a machine he had never before seen—a square black table braced on one side by a three-sided black box and on the other by a long metal rod with a scanner mounted to it. Inside the scanner was a laser, attached to a computer located inside the black box. The apparatus was able to scan crude three-dimensional images into the computer. The machine was called the Cyberware Scanner and had been created by a father-and-son team down in Monterey. Their original idea to stick the things in shopping malls and scan people's faces didn't pan out. The machine languished, waiting for someone to come along and find a use for it.

"I just thought it was so cool," Krishnamurthy says. "I thought there must be something cool I could do with this."

In that seemingly innocent impulse was the energy to trigger a chain of events that might conclude with the death of an old technology, the birth of a new one and millions of investors baying for shares of an I.P.O.

What Krishnamurthy did with the machine was to address a long-standing problem in computer graphics: How do you get an object from the real world into the computer? How do you translate every nook and wrinkle and shadow on a complex solid object into digital data, so that it is no longer a picture of that object but a kind of digital clone that can be reshaped and manipulated at the will of the programmer? How, in other words, do you break down the difference between real life and computer life? "Reality merge" is the term of art sometimes used by people in the field.

A Stanford professor named Marc Levoy had taken an interest in reality merge. Krishnamurthy joined Levoy's elite team of graduate students. Two years later, they had written software for the computer attached to the laser that more or less solved the problem.

Once again, the computer was being made to do something new. As Levoy's team progressed, Krishnamurthy came to know Domi Piturro, an artist who had worked with Sony developing models for their play stations division and with Viacom on television shows like "Star Trek: Voyager." In the technical progress of computer art over the past 20 years, Piturro saw an analogy to what had happened to the plastic arts during the Renaissance: the computer was groping toward more realistic depictions of nature. The Stanford technology represented a small Eureka! moment, the equivalent of Donatello's rediscovery of contrapposto. It meant you could quickly translate a human body into raw computer data; the data could be made to respond to a variety of manipulations exactly as an actual human figure.

"We had broken through one of the big barriers between working in real life and working in a computer," Piturro says. "As an artist I found that exciting. It was like being Masaccio or something."

There was a time not very long ago when Piturro would have been thinking chiefly of finding a gallery in SoHo to represent him and Venkat would have been thinking chiefly of tenure. But this was Silicon Valley in the beginning of 1997, and they were surrounded by young computer scientists who wanted more than anything else to become entrepreneurs. It took about three weeks and a few conversations with people around Stanford for the artist and the engineer to think their way to the next step: keep the technology and exploit it themselves.

"People will always pay to see a more realistic dinosaur," says Krishnamurthy, recalling his first commercial thought. "And we could now create a far more realistic dinosaur much more quickly and much more cheaply than anyone else." To create the dinosaur, they needed capital, a plan and someone to manage the business. They needed to figure out how many hundreds of millions of dollars their idea might be worth. They needed to learn how to sell their new machine to others. They needed, in short, to be plausible. "Me and Venkat running something alone," Piturro says. "It would be like just two tech guys doing cool stuff."

In April of last year Krishnamurthy and Piturro went to Stanford's office of technology licensing to secure the rights to the new software.

There, they found more or less waiting an engineer with business experience and a degree from the Stanford Business School named Brian Kissel. Kissel had just turned 38 and was himself looking to create his first company. And to create a company in Silicon Valley, you need a new technology.

. . . By the summer of 1997, Krishnamurthy, Piturro and Kissel had formed themselves into a believable enterprise now named Paraform. At some point, it occurred to them that they needed an office, and through a friend of a friend, they found the NASA Incubator. And once you are inside the Incubator, you're no longer three guys who had never started a business. You're a company that has been selected by the Incubator. Lawyers and accountants lined up to offer their services in exchange for a tiny piece of the new company. Needing capital, Brian Kissel called the Band of Angels [a venture capital group]; before the Angels called back, Brian was on the line with a dozen venture capitalists, most of whom wanted a piece of the action. Soon enough, the co-founder of Microsoft, Paul Allen, had a jet waiting for the three new entrepreneurs on the Tarmac at the San Jose airport. It took them up to Seattle. They showed Allen and associates the product in action. Allen had but one thing to say: "Cool."

"He said 'cool' twice," Piturro says. "Everybody told us we'd be lucky to get one 'cool.' We got two."

ACKNOWLEDGMENTS

Thanks to Jane von Mehren and Barbara Grossman of Viking Penguin for making a home here, and to Jane for her guidance and editorial skill. Thanks also to my agent, Joy Harris, for her business acumen and bedside manner. My parents were lured into editing and other acts of kindness. I am also very grateful to Karen Scofield for her generous support.

I also relied on the skills of several friends at various stages of this project. Jay Leibold contributed valuable research and ideas, especially regarding Native North Americans. Miles Kronby recommended important accounts, and edited a draft of the manuscript in his appropriately demanding fashion. Publishing expertise and sanity checks were offered by Marjorie Anderson, Laurie Brown, Marc de La Bruyère, Marion Ettlinger, Marguerite Holloway, Leslie Rossman, Stacy Schiff, Kathleen Spinelli, and Caroline Willis. I'd also like to thank Anne McCormick of Alfred A. Knopf for earlier efforts that encouraged me throughout this book, and which will undoubtedly continue to do so.

Once again, Alan Williams offered essential insight. He dismissed it as insignificant. I will miss disagreeing with him on that point.

SOURCES

To bring together five hundred years of Western history, I learned from several editors who focused on specific eras. *The Portable Western Reader,* edited by William Kittredge, is outstanding, especially for its presentation of contemporary writers. *Best of the West,* edited by Tony Hillerman, is just what it promises: the best book on "the Old West" of the nineteenth century. No mean feat in such a crowded field. *Native American Testimony,* by Peter Nabokov, is deservedly considered the standard in the genre. Bayrd Still's rare 1961 paperback, *The West,* is most interesting for its coverage of the movement from the Atlantic coast in the colonial era.

Regional works were no less absorbing. They included Kittredge's *The Last Best Place* (on Montana); *California Heritage,* by John and Laree Caughey; and *West of the West: Imagining California,* edited by Leonard Michaels, David Reid, and Raquel Scherr.

Readers who enjoy this volume will appreciate any of these books.

SELECTED BIBLIOGRAPHY

Angle, Paul, ed. *The American Reader*. New York: Rand McNally, 1958.

Berger, Josef, and Dorothy Berger, eds. *Diary of America*. New York: Simon & Schuster, 1957.

Bowman, John S., gen. ed. *The World Almanac of the American West*. New York: Pharos Books, 1986.

Caughey, John, and Laree Caughey, eds. *California Heritage*. Los Angeles: The Ward Ritchie Press, 1962.

Davie, Emily, ed. *Profile of America*. New York: Grosset & Dunlap, 1960.

Handlin, Oscar. *Readings in American History*. New York: Knopf, 1957.

Hart, Albert Bushnell, ed. *American History as Told by Contemporaries*, vol. I–V. New York: Macmillan, 1897–1929. [In the source notes, "Hart I"–"Hart V"]

———. *Source Book of American History*. New York: Macmillan, 1925. ["Hart VI"]

Hillerman, Tony, ed. *Best of the West*. New York: HarperCollins, 1988.

Hofstadter, Richard, and Michael Wallace, eds. *American Violence: A Documentary History*. New York: Knopf, 1970.

Michaels, Leonard, and David Reid and Raquel Scherr, eds. *West of the West: Imagining California*. San Francisco, Calif.: North Point Press, 1989.

Nabokov, Peter, ed. *Native American Testimony*. New York: Viking, 1991.

Snyder, Louis L., and Richard B. Morris, eds. *A Treasury of Great Reporting*. New York: Simon & Schuster, 1949.

———, and Richard B. Morris, eds. *They Saw It Happen*. Harrisburg, Pa.: Stackpole Co., 1951.

Still, Bayrd. *The West*. New York: Capricorn Books, 1961.

NOTES

The Return of Quetzalcoatl, from *The War of Conquest: How It Was Waged Here in Mexico,* by Sahagún, translated by Arthur J. O. Anderson and Charles E. Dibble (Salt Lake City: The University of Utah Press, 1978). Copyright © 1978 by Arthur J. O. Anderson and Charles E. Dibble. Reprinted by permission of the University of Utah Press.

The Aztec Metropolis, from Old South Leaflets, No. 35. In endnote: Buffalo and Grand Canyon accounts from *Narrative of the Expedition of Coronado* (1596), translated by George Parker Winship (Washington, D.C.: United States Bureau of Ethnology, 1896); Los Angeles smog account from *Relation of the Voyage of Juan Rodriguez Cabrillo, 1542–1543,* in *Spanish Exploration in the Southwest, 1542–1706,* edited by Herbert Eugene Bolton (New York, 1916).

The Wild West of the East, from Massachusetts Historical Society, *Collections* (Boston, 1792), I.

King Philip's War: The Death of Philip, from *A Brief History of the War with the Indians in New England* (Boston: printed and sold by John Foster, 1676).

The Pueblo Uprising, from *Revolt of the Pueblo Indians of New Mexico and Otermin's Attempted Reconquest 1680–1682* by Charles Wilson Hackett (Albuquerque: University of New Mexico Press, 1942). De Otermin quoted in Moquin and Van Doren; Naranjo quoted in Nabokov.

La Salle Claims Louisiana, from *Historical Collections of Louisiana* (New York, 1852), Part IV.

The Knights of the Golden Horseshoe, from *Memoirs of a Huguenot Family,* by Ann Maury (New York: Putnam, 1853). Quoted in Still.

Bering Reaches Alaska, from *Bering's Voyages: An Account of the Efforts of the Russians to Determine the Relation of Asia and America,* volume 2, edited by Frederick A. Golder (American Geographical Society, 1925).

Washington Parleys with the French, from *The Writings of George Washington,* edited by Worthington Chauncey Ford (New York, 1889). Quoted in Berger.

Pontiac's Rebellion Begins, from *Alexander Henry's Travels and Adventures,* edited by Milo M. Quaife (Chicago: R. R. Donnelley & Sons Co., 1921).

The Discovery of Paradise, from *The Discovery, Settlement and Present State of Kentucky, etc.,* by John Filson (Wilmington, Dela., 1784).

The Sacred Expedition Faces Disaster, from *The Portolá Expedition of 1769–1770* (Berkeley: University of California Press, 1911). Quoted in Caughey and Caughey.

Riot of the North Carolina Regulators, from *The Colonial Records of North Carolina* (Raleigh, N.C., 1890), VIII.

The Revolutionary War: The Conquest of the Old Northwest, from *The Capture of Old Vincennes,* edited by Milo M. Quaife (Indianapolis, Ind.: Bobbs-Merrill, 1927).

New Settlements on the Ohio, from *Col. John May, Journal and Letters . . . Relative to Two Journeys to the Ohio Country in 1788 and '89* (Ohio Historical and Philosophical Society, Cincinnati, 1873). Quoted in Hart III.

Lewis and Clark's Journey, from *Original Journals of the Lewis and Clark Expedition,* edited by Reuben Gold Thwaites (New York: Dodd, Mead & Company, 1904–5); and *Bird Woman: The Guide of Lewis and Clark,* by James Willard Schultz (Boston: Houghton Mifflin, 1918).

Zebulon Pike Is Robbed, from *The Southwestern Expedition of Zebulon M. Pike,* edited by Milo M. Quaife (Chicago: R. R. Donnelley & Sons Co., 1925).

The Aaron Burr Conspiracy, from *United States House Journal,* Vol. V, Eighty-ninth Congresses (1804–1807).

A Vicious Captain Leads Astor's Adventurers, from *Adventures of the First Settlers on the Oregon or Columbia River* (London, 1849), reprinted in *Early Western Travels,* edited by Reuben Gold Thwaites (Cleveland: A. H. Clark, 1904–7).

Tecumseh, from *Tecumseh: Fact and Fiction in Early Records,* edited by Carl F. Klinck (Englewood Cliffs, N.J.: Prentice Hall, 1961).

Johnny Appleseed, from *Johnny Appleseed: Man and Myth,* by Robert Price (Bloomington, Ind.: Indiana University Press, 1954).

Moses Austin Reveals His Plans for Texas, from "The Austin Papers," edited by Eugene C. Barker, in *American Historical Association Annual Report,* 1919, II (Washington, D.C., 1924).

Revival Meetings, from *A Condensed Geography and History of the Western States, or the Mississippi Valley* (Cincinnati, 1828), I. Quoted in Hart, *Source-Book.*

The Santa Fe Trail, from *The Commerce of the Prairies* (Chicago: R. R. Donnelley & Sons, 1926).

A Ball in Chicago, from *Winter in the West, by a New Yorker* (New York: Harper & Brothers, 1835).

Russian Fur Traders on the Pacific Coast, from *Two Years Before the Mast* (New York, 1840).

Kit Carson Fights at a Rendezvous, from *Journal of an Exploring Tour Beyond the Rocky Mountains* (Ithaca, N.Y., 1844). Quoted in Angle.

Davy Crockett Defends the Alamo, from *The Life of David Crockett, etc.* (New York: A. L. Burt Co., 1902).

"Remember the Alamo!," reprinted in *The South in Prose and Poetry,* edited by Henry Gill (New Orleans: F. F. Hunsell & Bro., 1916).

John Deere's Plow, recounted by L. Frank Kerns to the Moline *Dispatch,* January 13, 1902. Quoted in *John Deere's Company,* by Wayne G. Broehl, Jr. (New York: Doubleday, 1984).

A Smallpox Epidemic, from *Chardon's Diary at Fort Clark,* edited by Annie Heloise Abel (Pierre, 1932).

The Trail of Tears, from the New York *Observer,* January 26, 1839. Quoted in *Trail of Tears: The Rise and Fall of the Cherokee Nation,* by John Ehle (New York: Doubleday, 1988).

Colt's Revolver, from *Report to the Secretary of War.* Quoted in *The Story of Colt's Revolver,* by William B. Edwards (Harrisburg, Pa.: Stackpole Co., 1953).

Hospitality in Spanish California, from "In California Before the Gold Rush," *Century* magazine, XLI (1890). Quoted in Caughey and Caughey.

A Deadly Lottery, reprinted in *The South in Prose and Poetry,* edited by Henry Gill (New Orleans: F. F. Hunsell & Bro., 1916).

The Mormon Ghost Town, from *The Mormons: A Discourse Delivered Before the Historical Society of Pennsylvania: March 26, 1850* (Philadelphia: King & Baird, Printers, 1850).

Last of the Donner Party, from *History of the Donner Party,* by C. F. McGlashan, (Stanford, Calif.: Stanford University Press, 1940).

Against War with Mexico, from *Appendix to the Congressional Globe, 29th Congress, 2nd session* (Washington, D.C.: Blair and Rives, 1847). Quoted in Hart IV.

The Mexican War: At the Halls of Montezuma, from *Personal Memoirs* (New York, 1885), I.

Gold!, from *The Diary of Johann August Sutter* (San Francisco: Grabhorn Press, 1932).

Wagon Train, from *A Frontier Lady: Recollections of the Gold Rush and Early California* (Lincoln, Neb.: University of Nebraska Press, 1932).

The Panama Lottery, from *Seeing the Elephant,* edited by John W. Caughey (Los Angeles: The Ward Ritchie Press, 1951).

At the Gold Mines, from *The Shirley Letters from the California Mines,* by Louise Amelia Knapp Smith Clappe (New York: Knopf, 1949).

American Names, from *Discovery of the Yosemite and the Indian War of 1851,* by Lafayette Houghton Bunnell (Chicago: Fleming H. Revell, 1880).

The Committee of Vigilance, from *History of the San Francisco Committee of Vigilance of 1851,* by M. F. Williams (Berkeley, 1921).

The Gray-Eyed Man of Destiny, quoted in *Walker's Expedition to Nicaragua,* by William V. Wells (New York: Stringer and Townsend, 1856).

"Bleeding Kansas," from *House of Representatives' Report of the Special Committee Appointed to Investigate the Troubles in Kansas* (Report No. 200, Washington, 1856). Quoted in Hart, *Source-Book.*

Denver and Auraria, from *An Overland Journey from New York to San Francisco in the Summer of 1859* (New York: C. M. Saxton, Barker & Co.; San Francisco: H. H. Bancroft, 1860).

Death of the Pony Express, from *Alta Californian* and San Francisco *Herald.*

The Civil War in the West: The St. Louis Arsenal, from Chicago *Tribune,* April 29, 1861. Quoted in Commager.

The Civil War in the West: Quantrill's Raiders Ride into Lawrence, from *Quantrill and the Border Wars,* by William E. Connelley (Cedar Rapids, Ia.: The Torch Press, 1910). Quoted in Commager.

The Civil War in the West: The $150,000 Sack of Flour, from *Roughing It.*

The Civil War in the West: The Siege of Vicksburg, from the Cleveland *Herald;* and *My Cave Life in Vicksburg,* by "A Lady" (New York: D. Appleton, 1864). Quoted in Hart, *Source-Book.*

The Civil War in the West: Emancipation Arrives, from *The American Slave: A Com-*

posite Autobiography, edited by George P. Rawick (Westport, Conn.: Greenwood Publishing Company, 1972), vol. 5.

Buffalo Soldiers, from Senate records quoted in *Blacks in the United States Armed Forces: Basic Documents,* edited by Morris J. MacGregor and Bernard C. Nalty (Wilmington, Dela.: Scholarly Resources, Inc., 1977) Vol. III.

Wild Bill Hickok and Calamity Jane, from *The Life and Adventures of Calamity Jane* (Fairfield, Wash.: Ye Galleon Press, 1969).

Indian Agents, from *Condition of the Indian Tribes,* Senate Report no 156, 39th Con., 2d sess. (Washington, D.C.: Government Printing Office, 1867). Quoted in Nabokov.

Nature Sublime and Nature Ridiculous: A Volcano and an Earthquake, from *Roughing It.*

Race to the Last Spike, from *Collis Potter Huntington,* by Gerinda W. Evans (Newport News, Va.: The Mariners' Museum, 1954), I.

The First Woman's Suffrage Victory, from *The History of Woman Suffrage,* edited by Elizabeth Cady Stanton, Susan B. Anthony, and Matilda Joslyn Gage (1881; reprint, New York: Arno, 1969).

Lynching the Chinese, from "A Prophecy Partly Verified" by P. S. Dorney, *Overland Monthly,* March, 1886.

The Wonders of Yosemite, from *The Mountains of California* (New York, 1894).

Levi's, letter quoted in *Levi's,* by Ed Cray (Boston: Houghton Mifflin, 1978).

Buffalo Bill Takes the Stage, from *An Autobiography of Buffalo Bill* (New York: Cosmopolitan Book Corp., 1923).

"Surf-Bathing," *The Hawaiian Archipelago* (London: John Murray, 1881).

A First Buffalo Hunt, from *My Indian Boyhood* (Boston: Houghton Mifflin, 1931).

Custer's Last Stand, reprinted from *Black Elk Speaks,* by John G. Neihardt, by permission of the University of Nebraska Press. Copyright 1932, 1959, 1972, by John G. Neihardt. Copyright © 1961 by the John G. Neihardt Trust.

Nebraska, from *Across the Plains* (New York: Scribner's, 1904).

Pat Garrett Hunts Billy the Kid, *The Authentic Life of Billy the Kid* (Santa Fe, N.M.: New Mexico Printing and Publishing Co., 1882).

Leadville, from *Impressions of America, The Complete Writings of Oscar Wilde, Volume IX* (New York: Pearson Publishing Company, 1909).

Allotment, from *Big Falling Snow: A Tewa-Hopi Indian's Life and Times and the History and Traditions of His People* by Howard Courlander (New York: Crown, 1978). Quoted in Nabokov.

The Stockyards, from *American Notes* (Norman, Okla.: University of Oklahoma Press, 1981).

Boomers and Sooners: The Great Land Rush, from *Harper's Weekly,* May 18, 1889.

The Ghost Dance, from *Speaking of Indians,* by Ella Deloria (New York: Friendship Press, 1944), pp. 81–83. Copyright © 1944 by Friendship Press. Used by permission.

Wagons East!, from Emporia *Gazette,* June 20, 1895.

Butch Cassidy and the Sundance Kid Rob the Union Pacific, from Buffalo *Bulletin,* June 8, 1899. Quoted in *In Search of Butch Cassidy,* by Larry Pointer (Norman, Okla.: University of Oklahoma Press, 1977).

Going to the Territory, from *The Outlook,* January 4, 1908.

The L.A. Water Swindle, from *Los Angeles Times,* July 29, 1905.

The 1906 Earthquake and Fire and Their Aftermath, from *Special Report on Army Relief Operations at San Francisco* (Washington, D.C.: Government Printing Office, 1906); and the *San Francisco Chronicle Reader,* edited by William Hogan and William German (New York: McGraw-Hill, 1962).

Who Killed Governor Steunenberg? from *Attorney for the Damned,* edited by Arthur Weinberg (New York: Simon & Schuster, 1957).

The Birth of Silicon Valley, from *Father of Radio* (Chicago: Wilcox & Follett Co., 1950).

The First Close-up and Other Movie Innovations, from *The Movies, Mr. Griffith, and Me,* by Lillian Gish with Ann Pinchot (Englewood Cliffs, N.J.: Prentice Hall, 1969). Copyright © 1969 Lillian Gish and Ann Pinchot. Copyright © renewed 1997 James Frasher and Ann Pinchot. Reprinted by arrangement with James Frasher and the Barbara Hogenson Agency.

On the Run, from *The War, the West, and the Wilderness,* by Kevin Brownlow (New York: Knopf, 1979). Copyright © 1979 by Kevin Brownlow. Reprinted by permission of the author.

A Cowboy Star Is Born, from *My Life East and West* (Boston: Houghton Mifflin, 1929).

Racing an Avalanche, from *The Spell of the Rockies* (Boston: Houghton Mifflin Co., 1912). Quoted in Hart, V.

Sagebrush, Lava Rock, and Rattlers, from *Of Men and Mountains* (New York: Harper Brothers, 1950).

World War I in the West: The Zimmermann Telegram, from *War Memoirs of Robert Lansing* (Indianapolis, Ind.: Bobbs-Merrill, 1935). Copyright 1935 The Bobbs-Merrill Company.

Rich Man, Poor Man, Beggarman, Thief: The Teapot Dome Scandal, from "The True History of Teapot Dome," *Forum,* July 1924.

Fresno, from *The Saroyan Special* (New York: Harcourt, Brace and Company, 1948). Reprinted by permission of the Trustees of Leland Stanford Junior University.

"Manufactured Weather": The Invention of Air Conditioning, from *The Father of Air Conditioning,* by Margaret Ingels (Garden City, N.J.: Country Life Press, 1952).

Philo Farnsworth Imagines Television, from *The Box: An Oral History of Television, 1920–1961,* by Jeff Kisseloff (New York: Viking, 1995). Copyright © 1995 by Jeff Kisseloff. Used by permission of Viking Penguin, a member of Penguin Putnam Inc.

The Serum Drive, from *Seppala: Alaskan Dog Driver* by Elizabeth M. Ricker (Boston: Little, Brown, and Company/Atlantic Monthly Press, 1930). Copyright 1930 by Elizabeth M. Ricker.

The Appearance and Disappearance of Sister Aimee, from *Mrs. Astor's Horse* (New York: Stokes, 1935). Reprinted by permission of Joan Walker Iams.

Talkies, from *The American Film Institute/Louis B. Mayer Oral History Collection, Part I* (Beverley Hills, Calif.: American Film Institute, 1975). Copyright 1975, 1977 American Film Institute.

Taos, from *Georgia O'Keeffe* (New York: Viking, 1976). Copyright © 1976 by Geor-

World War II in the West: Henry Kaiser's Liberty Ships, from *Inside: USA* (New York: Harper & Bros., 1947).

World War II in the West: Navajo Code Talkers, from *The Navajo Code Talkers* (Philadelphia: Dorrance 1973).

World War II in the West: The Boeing B-17, from *My War* (New York: Times Books, 1995). Copyright © 1995 by Essay Productions, Inc. Reprinted by permission of Times Books, a division of Random House, Inc.

The Zoot Suit Riot, from *Eastside Journal.* Reprinted in Hofstadter, *American Violence,* pp. 337–38).

Get Your Kicks on Route 66, from *Route 66: The Highway and Its People,* by Quinta Scott and Susan Croce Kelly (Norman, Okla.: University of Oklahoma Press, 1988), pp. 148–149. Copyright © 1988 by the University of Oklahoma Press, Norman, Publishing Division of the University. Reprinted by permission.

Gangster's Daughter, from *New York,* July 27, 1981, and *Easy Street* (New York: Dial Press, 1981). Copyright © 1981 by Susan Berman. Used by permission of Doubleday, a division of Bantam Doubleday Dell Publishing Group Inc.

The Blacklist, from *Red Scare: Memories of the American Inquisition, an Oral History,* by Griffin Fariello (New York: W. W. Norton, 1995). Copyright © 1995 by Griffin Fariello. Reprinted by permission of W. W. Norton & Company, Inc.

I Love Lucy, reprinted by permission of The Putnam Publishing Group from *Love, Lucy* (New York: Putnam, 1996). Copyright © 1996 by Desilu, Too L.L.C.

Going on the Road, from *Jack Kerouac: Selected Letters 1940–1956* edited by Ann Charters (New York: Viking, 1995). Copyright © 1951 by Jack Kerouac (copyright renewed). Reprinted by permission of Sterling Lord Literistic, Inc., The Estate of Stella Kerouac, and John Sampas, Literary Representative.

Tripping, from *The Doors of Perception* (New York: Harper, 1954). Copyright © 1954 by Aldous Huxley. Reprinted by permission of HarperCollins Publishers Inc.

Baseball Moves West, from *The Era* (New York: Ticknor & Fields, 1993). Copyright © 1993 by Roger Kahn. Reprinted by permission of Houghton Mifflin Company. All rights reserved.

Blue Sky Dream, from *Blue Sky Dream: A Memoir of America's Fall from Grace* (New York: Doubleday, 1996; Harvest, 1997). This text is adapted from a version appearing in *The Atlantic Monthly* magazine, July 1993 (Vol. 287, No. 1718), p. 68. Copyright © 1996 by David Beers. Reprinted with permission.

Silicon Comes to Silicon Valley, from oral history prepared for the Santa Clara Historical Society by John McLaughlin. Copyright © 1997 by John McLaughlin. Reprinted with permission.

Alaskan Statehood, from *American Tapestry,* by Tom Tiede (New York: Pharos Books, 1988). Copyright © 1988 by Tom Tiede. Reprinted by permission of Tom Tiede.

Hell's Angels, from *Hell's Angels* (New York: Random House, 1965). Copyright © 1965 by Hunter S. Thompson. Reprinted by permission of Random House, Inc.

Watts, from *Soul on Ice,* by Eldridge Cleaver (New York: McGraw-Hill, 1968); and *Watts: The Aftermath—An Inside View of the Ghetto by the People of Watts,* edited by

Paul Bullock (New York: Grove Press, Inc., 1969). Cleaver reprinted with permission of the McGraw-Hill Companies.

The Grateful Dead, from *Living with the Dead: Twenty Years on the Bus with Garcia and the Grateful Dead* by Rock Scully and D. Dalton. (New York: Back Bay Books, Little, Brown & Co., 1996). Copyright © 1996 by Rock Scully and David Dalton. By permission of Little, Brown and Company.

Hippies, from *From Camelot to Kent State,* by Joan Morrison and Robert K. Morrison (New York: Times Books, 1987). Copyright © 1987 by Joan Morrison and Robert K. Morrison. Reprinted with permission of John A. Ware Literary Agency.

Like a Rolling Stone, from *The Rice Room: Growing Up Chinese-American from Number Two Son to Rock 'n' Roll* (New York: Hyperion, 1994). Copyright © 1994 by Ben Fong-Torres. Reprinted with permission of Hyperion.

Cesar Chavez and La Causa, from *Sal Si Puedes* (New York: Random House, 1969). Copyright © 1969 Peter Matthiessen. Reprinted by permission of Donadio and Ashworth, Inc.

State of Emergency at "The People's Republic of Berkeley," from *Reunion: A Memoir* (New York: Random House, 1988). Copyright © 1988 by Tom Hayden. Reprinted with permission of the author.

Eureka!, from *Quintana & Friends* (New York: A Henry Robbins Book, E. P. Dutton, 1979). Copyright © 1979 by John Gregory Dunne. Reprinted by permission of Janklow & Nesbit, Inc.

Siege at Wounded Knee, from *Lakota Woman* by Mary Crow Dog with Richard Erdoes (New York: Grove Weidenfeld, 1990). Copyright © 1990 by Mary Crow Dog and Richard Erdoes. Used by permission of Grove/Atlantic, Inc.

Independence Rock, from *Dateline America* (New York: Harcourt Brace Jovanovich, 1979). Originally broadcast on *Dateline America,* CBS Radio. Copyright © 1979 by CBS, Inc.

Looking for Work at Disneyland, Copyright © 1974 by Richard Stayton. Used by permission of the author.

Affirmative Action: Bakke v. University of California, from *Hunger of Memory* (Boston: David Godine, 1982). Copyright © 1982 by Richard Rodriguez. Reprinted by permission of David R. Godine, Publisher, Inc.

The Pipeline, from *Going to Extremes* (New York: Knopf, 1980). Copyright © 1980 by Joe McGinniss. Reprinted by permission of Alfred A. Knopf Inc.

Proposition 13, "1978: The Year the States Cut Taxes," *The Washington Post,* April 17, 1978. © 1978, The Washington Post. Reprinted with permission.

An Offer He Couldn't Refuse, from *Casino* by Nicholas Pileggi (New York: Simon & Schuster, 1995). Copyright © 1995 by Pileggi Literary Properties Inc. Reprinted with the permission of Pocket Books, a division of Simon & Schuster.

The Birth of the Personal Computer, from *The Road Ahead,* by Bill Gates with Nathan Myhrvold and Peter Rinearson (New York: Viking, 1995). Copyright © 1995 by William H. Gates III. Used by permission of Viking Penguin, a member of Penguin Putnam Inc.

White Nights, Dark Days, reproduced from *White Nights and Ascending Shadows,* by Benjamin Heim Shepard (London and Washington: Cassell, 1997). By permis-

INDEX

In every corner of the world, on every subject under the sun, Penguin represents quality and variety—the very best in publishing today.

For complete information about books available from Penguin—including Puffins, Penguin Classics, and Arkana—and how to order them, write to us at the appropriat_____election of books v

In the _____ _Ltd, Bath_
Road, I

In the _____ _89 Dept._
B, Neu

In Ca _____ _ue, Suite_
_300, To_

In Aus _____ _ingwood,_
Victoria

In Ne _____ _102902,_
North S

In Inc _____ _Shopping_
Centre,

In the _____ _us 3507,_
_NL-10_

In Ger _____ _rasse 26,_
_60594_

In Spa _____ _3, 28015_
Madrid

In Ita _____ _Corsico,_
Milan

In Fr _____ _Benjamin_
Bailla

In Ja _____ _2-3-25_
Korak

In S _____ _vate Bag_
_X14,_